Other Books by Harold Holzer

The Lincoln Image: Abraham Lincoln and the Popular Print
(with Mark E. Neely, Jr. and Gabor S. Boritt)

Changing the Lincoln Image
(with Mark E. Neely, Jr. and Gabor S. Boritt)

The Confederate Image: Prints of the Lost Cause
(with Mark E. Neely, Jr. and Gabor S. Boritt)

Lincoln on Democracy
(with Mario M. Cuomo)

The Lincoln Family Album
(with Mark E. Neely, Jr.)

The Lincoln-Douglas Debates:
The First Complete Unexpurgated Text

Washington and Lincoln Portrayed:
National Icons in Popular Prints

Mine Eyes Have Seen the Glory: The Civil War in Art
(with Mark E. Neely, Jr.)

Abraham Lincoln and his private secretaries, John G. Nicolay (left) and John M. Hay, in a photograph by Alexander Gardner in Washington, November 8, 1863. "We had a great many pictures taken," Hay recorded that day in his diary. "Nico & I immortalized ourselves by having ourselves done in group with the Prest." This is the only photograph of Lincoln with his staff aides. (The Lincoln Museum, Fort Wayne, Indiana)

DEAR MR. LINCOLN

Letters to the President

COMPILED AND EDITED BY

HAROLD HOLZER

ADDISON-WESLEY PUBLISHING COMPANY

Reading, Massachusetts Menlo Park, California New York
Don Mills, Ontario Wokingham, England Amsterdam Bonn
Sydney Singapore Tokyo Madrid San Juan
Paris Seoul Milan Mexico City Taipei

Library of Congress Cataloging-in-Publication Data

Dear Mr. Lincoln : letters to the president / [compiled by] Harold
  Holzer
    p.   cm.
    Includes bibliographical references and index.
    ISBN 0-201-63289-6
    ISBN 0-201-40829-5 (pbk.)
    1. Lincoln, Abraham, 1809–1865 — Correspondence.   I. Holzer,
Harold.
    E457.962   1993
    973.7'092 — dc20   93-8083
                                                  CIP

Cover design by Skolos/Wedell, Inc.
Text design by Karen Savary
Set in 11-point Bembo by Weimer Graphics, Indianapolis, IN

1 2 3 4 5 6 7 8 9-MA-969594
First printing, November 1993
First paperback printing, December 1994

For Bella Abzug and Mario Cuomo
Who taught me (among other things) the sanctity of constituent mail

I avail myself of the privilege exercised by the Humblest Citizen from the earliest ages of civil Government among Men to address the Executive upon great and important Measures of State policy and especially in times like these.

∽ *Opening words of a letter to Abraham Lincoln from Otho Hinton of Santa Rosa, California, January 1, 1864.*

It is the business of this desk to not neglect what they send.

∽ *Lincoln's clerk, William O. Stoddard, recalling his responsibilities as White House correspondence secretary, 1861–1864.*

Contents

Preface

THE CHARACTERISTICALLY American collection presented in this book can trace its roots to, of all places, Japan, where I travelled in September 1991 as press officer to New York Governor Mario Cuomo.

The trip was designed as an economic development mission—indeed, it did yield some important trade agreements—but while in Tokyo, the Governor also made news of the purely political kind by offering the first hint that he would bow to the hopes of his admirers and give serious consideration to running for the presidency the following year.

Ultimately he decided to remain governor (had he done otherwise, it might be noted, I probably would never have found the time to assemble this book). But four months of speculation about his candidacy served to trigger, along with other reactions, a huge outpouring of mail from all over the country and the world.

The overwhelming majority of letters urged him to run, but a surprising and substantial number recommended the opposite. And a tiny smattering of anonymous mail brought ugly ethnic slurs, and even an occasional threat. Out of that burst of public sentiment ultimately came the idea for this collection.

The Governor himself knew little about the mail that arrived throughout that precampaign winter. Reminding him not long ago about the voluminous burst of correspondence, I discovered that although he recalled that there were plenty of letters, he could remember reading only a few examples himself. And he had no recollection at all about the threatening or profane ones. Maybe, I thought, we had never told him about these in the first place.

It was just as well, I concluded; those letters were best forgotten. But almost immediately, I began wondering, too, what the flow of mail had been like for an earlier national figure whom Governor Cuomo and I both admire: Abraham Lincoln. How much mail did *he* receive? How much of what he received did he read himself? Did his staff, like Mario Cuomo's, keep the most abusive letters out of his sight? And how much of what Lincoln read did he act upon? What impact, if any, did correspondence have on his politics and policies? And, finally, what sorts of people wrote to their president during the Civil War? Just as important, what sorts of people did not?

I was astonished to find that almost no research had been done on the subject—that, in fact, no one had yet bothered to research and fully re-create for modern readers a sense of the White House office routine of America's best-known White House occupant. Precisely how that office was reinforced to respond to an avalanche of wartime visits and correspondence (still functioning as a bare-bones operation, however, compared to the bloated bureaucracy of today's White House) tells a remarkable story about an America at the crossroads between its ancient and modern histories. Surely it seemed the time had come to remind ourselves of an age in which ordinary Americans could still reach out to their president, and in many cases expect—and receive—a personal reply; of a government that grew at breathtaking speed to meet the requirements of a national emergency but somehow maintained a long-since vanished simplicity and accessibility.

The effort to reassemble the record of that political culture took me first to the Abraham Lincoln Papers at the Library of Congress—which comprise some 35,000 pages from the presidential years, on eighty-four reels of microfilm. From there, the search widened to embrace museums, libraries, historical societies, and private collections throughout the country where letters to Lincoln have also found homes—having once been forwarded by Lincoln's White House to the various federal departments, and undoubtedly sold years later to collectors. Today, such letters can be found in collections from Rhode

Island to California. The Lincoln Museum in Fort Wayne, Indiana, alone, I was surprised to learn, is the repository for 250 letters to Lincoln.

The results of the search—this book—aspires to offer no more than a taste of the dazzling diversity to be found in this largely untapped resource. But even in this sampling one hears again the passions of a troubled, hopeful, frightened, frequently admiring, occasionally resentful people, whipsawed by war and cultural upheavals that tore at the fabric of a society still only some fourscore and seven years old. And through these letters one imagines again, too, the sight of the endlessly patient president, reading and absorbing what he could, when he could, with the same forbearance with which he received ordinary citizens as visitors.

These are the very papers he held, read, considered, and answered.

And these are the voices he heard.

$$\mathcal{S}$$

A word on the editorial method is required. In reproducing the texts, I have attempted to perform as little editing as possible. Misspellings, however bizarre, are retained. Punctuation—or lack of it—remains unchanged. Individual styles of capitalization are preserved intact. There seemed to be no reason why modern readers should not see the texts just as Lincoln saw them.

I made exceptions only in letters I thought might prove simply too jarring for modern eyes. For example, when some correspondents of the day reproduced long quotes, they tended to use open quotation marks not once but at the start of every line of writing. The device looked cluttered and archaic then and seems even more so now; I eliminated it. To preclude a Babel of design, I also tried to simplify the form for return addresses and salutations: return addresses are here reproduced at the upper right of each letter, with the recipient's name at left, and the salutation indented. Writers of the day were hardly as consistent.

My comments and interpolations within letters appear in square brackets, and the use of square brackets around the date at the top right of a letter indicates that this date has been estimated based on the letter being preserved with a number of other letters on a particular day of Lincoln's administration.

The dreaded caveat *"sic,"* much to be avoided, is employed as sparingly as possible; misspellings and grammatical somersaults should be obvious enough without flagging them. But when correspondents accidentally repeat words (they did so most often when starting a new page of writing), or commit other, subtler transgressions, I have reluctantly but, it is hoped, usefully used *"sic"* to make clear, at least, that the errors are theirs, not mine.

An important point: for too long, I believe, historians have unquestioningly published underlined words in italics. Undoubtedly this improves the look of the printed page. Nineteenth-century letter writers, Lincoln included, used underlining a great deal. But that is precisely the point: they underlined; they did not italicize. I thought they should be permitted to underline here as well.

At the outset of this research effort, the task of deciphering and transcribing such a wild assortment of handwriting styles seemed daunting. Now, after reviewing more than thirty thousand pages of material in both microfilm and photocopied formats, I am surprised most of all by how few of their words proved so stubbornly indecipherable that they had to be so identified here—although, it must be admitted, correspondents such as Senator Reverdy Johnson are not represented anywhere on these pages for no better reason than that their handwriting was so completely unintelligible that it simply could not be read. The only wonder is how Lincoln or his clerks decoded it in the first place. Still, it is not suggested that the following pages will be free of error. But it is hoped that there will be no transcription errors as egregious as the one made by editor Emanuel Hertz in his 1938 book, *The Hidden Lincoln*—which was recently discovered and corrected by Professor Douglas L. Wilson of Knox College: Hertz mistook in the papers of Lincoln's law partner the word "darkey" for "donkey," and thus imposed the most bizarre miscalculation imaginable upon generations of readers.

Overall, the editor's greatest challenge came not in unearthing worthy letters but in eliminating those that deserved inclusion yet simply could not fit within this volume. In the end, I decided to focus principally on the letters from ordinary men and women, and with a few exceptions, to bypass famous letters and equally famous replies that are already available in other collections. This book, after all, is about the *vox populi,* not the official correspondence, although it is important to keep in mind that each day, letters of both sorts flowed across Abraham Lincoln's desk.

Finally, not all the letters reproduced here inspired replies, and among those that did, some replies have vanished—or are yet to be made public. I focused on those letters for which a response from Lincoln was available, yet many of the unanswered variety proved simply too good to ignore. Perhaps their appearance here may even spur the rediscovery and later publication of long-lost acknowledgments in Lincoln's hand, and in that way this book will help to keep the Lincoln mailbag alive and vital for years to come.

Acknowledgments

Just as Abraham Lincoln surely felt indebted to many of his correspondents for their ideas, advice, and productive criticism, I find myself enormously grateful to the friends and colleagues who filled my own mailbox this past year with words of encouragement, advice, and caution. Their efforts proved not only helpful but indispensable.

In particular, I am beholden to three Lincoln scholars who read and provided valuable comments on the early drafts of the text. One of them, my friend Frank J. Williams, president of the Abraham Lincoln Association, buoyed me with his enthusiasm and saved me from many errors. Another good friend, my frequent writing partner Professor Mark E. Neely, Jr., of St. Louis University, provided a typically insightful reading—and cheered on the project from the time it was a germ of an idea. Finally, Wayne C. Temple, chief deputy director of the Illinois State Archives in Lincoln's hometown of Springfield, proved again that he knows an astonishing amount about the most minute details of Lincoln's life. His scrupulous reading of the text prevented more misstatements than I would care to admit.

Along the research trail, many curators and collectors provided assistance, guidance, and photocopies, and I thank them all: Ruth Cook of the Lincoln Museum in Fort Wayne; Stephen G. Hague of the Abraham Lincoln Museum at Lincoln Memorial University in Tennessee; Jennifer B. Lee of the John Hay Library at Brown University; Rebecca Campbell Cape of the Lilly Library at Indiana University at Bloomington; Theresa A. McGill of the Chicago Historical Society; Stuart L. Butler at the National Archives; Donald McCue at the Lincoln Shrine in Redlands, California; Dona Sieden of the Minnesota Historical Society; Rex Scouten and his curatorial staff at the White House, along with Ruth Corcoran of the White House Historical Association; Mary Ellen Sinko of the Forbes Collection in New York; and Deborah Evans of the Library of Congress.

I appreciate, too, the support I received from my colleagues in the Lincoln fraternity. I must give thanks to John Y. Simon, executive director of the Ulysses S. Grant Association, for sage advice and sound warnings; W. Emerson Reck, for sharing much useful research material; Peter Kunhardt, for leading me to an extraordinary, hitherto-unpublished threat against Lincoln's life; Malcolm Forbes, Jr., for opening his family's peerless collection for this book; Cullom Davis, director of the Lincoln Legal Papers Project, for helping to decipher correspondence from Lincoln's old law partner; and, again, Wayne Temple, for sharing his published and unpublished writings alike. Also, I would be remiss if I did not acknowledge an additional debt to a scholar I do not know at all—Jack McLaughlin, whose recent book, *To His Excellency, Thomas Jefferson,* renewed my interest in assembling a grouping of letters addressed to Jefferson's successor, Mr. Lincoln.

I found and studied most of these letters on microfilm, and anyone who has ever used this medium to wade through hand-written nineteenth-century papers will probably sympathize with the task I faced in reviewing some 35,000 pages' worth for this book. My wife, Edith, thought she had made the ultimate contribution by encouraging me to purchase my own library-size microfilm reader, and then permitting me, with little complaint, to plant it rather prominently in our house. It would, she reasoned, keep me home and busy. As it turned out, it kept *her* busy, too—coming to my aid time and again to help me decipher some vital but illegibly scrawled word that I was attempting unsuccessfully to transcribe.

I cannot begin to estimate how many essential letters would never have been deciphered, much less reprinted here, without her keen eye and remarkable patience. My daughters Remy and Meg were occasionally summoned for similar duty, so the entire family helped these weary eyes comprehend words they could never have been understood otherwise. I thank them for that—and, of course, for their constant love and support.

It must be noted here that none of us would have had reels to read in the first place had it not been for Frank Williams. When purchasing microfilm became prohibitively expensive, Frank eased the potentially fatal research crisis by offering to lend me all the reels I needed from the complete set that graces his own incomparable collection of Lincolniana. He wound up sharing dozens, uncomplainingly sending some reels twice and three times each so the material they contained could be checked and checked again. It may sound like a cliché, but it is no exaggeration: without Frank Williams, this book could never have been written, and I thank him again for his boundless generosity.

Finally, I must express my gratitude to yet another group of people whose help was also vital: my agent, Geri Thoma, who always knew how and by whom this book should be published; my editor, Amy Gash, who returned to work from her maternity leave to help see this book into print; Meg Fry, Tiffany Cobb, and the rest of the team at Addison-Wesley, including my astute copy editor, Maggie Carr; and last but hardly least, Amy Varney-Kiet and Patricia Vaughan, who make John Nicolay and John Hay, Lincoln's secretaries, look like amateurs.

— HAROLD HOLZER
Rye, New York
August 1, 1993

Introduction

I doubt if there was any spot in the United States in those days, outside of a battlefield that was more continually interesting than was the correspondence desk of the Executive Mansion.
　　　　　　　—WILLIAM O. STODDARD, *White House secretary*[1]

*A*BRAHAM LINCOLN liked to call his White House office "the shop." And to his unrelenting distraction, it never lacked for customers.[2]

Virtually from the day Lincoln moved into the Executive Mansion on March 4, 1861, a crush of office seekers and favor seekers besieged its corridors, waiting rooms, and stairways—sometimes even hiding in the closets—until Secretary of State William H. Seward, for one, complained that official "ingress and egress" had become all but impossible.[3]

Lincoln's chief White House secretary, John G. Nicolay, agreed; he no longer had time to open the letters that arrived in even greater numbers than the visitors. "I am looking forward with a good deal of eagerness," he wrote home despairingly after only three weeks on the job, "to when I shall have time to at least read and write my letters in peace without being haunted continually by some one who 'wants to see the President for only a few minutes.' "[4] But Nicolay was waging a hopeless battle against both public prerogative and the President's own generous nature.

For generations, ordinary Americans had made the President's house their own, crowding into public receptions there and occasionally gaining personal access to the chief magistrate himself. The throng at Andrew Jackson's legendary "people's inauguration" in 1829 had not only done incalculable damage to the mansion's rugs and furniture but also provided irresistible encouragement to future pilgrims. No one but Nicolay seemed surprised that at the Lincolns' first White House levee, visitors too impatient to wait in the receiving line simply "climbed in at the windows."[5]

Public fascination with the nation's capital and its institutions extended to the legislative branch as well. The galleries of Congress had become the most popular tourist attraction in all America, and ordinary citizens, both male and female, like the heroine in Henry Adams's novel *Democracy* sought to learn how their government worked by observing legislators going about the people's business.[6]

On the other hand, even in this era of fervent interest in things political—an age in which politics had become what some scholars call "civil religion"—geography and tradition still conspired to inhibit unimpeded access to our leaders. America remained, in historian Philip Shaw Paludan's words, a nation of isolated, if "vital" communities, coupled with "a long tradition of weak national government." The result was a society whose overwhelming majority of citizens "seldom if ever saw a federal government official" in their entire lives—"other than the postmaster."[7]

With Abraham Lincoln's arrival in Washington, and especially after the onset of war seven weeks later, the last barriers between the people and their president seemed to melt away. One reason was that Lincoln was the first non-Democrat to occupy the presidency in eight years—the first Republican ever—and from the moment of his election, the victor was heavily lobbied for the long-coveted spoils. Patronage plunderers came from all over to make Lincoln's first months in office so hellish that finally, fearing he was paying too little attention to the secession crisis, he confided that he felt "like a man so busy in letting rooms in one end of his house, that he can't stop to put out the fire that is burning the other." Disunion and civil war failed to relieve the personal demands on Lincoln; quite the opposite. With the attack on Fort Sumter in April 1861, America's military class quickly and vastly expanded, and professional and would-be soldiers alike joined the office seekers crowding Washington, determined to win commissions, commands, promotions, and transfers—not to mention chaplaincies and potentially lucrative quartermaster's jobs—all, it sometimes seemed, from the hands of the President himself.[8]

The final contributing factors to this revolution in access to the White House can be attributed to both the unprecedented issues of the day and the unprecedented man in the White House. The Civil War brought wrenching changes to the fabric of life: the emancipation of millions of black slaves, the first national draft, the first income tax, and government suspension of constitutionally guaranteed civil liberties—not to mention a battlefield casualty rate so high that hundreds of thousands of women and children were left without husbands and fathers.

With such momentous questions dividing America, "every patriot became intensely interested in the strife," one of Lincoln's private secretaries explained, "and many after unburdening themselves in prayer before the Unseen, felt that they must sit down and give their thoughts on public affairs to the official head of the Republic." Those who did not live near enough or lacked enough wealth to finance a journey to the White House to do so in person, did the next best thing: they wrote.[9]

But there was something else motivating them to address the President. There was something about "the organization of the man" himself, the secretary observed, that seemed "calculated to draw forth communications from the trustful and sincere." As the aide put it:

> He was what we term a natural man. The prominent traits of his character had not been curbed nor repressed by scholastic discipline, nor had he ever studied the art of etiquette. In the Presidential chair he appeared to his neighbors essentially the same Abraham Lincoln that they had known when . . . he sat on the porch of the County Inn telling stories on the evenings of court week.[10]

For a while, the White House itself must have resembled the inn in Springfield during court week. Lincoln's bodyguard was surprised that the President "could get through with his work" at all, considering "the number of people who came there on all conceivable errands, for all imaginable purposes." Stubbornly, Lincoln at first opposed all efforts to limit access. "I feel," he insisted, "though the tax on my time is heavy—that no hours of my day are better employed than those which thus bring me again within direct contact and atmosphere of the average of our whole people." Besides, he pointed out about the throng, "They do not want much, and they get very little." As John Nicolay's daughter recalled her father explaining it, Lincoln considered himself the "servant of the people" not only "in the fulfillment of his oath" but also "by heart's impulse."[11]

But the crush eventually became too much even for Lincoln to bear, and his staff at last won from him major scheduling concessions. The daylong "promiscuous receptions," as he had taken to calling them, would be limited to twice weekly. At first scheduled to run five hours per session, from 10:00 A.M. until 3:00 P.M., they were later cut back further to three hours, running only until 1:00 P.M. Under this new system, Lincoln joked, every applicant had to take his turn "as if waiting to be shaved at a barber's shop." But even with a truncated schedule, each open house continued, Lincoln believed, "to renew in me a clearer and more vivid image of that great popular assemblage out of which I sprung. I tell you," he added, "that I call these receptions my *'public-opinion baths.'*" Their effect, he insisted, was "renovating and invigorating." At least that is what Lincoln said publicly. To one of his secretaries he wearily confided that at times the press of applicants seemed more to him like a "Beggars' Opera."[12]

Even though the revised office hours remained generous, not everyone who tried could get in to see the President. The doors were shut promptly at the appointed time, forcing countless visitors to leave disappointed. Others simply recoiled at the prospect of battling the crowds. They had but one recourse—and they took it: to set their cases before the President through the mails.

A typical admirer from Stonington, Connecticut, found himself repeatedly denied access to the President's office, and finally gave up, went home, and wrote instead. He had "made three trips to Washington to see you," his letter declared, "not because I had an Ax to grind but like the Jew in visiting Jerusalem I went almost to worship." He contented himself with worshipping on paper. The same fate might befall the famous. Joseph Medill, editor of the influential Chicago *Tribune,* arrived one day, cast one glance at the waiting throng, and departed without trying to see the President, returning home to write: "Not having either time or inclination to hang round waiting rooms among a wolfish crowd seeking admission to your presence for office or contracts or personal favors, I prefer stating in writing the substance of what I say verbally."[13]

Thousands of Americans did likewise, making up for their lack of direct access with letters that ran the gamut from contemplative tomes on the weighty issues of union, race, war, and peace to the most minor and frivolous requests for favors, pardons, and even payments of money. What all these letters suggest about their recipient is that he was a President who may have spent nearly as much time gathering public opinion by selectively reading his mail as he did by hosting the better-known public receptions that historians have been describing for generations. But until now, that influential archive has never been fully mined. This is the first peek at the entire Civil War White House correspondence archive since Lincoln's death in 1865.

∽

Lincoln's mailbag swelled to nearly unmanageable proportions almost as soon as the final votes were counted in the presidential election of 1860. "He received letters almost daily from the South," recalled one visitor, "on all sorts of subjects—some coarse, some witty, and others amusing . . . all of which never disturbed the equanimity of his temper."[14]

A full three months before he formally took office as president, he would invariably return from even a brief trip away from his Springfield base to encounter a huge stack of "accumulated correspondence." After one such absence, journalist Henry Villard observed that "a pile of letters greeted him before which a less determined soul might well have quailed." As Villard reported on November 28, 1860: "Until late last night and all day yesterday did it absorb all his attention. With a creditable patience he waded through the contents of several hundred letters, the perusal of which made him no wiser. Even his keen sense of the ludicrous begins to be blunted. . . . Bad grammar and penmanship, stylistic originality, frankness of expression, vain glorious assurance and impudent attempts at exaction may do well enough for the temporary excitement of humor."[15]

Villard was astounded not only by the volume of mail, but by its variety as well:

> Mr. Lincoln's correspondence would offer a most abundant source of knowledge to the student of human nature. It emanates from representatives of all grades of society. The grave effusions of statesmen; the disinterested advice of patriots reach him simultaneously with the well-calculated, wheedling praises of the expectant politician and the meaningless commonplaces of scribblers from mere curiosity. Female forwardness and inquisitiveness are frequently brought to

notice. Exuberant "wide awake" enthusiasm, with difficulty pressed into the narrow forms of a letter, is lavished upon him. Poets hasten to tax their muse in his glorification. A perfect shower of "able editorials" is clipped out and enclosed. Artists express their happiness in supplying him with wretched woodcut representations of his surroundings. Authors and speculative book-sellers frequently send their congratulations, accompanied by complimentary volumes. Inventors are exceedingly liberal with circulars and samples. More impulsive than well-mannered, Southerners indulge in occasional missives containing senseless fulminations and, in a few instances, disgraceful threats and indecent drawings. A goodly number of seditious pamphlets and manifestoes has also arrived.

To Villard, "all the 'light and shadow' of Anglo-American political humanity" was "reflected by the hundreds of letters daily received by the President-elect." But how long could Lincoln keep paying personal attention to his mailbag? The answer came by the start of the new year. Just before leaving for Washington and his inauguration, Lincoln's correspondence had increased "so wonderfully," Villard noted, that the President-elect found it "utterly impossible to read, not to speak of answering it all." Villard met Lincoln's servant on the night of January 19 toting "a good-sized market basket full of letters"—a single day's worth. The volume was now clearly outpacing Lincoln's ability to attend to it. "His private secretary opens them," Villard revealed, "and from the signature determines their relative importance. Those coming from obscure sources are invariably consigned to the stove without the least mercy. Petitions for office especially share this fate." Letters from prominent persons, and those boasting intriguing ideas on policy, presumably found their way to Lincoln. A routine for handling correspondence had been established, and it would be transported to the White House and followed, it might be said, to the letter.[16]

At first, Lincoln enjoyed the services of only a single staff assistant. His "entire office force," that force's daughter would recall, was a twenty-nine-year-old journalist named John George Nicolay (1832–1901).[17]

Born in the tiny town of Essingen, Bavaria, Nicolay was said to have spoken English with a German accent, although he had lived in America from the age of six. (Historians have never been quite able to

John G. Nicolay, White House chief of staff, as he looked when he arrived in Washington to take up his duties as presidential secretary. The Lincolns kept this carte de visite *photograph in their family album. (The Lincoln Museum)*

agree on the pronunciation of his family name, although it seems likely that it was Nico-*lay,* rather than Nico-*lie,* even though its original German spelling, Nikolai, invites the opposite emphasis.) Slender and bearded, Nicolay—"George" to his friends (although Lincoln always called him by his last name)—had been serving as editor of a pro-Whig Pittsfield, Illinois, newspaper, the *Pike County Free Press,* when he first heard the future president speak in 1856. The following year, Nicolay moved to Springfield, Lincoln's hometown and the state capital, to take up responsibilities as chief clerk to the Illinois secretary of state, Lincoln's friend and political ally Ozias M. Hatch.[18]

As "an assiduous student of election tables, the latest returns, or the completed record books," Nicolay remembered, Lincoln was a "frequent visitor" to the secretary of state's office, where he undoubtedly came to know Nicolay well. Like Lincoln, Nicolay had transferred his political loyalties from the dying Whig party to the new Republican party, and he grew into an ardent admirer of the tall, dark man from Springfield who had emerged as the party's leading westerner.[19]

In early 1860, Nicolay, who had continued writing for out-of-state journals on a freelance basis, contributed an editorial to his old Pittsfield paper advocating Lincoln's nomination for the presidency. "He maintains the faith of the fathers of the Republic," Nicolay effused. "He has the radicalism of Jefferson and of Clay and the conservatism of Washington and Jackson. In his hands, the Union would be safe." Nicolay may not have realized it at the time but he was paving the way for a future job.[20]

When the Republicans gave Lincoln the nomination that May, Nicolay at first hoped to continue contributing to his cause by writing a campaign biography. Instead he found to his disappointment that an Ohio journalist—the soon-to-be famous William Dean Howells—had beaten him to Lincoln's door with an identical proposal. "Filled with a jealous rage," Nicolay complained to mutual friends about this "usurpation." This disappointment may well have inspired Lincoln to console Nicolay by hiring him as his private secretary. Nicolay admitted that he was appointed "only a day or two later," although, he insisted, "without any solicitation on my part, or, so far as I know, of any one else, and I presume simply on account of the acquaintanceship formed." But he was not hired simply because he was a capable secretary with good writing skills. This was a political appointment, too, and Nicolay was a reliable Republican. He also knew how to keep himself out of the limelight; to his credit, friends confirmed, he never "said anything worth quoting."[21]

John G. Nicolay thus became the first—and the only—chief of staff Lincoln would ever have. Within months he would travel to Washington with the President-elect for his inauguration, station himself in an office adjacent to the President's on the second floor of the White House, and board in the Executive Mansion as well. The very first act of Lincoln's presidency was signing Nicolay's appointment papers. The chief secretary was paid $2,500 a year, exactly one tenth of Lincoln's salary as president. Over the next four years, Lincoln sent Nicolay on several delicate assignments outside Washington, for example, to help negotiate Indian disputes, but no one ever supplanted Nicolay, even temporarily, in the role of principal secretary to the President.[22]

At first, during the campaign, Nicolay's primary job was to help Lincoln avoid replying to inquiries about policy, since the candidate was determined "to thrust no letter before the public now, upon any subject." Lincoln eased some of these restrictions after his victory in

November, but letters continued to arrive that could not be answered by either man, among them threats, warnings, and ominous predictions of doom. "It is astonishing," Nicolay commented, "how the popular sympathy for Mr. Lincoln draws fearful forebodings." Nicolay failed to record for posterity that some of this so-called "popular sympathy" had inspired outright, obscene threats. That fact was hidden at the time and left for this study to unearth.[23]

On average, candidate Lincoln received fifty letters per day, but once elected, the number swelled, and Nicolay went to the President-elect to ask for help. It was Nicolay who proposed that John Hay accompany them to Washington to take up duties as assistant secretary. "We can't take all Illinois with us down to Washington," Lincoln supposedly complained when he first heard the idea. But then he quickly added: "Well, let Hay come." It was the start of a remarkable career in public service for a particularly gifted young man.[24]

Born in Salem, Indiana, John Milton Hay (1838–1905), like Nicolay, had lived for a time in Pittsfield; in his case he attended private school there. It was there that he first met his future White House staff colleague, and later he encountered Nicolay again when he moved to Springfield in 1859 after graduating from Brown University with honors as class poet. Articulate, debonair, and witty — as sprightly and irreverent as Nicolay was dour and sometimes officious — Hay set out to read law in his uncle's Springfield firm, Logan and Hay (whose senior partner, Stephen T. Logan, had once worked in partnership with a young attorney named Abraham Lincoln).

When the job offer came, Hay leaped at the chance to join the White House staff. After it was learned that the President's administrative budget allowed for only one secretary, Hay, always "John" to Lincoln, was placed on the payroll of the Interior Department as a clerk "detailed," in Nicolay's words, "for special service in the White House so that he gave me the benefit of his whole time." The twenty-two-year-old's salary was set at $1,600 per year and later raised to $1,800.[25]

Hay quickly learned to dislike Washington: it was as dull as "an obsolete almanac," he would complain, nothing more than a "miserable spreading village which imagines itself a city because it is wicked, as a boy thinks he is a man when he smokes and swears." But as long as he worked there he added sparkle to the Washington scene. "He laughed through the war," was the way Nicolay's daughter heard it. Whenever his workload became oppressive, Hay eased the boredom

John M. Hay in Washington in November 1861. This photograph by Edward Bierstadt, a carte de visite, *is also preserved in the Lincoln family album. "That one of me with the hat on is the best I have ever had," Hay wrote of this pose. "My friends stole all I had the first day." (John Hay Library, Brown University; gift of Kate Whitney, 1985)*

by amusing others. Letters that he was assigned to endorse for filing purposes, for example, were occasionally identified in unconventional ways: one particularly long, dull missive was filed as "Essay"; other letters were forwarded to the President's desk bearing endorsements in French ("events à Kentucky"). Hay also sporadically kept a diary of his years in Lincoln's employ, an incomparable source for historians, in which the President was usually identified affectionately as "The Ancient" or "The Tycoon" and his mercurial wife, Mary, with whom neither secretary was able to get along, as "La Reine" or "The Hell-Cat."

Lincoln grew deeply fond of Hay, seeing him perhaps as a replacement, and in all likelihood a more engaging one than the original, for his son Robert, who was away at Harvard during most of Lincoln's administration. Oddly, for all his irreverence, the junior secretary apparently disliked Lincoln's penchant for informality and spontaneity and complained of Lincoln's office routine that "there was little order or system to it," adding: "Those around him strove from beginning to end to erect barriers, to defend him against constant interruption, but the President himself was always the first to break them down." Asked once to describe his duties, Hay boasted self-confidently: "I'm the keeper of the President's conscience." In a more serious vein, he summarized the secretarial division of labor thus: "Nicolay received members of Congress, and other visitors who had business with the Executive Office, communicated to the Senate and House the messages of the President, and exercised a general supervision over the business." Hay, in turn, supervised the correspondence. Recalling the experience a year after the President's death, he said of Lincoln: "He wrote very few letters. He did not read one in fifty that he received. At first we tried to bring them to his notice, but at last he gave the whole thing over to me, and signed without reading them the letters I wrote in his name. He wrote perhaps half a dozen a week himself, not more. . . . He was extremely unmethodical."[26] In truth, Lincoln's voluminous *Collected Works* suggests that the President did far more letter writing than his assistant secretary gave him credit for.

Hay's work evidently met with the President's satisfaction. Lincoln would eventually secure for Hay a commission as major and assistant adjutant general of volunteers—probably a means of getting him a pay increase. Later he was promoted to lieutenant colonel, then colonel. Like Nicolay, Hay was also dispatched on several wartime presidential missions, one an abortive attempt to recruit loyal citizens of Florida in an effort to bring their state back into the Union; another was a delicate meeting with Confederate peace commissioners in Canada. But mainly Hay's duties remained in the White House.[27]

Nicolay and Hay did not share an office (Hay's workroom was across the hall, next to the main stairway), but they did share a bedroom, where, Hay reported early in the war, "we have some comfortable dinners and some quiet little orgies on whiskey and cheese." The prim Nicolay would allow only that the work space was "pleasant" and the bedroom "nice," although he did write home in time to confide that all the rooms in the house "sadly need new furniture and carpets." And when the city's first heat wave of 1861 forced the staff to throw open the mansion's windows, Nicolay was soon complaining that roaches, mosquitoes, and other insects were filling "the ceiling, the walls and the furniture," even his writing paper. But nothing, apparently, could seriously ruffle Nicolay for long, and he soon found a way to cope with not only the "little bugs" who besieged him, but also the big "humbugs" who filled his office, waiting for the chance to see the President. Lincoln's oldest son, Robert, was probably speaking for half of official Washington when he began a letter to the keeper of the gates with the salutation "Your private secretaryship." They were the odd couple of the White House: the cranky, nearly emaciated German who ushered away the uninvited and the baby-faced cynic who teased the visitors behind their backs.[28]

Not everyone appreciated the pair. Declaring, "the least said about them the better," war correspondent Noah Brooks hinted that both secretaries were "snobby and unpopular," referring to Nicolay as "the grim Cerberus of Teutonic descent who guards the last door opening into the awful presence." Another contemporary, A. K. McClure, recalled of Nicolay—some twenty-five years after Lincoln's death, and when he and the one-time White House secretary were feuding—that Nicolay "was a good mechanical routine clerk" but "utterly inefficient as the Secretary of the President." According to McClure, "his removal was earnestly pressed upon Lincoln on more than one occasion because of his want of tact and fitness for his trust, and only the proverbial kindness of Lincoln saved him from dismissal." But according to a young man who soon joined both secretaries on the White House staff, Nicolay and Hay seemed the ideal aides to Abraham Lincoln because they were entirely "without other associations or ambitions than such as bound them to himself." In turn, Lincoln's attachment to the secretaries became emotional as well as managerial. Nicolay's office, adjoining his own, and so close that visitors could hear laughter from the President's room even when the door was closed, was for a while the only place Lincoln could go in the house without being besieged by "loiterers, contract-hunters, garrulous parents on paltry errands, toadies without measure, and talkers without conscience," according to one visitor. That is because Lincoln could not even walk from his office to the family quarters without passing through a public reception room that was often crowded with strangers. Eventually Lincoln had a partition built in the room so he could pass along a makeshift corridor to the family library, unnoticed and

John Nicolay's copy of the Gardner photograph of Lincoln and his secretaries. Nicolay hired a miniaturist to paint in a background that depicts the President's office, complete with the portrait of Andrew Jackson that hung above the fireplace and the war maps that Lincoln kept on display nearby. (The John Hay Library, Brown University)

undisturbed. It was Lincoln's "only monument in the building," a contemporary noted—the only "addition" he made to the White House in his four years there. Not that this reduced his visits to Nicolay's adjoining room. For one thing, a newly installed toilet there, ordered during the Buchanan years, served the President and staff alike. And for another, Lincoln simply enjoyed his secretaries' company. He occasionally visited them after hours in their bedroom, his hairy legs visible almost to the thigh when he wore his short nightgown, looking from behind like the "tail feathers of an enormous ostrich," to read aloud from some passage that had aroused or amused him. Yet, all in all, Nicolay and Hay were *less,* not more intimate with Lincoln than previous secretaries had been with previous presidents, a fact overlooked by most historians. Before Lincoln's administration, such secretaries had usually been relatives of the president and routinely lived in the family quarters. Lincoln, a private man, kept his family sphere separate. This president's secretaries, for the first time, slept in the office wing instead.[29]

"There was never any red tape between us," Nicolay nonetheless testified of his relationship with Lincoln. But there was an extraordinary amount of mail, and at first it fell entirely to the two secretaries to handle it. "The President has not time to read all the letters he receives," Nicolay wrote home to Lincoln's onetime political manager, David Davis. Among a "hundred miscellaneous letters," he explained, "there will be a large portion which are obviously of no interest or importance. These the president would not read if he could." But the secretaries were obliged to examine every last piece of mail, and it quickly became clear that even their efforts together would not be sufficient to keep pace with the growing stream of deliveries. They were ready for a new aide. To "Nicolay" and "John" would be added "Stod."[30]

Like Hay a young lawyer, and like Nicolay a pro-Lincoln journalist, William Osborne Stoddard (1835–1925) was a native of Homer, New York, a graduate of the University of Rochester, and by age twenty-three the editor of the Republican *Central Illinois Gazette* in Urbana. In May 1859, a full year before the party was scheduled to choose its next standard-bearer, Stoddard came out for Lincoln in an editorial entitled "Our Next President"—the first such endorsement, Stoddard later claimed, "to nominate him."[31]

"We do not pretend to know whether Mr. Lincoln will ever condescend to occupy the White House or not," wrote the young enthusiast, "but if he should, it is a comfort to know that he has established for himself a character and reputation of sufficient strength to withstand the disreputable and corrupting influences of even that locality."[32]

By the following year, predictably, no one wanted to occupy

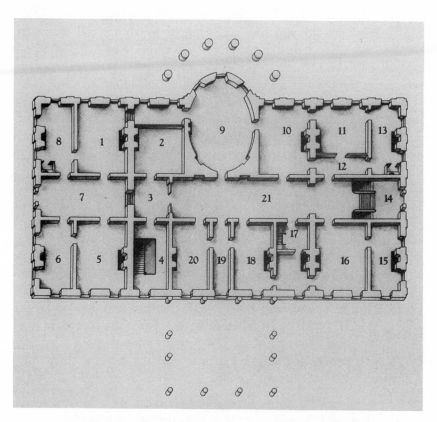

A floor plan showing the second floor of the White House in Lincoln's time: (1) the President's office and cabinet room; (2) the office reception room, showing the partition Lincoln had built to allow private access to the family library; (3) the office vestibule; (4) the office stairway; (5) Nicolay and Hay's bedroom; (6) the office shared by Hay and Stoddard; (7) the official waiting room; (8) Nicolay's office, complete with the office water closet; (9) the family library, or oval room; (10) Mary Lincoln's bedroom; (11) the President's bedroom; (12) the hallway for the master suite; (13) the Lincolns' dressing room, with private water closet; (14) the grand staircase landing; (15) Tad Lincoln's bedroom; (16) Willie Lincoln's bedroom, unused after his death in 1862; (17) a small room used for washing; (18) and (20) twin guest bedrooms separated by (19) a long corridor leading to a north window from which Lincoln occasionally delivered speeches; and (21) the central corridor that passed just outside the family's private quarters. (White House Historical Association)

that corrupting locality more than Stoddard himself—or thought he deserved to do so more. According to a memoir Stoddard wrote years later, Lincoln promised him a job shortly after the November election. "How would you like to come to Washington?" Stoddard recalled the President-elect asking. "Wouldn't you like to take a clerkship or something?" Stoddard remembered that he was ready to refuse the offer when some impulse made him blurt out: "Mr. Lincoln, the only thing that would tempt me to go to Washington would be a place on your personal staff." To which Lincoln replied, at least as Stoddard claimed, "Go right back to Champaign [Urbana] and write me a letter to that effect. Then wait till you hear from me."[33]

Stoddard did exactly that, but he was greeted with perfect silence. It is possible that Lincoln had advised the youthful aspirant to write simply to relieve himself of the need to disappoint Stoddard on the spot. If so, Stoddard was not about to take the hint. In his memoirs, a curious set of books in which everyone seems to talk exactly like William O. Stoddard—even Lincoln—the author remembers at last receiving the coveted summons from the new president early in December. But he was wrong: a surviving letter indicates that by the end of that month he still had not been satisfied. Four days before the start of the new year, Stoddard wrote "as to a confidential friend" to Lincoln's law partner, William H. Herndon, worried that his chances for a position with Lincoln were slipping away:

> As nearly two months have passed without my receiving any reply as to my application it is not unnatural that I should become a little nervous and desire to know what the indications are, if any. I am fully aware that the chances were from the first against my success, and am almost painfully conscious that my request was bold, even presumptuous. Very likely, also, others with greater ability . . . may apply for the same position. The "President-elect," knowing so little of me, must necessarily, if he has thought of the matter at all, have doubts as to my fitness for a post of so much responsibility, and hesitate about according to me the degree of confidence which a man must place in his "private secretary."[34]

Stoddard was desperate. "I would . . . be willing to begin 'on trial,' " he suggested, "as the Dutchman took his wife."[35]

Perhaps the joke resuscitated his chances, for after a few months' service in the Union army, Stoddard finally got his opportunity, at a salary of $1,500 annually, but not until July 20, 1861, the day Lincoln finally signed the commission appointing him, like Hay, to the De-

Lincoln's "third secretary," William O. Stoddard—"Lincoln's devil," as he called himself—around 1864, photographer unknown. This carte de visite *was owned by the Stoddard family. (The Lincoln Museum)*

partment of the Interior, as "Secretary to the President to sign patents for lands." On his first day at work he found himself doing precisely what the job description specified: attacking a huge pile of parchment land documents that had been left accumulating for him. He would later claim that this ongoing responsibility, which he was compelled to maintain throughout his tenure, required him to sign Lincoln's name nine hundred times a day.[36]

The White House staff was now composed of "three . . . young men," Noah Brooks scoffed (by then perhaps with an eye on the top job himself), but Stoddard contended that only "ill-natured people call us boys." As he put it, "we were young if you count by the almanac"—Nicolay 29, Hay 23, Stoddard 26—but quickly added, "that was a time when a day could be a year, and we grew gray internally."[37]

Stoddard was installed at a desk next to Hay's in the northeast corner office. But any resulting flush of glory quickly faded. He soon learned that he was expected to purchase all his own supplies himself—even pens and paper. Nor were official supplies plentiful: they were limited by a budget that had not increased, he complained, "since the days of John Adams"—only $250 a year for the needs of the President's entire staff (and from which Mrs. Lincoln attempted to skim funds to cover her own expenses). The White House ambiance was made even more difficult when Lincoln's undisciplined children ran wild—which was often. His usually serious middle son, Willie, came racing in one day to "slit into ribbons the cloth covering of the private secretary's table." Then the youngest boy, Tad, discovered the place where all the bell-wires in the house were "attached to a central pinion" (Lincoln used the bells to summon his secretaries) and set "all the bells, and human answerers of bells, in futile motion."[38]

Distractions notwithstanding, no secretary had more intense or prolonged experience with the presidential mailbag than William O. Stoddard, and none became as prolific in recalling the burdensome task in detail. While Nicolay and Hay, in later years, wrote a multivolume Lincoln biography—a collaboration that produced ten volumes of history but hardly a word about the office routine under which the authors had operated—Stoddard produced a shelf of reminiscences that focused on the inner workings of the White House. Although they have rarely been read in recent years, and although the details they present differ occasionally, one volume from another, Stoddard's was still the clearest window ever opened onto the comparatively primitive operation of the Lincoln White House.[39]

It became Stoddard's sole responsibility to receive, sort, and forward the 250 or so letters that arrived daily at the White House. To handle this "very curious department of American literature," as he jokingly referred to it, Stoddard developed what he called a "swift, decisive process of opening and disposing of the Executive correspondence" that kept arriving "in bales."[40]

Each morning, Saturdays included, White House guard Louis Bargdorf came in with what Stoddard described as "a full bag of . . . large parcels and small . . . many of them really weighty bundles," and poured them out onto the large, felt-topped chest of drawers that served as Stoddard's desk. Sitting there in a "swing-around armchair," Stoddard opened all of them, whether they were addressed to the

President, his wife, or his staff. The White House subscribed to journals of its choice, but additional newspapers and ink-underlined press clippings arrived as well and were immediately stacked in one pile. (The underlining, Stoddard scoffed, was apparently done "lest Mr. Lincoln . . . otherwise fail to be duly impressed"; Stoddard was originally assigned to prepare a digest of all press reports but gave up when the President failed to find time to review them.) Into another stack went official envelopes, easily spotted by their printed addresses (the War Department sent over so many communications they eventually printed up envelopes pre-addressed "The President"). Of the daily total, sometimes as many as three hundred pieces, Stoddard estimated that fully half were "simply misdirected, in the ignorance of the senders," involving business that belonged not with the President but with the federal bureaus and departments. These, together with "all the innumerable applications of the office seekers," were referred to more appropriate destinations, although they would have to be retrieved, usually with considerable difficulty, when individuals or delegations arrived to plead in person for favors or jobs that had not been granted in response to their letters.[41]

Of this last-named, voluminous category, Stoddard complained: "A curious idea appeared to have entered the minds of many men, that if a fellow had made good speeches and torn around actively in the presidential campaign," or perhaps had "done well with a flour mill or a country store," he was the right man to "lead a brigade." Such letters were rarely brought to the President's attention.[42]

The mail was littered, too, with diatribes from outright madmen. To Stoddard it began to seem that "whenever a man went out-and-out crazy, his first delirious impulse told him to sit down and write to Mr. Lincoln." Letters purporting to be written in blood, but looking to Stoddard's practiced eye more like cheap red ink, came regularly from the "Angel Gabriel." And enough missives came from "the spirit world" to prompt the secretary to joke that there must be "very badly conducted insane asylums in the other world." One missive purported to come from "the old worthies of the Republic" and not only bore the names of "George Washington," "John Hancock," "John Adams," and half a dozen other founders, but also was signed "as perfectly as the most expert forger could have done if he had traced the names over the printed copy of the Declaration of Independence." Inventors of both vision and delusion wrote frequently to herald new devices, most of them as outlandish as that perfected by an Illinois man who wrote to boast that he had created a "cross-eyed gun," a two-shooter with "diverging barrels," with which he proposed to arm an entire regiment of cross-eyed soldiers who could then be ordered up the Potomac to "clean out the Rebels from both sides of the river at once." The correspondent ended by declaring: "I know enough cross-eyed men to make a regiment, and by thunder, Mr. Lincoln, I'm cross-eyed enough to be their colonel."[43]

All such letters were subject to the "merciless business at the correspondence table," as Stoddard described it. He kept on either side of his desk a tall "willow-ware [ceramic] wastebasket," and into the baskets went "a very large proportion of the epistles, envelopes and all, without note or comment, the instant that their character was ascertained." Being assailed by such letters daily—and hate mail as well—Stoddard believed that the "paper-cutter on the correspondence secretary's desk" was an appropriate "defensive weapon." Much frivolous or offending mail was thus shredded before being discarded.[44]

Apparently, Stoddard's brusque handling of the mailbag became a poorly kept secret in Washington, for many letter writers pleaded that such treatment be spared their correspondence. "I hope the indulgence of your secretary may be trespassed upon for once," one such writer begged in 1864, "and that he will pass this over to your notice." A letter from a western governor began: "As within is one of the things which Mr. Lincoln would perhaps like to do to keep matters right . . . it might be well to show him the accompanying letter." And one worried Michigan woman opened her crude note with this entreaty: "Please place the foregoing under the eye of your well-meaning President, plain though it may be." Since far fewer than 250 letters per day survive in the Lincoln Papers, it is safe to assume that Stoddard turned a blind eye on nearly all such pleas.[45]

Oblivion also awaited notes from "volunteer statesmen," as Stoddard called them, whose "epistles were . . . long," but their "fate . . . short, owing to the handiness of the willow baskets." Assassination threats, which arrived with mind-numbing regularity, were similarly disposed of—at least if we are to believe Stoddard. "I was never permitted so much as to mention one of these," he insisted, "or, in fact, any other which did not immediately and beyond all question demand his personal inspection." But John G. Nicolay testified that while he directed all "threatening letters" to the War Department, he always showed them to Lincoln first. And Stoddard's successor on the White House staff recalled that the President kept as many as eighty of them in a special pigeonhole in his desk—in a file marked "Crazy and Poetry," an "odd . . . conjunction," admitted the secretary, but one that "was always filled with contributions." It seems likely that Lincoln saw at least some of the hate mail—threats included—that arrived at the White House.[46]

Stoddard may simply have been kept out of the White House loop on the matter of threatening mail. Nor was he entirely accurate, judging from the large amount of surviving correspondence in the Lincoln Papers, when he claimed that out of the daily "bushel-basketful" of mail, there were only "two or three letters that Lincoln would have to see—at most, a small handful," including letters from statesmen, petitions from citizen groups, notes accompanying gifts both lavish and homely, and letters from relatives. In his first days on the job, Stoddard remembered being inspired to bring the occasional disturbing letter directly into the President's room, and, he said, "got myself laughed at for the . . . interest I had taken." Stoddard quickly came to realize that the routine perusal of merely the printed circulars that arrived daily "would have required Mr. Lincoln to be set free from the trammels of time." And no such luxury was available. Stoddard was instructed: "When in doubt . . . consult Mr. Hay."[47]

Although Stoddard resorted to the wastebaskets "as rapidly as . . . decisions could be made," he was still horrified by some of the letters at which he was compelled to glance even briefly. "It seemed to me," he confessed years later, "as if the foulest blackguards on earth had made up their stupid minds that they could abuse the President through the mails." Most offensive of all, he felt, were the letters that "brutes" sent to Mrs. Lincoln. The First Lady handled her own correspondence "in her boudoir, where she had a desk," recalled a guard. But after confronting some horrifying letters herself, she asked Stoddard to screen her mail, too. Thereafter the only letters Mrs. Lincoln instructed to be delivered to her door unopened were those from her relations.[48]

Of all the letters Stoddard reviewed, only those of "exceptionally strong character," he insisted, were forwarded to Lincoln's own desk. But even these the busy President was not expected to read in full. On the back of each refolded letter, or on the envelope in which it arrived, a secretary wrote a brief summary of its contents. John Hay's distinctive handwriting appears on many such letters and envelopes from 1861; they were frequently brief and pithy ("Political," "Praises the President," "Colonization"). Stoddard penned longer, more straight-

The unfinished Washington Monument is visible outside the windows of Abraham Lincoln's White House office in this only known contemporaneous sketch of the room, drawn by C. K. Stellwagen in 1864. The table at center was used for cabinet meetings, and the desk against the door in the right background contained the pigeonholes in which Lincoln kept his files. Here all of Lincoln's official business was conducted, including the reading and answering of mail. (The Western Reserve Historical Society)

forward endorsements. And subsequent staff employees composed summaries that were nearly as long as the letters they were supposed to recap. But some letters apparently went to Lincoln's desk without any such commentary, for they bear no secretarial notations at all— only the unmistakable handwriting of Lincoln himself.

Lincoln usually went through the screened daily mail "in company with a private secretary," the *Boston Journal* reported in late 1863, filing some letters, putting others aside for further contemplation or reply, and returning still others to the clerk with instructions on how to answer them. He sat at his upright desk, or at the head of the table he used for cabinet meetings. There, "every letter receives attention," visitor Ben Perley Poore observed, "and all which are entitled to a reply receive one, no matter how they are worded, or how inelegant the chirography [handwriting] may be." Stoddard observed Lincoln one day, his "not handsome" face "cloudy" with thoughtfulness, as he silently pored over the mail that had been brought to him for his action. Stoddard's description provides perhaps the best portrait of the President's method of digesting correspondence of importance.

> He read or looked at letter after letter as he opened them, and for some he did not appear to care much. At last, however, he came to an epistle which I have since wished I knew something about. It was written on a square letter sheet, in a crabbed but regular and very black handwriting, page after page. It seemed to interest him at once, and he read on slowly, stopping at intervals as if to ponder ideas which were presented. His face at first grew darker, and the deep wrinkles in his forehead grew deeper. Then if you can imagine how a dark lighthouse looks when its calcium light is suddenly kindled, you may get an idea of the change which came into the face of Abraham Lincoln. All the great soul within him had been kindled to a red heat, and his eyes shone until he shut them.[49]

Lincoln answered personally only a handful of the letters he received, writing out his replies slowly in longhand, and sometimes copying them as well for his files. He rarely dictated. A few important letters were first "read over to confidential friends" and perhaps "corrected, or modified, before being sent." Occasionally he would ask that a gift or a greeting be acknowledged by a secretary, or that a draft be prepared for his signature. Most of these, Nicolay attested, he signed without bothering to read them. His pigeonhole filing system was apparently unaltered from his earliest days as a practicing attorney. His "second hand mahogany upright desk," as Stoddard described it, which looked as if it had come "from some old-furniture auction," provided ample pigeonholes for all the letters of the alphabet, and also for special categories that the President thought deserved individual space of their own. Editor Horace Greeley, for example, wrote so often that he was assigned his own pigeonhole. So were Union generals. When visiting artist Francis B. Carpenter, a longtime friend of Stoddard's, noticed one compartment mysteriously labelled "W. & W." he asked the President what it signified. "That's Weed and Wood—Thurlow and Fernandy," Lincoln replied, identifying, respectively, a New York State party leader and a New York City mayor, and adding with a laugh: "That's a pair of 'em!"[50]

Even with careful, perhaps overzealous, screening, the presidential mail took much of Lincoln's time, even if it is true, as Nicolay's daughter maintained, that he "read only about one in a hundred of the letters addressed to him." (Hay suggested it was more like one in fifty.) Years earlier, Lincoln had advised: "Leave nothing for to-morrow which can be done today," adding pointedly, "Never let your correspondence fall behind" (although, occasionally, he did so himself). If there was a constant impetus to move the mail through Lincoln's White House expeditiously it surely came from Lincoln himself. Nor was this the only correspondence to which he attended. When the Navy or War Department sent officers' commissions for his signature, Lincoln patiently affixed his name to piles six or eight inches high. And on those nights when he was anxious for information about the movement of federal troops, he walked to the War Department through the White House basement to read the news as it arrived in telegraphed dispatches. Even in wartime, the White House was not equipped with its own telegraph.[51]

Sometimes the press of work forced him to assign to others the task of reading even personal correspondence. On the back of one letter from an old friend, urging that blacks be allowed to fight in the war, Lincoln wearily alerted his secretaries: "I have not had the time to read this. Please read and return it." And when longtime ally David Davis forwarded an especially forbidding fifteen-page letter, endorsing it "entitled to be read," Lincoln found himself able to summon only enough energy to write on it: "Mr. Nicolay, please run over this and tell me what is in it." Later, Nicolay had to explain to Davis that Lincoln "has not time to read all the letters he receives," adding that of a "hundred miscellaneous letters there will be a large proportion" of no interest or importance. "The President is fighting today to get time to write a letter," Hay recorded in his diary on October 8, 1864, " . . . but is crowded as usual by visitors." A month before his reelection, the press of correspondence had evidently not eased.[52]

Nonetheless, there were times when his staff added to his burdens instead of easing them. One morning, Stoddard opened a long letter in a woman's handwriting, its pages "blistered" with tears "as if it had been sprinkled over with water." The writer merely wanted the President to know that she had lost all her sons on the battlefield but was still praying day and night for both Lincoln and the Union. Stoddard rushed into Lincoln's office bearing the letter, his own eyes moist, and watched Lincoln's eyes, too, well up with tears as he began to read it. Then Stoddard realized that "he wanted me to get out of his room and back to my own while he read it alone by himself," and the secretary silently withdrew, closing the door behind him."[53]

On the whole, however, sentiment did not rule the disposition of the Lincoln mailbag. How many letters were ultimately lost to history at the hands of Stoddard's paper cutter remains incalculable. Still, the surviving letters do make clear that Nicolay and Stoddard both may have underestimated the amount of material they actually allowed to reach the President's desk.

Some fifteen thousand individual letters from the White House days remain on deposit in the Lincoln Papers at the Library of Congress—letters and telegraph messages either endorsed by secretaries and then forwarded to the President, or those read first and endorsed by Lincoln himself. Since Lincoln served as president approximately fifteen hundred days, some two hundred of which were Sundays on which no mail was delivered, that means that on each work day of his presidency, eleven or twelve letters crossed his desk (with days on which the number was significantly higher). If we can believe Stoddard's estimate that some 250 letters arrived by sack each day, then the sampling brought before Lincoln's eyes was much closer to one in twenty than the one in one hundred suggested by John G. Nicolay's daughter. And this does not even take into account the letters that were later deposited in other collections. Abraham Lincoln, it would seem, did not escape the rigors of his correspondence—or the enlightenment much of it undoubtedly brought him—quite so easily as has been recollected. Nor did his secretaries; and eventually the routine began to exact its toll.

Both Nicolay and Hay suffered spells of illness during their years of service, and both grew weary of suffering Mary Lincoln. Stoddard alone got on with her, so well that "malicious people," he later bristled, "were afterwards . . . to speak of me as 'Mrs. Lincoln's secretary' "—as if no description could be more insulting; others called him "Lincoln's devil.") Even on the best of days, Stoddard understandably found his work becoming "mechanical." Yet the office triumvirate might have withstood boredom and the First Lady alike to survive the remainder of Lincoln's presidency intact had not serious sickness intervened. Sometime in 1864 Stoddard caught typhoid fever, probably from the contaminated Potomac River water unmindfully pumped into the White House.[54]

Stoddard's prolonged sick leave gave Lincoln the opportunity to hire the most talented and experienced—yet, to this day, one of

*Edward Duffield Neill as he looked in October 1861, three years
before he replaced Stoddard on the White House staff. This photograph was taken by Martin's Gallery in St. Paul, Minnesota.
(Minnesota Historical Society)*

the least known—of the secretaries who did service at his White
House. Edward Duffield Neill (1823–1893) was already a Presbyte-
rian minister, historian, and lecturer when he was recruited for duty
at the age of forty-one. Born in Philadelphia, he had been educated
at the University of Pennsylvania, Amherst College, and the Ando-
ver Theological Seminary. He was ordained in 1848, became an
emissary of the American Home Missionary Society in St. Paul,
Minnesota, the following year, and there grew active in that city's
public school movement. Later he served as territorial superintendent of schools, a member of the St. Paul board of education, and
chancellor of the University of Minnesota, which he helped found.
Clearly he was not only qualified to be Lincoln's secretary; he was
overqualified.[55]

It was as an historian that Neill probably came to the attention of the White House. In 1858 he had published a definitive *History of Minnesota.* Four years later, around the time Lincoln dispatched Nicolay to that state to confer on a Chippewa land treaty, the President borrowed the book from the Library of Congress and kept it a full five months. (Neill eventually sent Lincoln a copy of his own.) Nicolay apparently requested the volume, too; a letter he sent to Neill from Springfield midway on his journey to Minnesota thanked him for forwarding the book. "I am glad to have it to take with me on my trip up north," Nicolay wrote.[56]

By the time that the White House became interested in Neill, this peripatetic man had served as chaplain of the First Minnesota Volunteer Infantry and had returned to Philadelphia to become chaplain of the U.S. Military Hospital, which his brother headed. Then Nicolay apparently convinced Neill to come to Washington to step in for the ailing Stoddard. In February 1864 Neill received the identical commission his predecessor had held: clerk in the Interior Department, assigned to the White House to sign land patents. Like Stoddard, he would live outside the White House; Neill commuted by rail from a country house in summer (when the President, too, commuted from the Soldiers' Home, his summer retreat north of the city). And like Stoddard before him, Neill was asked to take over control of the presidential mailbag.[57]

Apparently Neill was even more carefully instructed than Stoddard had been, despite the fact that he was nearly twice the age of the "senior" secretaries who were supervising him, and rather stiff and pompous as well, judging by the style of his memoir writing. Before John Hay departed for a brief trip to New York, for example, he left a note for Neill admonishing him to "Refer as little to the President as possible." On the other hand, when Nicolay left on a mission of his own, his letter of instructions announced: "Take charge of the office, and get along with the work as well as you can." Even though Nicolay hastened to add, "when work can be deferred, defer it till my return," Neill unquestionably enjoyed access to Lincoln. For when Nicolay reported to the President from his mission two days later, he wrote on the envelope: "Mr. Neill please hand this to the President at once."[58]

Besides, deferring business may have become harder than ever by mid-1864, because the incoming mail appears then to have roughly doubled (which probably accounts for the rich trove of material that survives from that presidential reelection year). "A mailbag was brought to my room in the President's mansion," Neill recalled at this point, not once but "twice a day, well filled with letters upon various subjects." His job was to "open and read all letters directed to the President and select therefrom such as I thought needed his attention." Although he thought Lincoln's "capacity for work . . . wonderful," it was precisely because Lincoln was so busy "each hour" that Neill, like Stoddard before him, felt impelled to limit his mail. "To have read all the letters directed to him would have been a Sisyphean labor, never completed," Neill believed, "and it was necessarily delegated to another." Years later, Neill wrote several articles and delivered occasional lectures on the subject of White House correspondence, originally entitling one effort *Peeps into President Lincoln's Mail Bag.* But his recollections died with him, and when they were finally republished this century, they appeared only in a pamphlet issued quietly in St. Paul. His insights have been rarely consulted since.[59]

Neill's reminiscences show that in the years since Stoddard had begun opening letters to Lincoln, the diversity of correspondence had changed but little:

> Good and true men without foresight would mail twenty or thirty pages of anxious thought as to the course which they would pursue if in his place, and timid ones would forward manuscripts equally voluminous on the subject of peace at all hazards. School girls would mail their pretty photographs and in their sauciest little notes ask for his pretty face in exchange. College students afflicted with the autograph mania, stormed him with requests for his signature.

And while, Neill admitted, "the lunatics did not forget him . . . some letters were filled with the deepest heart sorrows [so] that the eyes of the reader flooded with tears." Lincoln continued to read and reply to those letters he found time to review. Neill was amazed at the President's ability to compose letters "amid distractions which would have appalled other men." He was equally impressed that Lincoln's writing "bore few marks of revision," but he seemed scandalized that the President "kept no formal letter-book" of copies.[60]

With two mailbags now arriving daily, and although Stoddard was planning to return to work, Lincoln apparently agreed to hire yet another aide—as long as he, like Hay, Stoddard, and Neill before him, could be hidden away on the employment rolls of one of the federal departments. On September 10, 1864, Charles Henry Philbrick (1837–1885) was also made a clerk in the Interior Department on assignment to the White House. As was likely the case with Neill, he appears to have been chosen not by Lincoln but by Nicolay.

The son of anti-slavery New Englanders born, ironically, on an East Feliciana, Louisiana, plantation owned by a great-uncle, Philbrick had been a longtime resident of Griggsville, Illinois, educated in classics at nearby Illinois College in Jacksonville. He had succeeded Nicolay in 1860 as the chief clerk to Illinois Secretary of State Hatch, serving in a "polished and courtly . . . manner" in the same building where Nicolay was then serving the President-elect.[61]

Three years later, Philbrick received the summons to follow Nicolay's path to the White House, having apparently overcome an unspecified character flaw that may at first have concerned the President. Philbrick may well have had a drinking problem, but in 1864, John Hay confirmed: "Charley is perfectly steady now, I am told. . . . I saw him when last in Springfield and he was straight as a string . . . thoroughly discreet and competent."[62]

Very little is known of Philbrick's specific White House assignments. However, it is clear that the new secretary did not live in the mansion, for within ten days of his arrival, John Hay reported that Philbrick had found a place to live: a "haven of rest in the family of some decayed Virginia gentry. Really a very lucky chance. Good, respectable & not dear," and within easy walking distance of the White House. Philbrick's arrival strongly suggests a new determination at the White House to deal more effectively with the mail. Stoddard was surely exaggerating when upon returning to the correspondence desk he had once managed alone he declared that the incoming mail was now "a third as large as it used to be." Stoddard conjectured: "All these victories have knocked the wind out of the abusive letter-writers; and the self-appointed critics and admirers are either tired of it, or they are satisfied, or they are dead, and as for the office seekers, the offices are mostly full." But there is no evidence to suggest that work was really dwindling, as Stoddard claimed—perhaps in an effort to make himself seem, in retrospect, more indispensable. By this time, according to Hay, who evidently came to dislike him, Stoddard's "assininity" was beginning to "advertise itself." By contrast, Philbrick was growing so worried about the overworked Nicolay's weariness and weight loss that he wrote home to their onetime employer, Ozias Hatch, joking: "I think if he and I could make an 'even divide,' he taking a part of my 163 lbs. weight, and giving me some of his indifference and industry . . . we should each be the better for the bargain." By then, Philbrick remembered, Hay was doing all the *"ornamental"* work of the office, while "the main labor is divided between three others of us who manage to get along tolerably well with it."[63]

Not long thereafter, Stoddard began campaigning for a new assignment, and in February 1865 he was named Marshall of the Eastern District of Arkansas. A few weeks later, Philbrick left to tend an ailing mother back in Illinois and never returned. Nicolay and Hay were offered posts in Paris, and Neill began promoting himself for Commissioner of Freedmen. Had Lincoln lived, an entirely new secretarial staff would have been installed in the White House, with journalist Noah Brooks replacing Nicolay.[64]

Meanwhile, additional clerks may have seen service at the correspondence desk, although almost nothing is known of their lives or their duties. In 1864, for example, Gustavus A. Matile joined the White House staff. Swiss born, two years older than the President, and trained in law in Berlin and Heidelberg, he signed some official letters in 1864 and later identified himself as the "late ap[pointmen]t. Sec. to President Lincoln." The Lincoln Museum in Fort Wayne, Indiana, owns an envelope addressed to a Fall River, Massachusetts, woman, franked "W. A. Browning" in the blank space above the printed title "Secretary to the President." And a faded 1928 obituary from a Pasadena, California, newspaper, identified a man named Stafford Ewing as "at one time one of President Lincoln's secretaries." Nothing else is known of these men. But the possibility that so many clerks—a huge staff for the time—coexisted so well for so long is probably attributable chiefly to Lincoln himself. Lincoln occasionally glared at his clerks "sidewise" but never made "verbal commentary" about their errors. "I do not know or believe," testified William O. Stoddard, "that he ever found fault with one of his private secretaries in all the onerous and delicate duties with which they were charged."[65]

∽

Although several of the secretaries who served Abraham Lincoln left behind reminiscences of the sum of the President's correspondence, they dealt little with its substance, beyond the obvious fact of its diversity.

Journalist Noah Brooks, a Lincoln admirer, a critic of John G. Nicolay, and the President's choice to replace his chief of staff in his second term. Lincoln died before he could appoint Brooks. (Courtesy Wayne C. Temple)

To modern eyes, the correspondence is perhaps less varied than Lincoln's clerks recalled—and as an ironic result, far more revealing. The Lincoln Papers are just as illuminating for what they do not contain as for what they do.

For example, there are hardly any letters from black people in the archive of Lincoln's correspondence. The ex-slave and abolitionist leader Frederick Douglass wrote but once, and his was an extraordinary, leader-to-leader communication on a matter of crucial national policy. But this proved a distinct exception.

Of course, blacks were largely illiterate in Lincoln's America, which accounts in great measure for the scarcity of letters from their pens. Yet even among the exceptionally rare letters sent to Lincoln by freed blacks, there is evidence of reluctance and distance not similarly expressed by white correspondents. One freedman writing from South Carolina used a white acquaintance to take down his words. And even a soldier from the fabled 54th Massachusetts—the best-known "colored" regiment of the Civil War—thought it proper to send his letter to Lincoln via white intermediaries rather than posting it to the President directly, perhaps concluding that with this imprimatur, it would stand a better chance of reaching the President. Even so, his well-written entreaty was promptly forwarded to a government department and not retained for Lincoln's files; perhaps Lincoln never even saw it. The fact is, in Lincoln's America, the White House was an aptly named destination for mail. It was for whites only.

Women, on the other hand, wrote often, and in the progressive change in the subjects that engaged them comes yet another revelation about the Civil War era. At first women wrote almost always on behalf of their husbands: seeking favors, promotions, jobs. The wives of two early wartime celebrities, John Charles Frémont, and Robert Anderson, both pleaded with the President to show more appreciation for their husbands. But later, when the war began desolating families and by necessity recasting Victorian-era gender roles, women began speaking up for themselves. Some wrote Lincoln as directors of huge charity fairs, asking donations. Other letter writers were female religious leaders. Widows wrote to demand their just due in back pay and pensions. In a more traditional vein, artists of the needle were generous with examples of their crafts: socks, shawls, pillows, rugs, quilts. But late in the war a letter arrived from one of the boldest women of her day, the notorious Rebel spy Belle Boyd. Her mission was astonishingly forthright: political blackmail. Of course, the Boyd letter is an anomaly. But Lincoln's own cousin by marriage was quick to make demands of her own. She pointed out that her loyal attendance on Mrs. Lincoln during the difficult first six months of her White House life surely entitled her to a job usually reserved for men: federal postmaster.

By and large, the Lincoln mailbag bulges with demands for favors—some as large as the emancipation of slaves, others as small as a request from a tavern-keeper that he be refunded a fine. Included in this volume is a mind-numbing avalanche of requests for jobs, petitions for jobs, and endorsements for jobs—this being the single largest category of letters in the surviving archive. Also included are pleas for pardons, requests for autographs, requests for passes through the lines,

A typical package label accompanying one of the innumerable gifts received by Lincoln during his White House years. (Library of Congress)

ideas on prosecuting the war, advice on political matters, pleas for private meetings, and letters accompanying gifts of all value and sizes, from a gold watch to a throw pillow, from a hand-carved cane to an ox. There are proddings to move more quickly on slavery, warnings to move more slowly on slavery; entreaties for favoritism, complaints about favoritism; compliments and criticism of the President, and of nearly all the cabinet and military officers he had appointed. And here, too, are the inevitable ravings of seers, soothsayers, and mystics, and threats both violent and profane—retained, inexplicably, in files otherwise purged of dross.

Writers as skilled as Edward Everett and Horace Greeley sent letters, as did ill-educated children, trembling veterans of the War of 1812, and frontier people barely able to forge a sentence—correspondents who spelled the President's name "Linkun" or called him "Uncle Abe" and "Father Abraham." It may have been the war that emboldened these simple, unlettered Americans to write their president, overflowing with patriotism; or, perhaps, a sense of close connection with a man who had risen from their ranks. As White House

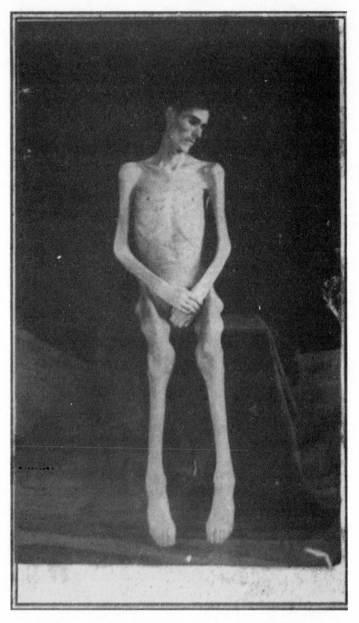

Ohio Senator Benjamin F. Wade sent Lincoln this frightening carte de visite photograph in 1864. It depicted a skeletal prisoner of war who had been starved by his Confederate captors. Lincoln kept the grisly piece of evidence in his files. (Library of Congress)

clerk Edward D. Neill confirmed, "The fact that he never with 'official awe' glanced at any one, and frequently relieved embarrassment by a little story, caused thousands of the sanguine and unsophisticated to take the liberty to write to him not only on the conduct of the war, but to unfold their tales of woe and personal misfortune."[66]

There is woe to spare in these brittle, fading letters. But they also contain affirmations of patriotism, reminders of astounding personal sacrifice and bravery, and the joyful welcoming of the liberation of a race. Reaction to all the incredible changes that wracked society filtered through the letters that came from as nearby as Georgetown and as far away as Europe. Here is Lincoln's true "public opinion bath"—not the ephemeral experiences he enjoyed from visitors who came and went, but those exultant, embittered, supportive, and critical, sometimes mad, sentiments carefully composed by his constituents, wearily but devotedly read by the President—and then retained for future reference because they had engaged his attention or his sympathies. Then they were filed away—for eighty long years.

$$\backsim$$

The story of Lincoln's mail has enjoyed a long, if shrouded, life of its own.

When Lincoln died, his son Robert summoned Supreme Court Justice David Davis to take charge of his father's affairs—and his father's papers as well. The judge kept the papers for nine years, finally shipping them to Robert in 1874. John G. Nicolay immediately urged the keeper of the President's flame "That not a scrap of paper of any kind be destroyed. The merest memorandum, mark, signature or figure," he warned, "may have a future historical nature. . . . The only good rule is to save <u>everything</u>."[67]

It was the fiercely private Robert who threw a cloak of secrecy over the Lincoln Papers and made them more famous for what they *might* potentially contain than for what they ultimately revealed. Weeks after the assassination he was telling visitors that some of the papers would, if made public too quickly, "be damaging to men now living." To one who sought access, he insisted that the papers were "in such a confused state" that they could not "be got at."[68]

Not until John G. Nicolay and John M. Hay embarked on the prodigious research for their mammoth Lincoln biography were the papers finally "got at," but even then, to the exclusion of everyone

PROCEEDINGS OF THE FIRST MEETING OF THE BOARD OF MANAGERS OF THE SPRINGFIELD HOME FOR THE FRIENDLESS. In accordance with the provisions of the Act of incorporation of the Springfield Home for the Friendless, passed by the Legislature of the State of Illinois and approved February 12th, 1868, a meeting of the officers and Board of Managers named in said act, was held at the residence of James C. Conkling, Esq., on Monday evening, March 2, 1868;

PRESENT—Mrs. Pope, Mrs. Conkling, Mrs. Dresser, Mrs. Bunn, Mrs. Campbell, Miss Eastman, Mrs. Lathrop, Mrs. Hay, Mrs. Dennis, Mrs. Cook, Mr. Bunn and Mr. Bowen.

The President and Vice President both being absent, Mrs. Conkling was elected President, pro tem.

The following communications were read:

From Hon. S. H. Treat, declining the office of President of the Corporation.

From Geo. Pasfield, Sr., tendering his resignation of the office of Vice President; and from the Secretary of State, enclosing a copy of the act of incorporation, and donating the fees for the same to the Society.

The Board filled the vacancies occasioned by the resignation of Judge Treat and Mr. Pasfield by electing S. H. Melvin, Esq., President, and James Campbell, Esq., Vice President

Mr. Melvin, being waited upon and informed of his election to the office of President, at the request of the Board, appeared and took the chair.

Mrs. Hickox having tendered her resignation as a member of the Board of Managers, Mrs. Fondey was elected to fill the vacancy.

On motion, the President, and Mrs. Pope, Mrs. Campbell and Mrs. Conkling, from the Board of Managers, were appointed a committee to visit Chicago Home for the Friendless and report to the Board upon the system and general management of that Institution, and also, to report a code of by-laws, rules and regulations for the government of this corporation.

On motion, the meeting adjourned.

S. H. MELVIN, President.

GEO. P. BOWEN, Secretary.

AN ACT to incorporate the Springfield Home for the Friendless.

SECTION 1. Be it enacted by the People of the State of Illinois represented in the General Assembly, That Eliza Pope, Mercy Conkling, Louisa Dresser, Susan Cook, Lydia Williams, Elizabeth Bunn, Harriet Campbell, Ann Eastman, Maria Lathrop, Mary Hay, Catherine Hickox, Mary Ann Dennis, and Elizabeth Matheny, and their associates, are hereby constituted a body corporate and politic by the name and style of the "Springfield Home for the Friendless," and by that name shall have perpetual succession and shall have power to contract and be contracted with, to sue and be sued, to plead and be impleaded, and to do and perform all such acts and things as are or may become necessary for the furtherance and advancement of the purposes of said incorporation as fully and completely as a natural person might or could do.

SEC. 2. The object and purposes of said incorporation shall be the relieving, aiding and providing homes for friendless and indigent women and children.

SEC. 3. Any person may become an annual member of said corporation who shall pay to the Treasurer thereof the sum of one dollar annually; and any person may become a life member of said corporation who has paid or shall at any one time pay to the Treasurer thereof the sum of ten dollars or more.

SEC. 4. The officers of this corporation shall be a President, Vice President, Secretary, Treasurer and a Board of Female Managers, not less than twelve in number, to be determined by the members of said corporation from time to time. The President, Vice President, Secretary, Treasurer and Board of Managers shall be elected annually by the members of said corporation on the first Monday in each year. All of said officers shall hold their respective offices for one year and until their successors

are elected. In case of any vacancy in either of said offices by death, resignation or otherwise, the board of managers shall have power to fill such vacancy until the next annual election. The regular annual meeting of the officers and managers of this corporation shall be on the first Monday in each year. The President and Secretary of this Corporation shall be ex officio President and Secretary of the board of managers, and shall be associated with and board in all matters of business pertaining to this corporation. It shall require at least seven of said board of managers to constitute a quorum to do business. In the absence of the President, the Vice President shall preside as President, and in the absence of both, the managers may elect a President pro tem, and in the absence of the Secretary, a Secretary pro tem may be appointed.

SEC. 5. The said corporation may receive, take and hold either by gift, purchase, devise, bequeath, or otherwise, any real or personal estate for the use of, and for the advancement of the purposes of said corporation, whether the same be purchased, given, devised, bequeathed or conveyed directly to said corporation or to any of its officers for the use of said corporation, and all real or personal property held by or for the use of said corporation or occupied by it shall be exempt from taxation not exceeding in value twenty-five thousand dollars.

No real estate to which said corporation shall acquire title shall be alienated or leased for a longer term than two years at one time, except by a majority vote of the managers at an annual meeting, or at a special meeting to be called for that purpose, to be specified in the notice of said meeting.

SEC. 6. The board of managers may at any time appoint such subordinate officers, agents and committees, as they may deem necessary for the more efficiently to carry out the objects of said corporation, and they may make and enforce such by-laws, rules and regulations as they may deem necessary for the election and government of officers and members of said corporation, and to govern the admission of applicants to the "Springfield Home for the Friendless;" also, for the government, discipline and disposal of those that may be received as inmates, and for the conducting and managing the general business of said corporation.

SEC. 7. The board of managers of said corporation shall be the legal guardians of all children that, by the provisions of this act, shall be surrendered to the said corporation, and they may, in their discretion, indenture such children to an honorable trade or employment, but in all cases provisions shall be made in the indenture by which said children are bound to service for securing an education proper and fitting for the condition and circumstances in life of such children.

SEC. 8. In case of the death or legal incapacity of a father, or in case of his absconding or neglecting to provide for his children, the mother shall be considered the legal guardian for the purpose of making a surrender of them to the charge and custody of this corporation, and in all cases when the person or persons legally authorized to act as the guardian or guardians of any child are not known, the Mayor of the city of Springfield may, in his discretion, surrender such child to said corporation.

SEC. 9. In case it shall be shown to any Judge of a court of record, or to the Mayor, or to any Justice of the Peace, within the city of Springfield, that the father of any child is dead, or has abandoned his family, or is imprisoned for crime; and the mother of said child is a habitual drunkard, or is imprisoned for crime, or is an inmate of a house of ill-fame, or if the mother of such child is dead, imprisoned for crime or has abandoned her family, and the father of such child is a habitual drunkard and an unsuitable person to have the care of such child; or that the parents of any child have abandoned or neglected to provide for it, then, such Judge, Mayor, or Justice of the Peace may, if he thinks the welfare of the child requires it, surrender such child to said corporation.

SEC. 10. Whenever complaint shall be made to the judge of any court of record, or to the Mayor, or to any Justice of the Peace of the city of Springfield, that any girl under the age of fourteen years, or any boy under the age of twelve years is abandoned by or is sustaining relations to its parents or guardians mentioned or contemplated in section nine of this act, it shall be the duty of such Judge, Mayor, or Justice of the Peace, to issue a warrant for the arrest of such child and its parents (if any it may have in Springfield) and if on testimony satisfactory to said Judge, Mayor, or Justice, it shall appear that such child has no parents, or is abandoned by its parents or guardians, or is sustaining relations to its parents or guardians contemplated in section nine of this act, the said Judge, Mayor, or Justice, may, if he believes the best interests of such child require it, surrender such child to the care of said corporation.

SEC. 11. The Hon. Samuel H. Treat shall be first President; George Pasfield, Sr., the first Vice President; George Bowen, the first Secretary; Jacob Bunn, the first Treasurer, and Eliza Pope, Mercy Conkling, Louisa Dresser, Susan Cook, Lydia Williams, Elizabeth Bunn, Harriet Campbell, Ann Eastman, Maria Lathrop, Mary Hay, Catherine Hickox, Mary Ann Dennis, and Elizabeth Matheny, shall constitute the first Board of Managers by virtue of this act; and shall hold their offices until the first Monday in January, 1869, and until their successors are elected.

SEC. 12. This Act shall take effect and be in force from and after its passage, and may be repealed or amended at any time.

[Signed]　　　　　　　　　　　　　　　E. A. BUCKMASTER,
　　　　　Speaker of the House of Representatives.
　　　　　　　　　　　　FRANCIS A. HOFFMAN,
　　　　　　　　　　　　　　　　Speaker of the Senate.

Approved, February 12, 1868.
[Signed]　　　　　　　　　　　　　　　RICHARD YATES,
　　　　　28673　　　　　　　　　　　　　Governor.

This painting by William Tolman Carlton, Watch Meeting/ December 31st 1862/Waiting for the Hour, *depicted slaves anxiously awaiting the dawn of the year 1863 and its promise of freedom under the Emancipation Proclamation. New England admirers presented the canvas to Lincoln as a gift, but abolitionist William Lloyd Garrison had to write personally to plead for an acknowledgment. (The White House Collection)*

else. Nicolay took custody of the entire archive, and when he died in 1901, the papers were moved en masse to the State Department, where his old junior clerk Hay was by then reigning as secretary of state. Entreaties for access by other scholars were routinely rebuffed. Finally, the papers went back to Robert, by that time an aging millionaire corporate executive with homes in Washington and Vermont.[69]

For the next dozen years, Robert's protectiveness grew to obsessive proportions. Although he no longer could cite the promise of exclusivity

Opposite: *This clipping was mailed to Lincoln by his old Springfield neighbors in 1863, who hoped it would inspire the President to donate to the charity it described. It did not. (Library of Congress)*

for Nicolay and Hay as an excuse to deny access to the papers, he adamantly refused to share them anyway. Journeying between his winter and summer homes, he invariably took trunks full of presidential papers along with him, never allowing them out of his sight. Robert's secretiveness—coupled with testimony by eyewitnesses that the old man threatened to destroy some of the letters ("I think I will burn them," he told historian Ida Tarbell)—prompted an entire generation to convince itself that Lincoln's sole surviving child had not merely preserved the precious archive but had also weeded out pieces he did not want posterity to see (including, it was rumored, evidence that members of Lincoln's administration had conspired in his murder).[70]

In truth, Lincoln's secretarial staff had accomplished the weeding out generations earlier, before Robert ever took control of the papers. Although Robert did restrict access to the documents, there is no evidence that he ever systematically purged the archive of their most scandalous contents—or, for that matter, that any scandalous contents ever existed in the first place, once Nicolay, Hay, Stoddard, Neill, and Philbrick all got through censoring the material as it arrived.

Robert finally deposited the entire collection in the Library of Congress in 1919. But still, it was to be kept under lock and key. Not until twenty-one years after his death, Abraham Lincoln's sole surviving child stipulated, could his father's papers finally be opened. He lived seven more years to the age of eighty-three, and just as specified, the papers remained sealed until 1947.

So much speculation had attended the papers for so long that when the archives were finally opened, it became a major media event. Breathless reporters gathered to watch a team of carefully chosen Lincoln scholars, including Carl Sandburg, break open the first packages. The nation tuned in to a live radio broadcast of the ceremony. But then, when the contents proved at first glance more quaint than shocking, the press and public promptly lost interest. A book was issued that brought to light a sampling of the correspondence, but it covered only the first few months of the Lincoln presidency. Scholars did begin turning to the papers for research, but they generally focused on the official letters from government leaders. The voice of the people was ignored, then forgotten.[71]

✺

As for the secretaries themselves, with one notable exception, they faded from history too.

John G. Nicolay was named by Lincoln as head of the U.S. legation and consul in Paris and confirmed by the Senate in March 1865. He assumed the post during Andrew Johnson's administration and served until 1869, when the new president, Ulysses S. Grant, replaced him. Later he aspired to a consul's post in Bogota, but that was denied him. Eventually he became Marshall of the U.S. Supreme Court. But no one ever thought that John Nicolay became anything more significant than Lincoln's chief aide—in a sense, for life. Noah Brooks would report, but not until more than three months after Lincoln's death, that the President had offered him Nicolay's post on January 1, 1865, at an annual salary of $2,500. "The President was then anxious for me to take the place near him," Brooks wrote, "but demurred at my sacrificing so much for the sake of serving him." He claimed Lincoln told him he could continue writing for the Sacramento *Union* under his nom de plume, "Castine," which stood to earn the journalist another $2,500 per year. But Brooks told Lincoln he would instead make the financial sacrifice as long as "all of the prequisites of the place, living, &c." were made as "liberal as possible." Said Brooks: "I would have made myself poor for the sake of serving a man so dear to me, for the sake of serving the Country by saving him for better and higher duties." That opportunity never came.[72]

Together with John Hay, Nicolay made an enormous success of his history of the Lincoln administration. *The Century Magazine* paid the pair $50,000 for the serial rights, and the ten-volume work, published in 1890, sold a respectable five thousand copies. But according to historian Mark E. Neely, Jr., the volumes eventually came to be viewed as a kind of "court history," which had been read, approved, and corrected by Robert Lincoln. Its diminished modern reputation notwithstanding, the books were both popular and influential in their time. Nicolay and Hay also went on to edit the first collection of Lincoln's speeches and writings, and Nicolay alone published a one-volume Lincoln biography that sold 35,000 copies.[73]

John Hay, however, eventually eclipsed his onetime supervisor. "Thoroughly sick of certain aspects of a life at the White House," he wrote in 1865, probably referring to frequent scrapes with Mrs. Lincoln, he was ready to leave by March. After travelling to Paris with Nicolay to serve as Nicolay's secretary of the legation, Hay became chargé d'affaires in Vienna, an editorial writer with the New York *Tribune,* a prolific poet and author, assistant secretary of state under Rutherford B. Hayes and secretary of state under William McKinley and Theodore Roosevelt. Alone among the White House staff during the Civil War, Hay escaped Lincoln's shadow and forged a reputation of his own. The "g-r-r-eat conflict," as the irrepressible onetime clerk took to calling the Civil War, proved for him but a stepping stone. But the vivid memory of his duties during those years never left him. Writing in his diary only days before his death in 1905, Hay confided: "I dreamt last night that I was in Washington and that I went to the White House to report to the President who turned out to be Mr. Lincoln." Even shrouded in the fog of forty-year-old recollection, Lincoln still seemed in the dream "very kind and considerate." And businesslike, Hay added: "He gave me two unimportant letters to answer."[74]

Edward Duffield Neill was the only secretary to keep his clerkship under Andrew Johnson, remaining at the White House, except for brief interruptions to work in the first (and short-lived) U.S. Education Department, until 1869. He was later named U.S. consul at Dublin, where he served until 1871, when he returned for good to St. Paul. There he helped found Macalester College, ultimately becoming its president. At the time of his death at age seventy he was a professor of history, literature, and political economy.[75]

Charles Philbrick never returned to the public eye after his trip back to Griggsville a few weeks before Lincoln's death. He lived on in his parents' house, never married, ultimately became an attorney, and was elected city clerk and, later, justice of the peace. If he ever wrote or spoke publicly about his days in Lincoln's employ, no accounts have ever come to light.[76]

The same cannot be said of William O. Stoddard. "Stod" outlived them all, and for the remainder of his ninety years produced a hundred books, including a virtual shelf of them about Abraham Lincoln. Sadly, his work of potentially greatest historical value, a mammoth autobiographical manuscript still in family hands, was issued only in a highly abridged version in 1949.[77]

∽

It is likely that only two of the President's secretaries were on duty at the White House on Saturday, April 15, 1865, the day Abraham Lincoln died. Nicolay was not one of them; he was at sea, returning from a cruise to Cuba. A pilot boat brought word of the assassination as Nicolay's ship left Charleston Harbor—the very site, ironically, where the first guns of the Civil War had been fired four years earlier. But Nicolay refused at first to believe the news; it was, he thought, just a wild rumor.

Stoddard and Philbrick had already left White House service. John M. Hay spent the night at Lincoln's deathbed, consoling his good friend Robert Lincoln. But Edward Neill was awakened at dawn by a pounding at his door. A railroad guard, tears streaming down his face, blurted out the news that Lincoln had been shot. Neill hurried to his office and probably met Hay there.[78]

Later that morning, Lincoln's body was brought back to the White House and "stretched upon a bed in one of the chambers" just down the hall from the offices. And, eerily, something else was delivered as well. As if nothing unusual had happened, the regular Saturday postal messenger arrived on schedule and "the last mail bag for President Lincoln was received at the Presidential Mansion."

"It was opened," Edward D. Neill remembered, "amid an awful stillness."[79]

This letter appears on page 46.

Westfield Chatauque Co.
N Y
Oct 15. 1860

Hon A B Lincoln
Dear Sir
                    My Father has
just come from the fair and brought home
your picture and Mr. Hamlin's. I am a little
girl only eleven years old, but want you should
be President of the United States very much
so I hope you wont think me very bold to write to
such a great man as you are. Have you any

little girls about as large as I am if so give them
my love and tell her to write to me if you cannot
answer this letter. I have got 4 brothers and part of
them will vote for you any way and if you will
let your whiskers grow I will try and get the rest
of them to vote for you you would look a
great deal better for your face is so thin. All
the Ladies like whiskers and they would tease

their husbands to vote for you and then you
would be President. My father is a going to
vote for you and if I was a man I would
vote for you to but I will try and get
every one to vote for you that I can I think
that rail fence around your picture makes it
look very pretty I have got a little baby
sister she is nine weeks old and is just as
cunning as can be. When you direct your letter
direct to Grace Bedell Westfield
Chatauque County New York
    I must not write any more answer
this letter right off Good bye
            Grace Bedell

[1]
Advice and Instruction

*A*S *PRESIDENT,* Abraham Lincoln became the national sounding board for ideas and counseling—good, bad, and ad-dled—on every issue that faced his divided country. Guidance, exhor-tation, advocacy, and remonstrance all poured in through the mails, leading the cynical correspondence secretary William O. Stoddard to conclude: "The average American, male or female, knows almost nothing about the machinery of the National Government."

His constituents' uninhibited eagerness to share their advice with Lincoln may well have been fueled by one of the earliest—surely still the best known—of such letters. It came, when Lincoln was still a presidential nominee, from an eleven-year-old girl who was so ap-palled by Lincoln's appearance that she wrote a now-legendary sug-gestion that the hollow-cheeked, lantern-jawed candidate grow a beard. Within months, a journalist would joke: "Abe is putting on [h]airs."

Young Grace Bedell was not the only correspondent to so advise Lincoln, or even the first. Three days before she penned her disarming recommendation, a group of self-proclaimed "True Republicans" wrote candidly to confide that the widely distributed campaign medals of the day "would be much improved in appearance, provided you

43

would cultivate whiskers and wear standing collars." Their letter was motivated, they apologized, only by "an earnest desire that 'our candidate' should be the best looking as well as the best" in the field.

It was Lincoln himself who immortalized Grace Bedell's apparently redundant suggestion when, two months later, he appeared in her hometown of Westfield, New York, aboard a train that was bearing him to Washington for his inauguration. Stepping into view of a crowd that had assembled there to greet him, luxuriant new beard sprouting from his face, Lincoln announced (in a talk widely reported in the press): "Some three months ago I received a letter from a young lady here; it was a very pretty letter, and she advised me to let my whiskers grow, as it would improve my personal appearance; acting partly upon her suggestion, I have done so; and now, if she is here, I would like to see her." When a little boy deep in the throng shouted, "There she is!" Lincoln made his way forward and "amid yells of delight from the excited crowd" planted "several hearty kisses" on her cheek. Grace Bedell's position in Lincoln folklore was forever secured. And so was the notion of Lincoln's receptivity to sound advice.

Over the next four years, a steady stream of such letters flowed into the White House, swelling into a torrent whenever a major political or military event captured the public imagination.

One of the first such events was the so-called Trent affair, a diplomatic crisis triggered when Confederate envoys bound for Britain were seized on the high seas by the Union navy. An angry English government demanded their release, and for weeks, as what was left of Lincoln's embattled Union hovered on the brink of foreign war, Americans both famous and unknown shared their recommendations on how best to wriggle out of the confrontation.

Emancipation, not surprisingly, was the issue that inspired more advice than any other. Lincoln was bombarded throughout the first year and a half of his administration with letters urging him, variously, to move with greater speed or to exercise greater caution. When General John C. Frémont took the nation—and Lincoln—by surprise by issuing his own emancipation order for areas of Missouri under his command, Lincoln's mailbag bulged with letters urging him either to sustain or rebuke Frémont. No other single incident of the war—and no other public figure save Lincoln himself—would inspire as much, or more fervent mail. Lincoln may well have had his finger on the pulse of public opinion when he finally decided, on October 24, 1861, to fire the troublesome general.

Lincoln surely came quickly to realize that his daily mail would reliably bring instant advice on at least two sides of every issue and personality of the day: The war was being prosecuted too quickly, some said; while others insisted it was being pursued too slowly. Peace must come now, at any price; peace must not come until the South had been punished and destroyed. Blacks must be encouraged to leave the country forever; blacks should be encouraged to serve in the army and stay.

If, by the end of his life, Lincoln was no longer paying much attention to public advice, it is understandable. But it is also tragic that he became so inured to these entreaties that he paid no heed at all to the earnest suggestion that arrived a month before his assassination, urging that Good Friday of 1865 be set aside for fasting and prayer.

Lincoln not only ignored the advice; he defied it altogether by attending the theater on that holy evening. And there he lost his life.

Grow a Beard

N Y
Westfield Chatauque Co
Oct 15. 1860

Hon A B Lincoln
Dear Sir

My father has just [come] home from the fair and brought home your picture and Mr. [Hannibal] Hamlin's [Lincoln's running mate]. I am a little girl only eleven years old, but want you should be President of the United States very much so I hope you wont think me very bold to write to such a great man as you are. Have you any little girls about as large as I am if so give them my love and tell her to write to me if you cannot answer this letter. I have got 4 brother's and part of them will vote for you any way and if you will let your whiskers grow I will try and get the rest of them to vote for you you would look a great deal better for your face is so thin. All the ladies like whiskers and they would tease their husband's to vote for you and then you would be President. My father is a going to vote for you and if I was a man I would vote for you to but I will try and get every one to vote for you that I can I think that rail fence around your picture makes it look very pretty. I have got a little baby sister she is nine weeks old and is just as cunning as can be. When you direct your letter dir[e]ct to Grace Bedell Westfield Chatauque County New York

I must not write any more answer this letter right off Good bye

Grace Bedell

∽ *Presidential candidate Lincoln answered this—probably the most famous piece of advice he ever received—with an equally well known reply a few days later (CW, IV: 129).*

P R I V A T E

Springfield, Ills.
Oct. 19. 1860

Miss. Grace Bedell
My dear little Miss.

Your very agreeable letter of the 15th. is received.

I regret the necessity of saying I have no daughters. I have three sons—one seventeen, one nine, and one seven, years of age. They, with their mother, constitute my whole family.

As to the whiskers, never having worn any, do you not think people would call it a piece of silly affect[at]ion if I were to begin it now? Your very sincere well-wisher

A. Lincoln.

Free Women, Not Blacks

Logan Co Ky
Jan 20nd 1861

Hon Abe Lincol [*sic*]
Dear Sir The negros have taken up the notion, or rather it has been taught them by beggers and Gipsies, that as soon as you were elected they would all be free. They have commenced their work of poisoning and Incendiaryism. Now all I want to know is, if you do not intend such a thing, is, for you to make them know it; so that they may go to work and wait until the next presidential Election to cut up again. I wish you would ask your Estimable Lady how she would Like, Just as she gets a good cook for some straggling begger, peddler, or fortuneteller to come along and persuade her that some one would give her higher wages on the other side of town, For God sake Dear Sir give us women some assurance that you will protect us, for we are the greatest Slaves in the South

Respectfully
Sue H. Burbridge

ఌ *No reply to this plea is known, but notwithstanding the writer's concerns, Lincoln would hardly have looked with disfavor on the prospect of domestic workers seeking the best wages they could obtain. Nor was he particularly sensitive to the concerns of women as an oppressed class, although early in his career he did favor their right to vote (*CW, I: 48*).*

Give Them "H——L"

N. York
Apl 10/61

Mr. President
Give those South Carolina villians [*sic*] h——l and we will support you.

A member of the 7th Regt. National Guard

This letter, which ironically was sent the day Fort Sumter was attacked in Charleston, contained a primitive drawing of the American flag flying on a pole above the palmetto flag of South Carolina.

"Be of Good Cheer"

Quincy [Ill.], Augt 19, 1861

My Dear Friend

In my last interview with you I was sorry to find you a little despondent, and not at all hopeful of your own individual future.

In this you are wrong most decidedly and do yourself great injustice. Be of good cheer. You have your future in your own hands, and the power to make your name one of the most justly revered and illustrious in the annals of the American race.

The people will stand by you, if you will stand by them. Give your own mind your own judgment, your own correctness of sight full scope. Hold the reins of government with a firm and steady hand, and let no man stand in the way of a glorious triumph for our cause. This rebellion must be put down, and the government, and the Union re-established on a firmer basis than ever.

The people are determined upon this, and prefer to do it under your leadership. You still have a strong hold upon their confidence, and their affections, and you can maintain it, and use it for great ends if you will; but you must be firm, earnest, and if need be, even inexorable. Let them see that their interests and the good and glory of the country are your first, last, and only care, and your power over them will be almost omnipotent.

God knows how earnestly, not only for the Country, but for your own sake, I desire the success of your administration. I want those troubles ended, and the Country made peaceful, happy and prosperous under your guidance, and it can and will be done if you follow the plain teachings of Providence. If you falter God may forsake you.

But all is in your own hands, and once more I say be of good cheer.

You know I have no selfish ends of my own to accomplish, and what I say to you I say in all sincerity of heartfelt, and faithfulness of friendship.

When at Washington, I was myself sometimes despondent, and half heart broken. Things did not look hopeful, and I should utterly have despaired, but for my confidence in you, and Mr. [William H.]

Seward [the secretary of state], and Genl McClelland [*sic*], and above all my faith in an all wise, just, and merciful God.

Mr. [Simon] Cameron [the secretary of war], whether justly or not, has lost, or rather failed to secure the confidence of the Country, and the administration is suffering greatly, and the cause of the Country is suffering from his continuance in office. There is a universal clamor in all the states through which I passed for his displacement, and the appointment of [former Secretary of War Joseph] Holt. Mr. Holt may be no better man, but the change would be of incalculable benefit at this time. I only make the suggestion. Pardon me, you know I am prompted by the highest regard for you, and the sincerest wish for your success.

Truly yours.
O. H. Browning

No reply to this letter from Lincoln's old friend Orville H. Browning has come to light, and although Browning made mention in his diary that he wrote this letter, he made no mention of receiving an answer (Browning, Diary I: 496–506).

Purge Frémont

Baltimore Sept 24th 1861

To His Excellency
Abraham Lincoln President U.S.

Oh for the Sake of our dear country remove Fremont[.] He is not fit to be entrusted in this critical hour with the Nation's interest.

Would McClellan or [General Irvin] McDowell have acted as he has. McDowell was only unfortunate—Fremont is either imbecile & unfit for his position or I fear, yes, dread he is worse. He is either an Aaron Burr or a conceited & imbecile fool.

A Southerner.

[General Nathaniel] Lyon!! sacrificed
Missouri! overrun.
Mulligan! left to shift for himself & compelled to surrender.
Our countrys Flag!! trailed by the existing miscreants in the dust!!!
The Union cause!!
The cause of our dear country!! dispirited, confidence lost & a stab to the cause of Liberty.

All of these lie at Fremont's door!!
Who can deny it?

P.S. Look at it in all its bearings! Give circumstances all their weight. Fremont's course is the very antipode of Genl McClellan or Gen. [John] Wool. They would have anticipated [Stirling] Price [Confederate general]

The country has the fullest confidence in them, that Fremont can never now enjoy No matter how brilliant his future success the country cannot confide in Fremont Mark me—

And another strong point is His impudent and unsoldierlike letter to you—he has to learn his Honor book over. The first lesson the cornerstone Obey!A man may obey with that sullen contempt that is worse than disobeying.

When he asked so insolently for a general order. Well for the country had the General order been his dismissal. Look to him! Look to him!! Beware of him ere too late. Better men than Fremont have been deposed for circumstances over which they had no control—that assume the lustre of virtues when compared to the acts & idealizing of this cold hearted & self conceited fool. He refuses audiences while the best sons of the States are sacrificed!

> *This unanswered letter was endorsed by a secretary: "One of many anonymous letters against General Fremont."*

Suϑtain Frémont

Brimfield Ill Oct 7th 1861

To President Lincoln
Dear Sir Fremont is the choice of the north west back him up and we will back you up

Respectfully Your obt srvt
John B. Day
One of Six Brothers who voted for Old Abe

> *Frémont's emancipation order ignited a firestorm of protest, as well as a significant amount of approval. Lincoln ordered the precipitant emancipation order revoked, and on October 24 he relieved Frémont of his command. The Frémont affair was the most difficult domestic political crisis of Lincoln's first year in office.*

50   Dear Mr. Lincoln

More Support for Frémont

Friend Abraham

Ambitious Politicians and <u>envious</u> Demagogues have held your ear too long. Listen a moment to the wishes of the People—<u>First of all</u>. Let <u>Fremont alone</u> and hang the <u>envious Hounds</u> that are trying to pull him down.

Secondly Adopt the same course towards McClellan & his enemies[.]

3d Send Adjutant <u>Granny Thomas</u> [Lorenzo Thomas] with some smart school marm to investigate that most Damnable Blunder of the whole war, the late deplorable affair at Edwards Ferry.

4th Send Cameron at the head of the War Department to Mackinaw to purchase <u>three Canoes</u> for the next attack at that point, and let [James W.] Ripley [the War Department's chief of ordnance] & Thomas see that there is no extravagance or peculation in the job.

5th Let those members of your Cabinet who so much fear Fremonts' popularity—employ themselves for the remainder of your term in <u>playing old sledger</u> for your cast-off shoes (Gordon Bennett, [editor of the anti-emancipation New York *Herald*] can keep a tally) for if they continue their present game, you will have no old shoes to leave for any of them—

Meanwhile stand up in your <u>Boots</u> and be what I a thousand times last year said you would be—"A man for the times" knowing nothing but right & shirking no responsibility—in short an honest man with a <u>good Backbone</u>.

Yours for justice & Right

P.S. Too late. The paper says that the order has gone out to supersede the War Patriot & hero Fremont. But he is not superseded with the People. He is their idol today—the man of their faith—who know the <u>cowardly</u> cause of his sacrifice—& are ready to rise in a mass to right him. While you for whom we enthusiastically shouted, so short a time ago, could not today get one thousand votes in the entire North West, aside from your office holders. I hope we have not been so fatally deceived as we now fear—I have faith in your good intentions yet & hope courage will be given you to do what you know to be right—I write in sorrow for I have loved your naim [*sic*], but I write the unanimous voice of the People of the North West as I have the best opportunity of knowing.

F. L. Tracy

∽ *No reply is known. This letter was merely preserved in Lincoln's bulging "Frémont" file.*

A Former President on Diplomacy

Buffalo, Dec. 16. 1861.

His Excellency Abraham Lincoln

Sir I have never, under any circumstances, presumed to offer my advice, as to men or measures, to those who have succeeded me in the administration of the Government; and I beg of you to consider the few crude suggestions which I am now about to make, as mere <u>hints</u> from one who will feel no mortification, personally, if they should be wholly disregarded.

I can in some measure appreciate the difficulties with which the administration of the Government is now embarrassed by this unholy rebellion; for I heard the threatening thunder, and viewed the gathering storm at a distance in 1850; and while I approve most cordially of the firm stand which you have taken in Support of the constitution, <u>as it is</u>, against insane abolitionism on one side and rebellious secessionism on the other, and hope and trust that you will remain firm; yet, it was not to speak of this that I took up my pen, but of a new danger which threatens more immediately our Northern frontier, but in its consequences, most fatally, the whole country. You of course will anticipate that I refer to a threatened rupture with England, for if we are so unfortunate as to be involved in a war with her at this time, the last hope of restoring the Union will vanish, and we shall be overwhelmed with the double casualties of civil and foreign war at the same time, which will utterly exhaust our resources, and may practically change the form of our government and compel it in the end to submit to a dishonorable peace.

I perceive that the telegram of this morning announces the fact from semi-official sources that, the law officers of Great Britain have given it as their opinion that the arrest of Messrs. Mason & Slidell and forcibly taking them from the Trent, a British merchant or transport vessel, was not justified by the law of nations; and that the British

Cabinet was united in sending a dispatch to Lord Lyon [the British Ambassador in Washington], protesting against the act, and demanding satisfaction by the restoration of the prisoners and a suitable apology for the insult to the British Flag. I still cherish the hope, however, that this statement may be heartily exaggerated—But suppose it be true—What then? It may be said that one of two things must happen—Either, this Government must submit to the demands thus made upon it by Great Britain, or take the hazards of a war at a most inconvenient time to settle a point of international law by by [sic] resort to arms. This alternative should be avoided if it can be with honor, and I venture to suggest that it may be by arguing in a firm but conciliatory argument in reply to the demand of Great Britain, our views of the Belligerent right to arrest these men, but conclude by saying that although we feel assured that we are right, yet if Great Britain after weighing our argument still adheres to the opinion that we are wrong; then as this is a purely legal question, where no insult was intended to the flag of Great Britain nor any intention to invade her rights, and as the point in dispute is one of international law in which all maritime nations are interested, we propose to submit it to one of the crowned heads of Europe for arbitrament, agreeing to abide [by] its word. It seems to me that Great Britain can not refuse so fair a proposition. But if she does, and insists on an unconditional compliance with her demand or war, all Christendom will then hold her responsible for the consequences.

I trust you will pardon these suggestions, which are made on the spur of the moment, without consultation with, or the knowledge of, any one, and may remain in <u>confidence</u> between us if you prefer that they should.

I am with sincere respect & great haste, Truly yours,

Millard Fillmore

∽ *There is no record of a reply to the ex-President's letter. The crisis to which he referred had been ignited on November 8, when the U.S.S.* San Jacinto *captured Confederate envoys James M. Mason and John Slidell, who were bound for England aboard the British mail-packet* Trent. *England demanded their release, hinting at war, and on December 26 the Lincoln administration finally freed the Confederates. Assistant secretary John Hay jeered that Fillmore never uttered "a sentiment that the asses around him did not at once recognize as an old acquaintance" (Monaghan,* Diplomat in Carpet Slippers, *182–184).*

A Bizarre Plan to End the Crisis

Washington D.C. Dec 30th, 1861.

A case has come to my knowledge which it may or may not be important for you to notice this point I propose respectfully to give you an opportunity of deciding upon yourself by stating the facts connected with it.

I hope and believe that this act the motives prompting it being good can produce no injurious effects and that if it be deemed impertinent that the motive will furnish a ground of acquittal.

There is in Washington a man so near purely a white man that no person unacquainted with his antecedents would suppose he was a slave and escaped to Canada where he has been made by residence and due legal form a British subject which he has papers to prove from the the [*sic*] Canadian Authorities endorsed by the American Consul.

The matter which I wish to bring to your notice is—if he is arrested under the Fugitive Slave Law as he can be by proper arrangements would or would not Lord Lyon upon the mans presenting his papers, demand his release? And what would be the result?

Here, the question takes its importance and presents complications to [*sic*] embarrassing for me. If I thought the man would be returned to slavery I should blush from this act, as he is only nominally any thing by a white man but if a way is seen clear to give him up to Lord Lyons I think he would be rather an impressive companion to Mr. Mason, the author of the Fugitive Slave Law, and quite a check to Mr. Mason's purposes in England. Being in the same category with this man excepting his former relation to slavery I make this communication with the hope of serving the countrys good and in perfect secrecy. If desired further particulars will be given and matters so conducted than no preconcert be discovered.

My reason for addressing you personally is that all others may be ignorant.

I must respectfully beg before closing that this may give no offense.

With the highest respects,

Charles H. Middleton

It may be proper for me [to] state that I think I am known to the Post Master-General as a man not likely to do any thing which I thought in the remotest degree improper and therefore if there be any impropriety in this act I hope it may be attributed to my want of better knowledge and an overzeal to sustain this Administration.

No allusion is made as to who this is to be directed to with the intention of connecting no one with it.

Lincoln forwarded this letter to William H. Seward with the following endorsement: "What thinks the Sec. of State of the within? A. Lincoln." Seward promptly answered: "The Secretary of State thinks that the scheme proposed would be injudicious." Presumably, the complex and rather offensive plan was dropped (CW, V: 83).

"Cultivate" McClellan

Chicago July 4th 1862

To His Excellency
Abraham Lincoln Prest. of the United States

Sir For the sake of our Country separate yourself from the Humbugs who surround you. Mr. [Edwin M.] Stanton [the new secretary of war] reminds those who know him of a learned Pig, exhibited by Dan Rice, the noted Showman, many years ago. His foolish aspirations for the Presidency will ruin you and our Country.

No one respects him, nor does any one pretend to, except those who are dependent on his whims. Messrs Seward & [Salmon P.] Chase [secretary of the treasury] do you credit, and outside of them you are sold. Congress will, if it can[,] ruin you or "any other man"—play Cromwell at once, dissolve them; if you do not, mark the prediction! "Some other man will."

Little Mac [the sobriquet of the day for General McClellan] is the idol of the Army and of one half of the civilians. Reflect! Now is the to [sic] cultivate him in time—He may be either a "Monk" or a "Cromwell" [McClellan would run against Lincoln for the presidency two years later]—Embrace opportunity take time by the forelock and Save our beloved Country. A Moments reflection will show you that this is not a fanciful posture—A glance at the history of the World will convince you of its truth—Send Stanton afloat—adjourn Congress— Send the Politicians home—stick to McClellan and and [sic] we can rest easily, and satisfied that our future is in the hands of honest men.

Very Respectfully Yours
J. P. Sanderson

∽ Sanderson was a Philadelphia politician and ally of the former secretary of war Simon Cameron, a fellow Pennsylvanian. This may explain Sanderson's hostility toward his friend's successor, Stanton. Cameron was sent into political exile as ambassador to Russia, and Stanton remained an intimate and trusted advisor to Lincoln until the latter's death (CW, IV: 174; ALE, 46).

Reshuffle the Cabinet

[December 1862?]

State	S. P. Chase	Ohio
Treasury	W. P. Fessenden	Me
War	N. P. Banks	Mass.
Navy	Jo. Holt	Ky
Interior	J. R. Doolittle	Wis.
P.M. Genl.	Preston King	N.Y.
Atty Genl.	Ed. Bates	Mo.

This cabinet would meet the expectations of the country and would end the War before spring.

[Unsigned]

∽ Lincoln filed away this anonymously provided list under the heading "New Cabinet advice." Of the names proposed, only one—that of the attorney general—was a holdover from the current administration. The President ignored each and every suggestion, although he did name Fessenden secretary of the treasury two years later, upon Chase's resignation.

"Dispose" of Free Blacks

Chicago May 1st 1863

Dear Sir,

The bearer of this, Dr. Delany, is a man who from the short acquaintance I have had with him, & what I have read of his operations & explorations in Africa, I think eminently qualified to conduct an enterprise of Colonization of the free colored people of the Country, should that be thought the best way to dispose of them. I therefore take great pleasure in reccommending [sic] him to your favorable consideration.

Yours truly,
Peter Page

To his Excellency, Abraham Lincoln President &c.

ℹ *By the time this letter was written, Lincoln had far more interest in inducting freed blacks into the Union military than in colonizing them in Africa. Peter Page was a Chicago real estate dealer who had once offered to serve as Lincoln's bodyguard (CW, IV: 177).*

Create a National Thanksgiving Day

P R I V A T E

Philadelphia Sept. 28th 1863.

Hon. Abraham Lincoln—
President of the United States

Sir,—Permit me, as Editress of the "Lady's Book" [*Godey's*], to request a few minutes of your precious time, while laying before you a subject of deep interest to myself and—as I trust—even to the President of our Republic, of some importance. This subject is to have the <u>day of our annual Thanksgiving made a National and fixed Union Festival.</u>

You may have observed that, for some years past, there has been an increasing interest felt in our land to have the Thanksgiving held on the same day in all the States; it now needs National recognition and authoritative <u>fixation</u> only, to become permanently, an American custom and institution.

Enclosed are three papers being printed these are easily read, which will make the idea and its progress clear and show also the popularity of the plan.

For the last fifteen years I have set forth this idea in the "Lady's Book," and placed the papers before the Governors of all the States and Territories—also I have sent these to our Ministers abroad, and our Missionaries to the heathens and commanders in the Navy. From the recipients I have received uniformly the most kind approval. Two of these letters—one from Governor (now General) Banks and one from Governor Morgan are enclosed; both gentlemen as you will see, have nobly acted to bring about the desired Thanksgiving Union.

But I find there are obstacles not possible to be overcome, without legislative aid—that each State should, by statute, make it obligatory on the Governor to appoint the last Thursday of November, annually, as Thanksgiving Day;—or, as this way would require years to be realized, it has occurred to me that a proclamation from the President of the United States would be the best, surest and most fitting method of National appointment.

I have written to my friend Hon. Wm. H. Seward, and requested him to confer with President Lincoln on this subject.

As the President of the United States has the power of appointment for the District of Columbia and the Territories; also for the Army and Navy and all American citizens abroad who claim protection from the U.S. Flag—could he not, with right as well as duty, issue his proclamation for a Day of National Thanksgiving for all the above classes of persons? And would it not be fitting and patriotic for him to appeal to the Governors of all the States inviting and commending these to unite in issuing proclamations for the last Thursday in November as the Day of Thanksgiving for the people of each State? Thus the great Union Festival of America would be established.

Now the purpose of this letter is to entreat President Lincoln to put forth his Proclamation appointing the last Thursday in November (which falls this year on the 26th) as the National Thanksgiving for all those classes of people who are under the National Government particularly in commending this Union Thanksgiving to each State Executive: thus, by the noble example and action of the President of the United States, the permanency and unity of our Great American Festival of Thanksgiving would be forever secured.

An immediate proclamation would be necessary, so as to reach all the States in season for State appointments, and to anticipate the early appointments by Governors.

Excuse the liberty I have taken

> With profound respect
> Yrs truly
> Sarah Josepha Hale
> Editress of the "Lady's Book"

∽ *No personal reply to Sarah Hale has come to light, but on October 3, 1863, Lincoln issued a proclamation urging all Americans "to set apart and observe the last Thursday of November next as a day of Thanksgiving"; it was the country's first national Thanksgiving Day, and the tradition suggested by Hale and established by Lincoln has been followed ever since (CW, VI: 496–497).*

Enforce Temperance

[Dec 4, 1863]

To His Excellency Abraham Lincoln
President of the U.S.

Dear Sir: The undersigned on behalf of the Temperance Association of Muskingam County, Ohio, respectfully address you as Commander-in-Chief of the Army and Navy of the United States.

At your call thousands upon thousands of brave and patriotic young men rallied round our Country's standard and hastened to the defense of our government.

Sorrowfully but freely we gave them up, more we could not do—less we dare not. Full well we knew that many a brave spirit must be sacrificed, that many a loved one would return to us, never.

We fondly hoped that the perils of war would not be augmented needlessly, nor its sufferings and evil, increased without cause.

We felt that we had a right to expect, that those whose good fortune it might be to have command, would so fully appreciate their proper responsibilities, as to be the soldiers best friend, and the guardian of his morals and his life and the promoter of his comfort and health.

While we are glad to know that in many instances this has been the case, we are constrained to believe that in more, the exact opposite is true.

We greatly fear that many officers have become addicted to habits of intemperance, and are not only leading their men by example, into ruinous habits of vice, but by their recklessness, and unfitness to command, have occasioned the needless sacrifice of thousands of valuable lives.

Much as we may admire their bravery or pity their infirmities we can not resist the conviction, that no drunk is fit to command in our armies or navy.

In no spirit of dictation, but out of the fullness of sorrowing hearts, we appeal to the Commander-in-Chief if it be possible, to mitigate this terrible evil.

We venture to suggest, that while intoxicating drinks are forbidden to the soldiers, the same restraint would prove equally salutary upon the officers. And that an established rule, by which all officers of notorious habits of intoxication shall be dismissed [from] the service, would do much to cure the evil.

But should all measures fail to accomplish all that is desired, yet the manifestation of the <u>will</u> of the President, to do all he can to conserve the morals, and save the lives of our brave soldiers, will afford consolation to many an anxious aching heart and call down the benediction of Heaven on his head.

With sentiments of unfeigned regard, and with fervent prayers, that you may be guided by Divine wisdom and sustained by divine grace we are truly yours,

Committee
A. A. Guthrie
John Taylor, Jr.
Henry Bandy

∽ *Busy preparing his 1863 message to Congress, Lincoln did not reply to the committee's letter, which may have been inspired by reports of General Ulysses S. Grant's drinking. The committee probably did not realize that twenty-one years earlier Lincoln had delivered a temperance lecture urging those tempted by liquor to drink instead from "the sorrow quenching draughts of perfect liberty" (CW, I: 271–279).*

Wage Vigorous War

Belleville [Ill.], Dec. 6, 1863

Hon. A. Lincoln, President &c.

You know I have never agreed with you in politics, but permit me to say one thing: Prosecute this war with the utmost vigor and put down this accursed rebellion against God and man and posterity north and south will bless you forever.

Yours truly
Wm. H. Underwood

∽ *Eight years earlier, Lincoln and Underwood had together defended a St. Louis banker in Carlinville, Illinois. No reply to Underwood's letter is known.*

Convert Capitol into Asylum

Washington D.C. Jan. 9th, 1864

Mr. President

Dear Sir I take the liberty of writing a plan for ending the War for your inspection as I have been advised by thousands of influential gents &

Ladies to do so and you will find it to your advantage to do so as I presume you understand the conqueror in all Wars becomes ruler after conquering the enemy therefore if the plan which I leve [sic] with you is carried into effect will place the Reins of Government into my hands and then I will give you the House and grounds where you reside and Five hundred thousand dollars besides as it is the will of God that some of my plans Shal be carried into effect before the War can be ended as he has taken me into his hands and compells me to do as he pleases and laid open before this plan and several others also plans for taking the piratical vessels if you cannot make this plan work I have another for taking Richmond by stratagem with 2500 horsemen armed with Revolvers only.

Yours with Respect, now for the plan

Dear Sir the plan I shal now lay before you is simply this which is to send for Jeff. Davis and his Congress and as many of his associates as possible General Lee in particular if you can get him to come so much the better send for them to come immediately to meet you and then hand them over to me and Resign your seat to me and I will Declare them Deranged according to the voice of God and have them taken care of as such until we can have the centre of the capitol converted into a Lunatic Asylum for them where Mr. Buchanan should have put them when they came to him to talk Secessionism thus you will perceive we put an end to all Wars forever as I prayed to god to assist me in getting up a plan to put an end to this war in such a way as to end all Wars forever he then took me in his hands and let me know that the Leading men of the south were deranged and it is the duty of Christians to get the Leading devils of the World which is J Davis and his associates by stratagem instead of fighting as it will be impossible to conquer by fighting as there are so many throughout the North that are in favor of the South that when they come into battle will not fight for the Union but give themselves up as prisoners and when another battle is to be fought they will be ready to assist the Rebels against us and in that way the War would be carried on until all are killed and everything Destroyed by fire and sword that can be I have had proof of this in traveling through Newyork City and state and other places as I traveled about six months for the purpose of getting all the information I could and I found most of the Democrat or demon party in that state of mind and feeling, so much so in N.Y. that I frequently found gangs of them collected on the corners of the streets and in Drinking places talking about making preparations to resist the Draft and saying among themselves if they had to fight they would fight their enemies at home which was the Republicans instead of going south to fight their Democratic brothers and by having the power of God I was enabled to face them and soothe them alone which I done last winter for three months and a lady I am engaged to being fearful of my being injured in some way by the crazy devils as they threaten to harm me every day in the streets she requested the chief of police to have me guarded by the whole police force which he did until the 21st of April last when I left for Washington therefore you perceive I have great power and courage I trust sufficient to carry through what I have undertaken although I am in delicate health and a beggar but I have always said am still of the same opinion that when God sees fit he can put a beggar to rule the Universe with his Christian laws and now he has compeld me to become a beggar and cannot help myself in any other way than by writing plans for your inspection for the benefit of all and I hope you will see the necessity and importance of carrying out some of my plans as it is the will of God. Some of this shall be carried into effect before the War can be ended you can see by the wording of this letter that it is written by inspiration and this plan was handed down to me from Heaven I wrote a plan about 6 weeks since and left with your secretary but never knew whether you received it therefore I give you this myself I have the right plans for taking the pirates on the Ocean if you want them I will write them yours with Respect

Samuel Connell

ဢ *After reading this diatribe, Lincoln replaced the letter in its envelope and scrawled on it, "Samuel Connell—crazy."*

Deport Rebels

Frankfort, Ky., June 2, 1864.

His Excellency Abraham Lincoln,
President of the United States:—

Permit an humble but, I trust, a true Union man, to recommend that you direct the Federal officers in Kentucky to clean out and send off out of the limits of the state, the refugee rebels, their wives, & families, and the families of all the rebels and traitors who have gone south, and all in the rebel army, or service of the States in rebellion and insurrection.

We have in this town refugees from Missouri, and Other states—some have been in Canada, others in the rebel army, and there is no doubt that they are plotting to overthrow the Government, and are the aides and abettors of those who call themselves "Conservatives," but who so silently act their treason that we cannot get evidence to convict them.

Show, by making our state cleaner, and thereby better, by the purging out of all rebels and traitors—male and female—that like the great Patriarch of old you are the "Father of the Faithful," and you will meet with the plaudit of "well done!" from tens of thousands of loyal people in Kentucky, who have no use for rebels and traitors, and especially for those whose treason has driven them thence from other states.

Yours most respectfully
Henri F. Middleton

∽ *Lincoln was doubtless sensitive to talk of treason in his border state birthplace. But no reply is known to Middleton's letter, which was written on the stationery of the* Frankfort Commonwealth, *a local newspaper.*

Cancel the Draft

[June 22, 1864]

To A. Lincoln President of United States
Mr. President.

Dear Sir, In your note to Congress the other day [probably his June 8 letter advocating repeal of the so-called "three hundred dollar clause" permitting persons to be excused from conscription in exchange for such payment], you say you "Want Men, Not Money," if so (and no one doubts it) Please dont try that Lottery game any more, for it is against the grit of a true Yank, Drafted, Never, we say, so long as we have 300$ in the locker Again we have no faith in these calls for 200,000 even 600,000. Again we are all doing well, and making money, and we do not like to leave, and have others Stay at Home, and continue to make the big wages, while we work at 16$ per month for the government. But all we want is, the right kind of a chance to Volunteer.

This is what we want you to do.

Issue a Proclamation, calling on the men to turn out in mass, and expect every one to use their influence to that effect suppose you come out about this way.

To All True Men

Fellow Citizens,

Whereas the Constitution made by our Fathers, Genl. Washington, and the rest of them, Declared in Art 6th, Sec 2d, that "This Constitution shall be the Supreme law of the land,["] and whereas there are a number of persons who, (being instigated by the Devil) are trying to set it aside, and refuse to be governed by it, now, I, A[.] Lincoln President of these United States—Call on Every Loyal Man to come up to my Help against these Rebels, and Traitors. I invite and urge ever[y] man to lay aside his business, and volunteer for One Hundred days. Let time Stand Still as far as business is concerned, That we may End this unhappy war, Save our Country, and Show to the World, that we are a Nation All powerful in ourselves (under God our King.) Let us lay aside all party strife and differences, and arise as one man. Trusting in God we shall Succeed.

Assemble together then, on Monday the 3d day of July, at your usual places of Election. And proceed to organize into companys chose your own field & company officers. And I will appoint Gens to command. And in order that provision may be made for the Families, let each County have its common Depot of Provisions, & county committee. Those able to supply their own Families will do so, and all able contribute to the common fund According to their ability.

Again, the Harvest must be cared for, Therefore, All those persons engaged in farming, will remain at Home, and they alone. But all others, between the ages of 18 & 50 years, of Every traid and profession, able to bear armes, are hereby exorted as they love our country, Our Constitution, and their Families to Volunteer[.] Those unable to go will remain [and] devote their time to the protection of Property, and will be organized as a Provo[s]t Guard. The County and District committees will see to the wants &c of the Families. All Business being Suspended for 60 Days.

The people will respond to such a call, and the Uprising of 1864 will far exceed that of 1861.

We are Satisified it is the Shortest, and Most Honorable Road to Peace.

Truly yours
One of the Million
W. M. C.

PS I have brought the above subject before many persons of every class during the last 2 years and have yet to finde one, who would refuse to obey Such a call.

Pittsburgh June 22/64

∽ Lincoln's secretaries filed this interesting letter with the endorsement "Draft of a Proclamation for calling out men for the army." In July, Congress ended the $300 commutation provision under which wealthier men could escape the nation's first military draft. But "substitution" remained a common practice. Lincoln himself paid for a substitute: a Pennsylvania man named John Staples. Lincoln received innumerable letters protesting conscription, with opposition coming from politicians who feared voter hostility, to Pacifists like the Shakers, who insisted they be declared exempt. An exasperated Lincoln eventually wondered: "Has the manhood of our race run out?" (CW, VI: 448).

Maintain White Supremacy

[T E L E G R A P H]
Hambrook, Bradford Co. Penn.
August 5, 1864

Sir

The following lines will give you to understand what is justice & what is truth to all men

My Dear Sir I hope you will be kind Enough to pay attention to these few lines

I am yours & c
John McMahon

Equal rights & Justice to all white men in the United States forever. White men is in class number one & black men in class number two & must be governed by white men forever.

∽ Presidential secretary John G. Nicolay sent McMahon a biting answer the following day, a letter some historians have speculated was written by Lincoln himself. This is the unsigned copy that survived in the Nicolay papers (CW, VIII: 483).

Washington, D.C.
Aug. 6, 1864

John McMahon
Hambrook, Bradford Co Penn.

The President has received yours of yesterday, and is kindly pay-ing attention to it. As it is my business to assist him whenever I can, I will thank you to inform me, for his use, whether you are either a white man or black one, because in either case, you can not be re-garded as an entirely impartial judge. It may be that you belong to a third or fourth class of <u>yellow</u> or <u>red</u> men, in which case the impartial-ity of your judgement would be more apparant [*sic*].

Introduce Negro Suffrage

Vincennes, State of Indiana,
September 14, 1864.

To His Excellency
Abr Lincoln, President of the U.S. of America

Sir Please excuse this letter claiming a few moments of your precious time. But the matter is too important to be overlooked. Let us be short then.

The time of Presidential Election is before the door: <u>Your Victory</u> over your competitor is <u>an absolute Necessity</u>, the Sinew of Life for the U.S.

Any other man would tear down what you succeeded by wisdom and experience to build up during three hard years. None but you can overcome this Storm and you are the only Pilot to lead the Ship into the Harbor.

Therefore, all <u>lawfull</u> means must be used to secure your Elec-tion. One of these lawfull means is the Votes of all Negroes over 21 years, being in the employ of the U.S. <u>as Soldiers</u> or <u>in any other capacity</u> what ever drawing pay from the U.S. Government; conse-quently virtually bound to support the Government. Be sure, all Ne-groes will vote for you, their Liberator and Benefactor.

The different States do allow Soldiers, Sailors &c counting their votes, not saying anything about the Color, soldiers must have. Con-sequently colored Soldiers, Sailors, Drivers, Cooks, etc. <u>employed in the U.S. Army</u> are entitled to vote.

Five Slaves are entitled to three votes [a reference to the three-fifths clause in the Constitution], why shall <u>free Negroes</u> in the U.S. Army be deprived of that prerogative?

Please, Sir, take this matter in consideration and, if possible, to act accordingly, this matter being of vital importance for our Nation and for the Posterity.

I remain most respectfully

> Your Excellency's most obedient servant
> Dr. F. W. Delang
> true Republican and Lincoln-man.

ᔒ *Lincoln was not nearly ready to raise the issue of black suffrage for the 1864 election. No reply to this letter has been found.*

Make "Peas" Now

Pittsburgh Jan. 16. 1865

Dear Friend it is with the opportunity that i take this Penn in to my Hand to in form you with a vew Lines and to say that i am well yet and i hope that these vew Lines will Find you the sam Dear Sir i have Left my Happie Home the Home you Left Last evre Person is Sollom and Sorry there I have Travlet throw a manny of Town befor I cam to Pittsburgh and i found it the same there. Dear friend the Peapple is in for making Peas yeas Peas they wand and thay pray that you will make it thay all say before the Lextion for you there was Bills posted up evrewhere that you would make a change in the cabnet and would make Peas the tok is about Peas but we cant see it and have not seen it. they say this cruel Ware has bin going long a nuf there is Thousands of Widdows Thousands and Thousands of orphans were there Fathers has Left there Happie Homes now slain up on the Field of Battle for the Love of his country. The Father has Left his Wife and his Beloved children the Brother has Left has his sister and Brother Father and Mother for to go and Battle for his Country the tears is Wiping evre day yes evre day that Gott gives to us and the harddest is now that you have made a nother call for Threehundred Thousand more with the Peopple will not stand thay say you have had a nuf of Men to crush this Rebilion and so thay will not stand the Draft anny more. Thay say you cann Settle this Ware if you want to do it and thay say thay have Elecded you for to make Peas so the copperheads would not have the canch to do it. Dear Friend do tell the Peopple wad your going to do My Hard weps with tears wenn i think of the Happie Counry we have hat wons but now it is destroyed it is in Morning all over it is Solom wath from from [*sic*] this cruel Ware yes it has Kield Thousends and crippled Thousends o how the Peopples Hards Fell you cand think of it and i cand tell you it as i ha say aloud about Draft it is not on count of me for i am to old for it and here is another thing wot I seen in Pittsburgh at the Provostmarshall office that thay will not exempt a Man unless he has a Leg of or an arm no i will tell you my on mind about that wath is this yous of sending a Man in the sirvis ween he is not fitt for it he will not stand it long untill he dies or gets discharght that is oll of the Doctors fould for he is paid for it and he dos not care ho he send out that is onley expens to you for i seen it myself i was there wen it was don he had a Man there that had the Kidnedeasseas vere bad and yussing Meddcine for 3 years and Father and Mother to prof if he said you will do to carry a gunn. Now i will close my Few Linse and my Best Respect to you and your Wife and children and Dear Friend try your best to settle this Ware and Draft for thay Peopple will not stand it were ever you you you [*sic*] here them say that eare please.

I your Truly optaind Servend
I am going on to see you my self if i can get to see you but i beleve i will not get to see you for in Pittsburgh i will not stay. my name i will not tell to you for i am a fraid you would hurd me for righting this to you. Dear Sir tell the Peopple wot you ar going to do. excuse bad righting for i am nervos and a poor schollor.

∽ *Although no response could be made to this anonymous plea for peace, Lincoln retained this letter for his files.*

Observe Good Friday

State of New Hampshire:
Claremont, March 16, 1865

To His Excellency, Abraham Lincoln
Honored Sir, I beg leave to express to you, the Chief Magistrate of our Country, my earnest request and desire that, if not inconsistent with your own views or with a decision already made, you will appoint Good Friday, the fourteenth day of April next—to be observed as a day of Fasting and Prayer throughout the United States. I have reason to believe that day would be agreeable to Christian people of all denominations.

Having made this brief suggestion, I beg to assure you of the high consideration with which I remain your Excellency's

Most Obedient and trustful servant
Carlton Chase
Bishop of the Diocese of New Hampshire

ᕫ *The President did not declare Good Friday of 1865 a national day of fasting and prayer. Instead, Lincoln went to the theater that night, where he was assassinated.*

This letter appears on page 112.

Brunswick Hotel. Jermyn St. London
24th Jany. 1865

Honble. Abraham Lincoln
President of the U. S. America

I have heard from good authority that if
I suppress the Book I have now ready for
publication, you may be induced to consider
leniently the case of my husband, S. Wylde
Hardinge, now a prisoner in Fort Delaware,
I think it would be well for you & me to
come to some definite understanding -
My Book was not originally intended to
be more than a personal narrative, but since
my husband's unjust arrest I had intended
making it political, & had introduced many

[2]

Requests and Demands

*A*NYTHING THAT KEPT the people . . . away from him he disapproved," assistant secretary John Hay wrote of Abraham Lincoln, "although they nearly annoyed the life out of him by unreasonable . . . requests."

For four years, the daily mail delivery inevitably brought to Lincoln's White House a huge pile of demands and requests—reasonable and unreasonable alike—for both jobs and favors. "Do you see what they are?" correspondence secretary William O. Stoddard recalled almost mockingly. "That pile is of applications for appointments to offices of every name and grade, all over the land. They must be examined with care, and some of them must be briefed before they are referred to the departments and bureaus with which the offices asked for are connected. We will not show any of them to Mr. Lincoln at present."

Nor was the President initially shown all of the countless requests for pardons that poured daily onto the correspondence desk once the war began. But these, Stoddard recalled, Lincoln wished to keep "where he can lay his hands upon them, and every batch of papers and petitions must be in order for him when he calls for it." According to Stoddard, Lincoln was "downright sure to pardon any case" that he

71

found "a fair excuse for pardoning," but, Stoddard added, "some people think he carries his mercy too far."

Stoddard and the other secretaries believed that an appalling number of Lincoln's correspondents went beyond the bounds of propriety, and there is enough evidence of presumptuousness in the surviving letters to support that belief.

For example, the sculptor Thomas D. Jones, who had posed Lincoln for a bust portrait from life back in Springfield, evidently came to the conclusion soon thereafter that his brief exposure to the future president somehow entitled him to diplomatic office. Not only did he write to demand the consulship in Rome—then considered the plum foreign posting for artists in search of underwritten, advanced education—but he also followed up with a letter to John Nicolay sneering that the appointment was "one of the smallest, or least" of Lincoln's many "favors." On this occasion, the favor was denied.

So was the favor requested by the old friend of Millard Fillmore, who wrote the White House to suggest that the former president's onetime secretary, "a good and true man," would be a perfect candidate to join Lincoln's staff. Not surprisingly, neither Nicolay nor Hay showed much interest in forwarding the suggestion to the President. They did forward a plea from another former president, James Buchanan, who wrote to request that his successor search for a set of books he had left behind in the White House. Far more touching—but in all likelihood even less favorably regarded—were the requests and demands that arrived over the signatures of less famous correspondents. A typical letter came in the late spring of 1862 from a self-described "lady who, worn out with fatigue, presented herself before you a supplicant for her husband's promotion." She wrote: "To err is human, to forgive Divine," making reference to some transgressions her husband had committed in the past—probably long since forgotten. It took a unique plea for patronage to win access to the President's desk—much less his eventual approval. But Lincoln, who loved Shakespeare, was probably both amused and impressed by one request that came in the form of a dialogue between Lear and Kent, ending with the appropriate line, "That which ordinary men are fit for, I am qualified in."

It is likely that no president before or since Abraham Lincoln was so routinely petitioned for help by ordinary citizens—not only for jobs but also for assistance in settling disputes so minor that some did not deserve the attention of even a village magistrate. And the fact that so many such letters survive in the Lincoln Papers suggests that a large number were in fact brought to his attention. They ranged from the insistent to the obsequious: one favor-seeking correspondent referred repeatedly to the President as "your highness."

William O. Stoddard remembered in particular a note from "a worthy soul out West, who had applied for a patent, and would be obliged if the President would step into the patent office and see about it and hurry up." Lincoln may never have seen that letter, but he did read the pleas from job seekers in search of a change of climate, charities begging for donations (which Lincoln seldom gave), admirers asking for autographs and locks of presidential hair, merchants offering their wares at supposed bargains, impresarios seeking permits, artists and photographers asking for sittings, investors offering opportunities, men of the cloth seeking appointments as military chaplains, and aggrieved transgressors appealing fines. Lincoln even received a letter in 1865 from the incoming vice president of the United States, Andrew Johnson, asking permission to skip the inauguration—a request Lincoln promptly denied.

To nearly all, Lincoln apparently paid at least cursory attention. William O. Stoddard would later claim that "after he became the chief magistrate of the nation he almost ceased to write personal letters, or even read them." But the Lincoln Papers bear ample evidence of exceptions to this rule.

Occasionally Lincoln would come to rue his generous impulses. Once, he learned that a correspondent he had obliged with a favor had repaid him by trying to use the President's name to extort $1,500. The citizen was promptly arrested in Philadelphia. John Nicolay explained the situation to Lincoln this way: "Do you remember, Mr. President, a request from a stranger a few days since for your autograph, and that you gave it to him upon a half sheet of note paper? The scoundrel doubtless forged an order above your signature, and has attempted to swindle somebody."

"Oh," replied Lincoln. "That's the trick, is it?"

But such experiences failed to inhibit Lincoln's overall eagerness to oblige his correspondents when he reasonably could, especially if they were needy or desperate. The "patent-leather kid glove set" may have known no more of him "than an owl does of a comet blazing into his blinking eyes," John Hay conceded. But Lincoln's humbler constituents seemed to know him well. The requests and demands from his mailbag—some impudent, some heartbreaking, some absurd—suggest that even those who misunderstood the office felt a connection to the man.

A "Gardner" Asks for Work

To Honorable Abraham Lincoln

    Dear Sir   As you are soon to occupy the Presidents house at Washington I would inquire if you would want to employ a gardner. I am an ornamental gardner by profession, and understand all the branches of gardning from the vegetable department up the flower garden, taking care of fruit trees shrubery &c I have been trained up to this business from a boy and think I could give perfect satisfaction Also am handy in keeping things in order about buildings I am a New-hampshire man and have always been a Republican I have a wife who is an experienced nurse in sickness and can do needle work Also have an educated daughter who can work at nice needle work, also a smart active boy who could wait upon your family My family are all pious, and members of the Presbeterian church. We can furnish the best Testimonials as to character and industry We would like a situation in your family Any thing trusted to our care could be depended upon I have lived in Rockford five years and have followed the business of Landscap and ornamental gardning.

    Should you wish for information I will refer you to the Rev L H Johnson of Rockton Ill our former pastor and minister Should you wish for our services we will be in readiness at your call. Will you please to have the gooness to give an answer

Your Obt servant
Samuel S Dimond

Hon Abraham Lincoln
P S Please to refer to Dr A. M. Catlin of this city. Also to Rev L H Johnson of Rockton Ill

∽ *There is no record of a reply to this offer of family service from the entire Dimond family—nor any record of their employment at the White House.*

Requesting a Presidential Mortgage

[February 27, 1861]

Mr. Abraham Lincoln
<u>Excellence</u>!

    I beg pardon to your Excellence! if I take the liberty to address to you without any introduction: but I hope, that your Noble heart will excuse me.

    I have wrot to your Excellence! during your permanency in New, York. Having not received answer! I hav take the determination to write to your Excellence! again. I am Italian married Lady—, with two american Sons. My Father was many years, in the Service of his Majesty George IV King of England. As a "Corriere di Gabinetto" and was Secretary of her Highness Caroline of Brunswick, wife to George IV. In my youth, I was very found of of music. I left my Country, (Milan) in the years (1835) at the age of 15 years, engaged for Mexico, as a "<u>Prima Donna</u>" in the Italian Opera troup in that Capital. I have been in Havana, New.Orleans, and in all the United States. I have many acquaitance in New.York: but, only one, good friend! this is Romaine Dillon Esq. God! father of my younger Son "<u>Cesare</u>" this good friend, hold a high position at Ryo Janeiro, Brazil, by the Government of Washington. In New.Orleans, we have lost all our money in Commertial speculations. With the remaining money, of our last engagement in Mexico, we purchase a Country Residence in Houghtonville, two miles south of Rahway New Jersey, were we reside. Adverces circumstances have trust us in a critical position. Nothing remain to us, but only our Country place, which is in Mortgag for ($1,200). Having no means to take up the Mortgag, and no means, to live in this Country, and not probability, to any Opera engagement: some time go, we advertised in the New.York Times, and Herald, our Country place, for Sale

> FOR SALE—A Very Handsome Villa in the township of
> Woodbridge, New-Jersey, two miles south of the City of
> Rahway, and five minutes' walk from Hougtonville dépôt of
> the New-Jersey Railroad, and one hour's ride from New-York.
> The house is new, well arranged, and handsomely built,
> surrounded with ornamental and all kinds of fruit trees,
> including 200 Isabella grape vines from Italy—stocked with all
> kinds of flowers. The villa is situated in the most delightful

part of the State on high and healthy land. A new stable, carriage house and out buildings, and about three acres of land all in garden style. Price $6000. Apply to A. Vattellina, on the premises. Letters for Rahway, N.J.

with the intention to take up the Mortgag, and with the remaining money, go to Italy. But, alas! we have not succeeded. In my despair, make me lay a Petition to the Prince of Wales, hoping he would help me, in name of my Father "Theodoro Majocchi".

The Honorable Daniel E. Sickles, in Washington, he give my petition to the English Ambassador, Lord Lyon. I have received answer from his Grace the Duck of Newcastle, that I have sended to your Excellence! in New York.

I have wrot to the President Mr. James Buchanan, upon the same petition. The answer from Mr. Buchanan, I deed sended to you, in New.York.

If our good friend Romaine Dillon Esq. could know our present circumstances, we ar sure, he would help us. His Brother Robert james Dillon Esq. in New.York, told me that his brother Romaine intention, was to come bak from the Brazil soon. With this hope we have weated for is coming! but in reeding the New.York Times, I see that Romaine Dillon was to remain in Brazil for long time yet. Now, is to late to address him, because, next month of March, the Mortgag will be forclos, and our Proprety, will be sacrified for the amount of one thousand and two hundred dollars. ($1,200) and of corts, myself and my childrens, on the Street! without hope to retourn to our Country.

The orrible future of our situation, fright me. I have tryd to find some persons in Rahway, to hold the Mortgag: but hunnaply, in the hard time, is impracticable. The thought com to me, to lay our circonnstances, to your Excellence! I heard spik very favourably of your magnanimity and humanity. Your Excellence! is blessed with Childrens! in name of <u>God</u>! and in name of your dear Childrens, I implore your protetion: Save me and my childrens. Do Sir! take up the Mortgag, and hold yourself our Property, until is sold, for a reasonable price. After, I will advertise immediately our Residence for Sale again. My lawyer, is Mr. Thomas H. Shafer of Rahway New.Jersey. I confess my temerity, but our situation is orrible and frightful, that make me daring, hoping in your Noble heart, a favorable answer.

<u>God</u>! bless you and your family. I will pray <u>God</u>! for your prosperity and happiness.

I have the Honor to be, Excellence! Your Loyal, Humbly and Respectfully Servant

Amalia Majocchi Valtellina

Rahway New.Jersey
February 27(1861

❧ *No reply is known—nor was one likely made. The letter was given this straight-forward endorsement: "Madam Valtellina asks the President to take up a mortgage on her villa, near Rahway, New Jersey."*

Two Dollars for His Picture

Green Bay Wis Mar 23, 1861

Hon Abraham Lincoln

Dear Sir I take the liberty of writing to you & making the following request for my little daughter, now about seven years old, which is, that you will send her your likeness. She is a very strong supporter of yours & has been ever since your nomination. Although all her little playmates are Democrats & almost every inducement has been used to make her turn she holds firm, Her Grandfather who is an old Henry Clay Whig tried to induce her to go for [John] Bell & [Edward] Everett [candidates of the National Union party for president and vice president in 1860] by all kinds of offers but it was of no use & one gentleman offered her a pound of Candy if she would only hurra once for Bell & Everett or Douglas, it was a great temptation but it was of no use, It is very surprising what an interest she takes in all that concerns you She reads everything in the papers and knows more of what is going on in politics than I do, & takes every occasion to defend you against all attacks from every source. A good many have tried to make her opposed to you but she sticks to you and tells them it will be all right now you are President. She has always been very anxious to have a Lincoln Medal but as I was unable to get her a good one here I have taken the liberty to make this request of you, which I hope you will grant as I think she really deserves to have a good likeness of you. Enclosed I send you Two Dollars to defray the expense.

Yours Very Respectfully
Joshua Whitney.
of Green Bay Wisconsin

∽ *Lincoln apparently answered this charming request, although no surviving copy is known. Whitney's letter bears the endorsement "Returned money & photograph May 23."*

An "Old Friend" Seeks Job

Springfield May 24th/61

Much Respected Friend A Lincoln

I take this opportunity of informing you of my present situation in life. Last fall as you well know I done all in my power for the Republican party. I was then threatened by Judge [Samuel H.] Treat that if I did not stop working for that party he would discharge me from the position which I held in the U.S. Court this he has done. He will not now permit me to sit as one of the jurors or to do any thing else about the Court. I am now placed in a sad position. The very means of my support has been taken from me for having done as I had a right to do. I now wish you to be so kind as to let me have or asist me in being appointed to the Registers Office in the Land Office in this City it is the wish of all your old friends of Springfield that I should have that office. now My old friend you know that I have a lot of old and helpless women to take care of I feel that it is not necessary to say any more as you know all about me.

Dr. Wallace [Lincoln's brother-in-law] can tell you that the Republicans & all good Union men are for old Arney as Register of the Land Office at Springfield.

I am with the highest Respect most greatfully

Your Obt. Servant
A. R. Robinson

To His Excellency
A. Lincoln
President of U States of America

∽ *No record has been found of an appointment for Arnold R. Robinson, or even a response to his letter. Lincoln may have remembered that Robinson had deserted the Whigs in 1848 to support opposition candidates. "Tell Arney to reconsider," Lincoln wrote at the time, "if he would be saved." Now, thirteen years later, it may have been too late to save "Arney" (CW, I: 490).*

Hero's Wife Seeks Promotion

Brevoort. [N.Y.]
May 30th 1861

To His Excellency The President

Sir, I pray you not to deem me intrusive or that I presume on the kindness you have already shown my husband, when I take the liberty of requesting that, in filling the Army appointments you will not forget <u>Major Anderson</u>. He has certainly a claim on your justice as well as on your generosity and on the Government which he as served <u>so</u> long <u>so</u> faithfully.

Mr. President, he would die rather than ask for or connive at getting an appointment for himself: and <u>his wife</u> is writing to ask for it for him <u>only</u> because she knows how gratifying such an acknowledgement of his success, on the part of his Government, would be to him. She knows, too, how kindly his sensitive nature would feel his juniors in the service being placed above him: and she could not <u>bear</u>, Mr. President, to see him endure <u>that</u> trial, after all he has already borne for the good of his country.

Whilst other appointments are made for political considerations, I hope it may not be presuming in me to remind you, that Major Anderson has had the good fortune to strike the chord which has reverberated through the whole country with such surprising effect.

You will, therefore, I am sure, excuse and grant the request I make of you. His whole military career places him equal to <u>any</u> command you may be pleased to confer on him; and, after the <u>very</u> kind manner in which you expressed yourself towards him when he had the pleasure of seeing you in Washington I hope and believe that you will give him <u>such</u> a position as you, his wife and his country deem that the <u>length</u> and <u>nature</u> of his services entitle him to.

Be pleased to present me to Mrs. Lincoln, whom I had the pleasure of seeing when she was in New York, and believe me, Mr. President, With sentiments of the highest Respect and Esteem

Your most Obt. Servt.
E. N. Anderson

Lincoln did not answer this appeal from Elizabeth N. Anderson, wife of Robert Anderson, the hero of Fort Sumter, probably because her husband had recently been given not only a promotion but command of Union forces in Kentucky.

Hometown Demands for Spoils

July 19 1861 Springfield Ill

Mr. Lincoln Dear Sir   I hope you may never feel as deep and bitter a disappointment as Mr. Moody and I felt last night when we heard you had given the Postoffice to Mr. Armstrong not but that he had as good a right to get it if he could as any one we felt the disappointment more for these reasons your wife told me the last time she called to see me that when you came to discharge offices you would remember Mr. Moody. Mr. Stewart told Mr. M a few weeks since that you was going to give the Postoffice to Mrs Grimsley [Mary's cousin, Elizabeth Todd Grimsley] and Mr. Moody he told him not to say anything about it till he got it more then that Mr. Duboice [Lincoln's friend Jesse K. Dubois] told Mr Moody that you told him when he was at Washington that you had made up your mind to give the Postoffice to Mr Moody he would have gone to see you about it but thought writing would answer the same purpose and save him the expence of the journey.

Mr Lincoln I hope you will not be offended with me the apology I offer is that we have bin very unfortunate in the Spring our oldest boy broke his leg in lifting and taking care of him I made my self sick and have bin sick ever since Mr Moody is out of business and no prospect of any. Dear Sir if you have one crum left cast to my husband and it will be thankfully received anything that would make us a living

Mr Moody dont know I am writing to you I dont wish him to

May God bless you and make you a blessing to our beloved country is my daly prayer

Yours truly
Mrs. S. B. Moody

P.S. Please give my sincere regards to your wife.

Few patronage offices plagued Lincoln as much as the postmaster's job in his old hometown. His own wife's cousin lusted after it but was denied. In August 1862

Lincoln offered Seymour B. Moody a post as either commissary or quartermaster, warning, "If appointed it must be without conditions." Moody replied that he would "prefer post Commissary if located at Springfield," but on August 22 he inexplicably declined both offers (CW, V:381).

Federal postmasters' jobs were especially coveted by office seekers. These political plums paid well. Sorting mail required only modest labor and offered free access to newspapers, a crucial source of information for aspiring politicians. Lincoln surely understood the job's appeal: he had held a postmaster's position in his own youth.

A Plea for "Some Help"

Chester [Penn.] July 8th 1861

Mr. Linkin

I have called on you for some help I am a widir woman with sixth children I was doing pirty well but since this war bisness commence it has cost me a good bit of truble I am willing to do with less for the sake of are union to stand I want you please to help me a little as I stand badly in need of som help please to rite and lit me know direct your letter to

> Mrs. Sarah H Vandegrift
> Chester

I shall put it to a good use.

ᦡ There is no record of a reply to this plea.

A Woman Wants Work for her Brother

Washington City
October 1861—

To his Excellency the President
of the United States.

The undersigned is the widow of Dennis Buckley who was employed for several years as a laborer in the Arsenal in this city, and whose excellent character is vouched for by officers of the Army, in letters which I have in my possession I am poor and the mother of six children, the oldest of whom is not more than 12 years of age. I ask for employment for my brother Michael Donovan, who has been out of work for two months and who kindly helps to support me. He is well known as an industrious, honest man who has been employed at the

Arsenal, and in various Departments of the Government and who is very poor.

Mrs. Mary Buckley

༄ *Lincoln endorsed this letter as follows: "Will Major [George D.] Ramsay [Commander of the Arsenal], or Capt. [John A.] Dahlgren, please find work for Michael Donovan? A. Lincoln." The following formal letter to Major Ramsay, written seven days later and now considered one of the most memorable of Lincoln's presidency, may have been in response to a renewed appeal for assistance from Mrs. Buckley (CW, IV: 556).*

Executive Mansion
Oct. 17, 1861

Maj. Ramsay
My dear Sir
The lady—bearer of this—says she has two sons who want to work. Set them at it, if possible. Wanting to work is so rare a merit, that it should be encouraged.

Yours truly
A. Lincoln

Former President Seeks Lost Books

Wheatland, near Lancaster [Penn.]
21 October 1861

My dear Sir
Pardon me for requesting you to refer this note to your private Secretary.

I believe that I left in the Library of the Executive Mansion Thier's History (in French) of the Empire (under Napoleon 1st) in some seven or eight volumes. It was covered in paper and has the name of its former owner, Geo W. Barton, written in each volume. Should it be found I would thank you to send it either to the State Department or to Dr. Blake.

Sincerely desiring that your administration may prove successful in restoring the union & that you may be more happy in your exalted station than was your immediate predecessor I remain yours

very respectfully
James Buchanan

His Excellency
Abraham Lincoln

P.S. Please to remember me kindly & respectfully to Mrs. Lincoln

∽ If ex-president Buchanan's missing books were ever found, no record of their discovery or return has been found.

"To the Victors Belong the Spoils"

Washington D.C. Dec, 27th 1861

Sir: I have been to your residence several times. I am ready and have but little to spare. I have lost all advocating the cause of our Party. I came here with letters from the most prominent men in the state of Illinois recommending the appointment of me, to some office I think I am duly entitled to some position under the present Administration. I was one of the first Republicans in Southern Illinois. I held out faithful—we were after a long time victorious and to the victors belong the spoils. If you can put me in any position I will be very greatful [sic] to you for so doing let me know this evening, As I am not able to remain here long.

Yours most Obt.
G. P. Edwards

Address Ebbit House
Washington D.C.

His excellency Hon. A. Lincoln
President of the U. State
Washington D.C.

Ↄ *Lincoln scrawled with evident annoyance on the back of this blunt note: "I do not know the position into which I could put Mr. Edwards. A.L. Dec. 28, 1861." The recommendations Edwards enclosed indicated he was an impoverished amputee who had once published a Republican newspaper in Shawneetown, Illinois.*

Pleading for her Father

April 22d 1862

Mr President Lincoln

Dear Sir I take my pen with a broken heart to try to write you a few lines. I am all alone I cannot write for weeping I am a poor little helpless girl of 13 years O Mr Lincoln if I could only see you and tell you all about O Mr Lincoln they have sentenced my papa Mr F. Petty to be shot. O Mr Lincoln wont you pardon him. O Mr Lincoln my papa is not gilty [*sic*] of what they charge him that very night he stayed at home with me and mother. O how can I live and no papa to protect me, O Mr Lincoln read the life of Mr Napoleon and see where he pardoned a man for his little girl and O can you be harder hearted than he was

O Mr Lincoln have you got no little girls and suppose you was in papa place and your little girl was to beg a man for mercy and he was to grant it. O would not you love him; O how papa would would [*sic*] love you. O how can i stand it. O pardon, O pardon my papa Mr Lincoln, O if I could see you, I would kiss your feet

O Mr Lincoln have mercy—have mercy—O pardon my papa. O how can I live, O how can you refuse, O hear the petition of a poor distracted child pleading for the life of her papa.

O if i knowed how to ask you in the humblest way I would a Servant for you for the pardon of my papa, O how can I how can i live, O Mr Lincoln show this to your little girls and ask them, to plead with you for my papa O God how can I live. O Mr Lincoln I do not know what to say I have said all that I can say—if you let my papa be killed it will kill me and mother too

Sally C. Petty

O Mr Lincoln my papa is in jail in Boon County Mo O let him stay there so I can see him sometimes they talk of taking him to Alton. O let him stay in Columbia till you pardon him O I know you will pardon him I know you cannot refuse look at your little girls and then think of me

Sally C. Petty

There is no record of a reply to this heartbreaking plea, nor can a record be found of the case of Mr. F. Petty. However, this letter was preserved without an endorsement by either Lincoln or his secretaries, which suggests that it may have been rushed to his desk by a sympathetic aide the moment it arrived and attended to immediately—perhaps to young Sally's satisfaction.

A Request for Portrait Sittings

[December 30, 1862]

My dear Mr. President—the bearer, Mr. E. D. Marchant, the eminent Artist, has been empowered by a large body of your personal and political friends to paint your picture for the Hall of American Independence. A generous subscription is made—and he visits you to ask your acquiescence, and to exhibit his testimonials. He will need little of your time. There is no likeness of you at Independence Hall. It should be there; and as Mr. Marchant is a most distinguished Artist, and is commanded by the most powerful influences, I trust you will give him a favorable reception.

Yours Truly
J. W. Forney

To the President
Washington Decr. 30, 1862

Lincoln agreed to give Edward Dalton Marchant his full cooperation. "My studio was for several months in the White House," the artist later recalled, "where I was in daily communication with the remarkable man whose features I sought to portray." The work, Marchant admitted, was "more truly a labor of love than I am often permitted to perform." But despite correspondent Forney's aspirations, the resulting canvas, depicting Lincoln as an Emancipator—literally breaking the chains beneath a statue of "Liberty" with a stroke of his pen—did not find a permanent home at Independence Hall. Instead it was sent to Philadelphia's Union League, where it remains to this day (Holzer, Neely, and Boritt, The Lincoln Image, 106–110).

Officers Want their Women

Campfr of the 19th Ind. Vols.
Near Belle Plain Va Jan 31. 1863.

To His Excellency
Abraham Lincoln
President of the United States

Respected Sir. Our wives are in Washington City, whither they have proceeded on their way to visit us, and are unable to come any further. They have repeatedly applied for passes to Belle Plain, and have as often been refused. We notice that ladies arrive at Belle Plain on every Boat from Washington, and this refusal to grant permission to our wives to visit us is to us inexplicable.

We have tried to do our duty. We have fought for our country at the Rappahannock Station, at Groveton, at Bull Run, at South Mountain, at glorious, ever glorious Antietam, and at Fredericksburg; and we trust that these services have earned for us some consideration. And we respectfully ask that our wives be permitted to visit us during the few days that we cannot move.

And we promise you sir, that we will not fight the less courageously because we have lately seen them. We will not falter on the day when it "rains lead and iron" because the kisses of our wives are still warm upon our lips, instead of 20 months old, and we trust that they yet may be permitted to visit us. Pledging ourselves, if you will grant our request to be your grateful debtors, we remain Yours &c

S. Williams, Lt Col Comdg 19th Ind Co
A. J. Makepeace Capt Co A 19th Ind Vol
William Ord, Capt. Co. 12. 19th Ind

∽ *No reply is known. (Original in collection of the Lilly Library, Indiana University, Bloomington.)*

A Woman Insists on a Job for her Husband

March 8th [1863]

To President Lincoln

It grieves me to think that the President should have misunderstood my motives in requesting of him an interview—after his kindness in the one already granted to me.

First, in the pressure of his business, I could not have expected him to carry my case upon his mind, nor would I have "importuned" him for an appointment which a Sec'y to whom he referred me, & who has his confidence, thought necessary to refuse me [probably John Nicolay, as John Hay was away from Washington at the time].

Mr. Stanton declined making another appointment to a Pennsylvanian, that State having more than its share of Paymasters. It was right—but I have been told that had I applied for Mr Phipps from Memphis—from which place he has a claim, Mr. Stanton w'd probably have nominated him—& that it is not now too late—

Upon the advice of these gent, I have been to the War Department—hoping to see Mr. S. (& thus far unsuccessful in seeing him) to tell him that Mr. Phipps was in business in Tennessee some years—& was driven from Memphis in the outbreak of the Rebellion—as an Abolitionist—He suffered in the loss of all he had accumulated for 3 years—his business was broken up, & after all personal violence, for persisting in his Loyalty. This persecution cast him upon the world penniless.

From that time, nearly 2 years, till now, he has been unable to get into any business—which has brought suffering to his family—& the deprivation of comforts essential to health.

The urgency of the circumstances is my excuse for appearing before the president—& Deportmenting for Employment, for a man Loyal to his country & true to the Administration.

When I see young men, without families, not more Loyal than he, certainly—& not possessed of his uncommon business talent receiving employment from the Government, I feel how very hard it is, when an honest man, industrious, & of unblemished reputation, having had an unusually large business experience, should by the Revolution in the Country be deprived of the power to support his family, or even to sustain himself. Can President Lincoln wonder at my coming to his aid in this way? The trial, I had rather endure alone than be dependent upon any intercession.

I feel no claim upon Mr Foster (but recently entered the family) who has large dependencies—in poor relatives—I have not thought fit to trouble him with a detail of our necessities—which I feel that I have his good wishes and his assistance, if I ask it. [Senator Lafayette Foster was George Phipps' brother-in-law.]

If there is no chance for a Paymastership for Mr. Phipps, from Tennessee, I have been wishing there could be some situation for him in Phila. such as in the Custom House—Post Office, or some office or agency in the <u>Presidents</u> gift which would enable him, while serving the Govt to be more with his family—than he could be of late years, through reverses—

<u>That</u> was my wish, in seeing you, to know if you could give him any Employment, which would give us some support, while you would have in his services a prompt & full return & without improperly importuning you, I most <u>earnestly</u> desire it—If there is such position in your gift—& for him you would have the heartfelt gratitude of

Most respectfully yours
(Mrs.) L. H. Phipps

To President Lincoln

↪ *Lincoln wrote the following two replies to this long plea—one to Mrs. Phipps, sternly criticizing her for her persistence; and another to the secretary of war, asking if a job could not, after all, be found for her husband. But because the angry note to Mrs. Phipps was found signed but apparently undelivered, still in the Lincoln Papers, it seems possible that the President wrote it, thought better about sending it, and instead decided to help the anguished Mrs. Phipps. Still, no record has been found of the appointment of Mr. Phipps (CW, VI: 114, 130–131; Dennett,* Diaries and Letters of John Hay, *54).*

Executive Mansion,
Washington, March 9, 1863.

Mrs. L. H. Phipps

Yours of the 8th is received. It is difficult for you to understand, what is, nevertheless true, that the bare reading of a letter of that length requires more than any one person's share of my time. And when read, what is it but an evidence that you intend to importune me for one thing, and another, and another, until, in self-defence, I must drop all and devote myself to find a place, even though I remove somebody else to do it, and thereby turn him & his friends upon me for indefinite future importunity, and hindrance from the legitimate duties for which I am supposed to be placed here?

Yours &c
A. Lincoln

Executive Mansion,
Washington, March 9. 1863.

Hon. Sec. of War:
Dear Sir

A few days since I gave the lady, bearer of this, Mrs. Phipps, some sort of writing, favoring the appointment of her husband to be an Additional PayMaster. She thinks she failed because the application was made as from Pennsylvania, and says that it could & can be justly made from Tennessee. Please let her have it, if you consistently can either from Tennessee or any where else.

Yours truly
A. Lincoln.

Tavern Owner Seeks Pardon

Washington Aug. 10 1863.

His Excellency Abraham Lincoln,
President of the U. States,

Sir, In the months of June and July I was fined by Justice Ferguson twice twenty Dollars, for having sold (as he said) Liquors to soldiers, at a Restaurant kept at 289 B. Street.

The true fact of the matter is this; A Civilian dressed in a blue Coat with brass buttons, was taken for a soldier, and seen drinking beer at my place; for which Justice Ferguson fined me $20.00 not giving me the chance to defend myself.

The second case is this: An Irishman I suppose a Soldier, came into my house begging for a glass of beer, saying that he was sick and would be oblige[d] to me for it; having refused to sell him any he persisted in me giving him some; my wife expecting troubles made him present with a Glass and told him to go—

Two hours afterwards he came back with a patrouille [a small formation of soldiers] had me arrested and Justice Ferguson, without asking me any questions fined me again $20.00.

A short time before this occured, the safe of my house was broken into, and the content of $700 with $200 deposited money taken therefrom; it was all I possessed, and I have now to refund the deposited money.

I pray now knowing the kindness and good heart of Our President, that your Excellency will cause those two fines to be refunded to me; my place has always been a place of order and my actions strictly to the Law of the United States, of which I am the truest citizen.

Hoping that Your Excellency will give a favorable consideration to this my petition I am with the truest sentiments

> Your most obedient servant
> Frederick Moelich
> 289 & 291 B. Street, between 2nd & 3d

∽ *Lincoln endorsed the letter as follows on September 10: "I can not listen to a man's own story, unsupported by any evidence, who has been convicted of violating the law; because that would put an end to all law. A. Lincoln."*

Help for a School

> Officer of the Commissioner
> of Public Buildings.
> Capitol of the United States,
> Washington City, Aug. 19., 1863

To the President
of the United States

Dear Sir, The War Department having taken possession of the school house of the First District of Washington for the purpose of converting it into a <u>Medical Museum</u>, the Trustees of the Public Schools were left without any place for the schools. They applied to me for leave to occupy Franklin Square <u>temporarily</u> for the erection of school houses. That square is owned by the U.S. & efforts have been made, in vain, for many years to induce Congress to cause it to be improved. It now lies a barren unsightly waste, and was occupied for several months by the barracks of the 12th N. York Regt. by <u>order</u> I suppose, of the Secy. of War.

This being the state of things when application was made to me, I thought it <u>only right</u> that the request of the School Trustees should be granted for the very laudable purpose intended. But, I said to them that I could not grant it without consultation with you, and obtaining your leave. I called on you, made known my business, & stated the facts. You asked me if the Square was the property of the U.S. to which I answered affirmatively. You then asked me if I thought the privilege ought to be granted, to which I also answered in the affirmative. You then advised me to grant it, if I saw nothing improper, in the way. The conversation ended by your saying emphatically, "Do as you think best in the matter," or words to that effect. I replied, "then I shall grant the privilege with your sanction."

I went immediately to my office and addressed a letter to the Trustees, stating that I had seen you, & with your sanction—, granted them the privilege asked for, for two years.

An appropriation was made by the City Councils for the building, and it was commenced, when a guard of Soldiers was sent by order, I learn, of the Secy. of War, and the building stopped by force.

All I have now to add, is, that I hope & trust you, as President of these United States, do not intend to permit the praiseworthy exertions of the Authorities of Washington to cause the rising generation of the City to be properly educated, to be thwarted by the bayonets of the army!

I most respectfully request, that you will take such measures as will result in granting the small boon that has been asked and once supposed to be granted, as it will neither injure any one, or interfere with either private or public rights and convenience,

> With high respect Your obt. Servt.
> B. B. French
> Com of Pub. Buildings

∾ *Lincoln replied as follows:*

> Executive Mansion,
> Washington, Aug. 19, 1863.

Col. B. B. French
Dear Sir:
I have just seen the Secretary of War who says he will return to the Trustees their own building now in the control of the Surgeon General.

> A. Lincoln

Pardoned to Desert Again

[*T E L E G R A P H*]

> Philadelphia
> September 19 1863.

Abraham Lincoln
Is John Gallagher to be shot Answer please

> Hughey Gallagher

ৎ Lincoln replied as follows:

Washington, D.C.,
Sept. 19 1863

Hughey Gallagher
Philadelphia, Pa.

I know nothing as to John Gallagher. The law does not require this class of cases to come before me, and they do not come, unless brought by the friends of the condemned.

A. Lincoln

ৎ Evidently the "friends of the condemned" did bring the case to Lincoln, for John Gallagher, also known as Jacob Watson, of the Fourth New Jersey Volunteers, sentenced to be executed for desertion, was ultimately pardoned. In April 1865, while on furlough, he deserted again (CW, VI: 466).

A Plea for Mistreated Blacks

Office Provost Marshal
War Department
Washington September 30th 1863

Abraham Lincoln.
President of the United States

Sir. I beg leave respectfully to call your attention to the facts below set forth.

The Colored people, Slave and freed, of this District and the adjoining Counties of Maryland are daily subjected to a more ferocious despotism and more flagrant and shameless outrages than were ever before tolerated by any Government claiming to be either wise or humane:

It is well known to you Sir, that large numbers of slaves, owned in Maryland, activated by a supreme desire to participate in the blessings of freedom enjoyed by their fellows in this District, are daily, almost hourly, making attempts to escape from their Masters and fly for refuge to this City.

The slave owners of Maryland, whose plantations are becoming desolate by this constant exodus of their chattels, no longer relying upon the protection of their own laws, and legally constituted authorities, have in many cases formed themselves into armed bands for the purpose of pursuing and recapturing escaped slaves.

Parties of slaves, men and women & children, have been pursued within the bounds of this District, have been fiercely assailed and shot down or remorselessly beaten and the survivors shut up in prisons or conveyed across the Potomac within the protecting arms of the rebel Confederacy.

Not less than forty slaves (human beings) have been killed in these lawless encounters, and I have information that no less than three dead bodies of slaves thus cruelly slaughtered are now laying in the Woods almost within sight of your home.

Not a month since an armed band of Maryland slave owners surrounded the house of a free negro woman less than three miles from the Capitol, broke open the door, presenting loaded pistols to the head of its frightened inmates and after exercising all their powers of abuse & insult took away by violence three free negroes.

Visiting this City and protected by the assumed authority of Mr. Commissioner Cox, these desperadoes break into the houses of colored citizens, thrust loaded pistols into the faces of terrified women and screaming children, and then, protected by legal papers bear off their victims to the tender mercies of the lash and prison, or the hopeless martyrdom of Southern slavery.

Along the borders of the Potomac below this City male slaves are now being mustered in gangs and sent over to Virginia as contributions by their Masters to the cause of the rebellion, if these men make an effort to escape they are pursued and shot to death by their merciless owners.

There is now in Marlborough Jail a negro man whose eyes have been utterly destroyed by a charge of shot fired into his face and not long since two colored girls were found chained in the garret of a private house in the neighborhood of this City, who after having been cruelly beaten by three men, one of them using a trace chain to inflict the blows, were left, with their backs one mass of festering wounds, to the farther horrors of chains and darkness.

An instance has just come to my knowledge where a negro woman and three daughters owned by a citizen of this City, still resident here, were sent to Baltimore a few days before the late Emancipation Act was passed, for the sole purpose of evading its provisions, one of those daughters, an intelligent woman, has succeeded in returning to this City and is now claimed as a Slave and threatened with seizure through the agency of Mr. Commissioner Cox's summary and illegal writs.

It cannot be that such atrocities will be longer permitted, and that men whose every sympathy is with slavery and its co-agent Treason shall be suffered longer to visit upon the poor slave the hatred they feel for Freedom and the Union.

I respectfully ask for such instructions as shall enable me to officially protect the now helpless victims of the Slave owners vengeance, and the perjured oaths of their friends, official and otherwise, in the City and District.

> I am Sir, Your Obedient servant,
> L. C. Becker
> Col & Provost Marshal War Department

No reply to this letter is known, but it was retained by Lincoln for his personal files—and, presumably, he intended to take action.

Requesting a Donation

Springfield Ills Dec 14th 1863.

Hon A. Lincoln

My dear Sir Still claiming you as one of our <u>citizens</u>, and knowing that you take an interest in our public enterprises, I take the liberty of calling your attention to the efforts now being made by our citizens to establish a "Springfield Home of the Friendless". A charter was obtained from the Legislature last for that purpose, a copy of which I enclose, together with a partial list of subscribers.

It is intended to commence building as early in the Spring as practicable.

We have raised by private subscriptions over $5,000. We desire to increase the Amt to $8,000. We have also received a pledge from the City Council for $2,000.

Maj Iles [Elijah Iles, one of Springfield's founding fathers] has donated an <u>entire block</u> of ground south of Mr Loose's residence, on which to erect suitable buildings.

If the project meets with your favor, a <u>substantial</u> endorsement will be gratefully received by your friends here.

A contribution accompanied by a brief note of encouragement from you, would do us more good than <u>double</u> the Amt from "any other man."

Hoping that we may have the pleasure of hearing from you on the subject.

I remain as ever.

Your faithful friend
S. H. Melvin

There is no evidence that Lincoln either endorsed or contributed to the cause described here by Samuel Houston Melvin, a Springfield retailer in medical supplies to whom the President had sold six chairs, a mattress, and a whatnot, among other possessions (for a total of $82.25), before leaving for Washington in 1861. Although the charter for the project proposed restricting its future occupants to "indigent women and children," such a "Springfield Home for the Friendless" must have seemed to Lincoln—particularly after reading one of the diatribes he received regularly from that city—a residence planned expressly with him in mind. But not enough so, apparently, to inspire a donation (CW IV: 189).

Plea for a Pardon

[T E L E G R A P H]

Fortress Monroe
December 30, 1863

President Lincoln

Jacob Bowers was sentenced to imprisonment for life by Genl. Order No. 37, from these Head Qtrs which sentence was approved by me Nov. 24th. for desertion. I now believe that he simply acted under a misapprehension of his duty, being a German not understanding his duty. Please permit me to remit this sentence if he returns to duty and re enlists during the war. I suppose I have the power now to do so but the papers are in Washington. This is the first time I have ever asked you to pardon any body.

Benjamin Butler
Genl

Lincoln replied the same day: "Jacob Bowers is fully pardoned for past offence, upon condition that he returns for duty, and re-enlists for three years or during the war." This is one of hundreds of such communications found in the files of the Lincoln Papers, all of which seek—and more often than not, receive—presidential pardons for offenses ranging from public drunkenness to desertion (CW, VII: 98).

A Shakespearean Job Plea

[1864?]

To the President of the United States:

Honorable Sir: I observe you are a patron of Shakspeare [sic]. I submit a particular passage:

King Lear. "How now, what are thou?"

Earl of Kent. (Disguised)—"A man sir."

L. "What dost thou profess? What woulds't thou with us?"

K. "I do profess to be no less than I seem, to serve him truly, that will put me in trust, to love him that is wise and says little,—to fight when I can not choose; and to eat no fish." (Especially Salmon) [a reference to Treasury Secretary Salmon P. Chase]

L. "What art thou?"

K. "A very honest-hearted fellow, and as poor as the King."

L. "What woulds't thou?"

K. "Service."

L. "Who woulds't thou serve?"

K. "You."

L. "Dost thou know me, fellow?"

K. "No, sir; but you have in your countenance authority."

L. "What services cans't thou do?"

K. "I can keep honest counsel (&c &c) and deliver a plain message bluntly: (as you discover) That which ordinary men (at least) are fit for, I am qualified in; and the best of me is diligence."

Now I pritheee read the first nine verses of S. John V Ch.

With respectful deference,
W. Harrison Grigsby.

1. "After this there was a feast of the Jews: and Jesus went up to Jerusalem.
2. "Now there is at Jerusalem, by the <u>sheep market</u>, a a [*sic*] pool which is called in the Hebrew Tongue, Bethesda, having five porches.
3. "In these lay a great multitude of important folk, of blind, halt, withered, waiting for the moving of the water.
4. "For an angel went down at a certain season into the pool, and troubled the water; whosoever then first after the troubling of the water stepped in was <u>made whole</u> of whatsoever disease he had.
5. "And a certain man was there which had an infirmity thirty and eight years.
6. "When Jesus saw him, and knew that he had been now a long time in that case, he said unto him, <u>Wilt thou be made whole?</u>
7. "The impotent man answered him, Sir, I have no man, when the water is troubled, to put me into the pool: but while I am coming, another steppeth down before me!
8. "Jesus said unto him, <u>Rise take up thy</u> bed and walk.
9. "And immediately the man was <u>made whole</u>, and took up his bed and walked; and on the same day was the sabbath."

S. John V: (1-9)

Mr. President:

Such is my predicament—minus the "thirty and eight years." I have the honor to refer to General Oglesby for particulars. I know it is a bold move to apply to <u>you</u> for help: Churches teach that "man is a poor worm of the dust," and yet they enjoin that <u>he</u> should pray even to the Great Jehovah!

Your Humble Friend
Grigsby.

∽ There is no record of a reply to this extraordinary job application—surely the most original of the hundreds of such letters sent to Abraham Lincoln. (Original in collection of the Lincoln Museum, Fort Wayne, Indiana.)

A Request for the Gettysburg Address

Boston 30 Jan. 1864.

My dear Mr. President, I shall have the honor of forwarding to you by Express, today or on Monday next, a copy of the Authorized Edition of my Gettysburg Address & of the Remarks made by yourself, & the other matters connected with the Ceremonial of the Dedication of the Cemetery. It appeared, owing to unavoidable delays, only yesterday.

I have promised to give the Manuscript of my address to Mrs. Governor [Hamilton] Fish of New-York, who is at the head of the Ladies' Committee of the Metropolitan fair. It would add very greatly to its value if I could bind up with it the manuscript of your dedicatory Remarks, if you happen to have preserved them.

I would further venture to request, that you would allow me also to bind up in the volume the very obliging letter of the 20 Nov. '63 [see page 134], which you did me the favor to write to me. I shall part with it with much reluctance, and I shrink a little from the apparent delicacy of giving some publicity to a letter highly complimentary to myself. But as its insertion would greatly enhance the value of the volume, when sold at the fair, I shall, if I have your kind permission, waive all other considerations.—

Regretting to add, in this way, to the number of annoyances of this kind, to which you are subject, I remain, Dear Sir, with the highest respect, very truly yours

Edward Everett

President Lincoln

ဢ *Lincoln replied a few days later with the following note, together with the priceless enclosure that later became known as the "Everett Copy" of the Gettysburg Address. The volume that Everett assembled sold to the highest bidder—for all of $1,000, and the copy of the Gettysburg Address was later acquired by the Illinois State Historical Society in Springfield (Kunhardt,* A New Birth of Freedom, *230).*

Executive Mansion,
Washington, February 4, 1864.

My dear Sir

Yours of Jan. 30th. was received four days ago; and since then the address mentioned has arrived. Thank you for it. I send herewith the manuscript of my remarks at Gettysburg, which, with my note to you of Nov. 20th. you are at liberty to use for the benefit of our soldiers as you have requested.

Yours very truly
A. Lincoln.

Hon. Edward Everett.

Horses for Sale

Rahway [N.J.], March 3/64

Hon. A. Lincoln,

My dear sir We wish to sell you the finest & most stilish pair of large red Bay horses that is to be found. they are 6 years old this spring 16 hands 2 inch high long tails to the ground & verry large full tails & mains black legs no white & good roadsters can trot a mile in four minutes together free from all bbbb & tricks not fearful of the cars good soddl horses. If you could se them you would like them & I think you would buy them If you wanted a team we hav a pair Bays 16 hand & A pair of Browns 15 3/ & a Pair of Grays I wish you could let your groom se them befor get a pair Yours truly Mooney & Vanfleet. Pleas let me hear from you Hon. A. J. Bozer can tel you all about the large bay horses I wish you would se him for reference to them

Yours truly Mooney & Vanfleet

∾ Lincoln made no known reply to this sales offer.

A Photographer Wants a Sitting

Whitehurst Gallery
434 Penna. Avenue
Washington March 4th 1864.

Hon. Abm. Lincoln.

Sir. I have been requested by the ladies of the Patent Office Sanitary Fair, to procure and present to them a large photograph likeness of yourself which I shall be pleased to do, providing you will be kind enough to give me a sitting at my establishment at such a time as will best suit your convenience. I would thank you for a line through the Post-Office, stating your intentions.

Considering your acceptance of this invitation a mark of honorable favor; I remain Sir

Very Respectfully
Wm. W. Metcalf
Proprietor of Whitehurst Gallery

ᔆ *Lincoln neither sat for nor replied to William Metcalf. He merely replaced this invitation in the envelope in which it came, marked it "Photograph," and filed it away. Although Lincoln was one of the most frequently photographed celebrities of his day, his indifferent reaction to this request from one of Washington's leading galleries suggests that there were times when he simply could not be bothered to pose, even when the results were earmarked for charity.*

Soliciting Advertising

[March 24, 1864]
New-York Abend-Zeitung
85 Bowery [New York]

To His Excellency
President Abraham Lincoln

Honored Sir, I do not know if you are aware, that my paper, the daily, weekly and Sunday German N.Y. Abend-Zeitung, published in New York city, has been advocating your cause against all other candidates for presidency. Upon inquiry you will find, that my paper is the leading Republican paper in the U.S. amongst the Germans, and has great weight in politics. The New York Abend-Zeitung will have to perform a very important duty during the next presidential campaign. But the beneficial results of the labors of this paper might be much increased, if something would be done to increase the circulation of the paper by sending a good many copies free of charge to the German population, who are now Democrats, or by publishing my paper twice daily, morning and evening. We have to compete here with a very dangerous and by no means unimportant foe, the N.Y. Staats-Zeitung, a Democratic and copperhead organ, which ought to be published in Richmond, or Fort Lafayette. Until now, I had to work on my own means, but to compete with a rich foe is very hard.

Men are born to assist each other and if you will lend me your hand, I think, we will make a strong pull. I submit these suggestions to you, and hope you will appreciate them. They come from a true heart. At the same time, I hope you will excuse the form in which this letter is written; I am obliged to write it in bed, to which I am confined by overworking, as the physician says, and I think he is about right, for publishing a newspaper is about as vexacious, and hard work as being President of the U.S. An early answer will oblige

Your obedient servant
Fred. Rauchfauss

New York, March 24, 1864

P.S. Any favors shown by publishing advertisements in the N.Y.A.Z., from the different executive departments will be thankfully appreciated. We had a few from the war department, but they are few and far between.

∽ *This rather brazen letter was filed under the heading "political" and apparently never answered.*

An Abolition Petition from Children

[April 5, 1864]

This heading was written by Mrs. Horace Mann, widow of Hon Horace Mann
Petition of the children of the United States, (under 18 years) that the President will free all slave children
This petition is designed only for the President—a sort of <u>private letter</u> from the children of Concord, Massachusetts. They have been delighted with the idea of speaking to our good President, & of giving one cent or more, for the benefit of the poor little slaves—
195 signatures

∽ *Lincoln endorsed these sheets as follows: "Little Peoples' Petition." Then he wrote to the widow of the famous educator. Senator Charles Sumner personally delivered Lincoln's thank-you letter to Mrs. Mann, but the acknowledgment surprised her, for as she quickly informed the President, the public use of her name had come "wholly without my knowledge." She hastened to add: "I cannot regret it, since it has given me this precious note from your hand" (CW, VII: 287).*

Executive Mansion,
Washington, April 5, 1864.

Mrs. Horace Mann,
Madam,

The petition of persons under eighteen, praying that I would free all slave children, and the heading of which petition it appears you wrote, was handed me a few days since by Senator Sumner. Please tell these little people I am very glad their young hearts are so full of just and generous sympathy, and that, while I have not the power to grant all they ask, I trust they will remember that God has, and that, it seems, He wills to do it. Yours truly

A. Lincoln

A Business Opportunity

Springfield Ills. April 15th 1864

His Excellency A Lincoln
President U S
Washington D C

When I returned from Washington to New York I concluded to write you asking if you wished to invest $5.000 in the First National Bank of Springfield Illinois, the stock holders would feel proud of your association with them as one of the share holders; If you desire to become so I will sell you 50 shares of my stock which is paid up in full in fact the entire stock is paid up and our organization complete After writing the above it occurred to me that possibly your position as President of the United States might make it improper for you to become a stock holder in any of the National Banks if so of course you will understand that the offer is made in all good faith & without any wish that you should to any thing that would compromise your high position.

I am Truly Your friend
John Williams

◡ This letter included a "Memo of Organization" and a list of stockholders, which included many familiar hometown names. No reply has ever been located, nor is there any evidence that the President invested in the scheme. A secretary simply marked the letter "Private," and Lincoln filed it away.

Seeking Support, Tartly

[April 25, 1864]

To the President:
Hon Abraham Lincoln.

Sir: The plan of the Home League having been warmly approved by several influential members of Congress—and no answer having been received from Secretary Chase, I made an appeal to Patriotic women through the Press. I thought it probable that both yourself and the Secretary prefered [*sic*] that women should take the responsibility of inaugurating a measure which was so exclusively their own, and then if it should not seem to be a good one, it would be perfectly easy for either of you, at any time to hinder its success by a single word . . . while if it promised to help the country, even a little, you would both rejoice to have it continue.

If I have made a mistake in thus expressing my own judgment, when I supposed I was purposely left to do so, I hope not to be severely censured. It has happened that I have found the wife of one of our distinguished Senators engaged to the same end as myself without our having any knowledge of each other's plans. Littell's Living Age [a magazine of the day] has an article in its last number upon the topic—and both in New York and Boston, some such movement is talked of. A Public meeting here is planned, where the reasons for and against will be presented.

After my appeal was in print I heard, indirectly, that Secretary Chase would not aid the League now although approving of its design. I have thought that as I had requested your permission to use Mrs Lincoln's name, which you had declined to give without grave and further consideration, that it was both proper and respectful to inform you of the present condition of the movement—

Very respectfully yours
(Mrs.) H. C. Ingersoll

A. L. Hosp'l
April 25/64

Hon Abraham Lincoln

∽ *Worried about military and political issues at the time this letter was received, Lincoln could hardly spare the time to mediate a quarrel between one of his cabinet officers and a women's charity. A secretary endorsed the letter: "Rather tart."*

An Autograph for Charity

Philadelphia, May 10 1864.

His Excellency A. Lincoln
President of the U. States
   Dear Sir I address you in this triumphant hour of the nation's glory on behalf of the Sanitary Commit.
   We are to have a great Fair in June to raise money for the relief of sick and wounded soldiers.
   We will present the greatest demonstration of modern times and believing that an autograph letter from yourself, who are the pre eminent personage of this remarkable era of our country, I have presumed to solicit your interest in this manner in behalf of the Great Fair. We desire to raise a million dollars for the fund of the Sanitary Commission, and I believe that no one object of interest would be more prized than a letter of commendation from yourself.
   I have a very fine one from Genl. Meade which has been so well thought of as to be the subject of printed cards to aid the subscriptions. Hoping that your many engagements may allow you to reply to me favourably, I am very respectfully

                    Your Excellencys Very Humble Servant
                    L. Montgomery Bond
                    Chm. Com. Labor, Income & Revenues
                    Central Fair for the Sanitary Commission

∽ *Lincoln apparently made no effort at first to comply with Bond's request, but he did demonstrate his support for the Philadelphia Fair by agreeing to make one of his exceedingly rare public appearances there. Two weeks before that visit, a Philadelphia citizen reminded John G. Nicolay about the overdue autograph. Finally Lincoln complied (CW, VII: 369).*

Executive Mansion,
Washington, May 31, 1864.

Mrs. Field

Mr. Sedgwick informs me that you desire an autograph of mine, to finish a collection for the Sanitary Fair. It gives me great pleasure to comply with your request.

Yours truly
A. Lincoln

A Freedman Pleas for his Land

St. Helena Is. S.C.
Frogmoor May 29th 1864

To the President of the United States
Abraham Lincoln

My name is Don Carlos, and I hope my letter will find you and your family in perfect health. Will you please to be so kind Sir, as to tell me about my little bit of land. I am afraid to put on it a stable, or cornhouse, and such like, for fear it will be taken away from me again. Will you please to be so kind as to tell me whether the land will be sold from under us or no, or whether it will be sold to us at all. I should like to buy the very spot where I live. It aint but six acres, and I have got cotton planted on it, and very fine cotton too; and potatoes and corn coming on very pretty. If we colored people have land I know we shall do very well, there is no fear of that. Some of us have as much as three acres of corn, besides ground nuts, potatoes, peas, and I don't know what else myself. If the land can only be sold, we can buy it all, for every house has its cotton planted, and doing well, and planted only for ourselves. We should like to know how much we will have to pay for it—if it is sold.

I am pretty well struck in age Sir, for I waited upon Mrs. Alston that was Theodosia Burr, daughter of Aaron Burr, and I remember well when she was taken by pirates,—but I can maintain myself and my family well on this land. My son got sick on the Wabash (Flagship at Hilton Head) and he will never get well, for he has a cough that will kill him at last. He cannot do much work, but I can maintain him. I had rather work for myself and raise my own cotton than work for a gentleman for wages, for if I could sell my cotton for only 8 cts a pound it would pay me.

What ever you say I am willing to do, and I will attent to whatever you tell me. Your most obedient servant

Don Carlos Rutter

P.S. After the Government Superintendent gave me leave to pick one of the new houses, I pitch upon the one I live in. Then I fill up the holes in the garden, and in the house, I laith it & fill in with moss till it is comfortable in the winter. I did a heap of work on it, and now it would hurt my heart too much to see another man have it. I should not like it at all.

A D D E N D U M

The letter above was dictated to me by a Freedman on St. Helena Island who is a refugee from Cedisto, and who was formerly confidential servant in the Alston family. He can read & write, but is too old to do it with ease. He, with other of the Freedmen, often expresses a wish to be able to speak to Massa Linkum feeling sure that he will listen to their plea for land & do what is best for them. At Carlos' desire, I took down from his own lips the words he was restless to speak to the President, intending to hand the letter to him at the Sanitary Fair, but I refrained from so doing that business might not be thrust in upon your pleasure. I have given my promise to Carlos that I will do my best to let his "own word" reach the ear in which he has unbounded trust & hope, and therefore I forward this letter to Washington, begging no one to prevent its reaching its destination.

> Very respectfully
> Laura Towne
> Teacher of Freedmen on St. Helena Is.

This unique letter was forwarded to the President's desk bearing the endorsement by a secretary, "Don Carlos Rutter . . . wants to purchase the land he is inhabiting." But if Lincoln replied either to Don Carlos Rutter or his friend Laura Towne, the reply has never come to light. Nonetheless, this is one of the few communications in the Lincoln Papers from a black American.

A "Widder Wumman" wants "Wurk"

Frederick, June 17, 1864

tu Abraham linkun President of the U. States at Washington—
Deer Sur: I take mi pen in hand to aske yu about the munney cum-
ming to me frum my husband Daniel Spielman who was a solger in
the 2d Mariland Ridgment in company C who was kill in a fite with
the rebs last fal near Boonsborrow M.D. I haint got no pay as was
cummin toe him and none of his bounty munney and now Mr. President I am a pore widder wumman and have no munney and have
borrered all what I lived on last winter and this summer toe—Now
Mr. President I can soe and cook and wash and du enny kind of wurk
but cant get none—see if you cant git me a plaice in one of your
hospittles and I will goe rite to wurk—but I dont want to leve mi little
gurl so I want to git a plaice what I can take her toe—I no yu du what
is rite and yu will se tu me a pore widder wumman whose husband
fote in your army your younion army Mr. President—So Mr. President I sign myself your servant to command

Catherine Spielman

ᔕ *Journalist Noah Brooks was so taken with this letter—"actually received by the
President and sent by him to the proper department of the government," he marvelled—that he published it in one of his reports from Washington. Brooks regarded it
as "an illustration of how the worthy Chief Magistrate is made the recipient of all sorts
of requests" (Staudenraus,* Dispatches of Noah Brooks, *360–361).*

From a Maker of Campaign Medals

No. 1 Park Place
New York June 18th/64

Hon Abraham Lincoln

Sir I intend circulating three or four million medals or metallic
cases containing likenesses of yourself & Andrew Johnson for President & Vice President, and want to get a perfect Photograph to copy
from, or the one that you would prefer to have circulated, I shall get
them up in the neatest manner.

If you would plan to send me a likeness, I shall be happy to use it
to copy from,
Respy. Your Obedt. Servt

John Gault

∽ *No reply has been located, but Lincoln or his aides likely obliged Gault. Most campaign medals of the 1864 campaign featured the easy-to-copy profile photograph taken at Mathew Brady's gallery in February 1864—the pose later engraved for the one-cent piece. Gault's letter suggests that for Lincoln's second campaign, as for the first, the creation of tokens, posters, and other images—so much a part of the strategy of today's presidential races—was left to independent artists and entrepreneurs, with only occasional assistance by the candidates themselves.*

Asking for Jewish Chaplains

Harrisburg, Pa. June 20th, 1864

To his Excellency
To the President of the United States!

Sir! We the undersigned—Board of the Hebrew Congregation Ohef Shalem of this City, take the liberty of adressing [*sic*] you briefly on a Subject of great Importance to us.

There are a large number of Israelites serving in the Army of the United States and this City and vicinity being the locality where many hospitals for the sick and wounded have been established, it is often the Case that a good many soldiers of our persuasion are brought hither in a Condition to require spiritual no less than bodily care.

It was therefore at our last meeting deemed highly expedient to have a Jewish Chaplain appointed under the authority of the President of the United States with all the Privileges, which pertain the ministers of other persuasions similarly appointed and as we have a qualified minister in our Congregation in the person of Rev. Reuben Strauss, we would therefore respectfully recommend you the same such.

The District might conveniently include York, Carlisle and other towns at not to [*sic*] great a distance where United States Hospitals are established.

In Trust that you will speedily comply with our request we remain respectfully your obedient Servants

> Board of the Ohelf Schalem Congregation
> Harrisburg, Pa.
> William Wolf, Pres. of Congregation
> Joseph Lowengart, V.P. of Congregation
> Joseph Schweitzer
> Abraham Gumbert

◇ *(Original in the collection of the Lilly Library, Indiana University, Blooming-ton.) Although this letter arrived with an enthusiastic endorsement from former secretary of war Simon Cameron, no reply is known, but Lincoln was probably favorably disposed to the request. Jewish chaplaincy had been an issue ever since the Volunteer Act of 1861 required that chaplains be "regularly ordained ministers of some Christian denomination." In December 1861 Lincoln pledged he would "try to have a new law broad enough to cover" this deficiency. A bill was passed in the summer of 1862, and that September the President appointed the first Jewish chaplain (Rubinger, Lincoln and the Jews, 53–61).*

Requesting a Lock of Hair

Pekin Tazewell Co. Ill.
August 22nd 1864

To his Excellency President Lincoln:

Sir, The loyal citizens of Pekin and vicinity have determined to hold a Sanitary Fair similar to those which have been held with such unprecedented success in several of our western and some eastern cities.

Well knowing the intense interest evinced by yourself and Lady in all efforts to relieve the suffering of our soldiers we sincerely trust you will grant our request, which is that each of you will send us a lock of your hair which will be woven into hair flowers, and be exhibited and sold at our Fair. The design forming a wreath of flowers made of the hair of our most noted patriots and wish yours for the center flower; as you are the center of political power and about you cluster all our national hopes.

We hold our "Town Fair" Oct. 17th.

Begging you in the name of our wounded soldiers not to disappoint us, (for doubtless such a wreath will bring a fabulous price) and breathing a prayer for your welfare, I remain a most enthusiastic supporter of your administration, and all else that's for the union.

Almira C. Lyman

P.S. Please direct to Miss Almira C. Lyman, Pekin Ill

◇ *If Lincoln sent the locks of hair, his letter accompanying them has not been located. Similar requests for locks of hair abound in the Lincoln Papers.*

Wants Boots Replaced

[November 9, 1864]

Dear Old Abe:

Yesterday I worked hard for you all day, and wore out my boots. Please send me a new pair by mail.

∽ *"A rude wag," White House correspondence secretary Edward D. Neill testified, wrote this letter to Lincoln "the day after his election for a second term." The original was not retained for the Lincoln Papers, but Neill quoted it word-for-word in his reminiscences (Blegen,* Abraham Lincoln and His Mailbag, *327).*

Begging Release of a Native American

Davenport [Iowa,] Nov 14th 1864.

To the President
Washington

You will remember me as the person to whom you were kind enough to give an order for release of the Indian "Big Eagle."

This order failed to effect his release. The person in charge and to whom I presented it, treated me very rudely. I may as well say that he insulted me most grossly. He treated also the order and yourself with great contempt because as he said, you ought to know better than to write an order in pencil, or to give it to a civilian.

I did not intend to trouble you again, but for reasons not necessary to be stated, I think I should report the facts to you, and request of you, that you will be kind enough to direct a note to the proper military officer, requesting him to issue the proper order for "Big Eagle's" discharge.

I write by the hand of my wife my own writing being quite illegible.

I am deeply sensible of the kindness shown me by yourself and by Mrs. Lincoln. And I remain

Your obt servant
Geo S. C. Dow

∽ *Little is known of the case of Big Eagle, who was confined at Davenport, Iowa. Lincoln had ordered on October 26: "Let the Indian 'Big Eagle' . . . be discharged at once," apparently to little effect. On November 19 he telegraphed Alfred Sully, the officer in command at Davenport, as follows: "Let the Indian 'Big Eagle' be discharged. I ordered this some time ago. A. Lincoln." Not until December 3 was the prisoner finally set free (CW, VIII: 76, 116).*

Asking Help for Seamstresses

Chestnut Hill, Phila. Pa.
Jany. 23, 1865

His Excellency
Abraham Lincoln, President U.S.

Sir: It is the glory of our free institutions that any citizen, however humble, may venture to address the chief magistrate of the nation on matters connected with the welfare of members of the community in which he lives.

Unknown to you, without any interest in the matter other than that of the commonest humanity, I venture to appeal to you directly, without the intervention of red tape, on behalf of about thirty thousand suffering people in the city of Philadelphia, who can, by a word from you as commander-in-chief of the army, be relieved of at least one half of their misery.

They are women who sew (on army work), and their children.

These women are now forced, instead of getting their work and then pay direct from the arsenal, to be at the mercy of contractors who give them sometimes not one half of the government rates, the whole of which they secure by an unholy combination, for themselves.

If an order were given (& you have the right to give it,) that they be allowed to get their work & their pay directly from the arsenal, instead of being given to contractors in the first place, the difficulty they labour under would be done away.

These women are, very many of them, the wives or widows of American Soldiers; & all they need is the show of fair play at the hands of the government for which their husbands are fighting or have died.

Sir, pardon my presumption in thus addressing you. You have a kind heart which cannot be insensible to human oppression & misery.

The hand which by a stroke of a pen gave freedom to an oppressed race can, if you will, secure, at the least, fair dealing with those who are dear to men who left them at home unprotected, to be able to back up your Emancipation Proclamation at the risk of their lives. The prayers of a poor wife, a helpless widow, & destitute children, will surely call down a blessing from Heaven upon you if you will but interpose in their behalf. I am, Sir, Very respectfully, Your Obedient Servant,

J. Andrews Harris
Minister of the Gospel

ᔕ *The minister enclosed with his letter a newspaper clipping entitled "Fair Play for Women," which listed typical prices paid by the government to clothing contractors, along with those paid by the contractors to seamstresses. The arsenal paid contractors 18¢ per shirt, but the seamstresses were paid only 7¢ per shirt, and they earned on average $1.44 per week. But it is not known whether this information moved the President; no record of a reply has been found.*

Notorious Spy Seeks a Bargain

Brunswick Hotel, Jermyn St. London
24th Jany. 1865

Honble. Abraham Lincoln
President of the U.S. America

I have heard from good authority that if I suppress the Book I have now ready for publication, you may be induced to consider leniently the case of my husband, I. Wylde Hardinge, now a prisoner in Fort Delaware. I think it would be well for you & me to come to some definite understanding. My book was not originally intended to be more than a personal narrative, but since my husband's unjust arrest I had intended making it political, & had introduced many atrocious circumstances respecting your government with which I am so well acquainted & which would open the eyes of Europe to many things of which the world on this side of the water little dreams. If you will release my husband & set him free, so that he may join me here in England by the beginning of March—I pledge you my word that my Book shall be suppressed. Should my husband not be with me by the 25h of March I shall at once place my Book in the hands of a publisher.

Trusting an immediate reply, I am Sir, Yr. obdt. Servt.

Belle Boyd Hardinge

∽ *Lincoln did not reply to this threat by the infamous Confederate spy, who went on to publish her book, which became a postwar sensation.*

Circus Needs Permit for Cuba

Custom House, New York
Collector's Office, Feb 4th 1865

Hon. A. Lincoln Esq.

Dear Sir. We are desirous of shipping our "Circus" to Havana, Cuba, to exhibit for a short time, and then return to the United States. We have ascertained from the Treasury Department that an Executive order prohibits the shipment of Horses out of the country, and we technically come under the order. Will you do us the favor of executing the enclosed <u>conditional Permit</u>. We are compelled to appeal directly to you to avoid Red Tape and bring the matter to a conclusion. We offer Howes & Macy, Bankers of this City as security upon any bond required by the Department.

Your Obt. Servant
S. B. Howes & Co

∽ *"The President makes no official order of this character," John Hay noted on the back of this unique plea, "except upon the concurrent recommendation of the Secs War & Treasury."*

Asking Autographed Photo

[Received March 1865]
Head Qrst 2nd Brig.
1st Divn. opposite Petersburg Va March 23

Mr. President

Sir As you are the tallest Father I ever had or ever expect to have again I hope you will do me the kindness of sending me your Autograph on the Photograph enclosed that I may have it as a keepsake in my Family I shall prize it much, as it comes from the Saviour of our Country.

Yours truly
H. C. Beemer

❧ Lincoln signed innumerable photographs of himself, which were preserved in the family albums of ordinary Americans when the fashion for such books dictated that they include political and military celebrities.

Seeking a Draft Exemption

Washington, D.C.
March 10th, 1865.

Hon. Abraham Lincoln
President of the United States of A.

Sir: I have the honor of presenting myself before you to solicit a favor at your hands.

My son Charles T. Dorsett having been drafted under the last call, and the favor I would ask of you is that you have him discharged. He has been employed in the Quarter Masters Dept nearly four years and those under whom he was employed all testify to the faithful discharge of his duty.

When the Rebellion first broke out he volunteered his services and served three months, and when hands were wanting to go to Virginia and also in July when the Rebel raid was made he again volunteered.

His object in asking to be discharged is not from any disinclination to serve his country but that he may be able to support a helpless family dependant entirely upon his labor.

Hoping this may receive your kind and favorable consideration I remain

Your Obt. Servant
L. R. Dorsett

❧ Eight days after this letter was written, Lincoln endorsed it: "Mr. Dorset, the father says he already has two substitutes in the army, that he yet has three unmarried sons subject to draft, who will not shirk and that he has still another son a prisoner among the rebels. He asks that this married son, now drafted, may be discharged. Let it be done. A. Lincoln." The additional information about the case was probably provided during a private interview. (Original in The Forbes Collection, New York.)

Requesting a Priceless Manuscript

National Soldiers Historical Association
Head Quarters, Cincinnati, Mar: 16th 1865.

Hon. Abraham Lincoln
President of U.S.

Desiring to secure original of your recent Inaugural Address to print fac-simile copies the receipts of sale of which will be devoted to printing history of the deeds of the private soldiers who have fallen in this war for the life of the nation. I respectfully appeal to you to honor me with the same in behalf of

<u>The National Soldiers Historical Association</u>—The enterprise has in view organizations of loyal women in all circles to form mite Societies for mental and moral improvement, by Committee of which record will be made of names and services of the true heroes of the war against rebellion. As the work is to be done by voluntary contributions of the people, it will not draw money from National or State Treasuries—

No such Anti-Slavery words have elsewhere been so forcibly used as those expressed in your Second Inaugural, and I bespeak an opportunity for the widest diffusion of the correct and original copy.—

In the cause of the Soldier

John D. Caldwell Secy.

Caldwell also wrote to Senator John Harlan, whose daughter was engaged to the Lincolns' son Robert, to use his "influence with Mrs. Lincoln" to secure the President's manuscript. But the original remained in the President's papers. At the time this request was made, it was possibly still at the typesetters, where Lincoln had sent it to be printed into a reading copy. This letter thus bears the inscription: "Answer that the ms. is not in the Prests posession. April 10, 1865." Ultimately, Lincoln presented it to his faithful assistant secretary, with the inscription: "Original manuscript of second Inaugeral [sic] presented to Major John Hay. A. Lincoln" (CW, VIII: 333).

This letter appears on page 133.

Eaglesmere Sepr 24th 1863

To

His Excellency
Abraham Lincoln
President
Of The United States
of America

It is with heartfelt
gratitude that I venture
to address you in order to
thank you for your kind-
ness to the Widow and
Orphan in nominating my
Son Horatio M. Jones as a
Cadet at West Point.

May you be rewarded
for your kindness by his
emulating his late father
Col I. Richter Jones, in

[3]

Compliments and Congratulations

*E*VERY ONE LIKES a compliment," Abraham Lincoln admitted to a correspondent near the end of his life. "Commendation," he had admitted earlier, "is all that a vain man could wish."

But Lincoln's vanity was rather infrequently fed, his thirst for
compliments seldom slaked, at least by the correspondence he received
as president.

Perhaps the rarest categories in all of the Lincoln Papers are the
unencumbered compliment and the unfettered congratulation.

Some such letters, of course, accompanied gifts—"tokens of respect," as one writer described his offerings—and these were in fact so
plentiful that this book devotes a separate chapter exclusively to such
presentations. But, otherwise, the occasional flattering letter typically
came weighted down not with gifts but with shameless requests for
favors, as if nothing could be more natural than demanding a personal
interview or a government job in return for the merest words of
praise.

There were exceptions: support for Lincoln's tough stand against
secession, praise for his speeches from exalted and ordinary Americans
alike, heartfelt gratitude for the Emancipation Proclamation, congratulations for election successes, and occasional expressions of gratitude

117

for pardons, clemency, and other assistance from the beleaguered chief magistrate.

Ironically—and rather touchingly—Lincoln's revealing "every one likes a compliment" admission came in response not to a genuine compliment but to a rather bland letter he evidently mistook as such. His eagerness to thank a correspondent for thanking *him*, misplaced as it was, suggests perhaps how much he yearned for such praise—and how infrequently it came his way.

A Vote of Confidence

Philadh. May 1st, 61

To His Excellency President Lincoln

Sir: It gives me much pleasure to enclose for your perusal, the Resolution passed "at Independence Hall" on the 18th of April by the "Men of the War of 1812." They were adopted unanimously and would have been forwarded before this date if they had all [not] been published by the newspapers. Some, however, were left out, & only referred to, since then. I have had them published for the Press & this morning they have all met the public eye. You Excellency will see that we go heart & hand in the good cause. Very Resptfully, I remain yours

J. B. Sutherland

These veterans of the War of 1812 had unanimously adopted a resolution stating that "after a lapse of nearly forty-seven years, we are again called upon to support our country, not from the invasion of a foreign enemy, but from the efforts of domestic traitors." The President was not specifically mentioned in the resolutions, and no reply to Sutherland has come to light.

"On the Right Path"

Pellham Farm [New York,] May 2 1861

President Lincoln

Dear Sir I can see in the future that an untimely death awaits Jefferson Davis, and his band of traitors, it is not his destiny to destroy our nation, the bones of his people will rise from the grave and curse him as he passes into eternity.

Thank God that might have been, but is not to be your fate, notwithstanding our flag is on the verge of ruin, our country rent by discord, and war staring us in the face, and even Maryland turned traitor to our most glorious cause, and they made her countrymen her foes by spilling their precious blood in her streets.

I cannot help feeling assured that you are now on the right path, and that the stand you have taken is the only one that justice and a sense of right would dictate, you have now repudiated the past, and stand forth the President of the United States. You are the man I like, because you have thrown off the trammels of your cabinet, and taken the advice of your best friend Mrs. L. and are now acting as plain common sense, and your own noble judgement dictates. The spontaneous gathering around you, plainly indicates how the nation feels. Thousands of bold and brave hearts respond to your call, and now rally around the star spangled banner held in your hand, heaven help it, and you.

They are willing and anxious to fight for their country, and their God. <u>But it must not be.</u>

Your cry for arms has been responded to from the East and the West, from the North, and even from the South, for there are brave Southern hearts that beat with the fire of Patriotism and who will stand undivided from their countries [*sic*] flag.

Be assured that the one foolish act of the Southern States, has been firing upon the American flag. It has aroused the hearts of men, from Pennsylvania to the far distant land that contains your home, and the martial cry has resounded from north to south; from hill and dale thousands are flocking to your banner; women have given up their husbands and sons like the heroines of old, and told them to begone, and return with honour or not return at all, and if necessary, bravely will they accomplish their task. Hearts would be made sad, homes desolate, were it not that God has watched over you and through you will bring forth our beloved land from under the cloud that now hangs over it.

If war should by any unforseen accident be inaugurated, it would raise the evil in mens hearts, and make them wish for blood.

Dear Mr. Lincoln you now are safe, you can defend the Capitol from all assaults, and are master of the country, and can conciliate the South on your terms, and with honour to yourself, without treading upon Southern rights.

Oh think of this in the name of humanity, and all you hold sacred, then in after ages your name will be honoured and beloved, let your own reason and judgment hold the sway, and you will never regret it. Give up Fort Pickens [a federal fort in Confederate Florida that Lincoln had determined to resupply], if any opportunity offers, which will show the South that you do not intend to invade their land, but stand by justice, and act on the defensive. If they attack you, which they will not do, exterminate them if you can. And you may count upon men, my sons, and my fortune to aid you. Take your own counsel, I know you wish this trouble settled without bloodshed, you have the matter in your own hands, let it be done quickly, call to your aid all the soldiers that are now prepared for war, so as to let the Southern people see you are invinceable.

Then a bright and glorious future will beam upon you, and our flag will float once more, over all our land, and not be dimmed by the loss of a single state, and will ever remain the harbinger of victory; having been born before the present generation of men flourished. In olden times, when tyrants have sought to crush it, it floated on the plains of Maryland, and summit of Bunker Hill, wherever it was unfurled the fight was victorious. I remember this, and though for a time it may be banished from some States, it only rests for you to show them the way, and they will most willingly crawl back, now they think they have right on their side, and rest assured, if you coerce them they will fight for those rights, step by step, until the whole Southern race white and black are exterminated.

You know what war can do, if once commenced, how it desolates the land. Commerce science and learning are hushed. Its messengers like vultures and tygers but look for prey. They will not only desolate and plunder those that are opposed to them, but when the war is over, fight each other, for when blood is once shed, it becomes a mania that few can resist, then do not let this war proceed, we of the North are safe, you have placed us by your pacific policy beyond the reach of the South.

Men have freely given their lives, their wealth, their all to aid you, there is not a craven heart so base as not to respond to your call for help; but it is past, be firm as you have already been, and you will step forth into the light of day uncontaminated by those around you, let your policy be your own, give us peace instead of war, and millions will bless the name you bear, and acknowledge you the Saviour of the greatest country on the face of earth. No man has ever lived possessed of the power that you now have, of becoming immortal.

I am with great respect your obedient servant.

Robt. L. Pell

ᔄ *No reply is known to this confused but flattering plea for peace and restraint. One of Lincoln's secretaries filed it under the heading "War and Politics." The day after Pell wrote, the President issued a proclamation calling for 42,034 volunteers, citing the need for "immediate and adequate measures for the preservation of the National Union." Reunion without bloodshed was not to be* (CW, IV: 333–334).

Announcing a Namesake . . .

His Excellency
A. Lincoln Pres. U.S.

Hon. Sir, Herewith please find record of the birth of Abraham Lincoln Potter.

Born in the village of La Crescent County of Houston State of Minnesota on the Morning of the 23rd of May 1861 at 8 o.clk

Abraham Lincoln Potter, son of George F. and Mary Anne Potter. The father ardently supported you for the Presidency and knows no better way to express his satisfaction with your administration than by naming his son after you feeling satisfied that the future will present no cause for regret. The sympathy of the people are with you and hope that this wicked rebellion of the very "brave" men who do not disdain to poison and murder may soon be effeccively crushed out.

Respectfully yours

George F. Potter

. . . And Another

Cochran Indiana June 23-1861

To His honor the president of this
United States of America

Mr. Abraham Lincoln you Will pleas pardon Me for taking the Liberty of Addressing you Apon this occasion. Honorable Sir Having had the pleasure of casting my Ballot for you the second father of My Country, I have seen fitt to name my youngest Son, Abraham Lincoln Tudor he Was Born february the 8th 1861 And Was Duly Crisond on the fourth of March the same Sir you may think it strange of Me taking this liberty but sir lett me asure you, that the Love for My Country And the presant choise of its Cheafe Executiv has induced Me to Take the Corse I have, As a Mechanic And An American I feel that all i can bequeath to him is his good Name And fitt him for his Country to the best of My Ability I have an other Son George Washington With those glorious names recorded in My Bible I feel confident of there success in life hoping dear sir you Will Take No offence of the liberty I have taken or of my remarks hear I have Made And With your Best Wishes for my little Linky, I Remain your humble Servent

Jacob L. Tudor

The Honorable Mr holman the Barer of this Note Will vouch for My sincerity.

∽ *If Lincoln replied to either of these letters, the acknowledgments have long since been lost.*

A Synagogue's Sentiments

Synagogue Chambers
Philad: April 23d/62

To his Excellency Abm Lincoln
Presdt of the U. States of America
Respected Sir In accordance with your Proclamation Our Minister The Revd. S. Morais on the following Holy day at our Synagogue delivered the Enclosed address & Prayer, and as it breathes Loyalty to the Union without exultation, or being Triumphant over the loss of our Misguided Brothers in the South, I take the liberty of Enclosing you a Copy & have the honor to Subscribe Myself

> Your Obt Sevt
> A. Hart
> President of the Congregation
> "Hope of Israel"

∽ *On April 10, Lincoln had issued a proclamation asking Americans to assemble "in their accustomed places of public worship" to thank God for recent "signal victories" by "land and naval forces engaged in suppressing the invasion." Several days later, on the Jewish holiday of Passover, Rabbi Sabato Morais responded with an address, at Congregation "Mikve Israel" in Philadelphia, in which he asked God to bless the President "for his sterling honesty . . . his firmness and moderation." Several weeks later Lincoln wrote Hart as follows to thank him for forwarding the newspaper report of the rabbi's sermon (CW, V: 185–186, 212).*

Executive Mansion
May 13, 1982

My dear Sir Permit me to acknowledge the receipt of your communication of April 23d containing a copy of a Prayer recently delivered at your Synagogue, and to thank you heartily for the expressions of kindness and confidence. I have the honor to be

Your Obt. Servt
A. Lincoln

A. Hart Esq
Prest. Congn. Hope of Israel
Phila.

Welcoming Emancipation

New York, Sept. 24, 1862.

Abraham Lincoln:
    God bless you for a good deed!

Theodore Tilton

Office of *The Independent*

∽ *Abolitionist editor Theodore Tilton had been a frequent critic of Lincoln.*

Philadelphia Sept 25/62

To his Excellency Abraham Lincoln
President of the United States
    Sir There is not a True Patriot or Philanthropist in the Union, that does not heartily approve your recent Message or proclamation, on the Subject of Slavery; and doubtless the almighty in his wisdom will bless the proposed measures with success.—I rejoice that the conflict between the North and the South, for which diversified causes have been assigned to suit the purposes of political brawlers, and crafty Rebels; has at last been brought to a focus, and that we now understand fully the principle upon which it is to be determined.— Allow me to congratulate you upon an assured and enviable immortality, whatever may be the result of this magnanimous vindication of the character of the Country and the rights of Humanity.—I enclose to you an able article of to day relating to this subject, and remain

Respectfully & Gratefully Yrs
David Paul Brown

∽ *Although Lincoln did not acknowledge this letter, it was filed under the endorsement "Congratulations."*

Lacon Ills 28th Sept 1862.

President Lincoln

My old Friend I say to you again all us [Stephen A.] Douglass [*sic*] Democrats are with you and we intend to be with you untill our whole country is free so that you can execute the laws in every town in the U.S. If they loose their negroes it is their own fault not ours. Every one says call men enough 2,000,000 and end it in Ninety days and make sure now and save life. It send this to let you know we all have confidence in you We all appreciate you most worthily and hope you will use any and all means to end this most unrighteous war accept my best wishes for yourself and our <u>whole</u> country and believe Truly your Friend

Chs Parker

Beaufort, S.C., Jan. 1. 1863.

To Abraham Lincoln
President U.S.A.

Sir, The Baptist Church in Beaufort, S.C., beg to submit to you the enclosed <u>Resolutions</u>, adopted by them unanimously at a special meeting held in their "Tabernacle" this first day of January, 1863.

The sentiments & the words of the Resolutions were dictated by a Committee of themselves, chosen for the purpose; & having been taken in writing <u>while</u> & <u>as</u> they were spoken, are their own.

The Committee have also, by direction of the Church, subscribed severally their names, or marks.

It seems proper to add, that the members of this Church, <u>now</u> resident on Port Royal & islands adjacent, are, with one esception, <u>people of color proclaimed free this day</u>, & numbering more than eleven hundred.

Accept, Sir, the assurance of my highest consideration, & of my own most hearty participation in the spirit & scope of the Resolutions.

By request of the Church,
S. Peck, Senr Pastor

∽ *It is not clear whether Pastor Peck was himself a person of color, or whether he was a white official speaking for his black flock. The resolutions themselves, sadly, have vanished.*

His Excellency Abraham Lincoln
President of the U.S.

Dear Sir: Amid the rejoicing & thanksgiving of three millions of enfranchised men, & the blessings they shower upon your head, the feeble voices of single individuals may be worth little or nothing, but nations are composed of individuals, & boys & girls (which we yet are) grow up into men & women, who all add their part to the public weal or woe. For this reason we hope you will accept these words kindly & in the same spirit in which they are spoken.

Language has no words to express how much we thank you for your glorious Proclamation. You have added glory to the sky & splendor to the sun, & there are but few men who have ever done that before, either by words or acts. We enthusiastically "went in" for you at the last presidential campaign, but pardon us if we candidly tell you that on the day when your Proclamation was issued, we said for the first time since your Administration, from the bottom of our hearts, "God bless Abraham Lincoln"! We know that no President has had to contend with so many difficulties as you, but we could not say it after what happened in consequence of Gen. Fremont's and Gen. Hunter's Proclamations [early emancipation orders that were rescinded by Lincoln], & we did not say it after your September Proclamation for the "day of Jubilee", was too far off then. The foul blot of many years on our own glorious flag, you have erased with one stroke of your pen. You have done a great thing, & perhaps God has never before, since the beginning of the world, given to any one man the great privilege, the golden opportunity, of doing such a great act. O! dear "Uncle Abe", only see the Proclamation carried out & how brightly will the name of <u>Abraham Lincoln</u> shine through all times & ages! How richly laden with blessings will your Proclamation be handed down to future generations, as great a document as the Declaration of Independence, & your memory as much honored and remembered as Washington! We are sure that every <u>really</u> loyal men blesses & loves you now, & the salute of hundred guns, fired in honor of that Proclamation, in Boston, must have awakened echoes in the hearts of all good people. How proud & happy you must feel, you a single man, the liberator of three million of our fellow-men, you alone accomplishing that object for which men have been writing & fighting for half a century, or more. But better than all blessing from men, is God's blessing, & we know that you have His. But once more we too repeat, "God bless you a thousand, thousand times."

Hoping that you will pardon us for troubling you with this letter, amid your many official duties, we remain yours very respectfully

Gertrude Bloede
Victor Gus. Bloede
Katie Bloede

Brooklyn, L.I.
Jan. 4th '63

ᔎ *No response is known to the letter from these young people, but Lincoln personally endorsed the envelope in which it came and presumably kept it in his own files.*

Thanks for West Virginia Statehood

Wheeling Va Jan 1st 63.

His Excellency, the President of the US—
Washington DC—

Sir, God bless you you have signed the <u>Bill</u> [giving statehood to West Virginia]. In the name of the loyal Ladies of West Va, we thank you for our blessed <u>New Year's Gift</u>.—As the wives of our state officers, we are doubly grateful you have saved us from contempt and disgrace.

The wildest enthusiasm prevails. The people are running to & fro; each one anxious to bear the "Glad tidings of this great day."

A Happy New Year to you Mr. President—May not another hair turn grey—May your cares be less, and may you live to receive the benedictions of our children's children.

Very Respectfully,
Mrs. F. H. Pierpont
Mrs. Saml. Crane
Mrs. L. A. Hagans

ᔎ *Excitement over statehood for the pro-Union counties of western Virginia was all but forgotten in the rush of even greater public attention to the Emancipation Proclamation, which took effect the same day.*

Support for an Open Letter on Civil Liberties

New York June 15, 63.

My dear Sir,

I desire to thank you for your letter to Hon. Erastus Corning & others, it is of more value to the cause than a victory. You have not left them a simple peg to hang on. There has at this time been ordered 50,000 copies of your letter in pamphlet form from the "Tribune" and before the present week closes these will have been printed and circulated of this letter at least 500,000 copies and you may safely calculate that by the end of June this letter will have been read by 10,000,000 of people.

Your friends in New York are taking steps to give every soldier in the field a copy of it. In a word it has done us all great good. God bless you for this as for every other good thing you have done. Your friends here who are not office hunters will never cheat or betray you, on the contrary they will stand by you to day & in 1864.

I am very truly

Wm. A. Hall

His Excellency the President

ᔕ *Hall was referring to Lincoln's now-famous letter, published in* The New York Tribune *on June 15, 1863, in response to resolutions passed in Albany condemning the administration for the military arrest of an antiwar ("Copperhead") Democratic Congressman, Clement L. Vallandigham of Ohio. Vallandigham's arrest, trial, and conviction for speaking out against the war—and Lincoln's subsequent decision to banish this critic to the Confederacy—created an uproar. Lincoln replied to the lengthy Albany attack with a famous public letter, an excerpt from which follows. On June 30 Albany Democrat Erastus Corning and his allies replied to Lincoln's scathing response, assailing the President's position as a "gigantic and monstrous heresy" and a "plea for absolute power." The American people, Corning and his committee insisted, "will never acquiesce in this doctrine" (CW, VI: 260–269).*

Executive Mansion
[June 12,] 1863

Hon. Erastus Corning & others

. . . I understand the meeting, whose resolutions I am considering, to be in favor of suppressing the rebellion by military force—by armies. Long experience has shown that armies cannot be maintained unless desertion shall be punished by the severe penalty of death. The case requires, and the law and the constitution, sanction this punishment. Must I shoot a simple-minded soldier boy who deserts, while I must not touch a hair of a wiley agitator who induces him to desert? This is none the less injurious when effected by getting a father, or brother, or friend, into a public meeting, and there working upon his feelings, till he is persuaded to write the soldier boy, that he is fighting in a bad cause, for a wicked administration of a contemptable government, too weak to arrest and punish him if he shall desert. I think that in such a case, to silence the agitator, and save the boy, is not only constitutional, but, withal, a great mercy.

If I be wrong on this question of constitutional power, my error lies in believing that certain proceedings are constitutional when, in cases of rebellion or Invasion, the public Safety requires them, which would not be constitutional when, in absence of rebellion or invasion, the public Safety does not require them—in other words, that the constitution is not in it's application in all respects the same, in cases of Rebellion or invasion, involving the public Safety, as it is in times of profound peace and public security. The constitution itself makes the distinction; and I can no more be persuaded that the government can constitutionally take no strong measure in time of rebellion, because it can be shown that the same could not be lawfully taken in time of peace, than I can be persuaded that a particular drug is not good medicine for a sick man, because it can be shown to not be good food for a well one. Nor am I able to appreciate the danger, apprehended by the meeting, that the American people will, by means of military arrests during the rebellion, lose the right of public discussion, the liberty of speech and the press, the law of evidence, trial by jury, and Habeas corpus, throughout the indefinite peaceful future which I trust lies before them, any more than I am able to believe that a man could contract so strong an appetite for emetics during temporary illness, as to persist in feeding upon them through the remainder of his healthful life. . . .

An Italian Nationalist Praises Emancipation

Caprera, Italy, August 6, 1863

To Abraham Lincoln:
Emancipator of the Slaves in the American Republic.

If in the midst of the danger of your titanic strife our voices may also mingle, o Lincoln, let us the free Sons of Columbus send a message of augury and of admiration of the great work you have initiated.

Heir of the thought of Christ and of [John] Brown, you will pass down to posterity under the name of <u>the Emancipator</u>! more enviable than any crown and any human treasure!

An entire race of mankind, yoked by selfishness to the collar of Slavery, is, by You, at the price of the noblest blood of America, restored to the dignity of Manhood, to civilization, and to Love.

America, teacher of liberty to our Fathers, now opens the most solemn Era of human progress, and whilst she amazes the world by her gigantic boldness, makes us sadly reflect that this old Europe albeit agitated by the grand cause of human freedom, does not understand, nor move forward to become equal to her.

Whilst the epicurian upholders of Despotisms intone the bacchic ode which celebrates the decay of a free people, let the free, religiously celebrate the downfall of Slavery—Parallel Mysteries of History!— the rapine of Mexico [the French had moved to conquer Mexico] and the proclamation of Lincoln!

Greeting to you Abraham Lincoln great pilot of freedom; greeting to all who for two years have fought and bled around your regenerating Standard,—greeting to you, the redeemed offspring of Ham. The free men of Italy welcome the glorious rupture of your chains.

> The Italian Liberals
> G. Garibaldi,
> M. Garibaldi,
> N. Garibaldi

∽ *The Lincoln administration had offered Giuseppe Garibaldi, Italy's liberator, a major general's commission in the Union army back in 1861, but the Italian leader had unrealistically insisted that he first be empowered to abolish slavery. No reply to this flattering letter is known (Mitgang, "Garibaldi and Lincoln," American Heritage 27 [October 1975]: 98).*

"Hearty Sympathy" for "Blessed Purposes"

Earlham Lodge
8th mo 18 1863

To The President of the United States
Esteemed friend
Abraham Lincoln

Many times, since I was privileged to have an interview with thee, nearly a year ago, my mind has turned towards thee with feelings of sincere and christian interest, and, as our kind friend Isaac Newton offers to be the bearer of a paper messenger, I feel inclined to give thee the assurance of my continued hearty sympathy in all thy heavy burthens and responsibilities and to express, not only my own earnest prayer, but I believe the prayer of many thousands whose hearts thou hast gladdened by thy praiseworthy and <u>successful</u> effort to "burst the hands of wickedness, and let the oppressed go free," that the Almighty Ruler of the Universe may strengthen thee to accomplish <u>all</u> the blessed purposes, which, in the unerring counsel of his will and wisdom, I do assuredly believe he did design to make thee <u>instrumental</u> in accomplishing, when he appointed thee thy present post of vast responsibility, as the Chief Magistrate of this great Nation.—Many are the trials incident to such positions and I believe thy conflicts and anxieties have not been few—"May the Lord hear thee, in the day of trouble—the name of the God of Jacob defend thee—send thee help from his sanctuary, and strengthen thee out of Lion—the Lord fulfill all thy petitions that are put up in the name of the Prince of Peace, of the increase of whose government and of whose Peace, he has himself declared, there shall <u>never</u> be an end.["]

I can hardly refrain from expressing my cordial approval of thy late excellent proclamation appointing a day of thanksgiving for the sparing and preserving mercies, which in the tender loving kindness of our God and Saviour, have been so bountifully showered upon us— for though, (as a religious people) <u>we</u> do not set apart especial seasons for returning thanks either for spiritual or temporal blessings, yet as I humbly trust, our hearts are filled with gratitude to our Almighty Father that his delivering arm of love and power has been so manifestly tossed about us, and I rejoice in the decided recognition of an all-wise and superintending Providence which is so marked a feature in the aforesaid document as well as the immediate influence and guidance of the Holy Spirit, which perhaps never, in any previous <u>state</u> paper, has been so fully recompensed before—especially did my inmost heart respond to the decision that the anger which has so long sustained this needless and cruel rebellion, may be subdued, the hearts of the insurgents changed, and the whole Nation be led, through paths of repentence and submission to the Divine will, back to the perfect enjoyment of Union and fraternal peace.

May the Lord, in his infinite compassion, hasten the day. I will not occupy thy time unduly, but in a feeling of true Christian sympathy and gospel love, commend thee and thy wife, and your two dear sons to the preserving care of the unslumbering Shepherd who in his matchless mercy gave his life for the sheep—who is alone able to keep us from falling, and finally, when done with the fast fleeting things of mutability, to give us an everlasting inheritance among all them that are sanctified through the eternal Spirit of our God.

Respectfully and sincerely
Thy assured friend
Eliza P. Gurney

ᔓ *Lincoln took more than a year to answer Mrs. Gurney, wife of a prominent antislavery & antiwar English Quaker. He replied with the following famous letter (CW, VII: 535).*

Executive Mansion,
Washington, September 4. 1864.

Eliza P. Gurney.
My esteemed friend.

I have not forgotten—probably never shall forget—the very impressive occasion when yourself and friends visited me on a Sabbath forenoon two years ago. Nor has your kind letter, written nearly a year later, ever been forgotten. In all, it has been your purpose to strengthen my reliance on God. I am very much indebted to the good christian people of the country for their constant prayers and consolations; and to no one of them, more than to yourself. The purposes of the Almighty are perfect, and must prevail, though we erring mortals may fail to accurately perceive them in advance. We hoped for a happy termination of this terrible war long before this; but God knows best, and has ruled otherwise. We shall yet acknowledge His wisdom and our own error therein. Meanwhile we must work earnestly in the best light He gives us, trusting that so working still conduces to the great ends He ordains. Surely He intends some great good to follow this mighty convulsion, which no mortal could make, and no mortal could stay.

Your people—the Friends—have had, and are having, a very great trial. On principle, and faith, opposed to both war and oppression, they can only practically oppose oppression by war. In this hard dilemma, some have chosen one horn and some the other. For those appealing to me on conscientious grounds [for draft exemption], I have done, and shall do, the best I could and can, in my own conscience, under my oath to the law. That you believe this I doubt not; and believing it, I shall still receive, for our country and myself, your earnest prayers to our Father in Heaven.

> Your sincere friend
> A. Lincoln.

Thanks from a Widow for an Orphan's Appointment

> Eaglesmere [Pa.]
> Sept 24th 1863

To His Excellency Abraham Lincoln
President of the United States of America

It is with heartfelt gratitude that I venture to address you in order to thank you for your kindness to the widow and orphan in nominating my Son Horatio M. Jones as a Cadet, at West Point.

May you be rewarded for your kindness by his emulating his late father Col. I. Richter Jones, in his love and devotion to his Country.

With much respect believe me

> Yours
> Anne E. Jones

∽ *No reply is known.*

Plaudits from the Principal Speaker at Gettysburg

> Nov. 20 1863

The President
My dear Sir,

Not wishing to intrude upon your privacy, when you must be much engaged, I beg leave, in this way, to thank you very sincerely for your great thoughtfulness for my Daughter's accommodation on the Platform yesterday, & much kindness otherwise to me & mine at Gettysburg.

Permit me also to express my great admiration of the thoughts offered by you, with such eloquent simplicity & appropriateness, at the consecration of the cemetery. I should be glad, if I came as near to the central idea of the occasion, in two hours, as you did in two minutes. My son who parted from me at Baltimore & my daughter, concur in this sentiment.

I remain, dear sir, most respectfully yours,

Edward Everett

I hope your anxiety for your child was relieved on your arrival. [Tad Lincoln had been ill before Lincoln left for Gettysburg.]

ᔄ *Lincoln replied as follows (CW, VII:24).*

Executive Mansion,
Washington, Nov. 20, 1863.

Hon. Edward Everett.
My dear Sir:

Your kind note of to-day is received. In our respective parts yesterday, you could not have been excused to make a short address, nor I a long one. I am pleased to know that, in your judgment, the little I did say was not entirely a failure. Of course I knew Mr. Everett would not fail; and yet, while the whole discourse was eminently satisfactory, and will be of great value, there were passages in it which transcended my expectation. The point made against the theory of the general government being only an agency, whose principals are the States, was new to me, and, as I think, is one of the best arguments for the national supremacy. The tribute to our noble women for their angel-ministering to the suffering soldiers, surpasses, in its way, as do the subjects of it, whatever has gone before.

Our sick boy, for whom you kindly inquire, we hope is past the worst.

Your Obt. Servt.
A. Lincoln

Election Day Good Wishes

836 So. 3rd St.
Philadelphia Nov 8th 1864

"Uncle Abe"

The American people, individually and collectively, generally exercise a great amount of freedom, Copperhead denials to the contrary notwithstanding, and assuming that you do not object to the greeting of any loyal man, allow me to present my compliments to Our Next President, Hon Abraham Lincoln.

To day the free people of this free country will say that thou shalt rule over us yet four years more and accomplish the good work thou hast begun; to day, the Chicago Platform [the opposition Democratic party platform], its admirers, supporters, and candidates, will receive such a shock that they will never recover from its effects "so mote it be."

I have a proud record to which I can refer when old age creeps on—yea a glorious record—to wit—: Three years in the good old Army of the Potomac, (Co "K" 2 Pa. Res.) a wound from the memorable "Fredericksburg" incarceration in the notorious "Libby" [Prison] and last though not least, my first Presidential vote cast for those good, sterling-patriot-statesmen Abraham Lincoln and Andrew Johnson, and better than all I vote on the winning side.

The frauds and conspiracies of Copperheadism will avail not.

[Clement L.] Vallandigham [antiwar Ohio congressman] will not be a member of the Cabinet for the ensuing four years, nor will the Messrs Wood [New York's Mayor Fernando Wood and his brother] exhibit their National devotion by throttling the free institutions of our country, and our own darling William B. Reed will continue to be a martyr.

Pardon my presumption in writing to you but as I never had the opportunity of giving your hand a hearty shake or of paying my compliments to our noble Chief Magistrate, and probably never will, I accepted the pen as the only medium through which I could wish you God Speed in restoring the supremacy of our glorious Star Spangled Banner.

May all your future efforts be crowned with success.

Excuse the caption of this letter [the irreverent salutation], but to day is "Election Day"

> I remain
> Very Respectfully Yours &c
> James F. Morrison

To Hon. Abraham Lincoln.

໑ *No answer is known; this letter was filed under "Complimentary."*

More Congratulations on his Reelection

Phila Nov 9 1864.

His excellency A Lincoln

George Washington made the Republic. Abraham Lincoln will save it[.]

James M. Scovel

Thanks for Clearing his Name

St. Nicholas Hotel,
Jan 26 1865

To His Excellency Abraham Lincoln Pres USA

Dear Sir: Accept my unfeigned gratitude for my prompt release from the malicious or profoundly ignorant charge of being a southern spy. To those who know me the charge is simply ridiculous. I may be justly charged of being impulsive, defiant, and precipitant, but never as a hypocrite or spy—never never. Sir, I have written this for other purposes than a return of my grateful acknowledgment for your confidence and friendship. I have at least succeeded this evening through my friends in prevailing upon the [New York] "World" the organ of the Democracy to declare on Saturday or Friday that to vote <u>for</u> or <u>against</u> the "Amendment" clause [the Thirteenth Amendment, abolishing slavery] on Tuesday next was no test of Democracy and rather indirectly to advise the Democracy to vote for it. I was thus promised this evening by its editor. So you need not have any apprehension now upon its passage. Gov [Horatio] Seymour [of New York] has declared that he had no interest upon the subject, and if it passed he would have no regrets. This he declared to George C. Jones, a former Dem member of congress whom I sent to test him. Mr. Seward first intrusted this matter to me, and I first won over Judge [Thomas A. R.] Nelson who introduced me to you and who has been indefatigable in his assiduous efforts to procure other Democrats to vote for it. The bill will pass and thus I will have discharged my obligations to eternal justice and an universal humanity. Had you not better have the article of the "World" copied in the [Washington] Chronicle the next day, to ease the Democratic scruples of some members of congress. Your friend

W. N. Bilbo

Bilbo had been released from prison on January 20 through a telegram from Lincoln to Maj. Gen. Dix: "Let W. N. Bilbo be discharged on his parole. A. Lincoln." Bilbo was a onetime Whig from Tennessee. (CW, VIII: 226).

A "Cripple's" Admiration

Jan 31 1865

Mr. President

Sir: Thinking it not amiss to address you a short missive, I now avail myself of the opportunity that I have had in contemplation, previous to your reelection. I am a cripple, probably for life. I devote most of my time to reading. 'Tis with pleasure that I perused your "Emancipation Proclamation." And your letter to "Col Hodges of Ky;" which I have cut out, and keep it in my dictionary. I can assert candidly before God & man, that I have not said aught against the Leader, or his Administration; which in my humble opinion, is executed according to God's will.

I am a warm friend of our dear soldiers, and have been, ever since the onset of the gigantic rebellion. My heart almost bleeds, to read of the intense sufferings of the prisoners in the "Chivalry" bastiles [Confederate prisons]. But their tribulation will not continue always; it must end sooner or later.

Convinced that you are well aware of their condition, I'll say nothing more of the matter. The year of 1865 has rolled its ample rounds, and still this cruel war rages; and the rebellion is still committing degredattions [sic], & outrages in our land. I am in hopes Generals Grant, Sherman, and Sheridan, aided by subordinate officers, acting as auxiliaries, will give the rebellion, Slavery &c, a Coup de grace by Spring.

Fully aware of the duties devolving upon you, I will not trouble you further with my remarks. Hoping you will read this, I'll close requesting you to give this an answer, if you don't write more than a dozen lines.

Your obt. servt.
Jno. W. Hawk

Dubois Co., Ludlow, Inc.

No answer was forthcoming.

Re-Inauguration Congratulations

Hamilton, Mass. March 4, 1865

Mr. Lincoln

Dear Sir I only wish to thank you for being so good—and to say how sorry we all are that you must have four years more of this terrible toil. But remember what a triumph it is for the right, what a blessing to the country—and then your rest shall be glorious when it does come!

You cant tell anything about it in Washington where they make a noise on the slightest provocation—But if you had been in this little speck of a village this morning and heard the soft sweet music of unseen bells rippling through the morning silence from every quarter of the far-off horison [sic] you would have better known what your name is to this nation.

May God help you in the future as he has helped you in the past; and a people's love and gratitude will be but a small portion of your exceeding great reward.

Most respectfully
Mary A. Dodge

ᔕᐧ *No reply is known.*

Misunderstood Praise

New York, March 4[, 1865].

Dear Sir,

The sour Weather has spoiled the Celebration, so I send you my Badge [probably an official identification badge for inaugural ceremonies]. It is prettily got up, though with by no means a flattered reflex [a photograph] of our President.

I learn that "Republican Robinson" is boring for a Judgeship. He is a second cousin of Judge White.

The reply to the Committee of Congress informing of your re-election, is not only the <u>neatest</u> but the most pregnant and effective use to which the English Language was ever put.

Very Truly Yours
Thurlow Weed

President Lincoln

⚬ Lincoln apparently took this to be a compliment not only for his reply to news of his reelection, but also for his second inaugural address, which Republican leader Weed never mentioned, for he gratefully replied as follows on March 15, in a rare admission of how important praise was to him (CW, VIII: 356).

Executive Mansion,
Washington, March 15, 1865.

Thurlow Weed, Esq
My dear Sir.

Every one likes a compliment. Thank you for yours on my little notification speech, and on the recent Inaugeral [*sic*] Address. I expect the latter to wear as well as—perhaps better than—any thing I have produced; but I believe it is not immediately popular. Men are not flattered by being shown that there has been a difference of purpose between the Almighty and them. To deny it, however, in this case, is to deny that there is a God governing the world. It is a truth which I thought needed to be told; and as whatever of humiliation there is in it, falls most directly on myself, I thought others might afford for me to tell it. [Best known for its magnanimous closing call for "malice toward none," the bulk of Lincoln's extraordinary speech was a scorching defense of the war as heaven-sent punishment for the sin of slavery.]

Yours truly,
A. Lincoln

This letter appears on page 153.

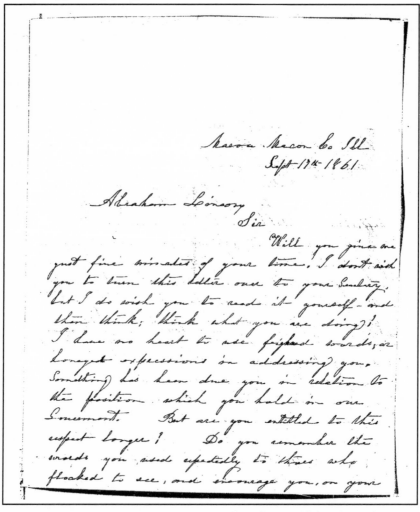

[4]

Complaints and Criticism

*T*HERE IS NO END to the fault finding," presidential secretary William O. Stoddard wrote of the complaints and criticism
that poured into the White House during the Civil War years.

Inevitably, every major decision Lincoln made—whether issuing
the Emancipation Proclamation, suspending the writ of habeas corpus,
or replacing unsuccessful generals—inspired not only letters of appreciation but letters of denunciation as well.

Yet criticism, occasionally of the most virulent and personal kind,
could be motivated by the most minor grievances too. One letter writer
was so offended that Lincoln brought his sons with him to a military
parade that he forwarded a long, abusive letter pointing out all of the
President's shortcomings in manner, bearing, and dignity. Disgruntled
office seekers, too, flooded the White House with their recriminations—including old friends, one of whom wrote to suggest that the
President would henceforth be held responsible for the imminent death
of the man's daughter because the President had refused to name the
ailing woman's husband to a government post in a hospitable climate.

As Stoddard put it, there was no end to "the brutalities, enmities,
and infamies of the President's letter-box." Unfortunately, most such
letters did not survive the scrutiny of Stoddard and his relentless paper

cutter—"witness . . . the litter on the floor and the heaped-up waste-baskets," he boasted—especially if the writers crossed the bounds of Stoddard's rather officious concept of propriety.

Stoddard's overzealousness was history's loss. But it helps explain the surprising dearth in the Lincoln Papers of surviving letters to Lincoln assailing his most important, and surely his most controversial presidential act, the Emancipation Proclamation, in marked contrast to the plentiful supply of surviving congratulations on the same subject. Stoddard himself left a valuable clue about how many negative responses in fact crossed his desk when he wrote:

> How does the country react to the President's proclamation . . . ? There is no telling how many . . . penmen within these past few days have undertaken to assure him that this is a war for the Union only and that they never gave him any authority to run it as an Abolition war. They never, never told him that he might set the Negroes free, and, now that he has done so, or futilely pretended to do so, he is a more unconstitutional tyrant and more odious dictator than he ever was before.

Although Stoddard recalled many letters announcing that soldiers would thereafter be reluctant to engage in battle, the correspondence secretary apparently felt justified in keeping such warnings from the President's desk. There is no evidence to suggest that Lincoln ever saw more than a handful of written complaints each month—a sampling of which appears on the following pages.

In Stoddard's defense, it is altogether possible that he had learned from personal, even painful, experience that his employer simply did not like to read such correspondence. On the envelope in which one such angry letter arrived, the President scrawled, "I understand my friend . . . is ill-natured—therefore I do not read his letter," and filed it away.

An Old Ally, Disappointed

Springfield 27 March 1861

Hon A. Lincoln

My Dear Sir I am sorely disappointed in all my expectations from Washington. I made olny [*sic*] two or three requests of you, One for the Northern Superintendancy of Indian Affairs for my Friend J. P. Luce [the correspondent's son-in-law]. My heart was set on this application for him, as in his appointment I could have transferred my Dying Daughter from the Wabash Valley to the healthy climate of Minnesota and perhaps prolonged her life. I would not go to Washington as I did not wish to trouble you, more than I could possibly help. I did feel as though I had some claims for the favors I asked for But in all I have been disappointed. I think I appreciate the peculiar and embarrassing circumstances under which you are laboring. It is your right to do as you have and still to do as you choose, and I do not Desire any more to intrude upon it. Hoping you may have a happy and prosperous reign and the country saved

I am Truly Your Friend,
Jesse K. Dubois

∽ *Lincoln regarded Dubois as one of his closest political allies, and Dubois, who had once pledged to him, "I am for you against the world," had named one of his sons after the future president. But Lincoln adamantly refused to appoint Dubois's son-in-law to the post in question. His reply to his old Illinois friend follows (LFA, 59; CW, IV: 302).*

Washington,
March 30. 1861

Hon. J. K. Dubois:
My dear Sir

I was nearly as sorry as you can be about not being able to give Mr. Luce the appointment you desired for him. Of course I could have done it; but it would have been against the united, earnest, and, I add, angry protest of the republican delegation of Minnesota, in which state the office is located. So far as I understand, it is unprecedented,

[to] send an officer into a <u>state</u> against the wishes of the members of congress of the State, and of the same party.

Your friend as ever
A. Lincoln

"De∂titute of Policy"

New York April 3d 1861

Mr. Lincoln

Dear Sir I voted for you thinking that <u>in</u> you the country would find a defender of its rights & honour. I am totally disappointed. You are as destitute of policy, as weak, and vassalating as was your predecessor when he begged the enemies of the country to defer the execution of their schemes of wickedness until he was out of office. Do you imagine your course is meeting the favor of republicans—even in New York? No Sir! Democrats rejoice over it, knowing that it will demoralize & overthrow the party, Give up [Fort] Sumpter, Sir, & you are as dead politically as John Brown is physically. You have got to fight. Issue a proclamation to the Union loving men of the Slave States & tell them, it is not them but their <u>enemies</u>—who would subject them to grievous taxations to support over them a military despotism—that you fight, You have got to do this thing Sir, else the country will do it <u>without</u> you, Do you think New York is going to sit quietly by & see its commerce diverted to Southern ports—foreign imports sent into the West & North West—<u>duty free</u> through the ports of of the South? No Sir, As the New York Times says this morning—"Your want of <u>policy</u> <u>& action</u> has demoralized the country more than all of the 3 months of Buchanans imbecility did all together"—As a republican I am sorry to have to <u>say</u> these things. But <u>facts vindicate</u> this statement, Either <u>act,</u> <u>immediately</u> & <u>decisively or</u> resign & go home.

A Republican

ᔕ *Lincoln had pledged in his first inaugural address in March to use "all the power at my disposal . . . to hold, occupy and possess" Fort Sumter and other threatened federal installations in the seceded states, but many northerners favored abandoning Sumter to avoid war. As Lincoln waited for the Sumter crisis to boil over, a number of concerned citizens, like the author of this letter, wrote to urge him not to waver. Similar sentiments were expressed by the author of the letter that follows (CW, IV: 254).*

Complaining of "Peace Policy"

Cincinnati O. April 4/61.

To President Lincoln:

Thirty days more of "Peace Policy" at Washington—and not only the Republican Party, but the Government itself will be gone to destruction or placed beyond remedy!

We have been beaten in our City election—the same in St. Louis—Cleveland—Rhode Island—Brooklyn—and lost two Members of Congress in Connecticut—all from the demoralization and discouraging effect produced by the apparent inaction and temperizing policy of the new Administration, and the impression that Fort Pickens was going to be given up also to the rebels!

The only possible salvation of the Administration—of the Government, and of the Union, depends upon a firm stand against Secession, and by all means and above all, upon the re-enforcement and holding against all opposition of Fort Pickens! That is the Key to this whole secession business! Hold that—and you hold everything within your own grasp, and everything "steady", until the disease runs its course, and either kills or cures itself—as it surely will in less than one year. If it be possible (no matter what the cost of money or life)—Fort Sumpter should be supplied with provision. It should be done by strategem, IT CAN BE DONE. Afterwards, it could be re-enforced with troops. But it will be better, thousand times, that the Fort be attacked, Captured, and Anderson and his men made prisoners of war, or all killed—than that it be evacuated! But if it must be abandoned, let it be done; we can bear it—provided Fort Pickens is held and reenforced for any emergency.

The most fatal infatuation that ever did or can possess a statesman is the idea of a Peace Policy in the present emergency! It only encourages and strengthens the enemy, while it disheartens the friends of the Union in the seceded States, as well as the real friends of the Union every where!

A "Peaceable Separation"—is an impossibility! Besides—that is not what is aimed at by the Secessionists and their abettors. All they want is to get the Administration, and the Republican Party committed to a "Peaceable Secession", and that moment the question will be sprung upon us—"Reconstruction, on the basis of the Southern Constitution, or Disunion"! and we will thus be placed on the side of disunion,—and beaten to death! The love of the "Union" in this Country is stronger than hatred to Slavery; and whatever that question—that issue comes (and it is coming)—the dissolution of the Union, on the adoption of the Jeff. Davis Constitution by all the States—the whole South, and the whole Democratic and Bell-everett Parties at the North, with a large portion of the commercial and Manufacturing interests besides—will be against us, and will carry us into the Southern Confederacy!

This scheme must be broken up—and at once!

1 Reenforce Fort Pickens. Let them attack it, if they will. (Who knows that they will?) If they do—the balls which they fire against its walls will rebound and strike them—kill them; that is all! No body, out of the range of the Forts' guns will be hurt! There need be no invasion—consequently no "Civil war". But we better have twenty years of civil war, than let the Government go to pieces—or than "recognize" the "Southern Confederacy",—which would be recognizing the Right of Secession—etc.

2—The Administration ought to do all it can—in the line of its legitimate duty—to encourage an attack or attacks by the Confederates: It should court and encourage, and bring it about, if possible. This—in order to induce them to raise, equip, and keep up a large military force, thus increasing their expenses, tax levies, etc, in order the sooner to break them down—force a reaction among the people—and in this way the thing would soon be crushed out.

3—Call Congress together—modify or abolish the Tariff: Raise an army of 60,000: make southern Kansas, the Indian Territory & West. Arkansas, the base of operation of our division of say 20,000 men, Send 5,000 to 10,000 down the Mississippi, to clear out the obstructions to commerce & navigation along that river. Hold 20 to 30,000 in and near Washington—Fill Fort Monroe && Gosport Navy Yard as full as they can hold: Then hold things steady—Collect the revenue on shipboard, or blockade the ports—and while all the war munition manufactures in the U. States are put to work, day and night, to their utmost—let the "Model Government" of the Confederate States flourish, for a few months,—giving its leaders as well as all the people of both the seceded States and those that talk of seceding, that after giving them sufficient time for reflection and a return to their loyalty in the Union if they dont do it, you intend to make them do it! Five hundred thousand of the men who voted for you are ready, willing, and <u>anxious</u>, to back you—in this course—in maintaining the <u>integrity of the Union</u>—the <u>old Constitution as it is</u>, and the <u>enforcement of the Laws</u>. But for God's sake! <u>Give not an inch</u>—and <u>dont</u> be afraid of <u>war</u>! <u>Do what you will</u>—<u>War</u>, (to some extent) <u>is inevitable</u>!

Truly Yours.
J. H. Jordan.

"You Need More Dignity"

New York
May 18th, 1861.

My dear Sir,

There are two things that worry people in this town, a good deal; one of which it certainly is in your power to modify, if not reform altogether—

1. The first is, fear that the government will not feed the troops as they ought to be fed, and keep their spirits up without which feeling, they will be good for nothing, however patriotic they may be at the start:—but it may not be in your power to regulate that thoroughly, while it cannot too quickly receive the notice of Mr. [Simon] Cameron and his [War] department.
2. The second source of worriment is your own personal manners—your drawing-room receptions will take care of themselves—In them you are not so particularly found fault with, but when you come to the receiving of military citizens (as all the volunteers are) it becomes a serious question enough, whether you please them or not—

Now then, soldiers write home to their friends in this town with reference to their disappointment in your bearing and manners when reviewing them—

They say when you are on horseback, and platoons of men marching by you, that you lean about and turn your head to talk with people behind you, when they claim that you should sit erect & talk to nobody and look straight at the saluting soldiers—that you ought to assume some dignity for the occasion even though your breeding has not been military—It makes but little difference whether the demand is reasonable or not—it dont require half so much sacrifice on your part to rectify it as it does of the men to go from their homes for the hardship they undertake.

And when you are passing lines of soldiers, receiving them, afoot, they say you take your boys along, and straddle off as if you were cutting across lots, to get somewhere in the quickest time you can, and pay a good deal more attention to your own getting along, than to the soldiers who you start out to review.

These things dont sound well at all—The influence is bad here— The complaint may be frivolous and based on a mistake: but such things are written home here and fortify [Henry] Raymond [editor of the *New York Times*] in his position of advertising for a "Leader." He has got over that, rather, but there is no need of your being so infernally awkward, if these things are true—For God's sake consult somebody, some military man, as to what you ought to do on these occasions in military presence—Nobody will volunteer advice, probably, and if you are arbitrary and conceited on these little things, as Webster used to be, you will alienate your friends and go where he went and John Tyler too, to wit where a man has no party—I don't mean a political party, but a great and universal body guard of men who speak well of you and will do anything to bear aloft and above reproach your administration—

The people here care a mighty lot about the volunteer soldiers— They feel that unless the spirit and loyalty of the soldiers are kept up and encouraged in every way, the country is to suffer immeasurably before these troubles are disposed of—and you, though you were autocrat, can never be popular with the army unless you try your best to lead them to think you appreciate their evolutions [an archaic term for parade movements] by addressing yourself to the business at hand when you are amongst them; and your manner is full as important as your talk. A lawyer in his office can put his feet on a table higher than his head, if he wishes to, but he cant come any such performance as Commander in Chief of the armies of the United States in their presence—Then he must pretend to be a soldier Even if he dont know any thing of tactics at all—

You had better let some officer put you through a few dress parades in your leisure moments, if you can get any, and get some military habit on you so you shall feel natural among military men— Dont let people call you a goose on these <u>very</u>, <u>very</u> important relations to the Army.

Mrs. Lincoln is growing popular all the while, because people say she is mistress of her situation—She aptly fits herself to the times—The dinner service she bought at Houghout's makes people think she is "in town"—They like to talk about her and say she has a good deal of sense and womanly wit about her—she is coming into excellent reputation in this naturally prejudiced city against you and her both—

My impression is that you will do well by paying more attention to your manners and make less effort at wit and story telling—All well enough in private but publicly it is a nuisance—Your talent is conceded—be a gentleman and courtly in your manners when you ought to be——now I dont care whether you take this well or ill—I voted for you and have a desire to be proud of your administration and I dont wish to see you over slaughed by these damaging stories when you can prevent it so easily.

I take it for granted that your temper is as clever as when you fought Douglass in the great campaign, and if it is, you wont be very mad at my writing you these things—Your position is a trying one, and when, on leaving Springfield you asked the people to pray for you, you did well, and millions do pray for you every day, and God is with you, on general principles, I really believe; but it wont do for you to be careless about any thing, not the least thing—

I am doing as I would be done by—In the general administration of your affairs as to this time none but fools and traitors, I imagine, find much fault—I think you have done wonderfully well—

If the stories I hear about Nicolay, your private secretary, are true, you ought to dismiss him—If he is sick, he has a right to be cross and ungentlemanly in his deportment, but not otherwise—People say he is very disagreeable and uncivil—That is wrong—and I dont think the amenity and popularity of the White house ought to be left too much to your wife—It is said here that clergymen and women are the getters up of secession in the South—Women and clergymen and every day people who have not much to do but criticize, are the people that make or unmake popularity more than representatives in Congress or statesmen in the Cabinet—And you know it—

You and I will probably never have any thing to do with each other personally, for we never have met and may never meet, and the greatest fault you can ever find with me, I imagine, is telling you what I think is true, to wit, You need more dignity.

I hope to gracious, you will take care of yourself in a way worthy of your position.

That is all I ask.

Yrs Respectfully
Robert Colby
47 Wall Street

President Lincoln
Washington—

P.S. There is one other thing conceded by every body but the secessionists, to wit: that you are a very warm hearted, honest, & patriotic man—I give you a good deal of credit in this "Soverign" [sic] communication, after all—

∾ *No reply was made to this presumptuous letter. On the back of the envelope on which it came John Nicolay wrote: "a curious specimen."*

"You Lack Nerve"

P R I V A T E

15 Murray St New York
Aug 10. 1861

Abraham Lincoln

For God's sake let a plain man say a few plain words to you—It is commonly reported and believed that Mr. Seward is <u>drunk, daily</u>; and it is universally believed that [Secretary of War Simon] Cameron is a thief—All men believe you, upright—but know you lack experience and fear you lack <u>nerve</u>—You require the best advisers in the land, and when necessary you must sacrifice men to country—While the whole country mistrusts Seward and Cameron you will become and you are becoming lukewarm in the war—If what I hear is true of Seward <u>you must know it</u>—If you want proof against Cameron, go to the Camp of the 14th Regt N.Y.S. VI at Arlington House and ask to see the <u>blankets</u> sold to them by the war department, to replace those they were ordered to throw away at the battle of Bull Run—The regulation army blanket is made of all wool and weighs 10 or 11 pounds per pair and is charged to soldiers at $2.42 each blanket or $4.84 per pair—These that have been sold to the soldiers since the retreat at Bull Run weigh less than 5 pounds per pair, are more than half cotton the balance being a miserable mixture of Hair & Wool of very common quality and are worth by the bale in New York about $1.25 per pair and yet the quartermaster was ordered to charge them to our poor soldiers at the full price of the regulation army blanket—viz—$2.42 each blanket or $4.84 per pair just about four times their value—When the quartermaster appealed to Major [Daniel H.] Rucker about it he said he had nothing to do with it, that Mr. Cameron had bought the blankets in New York through [Alexander] Cummings and that they had nothing to do but obey orders and charge full price—Now Mr. Lincoln this is, every way in which it can be looked at as a damnable robbery—I saw the blankets and pronounce it so—Your soldiers hate this man Cameron and will soon learn to despise the government which keeps him in it—if you mean to be faithful to your country investigate this matter for yourself, and if you find it as I say, then for your own sake for your country's sake for God's sake put him out of office—You must be a Marquis Posa now and sacrifice your friends—even if he be your dearest—for the welfare and friendship of millions—A holy regard for the right must force you to do it and May God help you—

In this time of our Country's due extremity a sot and a thief (plain & ugly but true names) ought not—must not, hold the chief offices You can call [Edward] Everett to the one and [Nathaniel] Banks or [Joseph] Holt to the other and fill them honorably honestly and capably I think —

I have almost venerated W. H. Seward and grieved when he lost the nomination at Chicago [to Lincoln] but I thank God sincerely that his will was not as mine then—God has put you where you are Abraham Lincoln—don't forget that—and he asks of you a faithful Stewardship.

That His Love and His Wisdom may inform every act of your life and office is my daily prayer and let me add it is my faith

faithfully yours
John P Cranford

When in the camp of the 14th looking for lost friends I saw the blankets—bought & brought home one and will send you if you wish the testimony of the most reliable blanket Merchants of this city as to their value.

Rumors of Secretary of War Cameron's corrupt purchasing practices abounded during the early months of the Civil War. Although he eventually dismissed Cameron (sending him off to Russia as U.S. Minister), Lincoln never joined the chorus calling for the secretary's censure. In 1862 the President even sent a special message to Congress criticizing its resolution condemning Cameron and Cummings. Lincoln argued that blame for irregularities could not in fairness "rest exclusively or chiefly upon Mr. Cameron . . . [that] not only the President but all the other heads of departments were at least equally responsible . . . for whatever error, wrong, or fault was committed" (CW, V: 242–243).

Protesting Treatment of her Husband

[September 12, 1861]

Mrs. Fremont begs to know from the President if his answer to Genl. Fremont's letter can be given to him without much further delay.

Mrs. Fremont is anxious to return to her family and takes the liberty of asking a reply by the messenger.

Willards Hotel
Sep. 12th

[September 12, 1861]

To the President of the United States.

I was told yesterday by Mr. F. P. Blair Sen. that five days since a letter was received from his son Colonel F. P. Blair, containing certain statements respecting Genl. Fremont and his military command in the Western Department which letter was submitted to you as President.

I was further told by Mr. Blair that, on that letter you sent Postmaster Genl. Blair to St. Louis to examine into that Department and report.

On behalf of, and as representing Genl. Fremont, I have to request that I be furnished with copies of that letter, and any other communications, if any, which in your judgement have made that investigation necessary.

I have the honor to be, Very Respectfully,

Jessie Benton Fremont

Willards Hotel, Washington City, September 12th.

∽ Frémont's proclamation of August 30 had freed slaves owned by pro-Confederacy citizens of Missouri. Lincoln, worried that it could trigger mass defections among Union supporters in border states, revoked it as "objectionable." Meanwhile, Frémont was feuding with the formidable Blair family, which was urging the general's dismissal, and the equally formidable Mrs. Frémont, daughter of Thomas Hart Benton, arrived in Washington to do battle for her husband. Lincoln answered her peremptory notes as follows (CW, IV: 519).

Washington, D.C. Sep. 12. 1861

Mrs Genl. Fremont

My dear Madam—Your two notes of to-day are before me. I answered the letter you bore me from Gen. Fremont, on yesterday; and not hearing from you during the day, I sent the answer to him by mail.

It is not exactly correct, as you say you were told by the elder Mr. Blair, to say that I sent Post-Master-General [Montgomery] Blair to St. Louis to examine into that Department, and report. Post-Master-General Blair did go, with my approbation, to see and converse with General Fremont as a friend.

I do not feel authorized to furnish you with copies of letters in my possession without the consent of the writers.

No impression has been made on my mind against the honor or integrity of Gen. Fremont; and I now enter my protest against being understood as acting in any hostility towards him.

Your Obt. Servt
A. Lincoln

"You Have Committed the One Great Error"

Mason, Mason Co Ill
Sept 17th 1861

Abraham Lincoln

Sir Will you give me just five minutes of your time. I dont wish you to turn this letter over to your Secretary, but I do wish you to read it yourself—and then think; think what you are doing! I have no heart to used feighned words; or honeyed expressions in addressing you. Something has been due you in relation to the position which you hold in our Government. But are you entitled to this aspect longer? Do you remember the words you used repeatedly to those who flocked to see, and encourage you, on your way to Washington? Let me quote "if the country is saved, it is the people who must save it—" "to you I must look for support."

Now tell me Lincoln; havent we (I must say here I supported you!) havent we sent our fathers; our Brothers; our <u>dear Husbands</u> to support you? Haven't they endured privation, and toil, suffering hardship—sickness—everything that mortals could endure, to support you, and sustain and perpetuate this our Beloved Union? and when you sent us a man who they could all rally around, and whom they could place confidence in; sufficient even to surmount every obstacle but those which you have yet placed in their way; I say after doing all this to support; now after these last instructions to Fremont, with what kind of courage do you suppose they will obey your future orders to their Generals.

Oh! to think that you whom they had elected; one from whom they had expected great and good things; could so fall from your high position; which these same brave Volunteers had placed you—all because of some of your advisers proclivities.

Beware—Lincoln—you are holding back the wrong man. Let the laws, when, we do happen to have good ones be executed, and that in the right place.

Lincoln you have committed the one great error of your life; and I now pray God as earnestly as I have hitherto prayed him to preserve, protect, and bless and give you wisdom, so now; I pray you may be soon brought to see the great error you have committed, and brought low in the vally [sic] of humiliation for it. We did look forward to a speedy termination of this war; but now what can we expect. How [can] we say to our loved ones—go—go—cheerfully—bravely—and God will protect you— Lincoln must we send our loved ones, to be shot down, butchered? and not use every means in our power to prevent it.

Had you a Brother in Mo. as I have who has had every thing taken from him, and he and his family obliged to sleep in the woods, nights, secreting themselves in the day time; I think then you would feel—that Fremont was all right. I do earnestly pray God to forgive you; and I do also pray that the thousand hearts here at the west may forgive you too.

You may think I have done wrong in so writing. I make no appology [sic]. I must speak—my heart bleeds at every pore for my Country.

> Very Respectfully
> Mrs. L. C. Howard

Mr. A. Lincoln.

✍ Few issues—or personalities—in the entire war inspired as many letters to Lincoln as General Frémont and his order of emancipation.

"You Stand on the Hearts of Widows"

[Dec. 30, 1861?]

Abraham Lincoln.

Put off your shoes now from your feet, for the ground whereon you stand is holy. You stand on the hearts of widows and orphans and childless mothers to be, and the voice of their wailing goes up to God this day.

It is written of Abraham [?] that though he loved not God, he found favor with the Angel because he loved his fellow-men. Where think you is there favor for him who places the interests of any party high above the life & liberty of his fellow men?

If you have the heart of a man, forget your party in this hour of your country's appalling peril, & pray to your Creator

> "The mercy I to others show—
> That mercy show to me."

In those other days that tried men's souls, when your ancestors & mine seceded from British rule, who think you would have fired the first shot if the red coats had held fortresses at New York? Think I pray you on which side all humanity ranges itself—on the side of a people struggling for liberty or on the side of a person forcing on the handcuffs? Granted that the South has committed an unpardonable sin in leaving the Union. We have some of us to answer for it. But there is a sin that we must answer for each man for himself at the awful hour of Final Judgement.

Tell me I pray you where are the slaves? How is it that their best friends seem to ignore their existence. One would think their interests were worth no more than the interests of thirty-millions of white people.

Hurrah! for Republican liberty of speech. We have heard of it always, it is upon us now. A man at the North has denounced this war as uncalled for & shameful, & patriots think hanging too good for him. His property is in danger they say. When preachers, lecturers, politicians of all rank & grades cursed slavery & slave-holders, meddling with matters over which they could never have one particle of control, & alienating forever their own brethren whom they might have won by kindness &

the commonest Christian charity, scattering seeds of disunion over the fairest land the sun ever shone on, the people shouted amen! & if one opposed by word of mouth or voice of the press a spirit so diabolical all were gagged at the North & might as well be slaves at once. Think of it! denied liberty of speech in a free country!!

Now say if you dare that there is any virtue or any patriotism at the South!

Hurrah for the liberty of the Press!

Hurrah for the Reign of Terror!

Hang men by scores! We are the people! & we will whip the South & keep it under. Bring me the fetters, forge the thumb-screws!

The South asked the right of buying forts on their own ground & were refused.

Did you ever hear of such a thing as a people fighting to have their own will? The British tried it to their total satisfaction.

Behold oh World! a great & wise nation ignoring a fact & fighting for a Theory!

We are no longer a Union. Fight & conquer ten men & put strong chains about them & then hurrah for Union & toast of Liberty.

There is a way that secureth right to a man but the end thereof is the way of Death! Will you submit to the shame & sin of fighting against God!

Ride as you may on the topmost crest of the wave of popular applause, rejoice in the insane shouts of men who curse their fellow men, but beware lest the Lord God smite you as he smote Herod on the throne with some foul & fell disease, & you perish in a day.

The wail of lost souls slain in faith makes mournful music to live and die by.

One who loves our country North & South

"You are Strangely and Disastrously Remiss"

[Aug 19, 1862]

The Prayer of Twenty Millions

To Abraham Lincoln, President of the United States:

Dear Sir:—I do not intrude to tell you—for you must know already—that a great portion of those who triumphed in your election, and of all who desire the unqualified suppression of the Rebellion now desolating our country, are sorely disappointed and deeply pained by the policy you seem to be pursuing with regard to the slaves of Rebels. I write only to set succinctly and unmistakably before you what we require, what we think we have a right to expect, and of what we complain.

I. We require of you, as the first servant of the Republic, charged especially and pre-eminently with this duty, that you EXECUTE THE LAWS. Most emphatically do we demand that such laws as have been recently enacted, which therefore may fairly be presumed to embody the *present* will, and to be dictated by the *present* needs of the *Republic*, and which, after due consideration, have received your personal sanction, shall by you be carried into full effect, and that you publicly and decisively, instruct your subordinates that such laws exist, that they are binding on all functionaries and citizens, and that they are to be obeyed to the letter.

II. We think you are strangely and disastrously remiss in the discharge of your official and imperative duty with regard to the emancipating provisions of the new Confiscation Act. Those provisions were designed to fight Slavery with Liberty. They prescribe that men loyal to the Union, and willing to shed their blood in her behalf, shall no longer be held, with the nation's consent, in bondage to persistent, malignant traitors, who for twenty years have been plotting, and for sixteen months have been fighting to divide and destroy our country. Why these traitors should be treated with tenderness by you, to the prejudice of the dearest rights of loyal men, we cannot conceive.

III. We think you are unduly influenced by the counsels, the representations, the menaces, of certain fossil politicians hailing from the Border Slave States. Knowing well that the heartily, unconditionally loyal portion of the white citizens of those States, do not expect nor desire that slavery shall be upheld to the predjudice [sic] of the Union, (for the truth of which we appeal not only to every Republican residing in those States, but to such eminent loyalists as H. Winter Davis, Parson Brownlow, the Union Central Committee of Baltimore, and to the Nashville *Union*,) we ask you to consider that slavery is everywhere the inciting cause, and sustaining base of treason: the most slaveholding sections of Maryland and Delaware being this day, though under the Union flag, in full sympathy with the Rebellion, while the free labor portions of Tennessee, and of Texas, though writhing under the bloody heel of treason, are unconquerably loyal to the Union. So emphatically is this the case, that a most intelligent Union banker of Baltimore recently avowed his confident belief that a majority of the present Legislature of Maryland, though elected as and still professing to be Unionists, are at heart desirous of the triumph of the Jeff. Davis conspiracy; and when asked how they could be won back to loyalty, replied—"Only by the complete Abolition of Slavery." It seems to us the most obvious truth, that whatever strengthens or fortifies slavery in the Border States strengthens also treason, and drives home the wedge intended to divide the Union. Had you from the first refused to recognize in those States, as here, any other than unconditional loyalty—that which stands for the Union, whatever may become of slavery—those States would have been, and would be, far more helpful and less troublesome to the defenders of the Union, than they have been, or now are.

IV. We think timid counsels in such a crisis calculated to prove perilous, and probably disastrious [sic]. It is the duty of a government as wantonly, wickedly assailed by Rebellion as ours has been, to oppose force to force in a defiant, dauntless spirit. It cannot afford to temporize with traitors nor with semi-traitors. It must not bribe them to behave themselves, nor make them fair promises in the hope of disarming their causeless hostility. Representing a brave and high-spirited people, it can afford to forfeit anything else better than its own self-respect, or their admiring confidence. For our Government even to seek, after war has been made on it, to dispel the affected apprehensions of armed traitors that their cherished privileges may be assailed by it, is to invite, insult and encourage hopes of its own downfall. The rush to arms of Ohio, Indiana, Illinois, is the true answer at once to the rebel raids of John Morgan [a Confederate cavalry raider], and the traitorous sophistries of Berrah Magoffin [the "neutral" Governor of Kentucky accused by unionists of being secretly pro-secession].

V. We complain that the Union cause has suffered, and is now suffering immensely, from mistaken deference to Rebel Slavery. Had you, Sir, in your Inaugural Address, unmistakably given notice that, in case the Rebellion already commenced were persisted in, and your efforts to preserve the Union and enforce the laws, should be resisted by armed force *you would recognize no loyal person as rightfully held in slavery by a traitor,* we believe the Rebellion would therein have received a staggering if not fatal blow. At that moment, according to the returns of the most recent elections, the Unionists were a large majority of the voters of the slave States. But they were composed in good part of the aged, the feeble, the wealthy, the timid—the young, the reckless, the aspiring, the adventurous, had already been largely lured by the gamblers and negro-traders, the politicians by trade and the conspirators by instinct, into the toils of treason. Had you then proclaimed that rebellion would strike the shackles from the slaves of every traitor, the wealthy and the cautious would have been supplied with a powerful inducement to remain loyal. As it was, every coward in the South soon became a traitor from fear; for loyalty was perilous, while treason seemed comparatively safe. Hence, the boasted unanimity of the South—a unanimity based on Rebel terrorism, and the fact that immunity and safety were found on that side, danger and probable death on ours. The Rebels from the first have been eager to confiscate, imprison, scourge and kill; we have fought wolves with the devices of sheep. The result is just what might have been expected. Tens of thousands are fighting in the Rebel ranks to-day whose original bias and natural leanings would have led them into ours.

VI. We complain that the Confiscation Act which you approved is habitually disregarded by your Generals, and that no word of rebuke for them from you has yet reached the public ear. Fremont's Proclamation and Hunter's Order favoring Emancipation were promptly annulled to you; while Halleck's No. 3, forbidding fugitives from slavery to Rebels to come within his lines—an order as unmilitary as inhuman, and which received the hearty approbation of every traitor in America—with scores of like tendency have never provoked even your remonstrance. We complain that the officers of your armies have habitually repelled, rather than invited the approach of slaves who would have gladly taken the risks of escaping from the Rebel masters to our camps, bringing intelligence often of inestimable value to the Union cause. We complain that those who have thus escaped to us, avowing a willingness to do for us whatever might be required, have been brutally and madly repulsed, and often surrendered to be scourged, maimed and tortured by the ruffian traitors, who pretend to own them. We complain that a large proportion of our regular Army Officers, with many of the Volunteers, evince far more solicitude to uphold slavery than to put down the Rebellion. And finally, we complain that you, Mr. President, elected as a Republican, knowing well what an abomination Slavery is, and how emphatically it is the core and essence of this atrocious Rebellion, seem never to interfere with those atrocities, and never give a direction to your military subordinates, which does not appear to have been conceived in the interest of slavery rather than of freedom.

VII. Let me call your attention to the recent tragedy in New Orleans, whereof the facts are obtained entirely through pro-slavery channels. A considerable body of resolute, able-bodied men, held [in] slavery by two Rebel sugar-planters in defiance of the Confiscation Act, which you have approved, left plantations thirty miles distant, and made their way to the great mart of the south-west, which they knew to be in the undisputed possession of the Union forces. They made their way safely and quietly through thirty miles of Rebel territory, expecting to find freedom under the protection of our flag. Whether they had or had not heard of the passage of the Confiscation Act, they reasoned logically that we could not kill them for deserting the service of their lifelong oppressors, who had through treason become our implacable enemies. They came to us for liberty and protection, for which they were willing to render their best service; they met with hostility, captivity, and murder. The barking of the base curs of slavery in this quarter deceives no one—not even themselves. They say, indeed, that the negroes had no right to appear in New Orleans armed (with their implements of daily labor in the canefield); but no one doubts that they would gladly have laid these down if assured that they should be free. They were set upon and maimed, captured and killed, because they sought the benefit of that Act of Congress which they may not specifically have heard of, but which was none the less the law of land—which they had a clear *right* to the benefit of—which it was *somebody's* duty to publish far and wide, in order that so many as possible should be impelled to desist from serving Rebels and the Rebellion, and come over to the side of the Union. They sought their liberty in strict accordance with the law of the land—they were butchered or reenslaved, for so doing, by the help of the Union soldiers enlisted to fight against slaveholding treason. It was *somebody's* fault that they were murdered—if others shall hereafter suffer in like manner, in default of explicit and public direction to your Generals that they are to be recognized and obey the Confiscation Act, the world will lay the blame on you. Whether you will choose to bear it through future history and at the bar of God, I will not judge. I can only hope.

VIII. On the face of this wide earth, Mr. President, there is not one disinterested, determined, intelligent champion of the Union cause who does not feel that all attempts to put down the Rebellion and at the same time uphold its inciting cause are preposterous and futile—that the Rebellion, if crushed out to-morrow, would be renewed within a year if slavery were left in full vigor—that Army Officers who remain to this day devoted to slavery can at best be but half-way loyal to the Union—and that every hour of deference to slavery is an hour of added and deepened peril to the Union. I appeal to the testimony of your ambassadors in Europe. It is freely at your service, not at mine. Ask them to tell you candidly whether the seeming subserviency of your policy to the slaveholding, slavery-upholding interest, is not the perplexity, the despair of statesmen of all parties, and be admonished by the general answer.

IX. I close as I began with the statement that what an immense majority of the loyal millions of your countrymen require of you is a frank, declared, unqualified, ungrudging execution of the laws of the land, more especially of the Confiscation Act. That Act gives freedom to the slaves of Rebels coming within our lines, or whom those lines may at any time inclose—we ask you to render it due obedience by publicly requiring all your subordinates to recognize and obey it. The Rebels are everywhere using the late anti-negro riots in the North, as they have long used your officers' treatment of negroes in the South, to convince the slaves that they have nothing to hope from a Union success—that we mean in that case to sell them into a bitterer bondage to defray the cost of the war. Let them impress this as a truth on the great mass of their ignorant and credulous bondmen, and the Union will never be restored—never. We cannot conquer ten millions of people united in solid phalanx against us, powerfully aided by Northern sympathizers and European allies. We must have scouts, guides, spies, cooks, teamsters, diggers, and choppers, from the blacks of the South, whether we allow them to fight for us or not, or we shall be baffled and repelled. As one of the millions who would gladly have avoided this struggle at any sacrifice but that of principal and honor, but who now feel that the triumph of the Union is indispensable not only to the existence of our country, but to the well-being of mankind, I entreat you to render a hearty and unequivocal obedience to the law of the land.

Yours,
Horace Greeley.

New York, August 19, 1862

Even though Greeley never sent the President a personal copy of this complaint, which was published as an editorial in Greeley's New York Tribune, *Greeley's letter is included here because it is the best-known letter of criticism Lincoln ever received. In response to the editorial complaint, Lincoln wrote a famous letter that seemed to minimize his interest in emancipation. Unknown to Greeley, Lincoln composed this after he had already drafted a preliminary Emancipation Proclamation, which he had determined to issue after the next Union military victory. Therefore, this letter was, in truth, an attempt to position the impending announcement in terms of saving the Union, not freeing slaves as a humanitarian gesture. It was one of Lincoln's most skillful public relations efforts, even if it has cast longstanding doubt on his sincerity as a liberator* (CW, V: 388–389).

Executive Mansion,
Washington, August 22, 1862

Hon. Horace Greeley:
Dear Sir

I have just read yours of the 19th. addressed to myself through the New-York Tribune. If there be in it any statements, or assumptions of fact, which I may know to be erroneous, I do not, now and here, controvert them. If there be in it any inferences which I may believe to be falsely drawn, I do not now and here, argue against them. If there be perceptable in it an impatient and dictatorial tone, I waive it in deference to an old friend, whose heart I have always supposed to be right.

As to the policy I "seem to be pursuing" as you say, I have not meant to leave any one in doubt.

I would save the Union. I would save it the shortest way under the Constitution. The sooner the national authority can be restored; the nearer the Union will be "the Union as it was." If there be those who would not save the Union, unless they could at the same time save slavery, I do not agree with them. If there be those who would not save the Union unless they could at the same time destroy slavery, I do not agree with them. My paramount object in this struggle is to save the Union, and is not either to save or destroy slavery. If I could save the Union without freeing any slave, I would do it, and if I could save it by freeing all the slaves, I would do it; and if I could save it by freeing some and leaving others alone I would also do that. What I do about slavery, and the colored race, I do because I believe it helps to save the Union; and what I forbear, I forbear because I do not believe it would help to save the Union. I shall do <u>less</u> whenever I shall believe what I am doing hurts the cause, and I shall do <u>more</u> whenever I shall believe doing more will help the cause. I shall try to correct errors when shown to be errors; and I shall adopt new views so far as they shall appear to be true views.

I have here stated my purpose according to my view of <u>official</u> duty; and I intend no modification of my oft-expressed <u>personal</u> wish that all men, every where could be free.

Yours,
A. Lincoln

Protesting a Military Arrest

Philadelphia
Oct 29th 1862

Respected and Dear Sir

The extraordinary arrest of Rev Mr Hay of Harrisburg for statements made by him in a published letter, inquiring why our <u>wounded & sick soldiers</u> at Baltimore, had less priveleges than <u>Traitor prisoners</u>; and of the Union investigating committee of Baltimore while ferreting out official military corruption in said city, have created profound surprise and the greatest indignation among loyal citizens.

For the sake of the Union and Constitution it behooves you to stop such illegal & high-handed outrages on loyal Union-loving administration-supporting citizens.

Were but <u>proved disunionists</u> incarcerated or even <u>tried & hung</u> none would complain.

But that life-long supporters of Union should thus be persecuted is shameful & unless stopped by the Government & the over zealous officials rebuked redounds to the defeat of the National Union men & strengthens the anti-war Democracy [Democratic Party]. Unless these injuries are publicly redressed, beware!, political defeat, and withdrawal of hearty support will undoubtedly ensue, [Horatio] Seymour & Co [then Democratic candidate for Governor of New York] will be elected and Republicanism thrown to the dogs. I have been a Sergt in Rushs Lancers Co K for 9 mos. untill I was sunstruck & discharged was a member of the Republican Invincibles of this city & strove earnestly for your election, and my only object in thus addressing you is to preserve Republican principles & Unionism from defeat. Unless prompt measures are taken to correct these abuses, the mouths of Administratuon men are stopped from its defence.

Yours for the Union without Slavery
G. D. Stroud 109 N. 6th Philadelphia Pa

No reply to this complaint is known. The Lincoln Papers are filled with letters complaining bitterly about the administration's policies of military arrests and the suspension of habeas corpus. Another writer, Judge George Gould, whose cousin had been arrested and thrown into prison, spoke for many unhappy Northerners when he argued in one such letter that "this kind of proceeding has gone too far." To Gould, and, undoubtedly, countless others, even "the rules of war" could not supersede "the common law of liberty, and the broad, great charter of the Constitution" (Gould to Lincoln, November 14, 1862, Lincoln Papers).

A Property Owner Complains—
and Lincoln Offers to Buy a Slave

[T E L E G R A P H]

Lexington Kentucky
Nov 19 1862

President Lincoln
   The conduct of a few of the Officers of the Army in forcibly detaining the Slaves of Union Kentuckians may provoke a conflict between Citizens & Soldiers; to prevent such a catastrophy [sic] we desire you to say as we believe you will that military force will not be permitted for the detention any more than for the restoration of such property & especially in resistance & contempt of the legal process of a Civil tribunal.

Yours Respectfully,
G. Robertson

The day after this wire was sent, Lincoln drafted the following reply—although he did not send it (CW, V: 502).

Executive Mansion,
Washington, Nov. 20. 1862.

Hon. George Robertson
My dear Sir.

Your despatch of yesterday is just received. I believe you are acquainted with the American Classics, (if there be such) and probably remember a speech of Patrick Henry, in which he represented a certain character in the, revolutionary times, as totally disregarding all questions of country, and "hoarsely bawling, beef! beef!! beef!!! [a scene from an 1841 book, *Life of Patrick Henry,* in which a Tory sues an army commissary for stealing steers, silencing "acclamations of victory" by "bawling . . . beef! beef! beef!"]

Do you not know that I may as well surrender this contest, directly, as to make any order, the obvious purpose of which would be to return fugitive slaves?

Yours very truly
A. Lincoln

✍ *After composing this unusual letter, Lincoln learned that Robertson, a judge from Lexington, Kentucky, was himself attempting to recover from a Union regiment there "a Negro boy" who "refused to go with him and <u>claimed</u> protection from the power of one whose cruel treatment . . . had already made <u>him</u> a <u>dwarf</u> instead of a man." The regiment's colonel appealed to Lincoln for "<u>protection</u>" from a charge of "<u>man-stealing</u>." Lincoln finally sent the following letter to Judge Robertson a few days later (CW, V: 512–514; Col. William L. Utley to Lincoln, November 17, 1862, Lincoln Papers).*

Executive Mansion,
Washington, Nov. 26, 1862.

Hon. George Robertson,

My dear Sir: A few days since I had a despatch from you which I did not answer. If I were to be wounded personally, I think I would not shun it. But it is the life of the nation. I now understand the trouble is with Col. Utley; that he has five slaves in his camp, four of whom belong to rebels, and one belonging to you. If this be true, convey yours to Col. Utley, so that he can make him free, and I will pay you any sum not exceeding five hundred dollars.

Yours, &c.
A. Lincoln

ᔕᕈ *Robertson refused Lincoln's offer. Instead he sued and nine years later won a judgment of $908 against the colonel. Not until 1873 did Utley get his money refunded—and it took an act of Congress to do so.*

Declining an Appointment

Canton Illinois
April 8. 1863

His Excellency Abraham Lincoln
Prest U.S.

Sir I am in receipt of a note from your private secretary informing me that as a "mark" of your "confidence and esteem" you had appointed me Consul at Valparaiso, Chile.

Certainly the Honor attached to the office ought to satisfy the Ambition of the most aspiring, and the salary (which would but little if any more than defray the expenses of myself and family to & from the place of duty,) is as much as a reasonable man should desire. Yet I feel myself compelled to decline the appointment.

At one time, I was indiscreet enough to indicate to your Excellency a desire to an appointment to an office, for which, I was vain enough to believe I was qualified but from the position now offered, I am forced to conclude, that your Excellency held a decidedly different opinion from my own on that subject, or that my political status was such that the administration would suffer by my appointment to an office of the grade if those held by [Ebenezer] Peck, [David] Wilmot [judges on the U.S. Court of Claims], [Abraham B.] Olin, [George B.] Fisher [named to the U.S. Court for the District of Columbia], [Leonard] Swett [an old friend of Lincoln's, he was appointed commissioner of Peruvian claims], [John A.] Gurley [named Governor of Arizona] and [David K.] Cart[t]er [also named to the U.S. Court for the District of Columbia] and many other recent appointees—

If I have lost the confidence and regard for whom I have had a most ardent esteem and whom I have most faithfully served, I must not loose [*sic*] my own self respect. I am therefore compelled to decline the position tendered.

Sir my first and strongest desire is that your administration may be successful in maintaining the supremacy of the Government and in restoring peace and prosperity to our distracted country and for your own happiness & success permit me to hasten you my best and sincere wishes.

I am sir your obt svt

Wm. Kellogg

∽ *Lincoln never opened this complaint from a disappointed office seeker. Instead, he wrote on the envelope in which it arrived: "I understand my friend Kellogg is ill-natured—therefore I do not read his letter. A. L."*

Criticizing a Newspaper Shutdown

[T E L E G R A P H]

Chicago, June 3d 1863

Hon Abraham Lincoln.
President.

At a meeting held to day in reference to the suppression of the Chicago Times by order of General [Ambrose E.] Burnside, the following was adopted.

Whereas in the opinion of this meeting of citizens of all parties, the peace of this City and State, if not the general welfare of the Country are likely to be promoted by the suspension or rescinding of the recent order of General Burnside for the suspension of the Chicago Times, therefore:

Resolved that upon the grounds of expediency done, such of our citizens as concur in this opinion without regard to party are hereby recommended to write in a petition to the President, respectfully asking the suspension or rescinding said order. The undersigned in

pursuance of the above resolution respectfully petition the President's favorable consideration and action in accordance therewith.
Chicago June 3d 1863.

(signed) F.C. Sherman, Mayor of the City of Chicago

Wm B. Ogden	Theo Hoyne	C. Beckwith
E. Van Buren	Wirt Dexter	Henry G. Miller
Samuel W. Fuller	Van H. Higgins	Wm F. Feeley
S. S. Hayes	A. C. Coventry	
A. W. Arvington	N. A. Hahn	

We respectfully ask for the above the serious and prompt consideration of the President

June 3d. 1863.　　　　　(signed)　Lyman Trumbull
　　　　　　　　　　　　　　　　　　Isaac N. Arnold

ᔣ *Lincoln wrote to the secretary of war the next day, and on the same day, Burnside revoked his order suspending the publication of the* Times *as well as of the New York* World, *both of which had criticized the President for the arrest of antiwar Ohio Congressman Clement L. Vallandigham (CW, VI: 248).*

Executive Mansion,
Washington, D.C., June 4, 1863.
Hon. Secretary of War:
My Dear Sir: I have received additional dispatches which, with former ones, induce me to believe we should revoke or suspend the order suspending the Chicago Times, and if you concur in opinion, please have it done.

Yours truly,
A. Lincoln

Against Usurpations of Constitution

Palace Hotel
Buckingham Gate
London August 29th 1863

To the President of the United States
& Cabinet—Washington
I claim your attention to within. You are responsible for the liberties of the people & the Constitutional rights of the States. Your

usurpations of the Constitution has secured the bitter unrelenting hostility of the south & a division of the North. Continue a slave proclamation war policy & a gradual undermining of the foundation stone of the liberties of the people & refuse a just tribunal hearing to the South & North, you will force the Northern States to rise up in judgement against you, for the purpose of overrulling [*sic*] your power under State Constitutional right.

I now inaugurate this policy, as set forth in my address to England containing an appeal to France—as an independent advocate of the interests of the American people & as due to my Constitutional claim as a Citizen of the United States.

This course must be pursued to prevent the result of your at-present despotic policy, terminating in a declaration, under a military war plea, to maintain your government against the will of the people, until the war is settled. I am justified in this conclusion, inasmuch as you have not hesitated, to violate the constitution in conducting the War. Why should you not then do so—to prevent the people changing rulers? I urged the President at the time of his inauguration to a policy, through a representation of the South as Secretary of State, that would have prevented the War. I continued to urge a policy, after the War, based upon the Constitution & the Union, as the only reliable chart of safety—with the word slavery, buried. The result of a contrary course, is before the world, for which the American people hold you to an account—in destroying them in the height of their national prosperity, & the world—for the injury thereby to humanity & the cause of human liberty.

But one course now remains, for you to retrace your steps, or see your now weak power, transferred to the States, which if so, God grant it may be through a "military necessity"—State policy, under the gallant, brave & true-hearted Vallandigham, as Governor of Ohio, to reestablish American Liberty—to the South, North & people & to secure an honorable peace.

Wm. C. Jewett

There is no record of a reply to William Cornell "Colorado" Jewett's letter.

This letter appears on page 191.

Georgetown D.C Feb. 9. — 1865

To his Excellency, President Lincoln.

Sir; Please allow me, to demonstrate the practicability. by a Mathematical problem easy to be understood; of the absolute existence of a self=moving machine yet to be developed for the glory of God and the happiness of the human family.

Mr President; I will not detain you forty minutes. I have been forty years, struggling to find the mechanical actions to the problem, and have at last found them. and there is no dis=pute; I bid defiance

The problem has been examined by your private Secretary; Capt. J. M. Gilliss; Capt C.H. Tompkins; Prof. Henry Mitchell; and they all concur in the one opinion, that the problem is correct; and that if the mechanical action can be effected, it is a discovery of great magnitude to the world.

Now, Mr President; this war was foretold to me in a vision, Oct 20th 1846, at the same time, this.

[5]
Inventions and Innovations

WHEN THE FIRST ironclad warship of the Civil War, the hulking Confederate vessel *Merrimack*, steamed into Hampton Roads, Virginia, like a vision from hell in May 1862 and promptly decimated an entire federal blockading squadron without suffering a scrap of damage herself, more than one northern official expressed the belief that the conquest of the Union was inevitable.

But the very next day, the Union dispatched its own newly produced ironclad, the *Monitor*, setting the stage for an epic, if not particularly picturesque, battle between the two modern warships. Their May 9 duel ended without a clear victor, and some time later, both ships were lost. But they were promptly replaced by ironclads aplenty.

Technology was changing the face of war. Hot-air balloons were offering new possibilities for reconnaissance. Improved rifle mechanisms made reloading easier and more accurate rapid fire possible. Artillery was soon reaching greater distances than ever.

Practically from the moment the first guns were fired, inventors, innovators, and technicians sent the Commander-in-Chief novel ideas for introducing the latest—and often the most dubious—technologies to battles on land and sea.

"It looks like war," one such correspondent wrote to Lincoln even before he took office. "I have invented a machine which will fire 400 bullets simultaneously; write me if you wish me to explain it to you." But Lincoln endorsed the plea: "Need not answer this." Neither did he respond to the soldier who confided, "<u>You</u> are the only man with whom I will trust the secret"—that of a newfangled projectile. Not that Lincoln was immune to or uninterested in such letters. Before many more months had passed, he had begun appearing so often in the waste fields between the White House and the unfinished Washington Monument to test-fire new guns that the area became known as Lincoln's Firing Range.

"Not a few of the letters he received," presidential secretary William O. Stoddard recalled, "asserted remarkable improvements in guns, cannons, and other war materials." But a huge proportion of the proposals simply seemed too good to be true—and it turned out that they were.

One young man from Brooklyn, for example, offered to perfect "an Air gun, made in a different way from any gun that I ever saw"—provided Lincoln guaranteed "not less than $800." Another inventor, from the antiwar Quaker sect, wrote Lincoln "to send thee a diagram of an improved shell." An elderly Boston man forwarded a plan to defend Boston Harbor with a crescent of warships, all programmed to fire at the same instant. And a semiliterate correspondent from Kentucky contended that he had "a moddle of" an invention for the President that was so important he could not trust it to the regular patent route, for fear that "in that way the rebels would get hold of it."

"Lunatics and visionaries are here so frequently," private secretary John Nicolay wrote home midway through the war, "that they cease to be strange phenomena to us, and I find the best way to dispose of them is to discuss and decide their mad projects as deliberately and seriously as any other matter of business." Historian Robert V. Bruce aptly called such entreaties "patent nonsense." Stoddard, for example, remembered the crank who sent a "pretty blue shell of polished steel," a prototype for body armor that was certain to make Union soldiers invincible in battle. It remained in Stoddard's office until Lincoln reportedly suggested that the inventor should volunteer to prove its effectiveness by testing it in battle himself.

But with a fearsome war raging, Lincoln was careful not to dismiss any but the most ludicrous proposals out-of-hand. Even the notion of body armor was seriously entertained—for a while. As president-elect, Lincoln had received an offer from a Philadelphia chemist to make an undershirt of chain mail for his own use—"plated with gold, so that perspiration shall not affect it." Apparently, some soldiers were ultimately sent into battle so attired. Lincoln's friend Lucius Chittenden recalled once seeing a dead body on a battlefield, his chest covered with "a shield of boiler-iron moulded to fit . . . and fastened at the back by straps and buckles." Certain he was fully protected, the soldier had exposed himself to enemy fire and taken a direct hit—leaving over his heart, Chittenden recalled, "a hole large enough to permit the escape of a score of human lives," armor notwithstanding.

The war did inspire its share of technological miracles, however, and Lincoln proved as enthusiastic about the genuine articles as he was wary of the frauds. With the head of the Smithsonian Institution openly advocating scientific breakthroughs for "destroying life, as well as . . . preserving it," Lincoln applied his long-standing curiosity about mathematics and science to military technology and quickly became the national sounding board for such innovations. A onetime would-be inventor himself—he had patented an unworkable device to lift vessels over shallow shoals—Lincoln approved in 1863 the creation of a "Permanent Scientific Commission" to handle the outpouring of ideas from inventors (and to protect him from making all judgments on his own).

Meanwhile he continued to test or observe new equipment personally. Visiting George B. McClellan's army headquarters, he looked on in amusement as a sharpshooter aimed at an effigy of Jefferson Davis from 600 yards away—and struck it in the eye. Lincoln himself tested a new crank gun in the loft of a carriage shop near Willard's Hotel. And experimenting once with a new kind of shot that could not quite reach its target, he laughed merrily as spent balls began striking the shoes of bystanders.

Such mishaps failed to sour Lincoln on the notion that the war required him to balance old wisdom with new ideas. Never was that juxtaposition more apparent than during his wartime visit to West Point to confer with retired General Winfield Scott, hero of the Mexican War. After their meeting, Lincoln journeyed to nearby Cold Spring, New York, and there visited Robert B. Parrott's futuristic gun foundry, then "in full blast," in the words of one eyewitness.

Still, Robert V. Bruce has concluded that notwithstanding the Civil War's reputation as the first modern war, "neither Southern desperation nor Yankee ingenuity gave birth to any fundamental *war-time* breakthroughs" in weapons technology. Breech-loading and repeating rifles, ironclads, machine guns, sea mines, and rifled cannon, Bruce pointed out, may have been used successfully during the Civil War, but all had been developed before it started. Aerial balloons, submarines, and war rockets, he added, had been introduced into combat "generations before."

Some two hundred letters to Lincoln from inventors survive in the National Archives—at least thirty of them bearing long, handwritten endorsements from Lincoln himself. A handful more reside in the Lincoln Papers—those notes and entreaties which Lincoln thought promising or bizarre enough to retain in his own files. The existence of so many letters suggests that Lincoln's secretaries exercised far more restraint in disposing of such letters, even the most farfetched ones, than they did with any other variety of correspondence. Yet Lincoln apparently remained, to the end of the war, more curious about innovation than he was effective in introducing it.

Not all the surviving letters are concerned with military technology. Lincoln also heard from the inventors of new devices to wipe the ink from pens, new ventilating overshoes to keep the feet dry and warm, and new pleasure saddles to make riding more enjoyable.

But such diversions proved the exception, not the rule. William O. Stoddard remembered that "every proposed vendor . . . was possessed by the idea that he might make a sale" of new firearms if only "he could induce the President to overrule the decisions of the Bureau of Ordnance." In such cases, Stoddard added, "I was likely to have a specimen gun deposited in the corner." Before long the correspondence room "looked like a gunshop," crowded with grenades, rifles, steel cuirasses, and swords. And if Lincoln failed immediately to appreciate the value of each invention and inventor, "oh, how that genius did abuse the President," not only for failing to endorse the innovation, but "for his general bad management of the war" as well. What is remarkable is that through it all, Lincoln never seemed to lose his curiosity about science and technology, for both war and peacetime uses alike.

The day before leaving for Gettysburg, for example, Lincoln presented his ailing attorney general, Edward Bates, with an "elastic pen-holder," which, a grateful Bates acknowledged, "pleased me well, as fitting my rough hand exactly." Lincoln had perhaps grown weary of struggling to decipher Bates's all-but-incoherent handwriting and was hoping the new device would help matters. Subsequent communications from the attorney general, however, all as indecipherable as before, show that like so many other inventions sent to Abraham Lincoln during the Civil War, this one failed to live up to its promise.

A Better Lightning Rod

Indianapolis, Inda.
Decr. 8, 1860

Hon. A. Lincoln; —

Respected Sir: I shall be under lasting obligations if you would favor me with an autograph recommendation of my Lightning rod. It may seem a piece of small impertinence to approach you thus, but I have already the approval of the most eminent scholars in the Country, and your <u>name</u> can do me incalculable good. It is my enterprise and all I look to for a living, & I am making the most of it. I claim more conducting surface, in better form and better connection at the joints of the sections than any other rod. Your Opinion will be thankfully and gratefully received, & cherished as a <u>priceless Souvenir</u>. Begging pardon for this intrusion, believe me, I am, ever,

Your most fervent friend,
Wm. Hall.

ꝏ President-elect Lincoln evidently did not provide this inventor with the "priceless souvenir" endorsement for which he yearned. Instead Lincoln endorsed the letter thus: "Needs no answer." A quarter century earlier Lincoln had scoffed that lightning rods were designed "to protect a guilty conscience from an offended God." But later he installed rods on his own house in Springfield (Shaw, The Lincoln Encyclopedia, *189).*

A Faster Steam Ship

Milwaukee, Feb. 18, 1861.

To his Excellency, Abraham Lincoln,
President of the United States:

Excellent Sir: This is but an office begging letter. Your Excellency may lay it aside until an office of Post Master here (now vacant) is, in its proper turn, under consideration, when please read this.

I am a Lawyer by profession, and now over 64 years old. More than twenty five years since my attention was directed to an improvement in the Steam Engine. I have spent some ten years of time in building models & making experiments, and about fourteen thousand dollars in money upon it. I have now two Patents for it, both of which I esteem valueless by reason of subsequent improvements made by me. I am positive (inventors are always <u>positive</u>) that with my improvement & the same amount of steam, any Steam-ship now running upon the Atlantic can be propelled from New York to Liverpool in a week. I desire to try it. To build a Steam Ship engine [requires] the expenditure of about half a million dollars—the trifle of about $475.000 more money than I can command. As I cannot now command the means to build an Ocean Steamer, I must content myself, on the start, to build as large as I can pay for; e.g. a Mississippi River Steam Boat costing about $30.000, and depend upon a sale of my improvement for that stream and tributaries to bring me the means to build the Ocean Steamer. But this $30.000 is dependent upon the sale of my real estate here, and near the city, esteemed worth double that sum, but which, in reality, at present, cannot now be sold for more than half that sum.

Getting old, and impatient to realize the means to put my invention into operation upon the Western waters upon a scale as large & profitable as the means at my command will admit, I desire the appointment of Post Master at Milwaukee <u>as a means to this end.</u> Let some one be found to loan me, upon good security and 7 per cent int. $12.000 for 4 years, (the probable nett profits of that office, for that period,) or, as still more desirable, some one to purchase my property at a discount of $12.000 below its estimated value, and I would much prefer the sale, or the loan, to the office, for the reason that it would enable me to do now, what is contingent upon my health & life at the expiration of that period.

Solicitous to convert my real estate into money, and believing that new buildings & extensive improvements would most speedily effect the object, I came on to my farm of 80 acres, half a mile from the city, four years ago the ensuing spring, where the revulsion in financial matters has left me minus $5.000 in cash extended in buildings & improvements, and unable to sell now for twice that sum less than I then refused as insufficient, and every day less induced to resume the practice of my profession which I then relinquished.

I voted against Jackson in 1828, & 1832, and against his foot-step treaders, high and low, ever since. Am an old fashioned Whig, opposed to the compromise of 1850 and every other compromise offered since to this hour, <u>and never a Democrat in my life.</u>

If for all the foregoing reasons, or any of them, your Excellency is inclined to assist me in this way to bring my invention into public use—the sole end and object of my soliciting the appointment—you have but to address a note to my friend, Hon. John F. Potter, our Representative, to find a corroboration of my "yarn." I have written him in substance as I have to your Excellency, and he can by direct application, if necessary, to our Senators, acquaint you in advance whether there be any objection to my confirmation to the office. I presume there is not. I have not addressed them directly nor indirectly upon the subject, nor will I. Doubtless they have favorites, and, possibly, schemes of ambition of their own, and I have no faith, judging them as politicians usually judge of and act to inventors, that the object or reason why I desire the office would either be appreciated by them or enlist their sympathy.

Your Excellency can fully appreciate the motives, or rather heart yearnings of the inventor who for more than a quarter of a century has given his time, his money and his health to the perfection of what he esteems, if he can but find the means and theatre for its display, an enduring monument of his fame and in the vast commerce of offices at your disposal, manifest your sympathy to the most worthy by a "discriminating tariff" to the encouragement & reward of those who seek office for the most laudable ends.

Humbly trusting that the end sought by me will be a sufficient pardon for the unusual mode of soliciting the nomination I ask, I subscribe myself in every contingency and event—

Your Excellency's great admirer, sincere friend

& most obt. Servt.
Peter Yates

There is no record that Lincoln replied to this lengthy plea for scientific subsidy. John Nicolay endorsed the letter with one word: "Office." Yates persisted until October 1864, when the Navy Department's so-called Permanent Commission, which was created to evaluate proposed inventions, rejected Yates's steam engine once and for all. The Commission's decision prompted Yates to compose a new eight-page letter to the President, which ended with this plaintive assurance: "Mr. President, I may write like a crazy man—In truth my parents, while living, my sisters & brothers & many of my friends and clients, have all accused me to my face of being a monomaniac upon this subject, & this for the last 15 years—but I am not crazy . . . and I assure you, that however crazy I will not bite." But where Yates's dubious invention was concerned, neither did Lincoln (Peter Yates to Lincoln, October 4, 1864, Lincoln Papers; LTW, 224).

"First Balloon Dispatch"

[*T E L E G R A P H*]
Balloon Enterprise June 16 1861
To President United States

This point of observation commands an area near fifty miles in diameter—the city with its girdle of encampments presents a superb scene—I have pleasure in sending you this first dispatch ever telegraphed from an aerial station and in acknowledging indebtedness to your encouragement for the opportunity of demonstrating the availability of the science of aeronautics in the military service of the country.

T. S. C. Lowe

Thaddeus Lowe's balloons provided the means for early surveillance of enemy encampments during General McClellan's ill-fated Peninsular campaign in Virginia. Lincoln endorsed this telegraph in his own hand: "First Balloon Dispatch."

On Spreading News by Balloon

Phila. July 6th. 1861.
President Lincoln

Dear Sir. Would it not be a grand idea to strike off hundreds of copies of your noble message and let Mr. Lowe ascend in his balloon and scatter them in Southern camps and all over the South—Depend upon it, if the poor deluded beings who cannot see a Northern paper were to read your address the South would be electrified, and the Union would triumph—They know not what they do, many of them are held in ignorance by the greatest villains the world ever knew, light would in many cases prove a blessing, but alas!! I know too many glory even in the wrong—Pardon the Liberty I take, but a woman's mind is full of inventions—

Yours respct—
Union.

The noble message this writer refers to is Lincoln's July 4, 1861, special message to Congress, which declared: "This is essentially a People's contest. On the side of the

Union, it is a struggle for maintaining in the world, that form, and substance of government, whose leading object is, to elevate the condition of men—to lift artificial weights from all shoulders—to clear the paths of laudable pursuit for all—to afford all, an unfettered start, and a fair chance, in the race of life." There is no evidence that the President consented to this anonymous writer's proposal that these words be spread throughout Southern territory by balloon (CW, IV: 438).

New Plating for Warships

Philad Pa. 919 Morgan St
July 17th 1861.

Hon. Abram Lincoln
President United States

Dear Sir   Enclosed you have a description of the process of making the iron and Steel armour plates for War Vessels adopted by the English Government. I clipd it from a publication just received from my Brother (native of that Country). I have several times seen it announced in our papers that it was the intention of the (US) Government to build some small Vessels for River purposes to be furnished after this process and also to give some of the larger ships now afloat a Coat of Armour. If such be the case, something worthy of the notice of our scientific men may be gleaned from this information. Being familiar with the Iron business in all its branches I comprehend the whole process. With a prayer to the giver of all good that He may guide and sustain you in this dark and trying hour of the Country's peril and endow you with wisdom from on high amidst the dark storm which like a thunder bolt has been hurled from the Southern hemisphere against the Constitution and the Country's peace and happiness, and as President of the United States enable you to conduct the affairs of the Nation to a triumphant and victorious peace and in the end bring you out more than Conqueror—With much respect I am Dr Sir

Yours truly
John Horton

Horton enclosed a clipping from the Sheffield Independent bearing the headline "Rolled Armour Plates for Vessels of War." The introduction of ironclad warships in the United States was still a year away.

A New Rifle Rest

Jonica La Salle Co Ill.
Oct. 3rd 1861

Abraham Lincoln, President of the U.S.

Dear Sir I shall in a day or two send by Express two Rifle Rests, suitable for the sharpshooters in our army. I was induced to invent them, in the following manner for a number of years at my leasure [sic] moments I have been trying to invent a Rifle rest that a man could put on under his coat, and not impede him in his movements a gentleman who was a friend of mine, but who I am sorry to say is now a rebel, knew of my invention and writes me that if I would go south and simplify my invention so as to adapt it to the army uses I could command my own price for them or sell it to the Government for any price that I might ask. Since I received his letter, I have been devoting my time to the invention and think I have reduced it down to a useful implement of war, by which our army of sharpshooters will be made more than twice as efficient because they will always fire from a rest.

I intend to take out a patent for it but in the mean time I forward it to you so that you may judge whether it is an object so to increase the efficiency of our forces, and thus help to shorten the war. My advice would be to manufacture the rests in a quiet way so that when our forces are ready to march they can have the rests a few days before hand to practice with, and prevent the enemy from gaining any knowledge of them.

Should you think it necessary I will come to Washington immediately on receiving your direction to do so there is no telegraph station here but you can telegraph to La Salle and direct the agent to send the message from there by mail or special agent, it is only nine miles distant.

Very Respectfully
Wm. Watson

P.S. I send this direct to you believing that it will receive proper attention sooner than if sent any other way. I enclose the directions I received on how to send the letter &c. South. W.W.

There is no record of a reply, but the interesting advertisement Watson enclosed with his letter offered a "Private Letter Mail" service "to and from the Federal [Union] States" for residents of the Confederacy, promising to deliver letters from Nashville, Tennessee, to Franklin, Kentucky, and there mail them safely to "the Old States." The service cost ten cents.

A Navigation Balloon

Georgetown January 27—1862

Most Excellent Sir

Please read the within synopsis of my useful life [a printed letter to members of Congress] and say in your heart, if I do, or do not deserve your hug patronag.

I have told you, that war is of God to liberate the Slaves, but that you must have my balloon to put down all foreign foes. I again warn you against secret Enemies. Watch well, and you will find the golden wedge, and the acorn too [a reference to Joshua in the bible].

I say you cannot conquer without my navigating Balloon. Have it examined speedily, and do your duty to God, for 1864 is drawing nigh. Very Respectfully

Your Loyal friend
Edward D Tippett

"In 1816," according to Tippett's "Synopsis of Reason," on the back of which this letter was written, "three inventions were mysteriously put into my heart." In addition to his navigation balloon, Tippett claimed to have devised a cold-water steam engine for riverboats. "These magnificent inventions," he claimed, were "calculated to reflect honor upon American ingannity [sic]," even if they were at the time being ridiculed by "outside, ignorant, enemies" who "blow hot and cold with the same breath." All Tippett asked was $10,000 to complete his experiments. Lincoln did not honor his request (LTW, 131–132).

Promising Better Military Engineering

[March 31, 1862]

Mr President

For the purpose of improving the time promised, to the best advantage, I will briefly state my object in writing. First. Some Six years ago I told Speaker of the House N. P. Banks, Gov. Seward Senator Hale, and others, and that the foundation was not sufficient for the new Dome of the Capitol. This defect, though then denied by Capt. [Montgomery] Meigs [Quartermaster-General, in charge of construction of the new Capitol dome] and others, is already manifesting itself in gaping and increasing fractures in the walls, and is thus <u>proving</u> that I understand such matters better than Meigs and his associates. Second. I have demonstrated, mathematically and experimentally, that our reputed highest Engineers are governed by false theories as to the action of forces in beams, girders, roofs and bridges. The loss of strength resulting from their errors amounts to <u>one third</u>. Now on these two highly important facts, and many others of a similar nature that I am prepared to show, I base a claim for prefference [sic] over military, and other Engineers for conducting civil construction for Government. And I will add that I am quite confident that I could make important improvements in military and Naval matters. That I could sink the Merrimac in ten minutes, the Monitor in fifteen minutes, and that I could have reduced the rebel works on Island Number 10 [a Confederate stronghold on the Mississippi River, 60 miles south of Columbus, Kentucky, where initial Union efforts to take enemy batteries were defeated in April 1862] in half the time our forces have already spent upon them. In support of these views I desire to call attention to the well known fact that most of the <u>improvements</u> made in military matters is done by civilians.

Very Respectfully Your Obt Servt.
B. Severson
359 E St. West

Washington March 31. 1862.

〜 *Lincoln forwarded this letter to the Office of the Chief of Engineers with the following endorsement: "Will Gen. [Joseph G.] Totten please look over this, and the accompanying drawings, & give me his opinion of them. A. Lincoln." On April 12 Totten reported back that he had "examined the papers of Mr. Severson" and found "his claims . . . so superlative and at the same time so unsupported, that, I can only avow myself unable to credit them." Lincoln made no further effort to investigate Severson's claims (CW, V: 176–177).*

The Monitor's *Designer Recommends a Rifle*

[Aug 2 1862]

His Excellency Abraham Lincoln
President of the United States

Sir   I most respectfully call your attention to Mr Rafaels repeating rifle—I have examined this formidable war instrument carefully and find it free from those imperfections which invariably defeat the usefulness of such contrivances. My long practical experience together with my knowledge of military matters, enable me to judge with sufficient accuracy of the utility of this weapon. By its adoption the detached bodies of men necessary to retain possession of the places captured from the rebels, will at once be able to hold out against and defeat the concentrated force which the cunning enemy will, from time to time, hurl upon your small and necessarily isolated detachments.

The time has come, Mr President, when our cause will have to be sustained not by numbers, but by superior weapons. By a proper application of mechanical devices alone will you be able with absolute certainty to destroy the enemies of the Union—Such is the inferiority of the Southern States in a mechanical point of view, that it is susceptible of demonstration that if you apply our mechanical resources to the fullest extent, you can destroy the enemy without enlisting another man.

As a beginning you will do well to put into the hands of your exposed Western detachments the little war engine to which I have called your attention—One regiment of intelligent men provided with one hundred of these effective weapons can most assuredly defeat and destroy a four-fold number of enemies.

I am with profound respect Your most obd Servant

J. Ericsson

New York August 2, 1862
To save you the trouble of making out my peciliar hand, I have resorted to the [illegible word] of employing a copyist.

༠ *A Swedish-born engineer, Mr. Ericsson had designed the first Union ironclad, the* Monitor, *which halted the brief but terrifying reign of the Confederate ironclad* Merrimack *at Hampton Roads five months before this letter was written. Although* no response is known, Lincoln doubtless took Ericsson's recommendation seriously, because the President granted Mr. Rafael an interview. Lincoln eventually visited the Washington Navy Yard to watch a demonstration of the Rafael Repeater, a precursor of the machine gun, and pronounced it "well worthy the attention of the Ordnance Bureaus." Lincoln seemed particularly amused when he learned that the new gun minimized the amount of gas released from the breech. "Well," said Lincoln, in the presence of an observer from the New York Tribune, "have any of you heard of any machine, or invention, for preventing the escape of 'gas' from newspaper establishments?"

Lincoln's strong recommendation sent the War Department into action on the Rafael Repeater, but because its cost was estimated at $850 per unit, no orders were ever placed (LTW, 209–211).

Endorsing Another New Rifle

New York August 19, 1862.

To his Excellency Abraham Lincoln.
President of the United States.

Dear Sir.   I have examined with care the Breech Loading Musket and Carbine (the mechanism of both being the same) the invention of the bearer, Mr. I. Wood.

These arms are, in my judgment, better adapted to the U.S. service than any which have yet been made. The mechanism is simple, substantial, and less liable to get out of order than the Springfield Musket. Mr. Wood, I think, has succeeded in securing the advantage of breech loading without the objections of some one or more of which all other breech loading arms that I have seen are liable. Mr Wood will submit to you the opinion of a military Board, and other competent persons who have given them an attentive examination. The advantages to be obtained by the introduction of these arms into the U.S. service are so great, that I have taken the liberty of calling them to your attention in the hope that measures may be taken to have them brought into use.

I will add that I have no interest direct or remote in the patent for these arms or in their Manufacture.

Your most Obt Servant
Peter Cooper

No reply is known. This recommendation came from the respected financier who had designed and built the first American locomotive, and promoted and helped back the laying of the Atlantic cable, which made possible the first overseas telegraph transmissions. Cooper dedicated the school named for him in New York—Cooper Union—to the "advancement of science and art." Lincoln spoke there in 1860.

A Cure for Soldiers' Sore Feet

Washington Jan 19 1863

To the President of the United States

Sir: Some three months since I proposed to the Secretary of War to furnish two million pair of of [sic] the patent [-leather] military sandals for the cure and prevention of sore feet in the army.

This invention being improperly designated and described was referred to the Quartermaster General by the Secretary, whereas I am informed that if my proposal had been properly worded it must have been referred to the Medical Department where the facilities for testing and the experience for judging of its importance must have secured its introduction into the army.

If only the comfort and well being of the soldier was sought to be, as they undoubtedly are attained by this invention, I should not presume to trouble you with its reference or adoption, but military and medical men of the highest distinction in their respective professions inform me that there can be no doubt that its general introduction must increase the mobility and consequent efficiency of the army at least twenty five per cent.

This is accomplished by protecting the feet of the infantry, where the first and ultimate failure occurs in all armies. The accompanying report or statement of the Medical Inspector General will inform you of the suffering and demoralization of the infantry resulting from the present insufficient clothing of the feet, and of his opinion of the proposed supplement to the ordinary military stocking as a remedy for the evil in question.

Hoping that these considerations justify me in troubling you with this apparently trifling but really important matter I have to request in conclusion that you will refer my proposal to the Medical Department, where it properly belongs and that you explain to the Secretary of War the reasons for making this request. I have offered to supply two million pair at forty cents per pair. I am very respectfully

Your Obdt Servt
E. Harmon

Lincoln kept this letter on his desk for two months, then forwarded it as requested with the following endorsement: "Submitted to the Surgeon General for his report. A. Lincoln." Two days later, on March 19, Surgeon General William A. Hammond replied that whereas "the sandal referred to is perhaps useful I do not regard it as indispensable." Besides, Hammond pointed out, he had no authority to purchase ordinary clothing for the troops; that duty belonged by law to the quartermaster. But there is no evidence Lincoln referred Harmon's plea afresh. The following April, however, another correspondent wrote to Lincoln, enclosing testimonials about "Harmon's sandal socks," wash leather stockings designed to be worn over regulation socks, and useful for "the preservation of the feet, on long marches . . . and the prevention of straggling." It was undoubtedly the same invention that Harmon had written about the year before, and when his new booster offered to go to the front himself and "put a pair on" General Grant's feet, Lincoln wired his commander to warn him that Harmon's admirer "wishes to visit you with a view of getting your permission to introduce into the Army 'Harmon's Sandal Sock[.]' Shall I give him a pass for that object? A. Lincoln." There is no further record of Lincoln's involvement with the Harmon sandal (CW, VII: 416).

Service from a Would-be Meteorologist

FOR THE <u>WAR</u> DEPARTMENT

Sat. Ap. 25th 1863.

His Excellency
The President
    Dear Sir, It would give me great pleasure to assure you of the <u>fine weather</u> suitable for a visit to the front or for starting an Expedition fraught with momentous interests to the Country, & not less important—in its <u>economical</u> aspects, like the recent Cavalry movement.
    Please refer me, favorably to the <u>War</u> Department. I will guarantee to furnish Meteorological information that will <u>save</u> many a serious sacrifice. Most respectfully

F. L. Capen

Enclosed with this letter was Frances L. Capen's calling card, on which he wrote further: "Thousands of lives & millions of dollars may be saved by the application of Science to War. Frances L. Capen, Certified Practical Meteorologist & Expert in Computing the Changes of the Weather." But a few days after Capen wrote and evidently met the President in person storms engulfed Washington, and an annoyed

Lincoln scribbled on this letter: "It seems to me Mr. Capen knows nothing about the weather, in advance. He told me three days ago that it would not rain again till the 30th of April or 1st of May. It is raining now & has been for ten hours—I can not spare any more time to Mr. Capen. A. Lincoln" (CW, VI: 190–191).

A Repeating Rifle

Armory of the Spencer
Repeating Rifle Company
Boston Aug. 13 1863.

His Excellency Abraham Lincoln.
President of the United States.

Sir. This will be handed you by Mr C. W. Spencer who is the Inventor of our arm.

Mr. Spencer will deliver to you the Rifle and ammunition which Mr. Cheney promised to send you.

It would give us much satisfaction if you would allow Mr. Spencer to make a trial of the rifle in your presence, and we would suggest that as the Hon. Secretary of War, Gen. [Henry W.] Halleck [then the Union army's general-in-chief] and others were Knowing to the mishaps of our gun at its former trials before you, that it would be very desirable that they should be present if possible.

If you can conveniently arrange such an exhibition we should esteem it a very great favor.

Mr Spencer will hold himself at your disposal until such time as may suit your pleasure and opportunity.

We have the honor to be

Your most obd servant
Warren Fisher Jr. Treasurer
Spencer Repeating Rifle Company

Lincoln did not reply, but four days after this letter was written, Christopher W. Spencer arrived at the White House to give Lincoln a rifle and show him how to assemble it. Then, on August 19, John Hay recorded in his diary: "This evening and yesterday evening an hour was spent by the President in shooting with Spencer's new repeating rifle. A wonderful gun, loading with absolutely contemptible simplicity and ease with seven balls and firing the whole readily & deliberately in less than half a minute. The President made some pretty good shots." Two thousand rifles were promptly ordered (Dennett, Diaries and Letters of John Hay, 82; LTW, 261–264).

Improved Gunpowder

Washington City, D.C. October 31, 1863.

Sir: I have the honor of submitting the following Report on a new and secret art of making Gun Powder. I have the honor to be,

> Very Respectfully
> Your Ob't Serv't.
> Isaac R. Diller

To the President.

∽ *Diller was an old friend of Lincoln's from Springfield. Acting as an agent for a German developer of chlorate-based gunpowder, he enclosed a "sealed package" bearing the encouraging but still inconclusive results of secret experiments Lincoln had authorized Diller to conduct at Timber Creek, New Jersey. Worried that England might yet cut off its supply of niter—the Union's sole source of gunpowder—Lincoln had reacted with enthusiasm to the notion of developing new powder made of chlorate. But its inventor never solved the challenges of its cheap manufacture or safe transport, and eventually the Union stockpiled enough English niter to last through 1866.*

Although the Diller project was dropped, historian Robert V. Bruce sees Lincoln's strong commitment to the experiments as a precursor to Franklin D. Roosevelt's Oak Ridge Project eighty years later (Bruce, Modern American Science, *311–312). The following memorandum, outlining specific instructions on how Lincoln wanted tests to proceed, is the most detailed response in the Lincoln canon on matters of scientific experimentation (CW, VI: 559–560).*

[ca. November 2, 1863]

I select you to make the test of the new gun-powder, according to the foregoing documents. Having expended some five thousand dollars to be prepared for making the test, it is desired that it be most carefully and thoroughly made, and answers thereupon given to all the following questions, and any others which may occur to you as pertinent.

Does this powder contain saltpetre or sulphur?

Does it bear any relation to gun-cotten?

Can the ingredients for making it always be obrained in sufficient quantity in the United States?

Is it's manufacture simple, requiring no complicated apparatus, and is it atteded with less danger than the manufacture of ordinary gun-powder?

Do atmospheric changes, whether of moisture or heat, injure the powder?

Will it explode with as little or less pressure than ordinary gun-powder?

Will it ignite under 300° Celsius?

Will it ignite by a spark, or percussion-cap, like common gun-powder?

Are <u>seven</u> parts of it, in weight, as effective in smooth bored guns as <u>nine</u> parts of common gun-powder?

Is <u>one</u> part of it, in weight, as effective in rifled guns, as <u>two</u> parts of common powder?

Will it, or the ingredients of it, deteriorate in store?

Will it heat a gun less than common powder? and in what pro-portion?

Does it give a weaker report?

Does it make less smoke?

Does it foul a gun less?

Is it less liable to burst or damage a gun?

In proportion to effect produced, is it cheaper than common gun-powder?

Has it any fault or faults not stated, or suggested in and by the answers to the foregoing questions? and if so, what?

Better Eyeglasses

Springfield Mass.
March 3d 1864

To his Excellency Abraham Lincoln
President of the United States of America

Sir/ I have very recently succeeded in producing very beautiful & peculiar lenses, of much service to decayed or failing sight, the lenses are of the periscopic form and most beautifully tinted, and they can be adapted to almost any eye. Might I have the honor & satisfaction of supplying your Excellency with a pair? I shall have the greatest plea-sure in waiting on your Excellency, at any time you might specify after the 26th inst.

Trusting for a favorable reply, I am Sir Your Excellency's

Humble & obedient Servant
Barnett Lazarus

cs White House secretary Edward D. Neill noted on the back of this letter that the writer "would like to supply the President with a pair of spectacles, with beautifully tinted lenses." But there is no record of Lincoln's asking for an examination or demonstration of the eyeglasses.

Ventillating Overshoes

New Brunswick, N.J.
January 19, 1865

His Excellency Abram [sic] Lincoln
President of the U. States
    Dear Sir: Will you please do us the honor to accept a pair of Felt, Union, Ventillating, traveling, overshoes. The advantages of these shoes is, while they keep the feet warm, to not cause and retain perspiration. After trial, if convenient, please allow your secretary to Express your opinion of them & greatly oblige. Very Respectfully

Your Obedient Servant
Meyer Rubber Co.

cs The letter was marked "Ack[nowledged] Jan 22, 65," but no reply has been found. By the time he received this offer, Lincoln had long been wearing shoes made to order for his difficult-to-fit size 14 feet.

A Gravity-Powered Miracle Machine

Georgetown D C Feb 9—1865
To his Excellency President Lincoln.
    Sir; Please allow me to demonstrate, the practicability; by a mathematical problem, easily to be understood; of the absolute existence, of a self-moving machine, yet to be developed for the glory of God, and the happiness of the human family.
    Mr. President; I will not detain you forty minutes. I have been forty years, struggling to find the mechanical actions to the problem, and have, at last found them, and there is no dispute; I bid defiance.
    The problem has been examined by your private Secretary; Capt J. M. Gilliss; Capt C. H. Tompkins; Prof. Henry Mitchell; and they all concur in the one opinion, that the problem is correct; and that of the

mechanical actions, can be effected; it is a discovery of great magnitude to the world.

Now, Mr President; this war, was fourtold [*sic*] to me in a vision; Oct. 20th 1816; at the same time, this wonderful invention, was shown me, and it was made obligatory on me, laboring it out as a sign of a future want, just before us. As I understand in the vision, this war was not to close, until this invention was in operation. From 1849 to 1860, I beged [*sic*] the Southern Senators, to desist in their determination of secessionism; Stating to them my vision, and declaring to them, that it would cause the most horrid war ever known, but they laughed at my vision, and treated it as nonsense.

In 1861; they acknowledged my prophesy and desired to know how long it would last. I told them 4 years and longer; if they did not reelect Abraham Lincoln. It was then a question, how long after that? The answer was one year and better; perhaps two.

Sir; I now say it will not close until self moving power is out; this is my impression from the vision in connection with the signs of the times. I cannot believe that any thing like a peace has been affected, by the late conference, with the Rebel Commissioners; I believe it all, a trick well played for time by them.

Once more, if you please; allow me to say; if I can show all the mechanical actions, to the problem, as required, to constitute a perfect machine, which will run without any other aid but that of gravitation, when completed; would you not say, that it ought to be immediately tested in the best manner? You will most undoubtedly answer in the affirmative. I say then, please examine my problem, as we now live in an age of wonders, and cannot tell, at what point, the arts and sciences, will end. We cannot tell what a day will bring.

Your success has been great; but if you bring this invention to light, you will have accomplished more than all your predecessors together. The problem was examined by President Tyler; and by his order submitted to three eminent Professors; whose reports were favorable, and one trial made; but the action then, was not perfect; but now it is and only requires finishing in a proper [*sic*] mechanical manner.

Tyler; got $4000, appropriated for my experiments, upon that and my safety steam engine; but I only received $1000. I am entitled to the balance; but a small sum, is only required now; to put this great invention in operation; thousands of dollars have I spent, for the future honor of my Country, with a view to coming events.

Since writing the past; Thursday January instant; 6 oclock, the news came to me of the death of Capt. J. M. Gilliss; who examined my problem as before Stated. I found him a man of talents, easy of access, and well disposed to inventive genious [*sic*]; I have lost a friend, who promised to examine my model machine, in a few days; <u>in the midst of life we are in death</u>; let us not neglect any duty, made binding and obligatory for the spread of human knowledge.

I am sir; respectfully;

Your humble friend
Edward D. Tippett

P.S. I will call tomorrow

&cn; *It is doubtful that Lincoln received "inventor" Tippett if he called at the White House the day after delivering this diatribe. Lincoln filed this letter after providing the following handwritten endorsement: "Tippett: Crazy-Man."*

This letter appears on page 229.

To My much Esteemed President—
Abraham Lincoln,
Dear Sir
Please allow
an oald ladey of thirty one years of age to present
you a very humble testimony of esteem & confidence
in the shape of a paie of sooks knit with my own hand
& allow me to say that I remember the trijels pased
through in revoculition days, I lost two Brothers
out of three that was in the survis of the cuntry.
besides Uncles & a number of cousins. & My prayer to Him
that doithe all things well, that holde the their nation
in the hollow of his hand & huth continued my life
to this time, & has Enabled me to worke almost dailey
from the comment of this rebelion to the present
hour for the soldiers (God bless) that you might be
richley indowed with that wisdom which you have so
much kneaded to enable you to bare so grate responsibilities
& to do that that is for the good of our bleding Cuntry
& I do pray that you may live to see this rebelion crusht
& with it slavery (which I do abomonate) wiped
from our land, & being thereafter to witness & Enjoy
the fruits of your labour—You will pardon this intrusion
upon your time & belive me to be your frind
& frend of my bleding cuntry, Sarah Phelps.
Groton. N. H. Jany. 1865.

[6]

Gifts and Honors

*L*ESS THAN FOUR MONTHS after Lincoln became president, his secretary of state, William H. Seward, wrote to inform him that the trustees of Columbia College in Seward's home state of New York has come to Washington "to deliver you the diploma conferring upon you the degree of L.L.D."

Writing in reply, Lincoln accepted the honor "with feelings of deep gratitude not unmitigated with diffidence." If such florid sentiments seem alien to the Lincolnian style, there is a good reason: the response was drafted by a secretary and merely signed by the President.

Barely one hundred days into his presidency, apparently Lincoln had already run out of the time and patience needed to respond to the gifts and honors that were only just beginning to pour into the White House. "There was little time," presidential secretary William O. Stoddard later admitted, "for mere courtesies in those days." Over the next four years, Lincoln would take the opportunity to thank only a few of his innumerable gift-givers personally; but his seeming ingratitude in no way inhibited the unending supply of presents, large and small. They kept arriving until the week he died.

In Lincoln's day, neither law nor custom forbade presidents from accepting such tokens or even required that they account for gifts publicly or pay taxes on their value. And Lincoln apparently accepted nearly everything he received (except the elephants offered by the King of Siam). Such gifts began arriving right after his nomination—and while he still had the leisure, inspired some amusing acknowledgments. For example, Lincoln told one admirer that he could not fully appreciate the gift of soap because "Mrs. L . . . protests that I have never given sufficient attention to the 'soap question' to be a competent Judge." The outpouring increased after he won the election, when so many new suits and hats arrived in Springfield that Lincoln purportedly told Mary, "Well, wife, there is one thing likely to come out of this scrape, any how. We are going to have some *new clothes.*"

But nothing could have prepared Lincoln for the tangible outpouring of respect and affection that flooded the White House once he assumed the presidency: all manner of food (fresh fish, fruit, and meat, to name a few examples), as well as drink (champagne, red and white wine, bourbon, rum, and rye whiskey), even though the President did not imbibe alcoholic beverages. Some of the food the Lincolns presumably ate, although they donated much of what they received to local hospitals.

Amateur bards sent examples of their questionable talent, and professional writers and publishers obliged, too. "There were of course a great many curious books sent to him," a visitor recalled, "and it seemed to be one of the special delights of his life to open these books at such an hour, that his boy could stand beside him, and they could talk as he turned over the pages."

Artists sent their photographs, prints, paintings, and sculpture, and country women sent all manner of needlework: socks, shawls, throw rugs, pillows, and quilts. Craftsmen sent a closetful of canes. Theatre owners sent free tickets for opening night galas. A westerner sent gold and silver ore from a mine in Arizona.

Not all of the gifts could be sent through the mail—although it was a letter that brought Lincoln the news that he had received the largest gift of his entire presidency—a "mammoth ox" named after General Grant. Lincoln promptly wrote back to donate it to charity, before the animal could be shipped to him.

Of the hundreds of presentation letters—formal and simple alike—in the Lincoln Papers, only a representative fraction can be included here. Among the charming presentation letters omitted are those that accompanied, for example, the flag once used by the martyred Zouave colonel Ephraim Elmer Ellsworth; a cane made from the

Confederate ironclad *Merrimack;* a gift of "pine apples" from his chiropodist, Isachar Zacharie, who sent gifts often; and a number of epic-length poems by ardent if untalented admirers.

Christmas gift giving was evidently not in vogue during the Civil War years—at least not from constituents to the President—for there are surprisingly few letters in the Lincoln Papers bearing evidence of holiday inspiration. A few gifts *did* arrive for New Year's, and one for his birthday. And half-barrels of hams arrived from a Baltimore admirer "on the occasion of the [Emancipation] Proclamation." But by and large, presidential gift giving appears to have been as spontaneous as it was generous. And it seems to have reached new proportions during 1864, when presents arrived by both mail and express in unprecedented volume—inarguable testimony to Lincoln's growing national popularity.

Amid the gifts came honors, too. A few months before the Battle of Gettysburg, a letter arrived from Portland, Oregon, bearing the news that Lincoln had been made an honorary member of the American Board of Commissioners for Foreign Missionaries; he was also sent a certificate of membership. The honorary doctor of laws degree he received from Columbia College at the start of his presidency was nicely complemented by the signal college honor he received near the end—word from his home state of Illinois that an entire university there was to be named for him.

The volume of gifts made it all but impossible for Lincoln—or even his clerks—to keep up with the obligations of acknowledgment. Although some such notes have surely vanished or remain hidden— many letters to Lincoln bear endorsements indicating that responses were sent, although these have yet to be located—there is no doubt that Lincoln became increasingly slow in acknowledging these favors. An artist who had made a personal seal for the President but had been sent no letter confirming its arrival sent several exasperated notes to Lincoln and his secretary in an effort to find "if the same has been received—and how the President likes it." There is no evidence that he ever found out. Similarly, a Philadelphian wrote to inquire whether a framed piece of needlework had arrived at the White House. Its maker was worried, for some inexplicable reason, that "it may have fallen into the hands of enemies."

Once—as correspondence in this chapter shows—even the noted abolitionist leader William Lloyd Garrison felt compelled to write to ask if a valuable gift had been received at the White House and to plead for a presidential acknowledgment. Lincoln finally wrote the letter—that is, he signed the usual draft prepared by a secretary— prompting Garrison, perhaps at that point feeling guilty, to write yet again to thank Lincoln for "putting me in possession of what I shall value very highly—namely, your autograph." Garrison suddenly seemed surprised that Lincoln had taken any notice of his request at all, acknowledging that the President must be "not only over- whelmed, but almost literally crushed, by the multitudinous matters constantly pressing upon you." Added Garrison: "My astonishment is that you are above ground. Happily you are blessed with an elastic and cheerful spirit." Remarkably, this was the only occasion that ever prompted Garrison to write to Lincoln, and it involved not a political issue, but a present.

Gifts undoubtedly made Lincoln more cheerful; but the record shows neither his spirit nor his time were in truth sufficiently "elas- tic" to guarantee all donors the thank-you notes for which they yearned.

A John Hancock Autograph

105 Bleeker St.
New York March 22 1860[1]

Honored Sir

A niece to John Hancock, I take pleasure in presenting to you, an interesting relic of the past, an autograph of my uncle, having the endorsement of your ancestor, Abraham Lincoln, written nearly a century ago: humbly trusting it may prove an happy augury of our countrys future history "The cradle of Liberty," "re-built" by John Hancock, and Abraham Lincoln. I remain

With highest respect
Mary Hancock Colyer

His Excellency Abraham Lincoln
President of the United States

∽ *Mrs. Colyer enclosed a lottery ticket for the benefit of the rebuilding of Faneuil Hall in Boston, signed by John Hancock and endorsed by an earlier Abraham Lincoln. The President replied as follows (CW, IV: 319):*

Executive Mansion April 2. 1861

My Dear Madam   I have the honour to acknowledge the receipt of your favor of the 22nd of March.

Permit me to express my cordial thanks for the interesting relic you were so kind as to send me, as well as for the flattering sentiment with which it was accompanied. I am with great respect

Your Obdt Servt.
A. Lincoln

Mary Hancock Colyer   105 Bleeker St New York

A Regiment in his Honor

Chicago Feb 4th 1861

To the Hon. A. Lincoln

Dear Sir: We have organized a company of Militia, in this city, composed of men of Hungarian, Bohemian & Sclavonic origin. Being the first company formed in the United States, of said nationalities, we respectfully ask leave of your Excellency to entitle ourselves "Lincoln Riflemen of Sclavonic Origin."

∽ *Lincoln wrote at the bottom of this letter: "I cheerfully grant the request above made. A Lincoln." (Original in the Chicago Historical Society).*

Fresh Butter

Rome [N.Y.,] Mar 25. 1861

To His Excellency, Hon
A. Lincoln President

Dr Sir   I have this day shipped you by Express a very nice pkge of Fall Butter, which please accept from one of your staunchest political friends—

I observe that you are constantly besieged with applications for office & the rumor is you are working too hard, it therefore occurred to me that something nice & palatable in the way of good butter might do you good, & help to preserve your strength to perform your arduous duties. I am a dealer in the article entire in this Town, & can assure you that this is something extra nice, which will suit you & your Family—

I am not asking for any office & only desire good government, & to have honest & true men appointed to office: So far, the President has been fortunate in that respect

I[n] conclusion allow me to beg of you for the sake of our country to use all the means in your power to sustain your health & strength & take time from your severe labors for necessary exercise—

That you may be the means of restoring our country to its former prosperity, is the ardent wish of my heart, & I have great faith, if your life is spared that order & good Government will be surely established under your administration

I am an old citizen of this Co. (Oneida) & formerly one of the strongest supporters of our noble & deeply lamented Henry Clay, the greatest statesman & Patriot that ever lived in these United States—

Knowing, too, that you were one of his ardent friends & admirers—is one great reason of the strong & sincere attachment I feel for you, & that you may succeed in your endeavors to bring order out of chaos is my great & earnest desire—

I am very Respectfully your Friend & obt Servt.

John B. Bradt

P.S. Keep a goot strong pickle in this butter & in a cool place then it will keep sweet till July

J. B. B.

Offering Toll-Free Passage

Washington June 4. 1861

To His Exclency The President of
The United States

I was introduced to you by Judge James of New York but knowing that your time was fully occupied have not done myself the honor to call since except at your public receptions.

Am please [sic] to see that your family pass over our Seventh St. Turnpike and I have given direction to our toll gather[er] not to detain your carriage or to receive any compensation for its passage.

Wishing your administration entire success   I am your Obdt Servant

J. C. Lewis
Hopeton
North of Washington D. C.

ᗌ *No reply is known. The Lincolns likely used the road described during the summer months, when they lived at the Soldiers' Home outside Washington, and the President commuted from there to the White House daily.*

Penobscot Salmon

Bangor June 21. 1861

My Dear President

I send you this morning a Salmon, fresh from the waters of the Penobscot, which I hope will reach you in good condition, and prove acceptable.

As I have never had the pleasure of a personal acquaintance with [you] I a few days ago requested Wm. Seward to apprise you of my intention to present you with this offering and to assure you that it would be from a friendly source.

> Your Friend & obdt Servt
> Rufus Daniel

His Excellency Abram Lincoln
Washington D.C.

∽ No acknowledgment of the fish has been found. Salmon seems to have been a favorite gift to the President. Six days after this letter was sent, Massachusetts Governor John A. Andrew sent "a codfish and a salmon, both fresh and dripping from our New England waters."

Patent Medicines

> Fredonia Chautauqua Co. N.Y.
> June 27. 1861

Hon A. Lincoln

Dear Sir   Having been engaged the last three years in the sale of medicines from Pierpont & Co. of Rochester N.Y. and having witnessed the instant relief, and permanent cure of many of the various ailments for which Dr. E. Cooper's Universal Magnetic Balm is recommended—such as Paralysis, Cramps, Colics, Burns Bruises Wounds Fevers, Cholera Morbus, Camp Disease, &c. &c. &c. I have thought it might be well to send "Our President" a small supply of the Mag. Balm; and therefore sent it, a few days since, via Pierpont & Co.

Please accept the same and do not fear to trust it as you would a true friend,—administer to your own family and friends, (especially to Gen. Scott), note its effects, and write to me giving a result, and you will much oblige.

> Yours Respectfully
> P. Miller Jr.

P.S. On receipt of this please write, and let me know if the med. is received.

> P. M. Jr.

No acknowledgment of Dr. E. Cooper's Universal Magnetic Balm has come to light. Nor do we know whether the President recommended it, as requested, to the aged Winfield Scott, whose rheumatism was evidently common knowledge.

Unfermented Bread

111 East 14th St
New York July 12. 1861

To his Excellency Abraham Lincoln
President of the United States

Dear Sir, We have this day sent to you by Adams' express, freight paid a large basket of our Patent Unfermented bread, for the use of your table, with the hope that it may be regarded as a heart felt tribute of our great respect to your character and great qualifications.

We are supplying the Sickles Brigade, and the Plymouth Regiment (H W Beecher's) with the same bread—The faculty pronounce it the finest in the world.—Accompanying the basket will be found a full description of its manufacture by our patented process, and trusting you and your family, will be gratified by its use, and that the best blessings of Providence may attend both you and them. We are Dr Sir

Yours most truly
Davies & Co.

Enclosed are the 2 keys to unlock the basket

The President did not acknowledge this gift. Accompanying the letter was an illustrated pamphlet entitled Pure Bread: An Essay on Its Chemistry and Manufacture, *which contained a description of how the new process avoided the "filth" associated with customary baking processes, and "the untold abominations possible with careless, dirty, or diseased workers."*

A Son's Ode

[December 9, 1861]

To His Excellency Abraham Lincoln
President United States

Allow me to present you with an ode written by my Son, Mr.

Appleton Oaksmith, in memory of the great Union meeting in the City of New York.

> Very Respectfully
> Elizabeth C. Smith

> New York 9th Dec
> 1861

> The Union Marseillaise
> Song of The "Union League"
> by Appleton Oaksmith April 1861.

Ye sons of the Union wake to duty!
Your sires' great spirits bid you rise;
From yonder Heaven, in holy beauty,
They watch your acts with tearful eyes:—
They bid you now be firm and wise.—
Though madness, erring brothers leading,
May seek to desolate the land,
We will not raise a single hand
Till Liberty herself lies bleeding.
> God keep us firm and brave—
> The union must be saved
March on, March on, all hearts resolved
> On Union, Peace, or Death

But should the hopes of Freedom falter—
Should Liberty's expiring cries,
From the ruins of this Union's alter [*sic*],
Shriek in dying accents to the skies—
We then will for this Union rise:
And like the mountain torrent rolling,
> its irresistible, our band
Will sweep forever from our land
The curse its greatness now controlling.
> God keep us firm and brave—
> The Union must be saved—
March on, March on, all hearts resolved
> On Union, Peace, or Death.

Henry Clay's Snuff Box

Ashland Near Lexingon
4th August 1862.

To His Excellency Abraham Lincoln
President of the United States

Dear Sir, I send you through Adams Express a snuff box, not of much intrinsic value, but which belonged to my late father, whose avowed sentiment "that he owed a higher allegiance to the Constitution and Government of the United States than to the Constitution and Government of any State," is mine, and whose other noblest sentiment "that he would rather be right than President" I hope may ever be yours.

My mother now past eighty one years of age consents for me to send you the snuff box. With Great Respect

Your friend & Obdt Servt
John M. Clay

ᓚ *Lincoln replied to the son of his great political hero a few days later (CW, V: 363–364).*

Executive Mansion,
Washington, August 9, 1862.

Mr. John M. Clay.
My dear Sir:

The snuff-box you sent, with the accompanying note, was received yesterday.

Thanks for this <u>memento</u> of your great and patriotic father. Thanks also for the assurance that, in these days of dereliction, you remain true to his principles. In the concurrent sentiment of your venerable mother, so long the partner of his bosom and his honors, and lingering now, where he <u>was</u>, but for the call to rejoin him where he <u>is</u>, I recognize his voice, speaking [Lincoln first wrote, then crossed out, "from on high"] as it ever spoke, for the Union, the Constitution, and the freedom of mankind.

Your Obt. Servt.
A. Lincoln

Stolen Money Returned

[March 2, 1863]

"Inter nos"

To his Excellency Abraham Lincoln
President of the United States

Enclosed you will find Eight hundred and sixty eight dollars which came by in a dishonest manner and which I return to the United States through you

Being tempted, in an unguarded moment, I consented to take it being very much in want of money but thanks to my Saviour I was led by the influences of the Holy Spirit to see my great sin and to return it to you as the representative of the United States

Hoping you will pardon, me in the name of the government you represent as I trust I will be pardoned by my Father who is in heaven (through the merits and mediation of Jesus Christ his son) I remain

Your penitent supplicant
"Candide secure"

Brooklyn, March 2nd 1863

Please acknowledge receipt

ᔆ *Lincoln endorsed the envelope, "Stolen money returned," then wrote out the following receipt in his own hand: "Received, March 5, 1863, of A. Lincoln, President of the United States the sum mentioned within, in 'Green-backs.'" The receipt was then signed by F. E. Spinner, Treasurer of the United States.*

An Actor's Thanks—and Faux Pas

New York, March 20, 1863

To President Lincoln
Washington D.C.

Your Excellency favored me last Friday evening 13th inst. by a spontaneous visit to the Washington theatre to witness my personation of the Falstaff of King Henry IV, and I would respectfully ask your acceptance of a volume I have recently published and the concluding portion of which refers particularly to the remarkable points of that renowned character—

I have sent said Book through Adams' Express Company and venture to hope that at your convenient leisure you may find therein some agreeable relaxation from your cares of the State—

Your Excellency's obedient Servant
Jas. H. Hackett

∽ *It took Lincoln five months to write the celebrated Shakespearean actor James H. Hackett to acknowledge the gift of his book* Notes and Comments upon Certain Plays and Actors of Shakespeare, with Criticisms and Correspondence. *The President probably wished retrospectively that he had never replied at all, because the letter that follows became something of a public embarrassment for him.*

Executive Mansion,
Washington, August 17, 1863.

My dear Sir:

Months ago I should have acknowledged the receipt of your book, and accompanying kind note; and I now have to beg your pardon for not having done so.

For one of my age, I have seen very little of the drama. The first presentation of Falstaff I ever saw was yours here, last winter or spring. Perhaps the best compliment I can pay is to say, as I truly can, I am very anxious to see it again. Some of Shakespeare's plays I have never read; while others I have gone over perhaps as frequently as any unprofessional reader. Among the latter are Lear, Richard Third, Henry Eighth, Hamlet, and especially Macbeth. I think nothing equals Macbeth. It is wonderful. Unlike you gentlemen of the profession, I think the soliloquy in Hamlet commencing "O, my offence is rank" surpasses that commencing "To be, or not to be." But pardon this small attempt at criticism. I should like to hear you pronounce the opening speech of Richard the Third. Will you not soon visit Washington again? If you do, please call and let me make your personal acquaintance.

Yours truly
A. Lincoln.

James H. Hackett, Esq.

⌒ Hackett had the poor judgment to publish Lincoln's reply under the title, "A Letter from President Lincoln to Mr. Hackett . . . Printed not for publication but for private distribution only, and its convenient perusal by personal friends." Not surprisingly, the press got hold of copies of the letter and published the text along with derisive comments on the President's taste. Horrified, Hackett wrote the President again.

October 22, 1863

To President Lincoln
Washington D.C.

About a month since my son John K. Hackett of New York [an attorney there] wrote to me how vexed he had been at the unwarrantable liberty taken by certain Newspaper-Presses in publishing your kind, sensible & unpretending letter to me of "17 Augt." last & more particularly at the Editorial remarks upon & perversion of its subject-matter to antagonistic political purposes, accompanied by satirical abuse in general.

In order to calm my son's fears that it might give you cause to regret your having thus favored me, with such original materiel [*sic*], I replied that I felt assured that, as a man of the world now and an experienced politician you were not likely to be so thin-skinned, and that in my humble opinion such political squibs would probably affect your sensibility about as much as would a charge of mustard seed shot at forty yards distance, fired through a popgun barrel at the naturally armed Alligator, touch his nerves. Pray excuse the illustration! But, my son being a first rate shot with gun or pistol & thoroughly aware of their comparative effects, it was therefore an <u>argumentum ad hominiem</u>.

I have just recd. from my son the enclosed cut from the N.Y. Herald of the 16th inst, transcribing an Editorial from <u>"The Liverpool</u> (Eng.) <u>Post of Oct 1st"</u>; and as I perceive your letter was not quite correctly quoted therein & has been very improperly in Sept. last by the <u>Boston Courier</u>, and also because you may not have retained a copy, allow me to send you one of some which I caused to be printed for my friends' perusal without subjecting the original to consequent mutilating.

I wrote your Excellency hence dated "3d Oct." inst. with a small package by mail which I hope came duly to yr. hand; and I intend to depart hence within a week for New York, there to pass the Winter.

Your Excellency's obedient servant
Jas. H. Hackett

∽ *Hackett's explanation prompted the following response from Lincoln—this time carefully marked "private."*

P R I V A T E

Executive Mansion,
Washington, Nov. 2. 1863.

James H. Hackett
My dear Sir:

Yours of Oct. 22nd. is received, as also was, in due course, that of Oct. 3rd. I look forward with pleasure to the fulfilment of the promise made in the former [on October 3 Hackett had invited the President to "each or either" of a series of performances he planned for Washington on December 21–23].

Give yourself no uneasiness on the subject mentioned in that of the 22nd.

My note to you I certainly did not expect to see in print; yet I have not been much shocked by the newspaper comments upon it. Those comments constitute a fair specimen of what has occurred to me through life. I have endured a great deal of ridicule without much malice; and have received a great deal of kindness, not quite free from ridicule. I am used to it.

Yours truly
A. Lincoln

∽ *Evidently Lincoln meant what he said in his forgiving letter. John Hay recorded in his diary for December 13: "Tonight Hackett arrived and spent the evening with the President . . . the Tycoon [Hay's pet, private name for Lincoln]showing a very intimate knowledge of those plays of Shakespeare where Falstaff figures." The following night Lincoln took his family to Ford's Theatre to see Hackett portray Falstaff in* Henry IV, *and the very next evening, the President brought his secretaries, Nicolay and Hay, to see the "admirable" performance yet again (with Hay recalling that Lincoln "criticized H.'s reading of a passage where Hackett said, 'Mainly thrust at me,' the President thinking it should read "Mainly thrust at me"). His criticism notwithstanding, Lincoln returned to Ford's the very next night to see Hackett yet again, this time in* Merry Wives of Windsor. *And thus ended—happily—the affair of the actor and the President (CW, VI: 392–393, 558–559; LDBD, III: 227; Dennett, Diaries and Letters of John Hay, 138–139).*

A Dictionary

Washington D.C.
1 April 1863.

Mr. President,

I am requested by Messrs. G. & C. Merriam, the publishers of Websters Dictionary, to present to you in their name, a superbly bound copy of that great National Work.

Regarding it as the most valuable contribution of American Genius to the learning of mankind yet produced, I feel honored in being requested to offer it for your acceptance.

Noah Webster has been the Great Schoolmaster of our Republic from the publication of his Spelling Book in Washingtons time. He has educated three generations of Americans; and so omnipresent is his influence that no human being who steps on this continent can escape it. I doubt not that his Dictionary has been your companion from your boyhood, and that you will cheerfully pay your venerable master your manhoods gratitude.

I have the honor to remain, with the greatest respect, Your Servant, Friend, and Fellow-citizen

C. Edwards Lester

No reply has been found.

A Sofa Cushion

[July 9, 1863]

Our Respected Friend Abraham Lincoln

Will please accept the accompanying Sofa Cushion, which was purchased by subscription, from the table of "The Penn Relief Association for Sick and Wounded Soldiers," at the Grand Floral Fair recently held in this city.

On behalf of the Association

Rachel S. Evans, Pres.
N.E. cor. 11th & Vine Sts.

Philadelphia
7th Mo. 9th. 1863.

ᴄᴏ *An acknowledgment of this gift was forwarded a month later, written in John Hay's handwriting and signed by Lincoln (CW, VI: 375).*

Executive Mansion,
Washington, August 10, 1863.

Dear Madam

I thank you very cordially for the beautifully-finished Cushion, received, through your courtesy, today. But grateful as I am, it must be your greatest satisfaction to reflect that the brave soldiers who reap the benefit of your compassionate kindness and liberality, are this day more grateful still. I am very truly

Your Obt. Servt
A. Lincoln

Mrs. Rachel S. Evans
N.E. Cor. 11th & Vine

To Relieve Presidential Constipation

[Washington]
Sept 12. 1863

My dear Sir

This is the season when you and I are apt to be afflicted with disordered bowels; & as my black berry cordial, like the rebellion, is pretty well "played out," or "used up", I send you for trial, an article which is <u>highly</u> reputed, but which I have not had occasion to try since its appearance in the shops. I hope you will find it beneficial. With good wishes & congratulations, I am

Most respectfully
N. Sargent

ᴄᴏ *A secretary filed this with the endorsement "Sends to the President <u>something for his bowels</u>."*

Lincoln Win*s* a Watch

Chicago, Nov. 26th 1863

President Lincoln

Sir: Among the many remarkable incidents of our recent Fair, not one has been more pleasant, than the duty that devolves upon us, of consigning to you, on this National Thanksgiving Day, the accompanying watch; of asking you to accept it as a memorial of the Ladies N. Western Fair. During the progress of the Fair, Mr. James H. Hoes, Jeweller of Chicago, a most loyal and liberal man, after giving very largely himself, in order to stimulate donations from others, proposed through the columns of the Tribune, to give a gold watch to the largest contributor to the Fair. "Thou art the man." Your glorious Emancipation Proclamation world wide in its interests and results, was sold for $3000, the largest benefaction of any individual. This termination seemed to be all that was needed, to complete the history of this remarkable Fair. The little one has become a thousand. I have the pleasure to announce to you that the precious Document, has already become the cornerstone of a permanent Home for Illinois soldiers. It will also be the cap-sheaff & glory. It will be built in a frame, in the wall of this Noble Institution, & stand as a lasting monument, of your wisdom, patriotism, liberality, & fatherly tenderness for the brave boys, who at your call, so promptly "rallied round the flag," and so gallantly defended it. May the God of peace be with you, as the God of battle has prospered you. May the God of Jacob be your Counsellor, is the earnest prayer of your grateful friends & admirers

Mrs. A. H. Hoge
Mrs. D. P. Livermore
Managers Northwestern Fair

ᴄᴏ *The document Lincoln donated to the fair—his manuscript of the Emancipation Proclamation—eventually found its way into the Chicago Historical Society, where it was destroyed in the great fire of 1871. He acknowledged this gift in the following letter addressed to the jeweler who donated the timepiece—and he wore the watch for the rest of his life* (CW, *VII: 75; Kantor and Kantor,* Sanitary Fairs, *172–174*).

Executive Mansion,
Washington, December 17, 1863.

My Dear Sir

I have received from the Sanitary Commission of Chicago, the Watch which you placed at their disposal, and I take the liberty of conveying to you my high appreciation of your humanity and generosity, of which I have unexpectedly become the beneficiary.

I am very truly yours

A. Lincoln

James H. Hoes Esq

A Flawed Scarf

Ft Howard [Wisc.,] Jan 11th/64

Dear President Lincoln

Please excuse the freedom I use in encroaching upon your time for a moment, and also accept the emblem of our Country's Freedom which accompanies this note, from one that greatly admires the Fidelity Patriotism and Wisdom which you have manifested throughout this wicked and terible [sic] Rebellion, I send it to you with the sincere hope that our great banner may soon wave over every foot of this great republic and over a freed and happy People, and I believe you are destined through Providence to guide the great Ship of State safely through this Storm into the Harbor of peace and Freedom, therefore I hope you may be sustained by grace and live to be our next President (no very enviable position I should judge at present however).

Your sincere friend
Mrs H S Crocker

PS the scarf is some of my own knitting and inventing it I tried to knit a spread Eagle over your name but did not succeed——

H S C

No acknowledgment of this gift of an imperfect scarf has yet come to light, although a secretary's endorsement on the back of Mrs. Crocker's letter included the notation "Ansd Feb. 13. 1864."

A Saddle of Venison

Carthage [N. Y.,] the 11th of Feb 1864

Mr Abraham Lincon Esq
President of the United States

I have sent you two sadles of Venison and if you should not wantit [sic] if you will send your Servent to the Market with it you may depend on it being good Mr A. W. Clark the Congressman from Jefferson Co Knowes me and has for 20 years he will inform you all a Bout me in hast & most obedent Servent

E. Willars
To A. Lincoln President of the United States of America

ᔓ *No acknowledgment is known. A White House secretary filed this letter with the amusing endorsement "Has sent the President two saddles of venison & if he dont want it, he can send it to market."*

An Afghan From Buffalo

Buffalo March 9th 1864

President Lincoln

Please accept this "Afgan" [sic] from your little friends who desire to express their regard for you in these terrible days of war. The afgan was exhibited at the "Central Fair" recently held here, and now we are very happy in sending it to our Dear President

Please remember that you have little friends in Buffalo who pray for you, that you may be cheerful, strong, and wise.

With much love
Clara & Julia Brown

ᔓ *The Brown girls, age eleven and thirteen, received the following note from Lincoln a few weeks later (CW, VII: 258):*

Executive Mansion Washington
March 21 1864

Misses Clara & Julia Brown

The Afgan you sent is received, and gratefully accepted. I especially like my little friends; and although you have never seen me, I am glad you remember me for the country's sake, and even more, that you remember, and try to help, the poor Soldiers.

Yours very truly
A. Lincoln

A "Choice Cut of Bullock"

Washington Mar 22/64

To the President of the United States
Dear Sir The box accompanying this letter and which is addressed to you in my care comes to me from a highly respectable constituent of mine—Hon James J Lewis late State Senator from my District. Mr Lewis states in his letter that the content of box is "the choice cut from a bullock weighing when dressed nearly 2400 lbs.["] He desires me to present it to you in the name of the Farmers Meat Company—a corporation composed mainly of my constituents. Will you do me the favor to accept it as a small token of their regard.

Your very truly
J. M. Broomall
7th Cong Dist Pa.

∽ *No reply is known.*

Wine from a Grateful Political Appointee

New York April 9th 1864

To His Excellency Abraham Lincoln
President of the U.S.
Washington D.C.
Sir: We beg to enclose Adams Express receipt for one case wine, received from Theo. Canisius Esqr. U.S. consul at Vienna; and shipped to your address by his order.

Your obed't servants,
L. E. Amsinick & Co.

∽ *John Hay endorsed this letter with a note of instruction to the junior clerks of the White House: "In all this class of cases . . . please ascertain . . . whether the present*

*has been recd. & then prepare a note of acknowledgement." But if Lincoln acknowl-
edged this particular gift, the note has vanished. The President did not drink wine,
except an occasional sip or two, on doctors' orders, to relieve stress, and usually he
ordered such gifts sent to local hospitals. The German-born Dr. Canisius had been the
editor of a German-language newspaper in Springfield, the* Illinois Staats Anzeiger,
*a sheet owned by Lincoln himself. Early in his presidency, Lincoln decided he must
reward Canisius, so he instructed Secretary of State Seward to make Canisius Consul
to Vienna, explaining almost apologetically in a note to Seward: "The place is but
$1000 and not much sought; and I must relieve myself of the Dr. Illinoisian, tho, he
be" (CW, II: 524; IV: 418).*

A Pair of Eagles

On Board the U.S.N. Str. "Newbern"
From Beaufort, N.C. May 1st 1864

To his Excellency,
Abram [*sic*] Lincoln,
President of the U.S.

Please accept this Pair, (Male and Female,) American Eagles,
taken young, now two thirds grown, captured on the banks of the
Neuce River, N.C.—captured by Miles C. Bradley, and forwarded to
you, by your ob't. serv't. the undersigned.

There seemed to be an appropriateness, in making this present to
you, as the Chf. Magistrate.

They were hatched in a <u>tree</u>, that also is worthy of a passing
remark, cut, to be wrought into a monitor, in Brooklyn Navy Yard,
the dimensions, when hewn, was thirty inches at the butt, twenty
eight inches at the top, and eighty four ft. long.

There are so many patriotic associations, about this proud bird,
that as President of the United States, I trust you will receive them, in
the spirit they are donated to you, and give them the full benefit of
their emblematical character.

Accept the assurance, of my distinguished regard, from your Ob't
Servant

John S. Bowen
Cap't and A.Q.M.

ᔧ *There is no record of an acknowledgment of these unusual gifts.*

Likeness of a Presidential Look-alike

> Post Office, Chicago, Ill.
> May 30—1864

Honred Sir

I have not the pleasure of your acquaintance, but I am often calld. Abraham Lincoln. Especially during the last Presidential Campaigne, I was often Saluted by young urchins of Boys & Girls by the honorable Cognomen. I Suppose, for the reason we were not so favored in the game of Snatch, when <u>Beauty was passd</u>. last winter, when we clerks of the Postoffice made a present of our Vizes and an album to our worthy Postmaster John L. Scripps Esq. I promised the Clerks that I would ask your honor to Exchange with me, & now at this late hour I ask it—I hold no grudge against any one on a/c of their beauty; the heart they possess, and that in the right place, is worth more than all the "<u>Beauty</u>" Extant. ["]Yours before, <u>Yours this time</u>." With all my might & Strength—I. N. Arnold Esq [an old friend of Lincoln's] will vouch for, that I have been personally acquainted with him over 15 years and a worthy Gentleman he is too.

> Daniel T. Wood

To Hon. A. Lincoln

∾ *"Sends his photograph and wishes an exchange,"* reads the endorsement on this *letter from a homely Lincoln look-alike. If the President obliged, the correspondence has been lost, and sadly, so has the photograph of Mr. Wood.*

An Updated Biography

> Moore, Wilstach & Baldwin.
> Publishers, Wholesale Booksellers, Stationers . . .
> Cincinnati June 24 1864

President Lincoln

Dear Sir   Thinking that you might like to see what Mr. Barrett has done in his new book, I have just sent you two copies by mail [undoubtedly Joseph Hartwell Barrett's new, updated edition of his 1860 Lincoln campaign biography, still entitled *Life of Abraham Lincoln,* which was republished in 1864 to include presidential messages and proclamations, "and a concise History of the War"]—

I hope Mr Carpenter [artist Francis Bicknell Carpenter, then painting Lincoln from life in the White House for an Emancipation history painting] will not feel jealous of his friend Mr. [Alexander H.] Ritchie [an accomplished New York engraver], when he sees how very successful Ritchie has been in engraving your portrait from Brady's photograph: your friends here—the few who have seen it—pronounce it much the best likeness that has ever been published—

I trust you will be pleased with it—

We might have waited to send you finely bound copies, but I thought you would like to see the volume as it goes forth to the people, and so have forwarded copies from those first received from the Bindery

Very Respy Yrs
Wm H. Moore

∽ *Lincoln may well have shown the book's Ritchie engraving to artist Carpenter, then working in the White House, for when Carpenter was ready to choose someone to engrave his painting, he selected Ritchie (Monaghan,* Lincoln Bibiliography *I: 6).*

A Pipe

Totten U.S.A. General Hospital
Louisville KY. Aug 26th 1864.

A. Lincoln
President U.S.A.

Sir. I have the pleasure of herewith transmitting a Smoking pipe made expressly for you. It was manufactured by Henry Meier a private of the 5th Connecticut Regiment. He is a German, 39 years of age, came to this country, enlisted in the Union Army, was in the battle of Resaca [an engagement in Georgia in May 1864], came to my hospital Several weeks Since Suffering with rheumatism. He has lost his right thumb, and manufactured the accompanying pipe with <u>a pen knife held between his fingers.</u>

The Laurel root is from Cumberland mountains—the Shells from Stone river.

He has a wife and two Small children in Germany, of whom he often Speaks with deep emotion. He is now marked for the "Invalid Corps."

Accept the pipe as an offering of high regard from a Sick, but brave, Soldier, for the President of the United States of America. I would be pleased to have its receipt acknowledged, that I may have the pleasure of assuring him that his design and labor were not in vain.

Praying that you may be triumphantly elected, that God will direct you in the midst of your great responsibilities, and grant that you may live to See a glorious peace conquered, and that this Government may be permanently established.

I am yours with great respect,

> Washington M. Grimes
> Hospital Chaplain, U.S.A.
> Louisville, Ky.

ᔢ *No reply from Lincoln has been found, but secretary Edward D. Neil endorsed the letter: "Receipt acknowledged Sep 2 1864 E.D.N." Lincoln did not smoke.*

Pennies for the Soldiers

[September 2, 1864]

To His Excellency Abraham Lincoln
President of the United States

Honored Sir   I take the liberty to enclose to your care Five dollars, being the proceeds of some German currency, sent to me by my only child, James B Meier, for the last eighteen months at school in Dusseldorf.

He writes me that he has been "saving up his pennies," in order that he might "help the sick and wounded of our brave boys, fighting for the glorious cause of truth and freedom" as he is "not yet old enough to fight."

Will you respected Sir accept my "Boys offering," even tho' small, and may I ask you the great favor of one word of acknowledgement, in his behalf, it will tend to encourage our true hearted Girls & Boys in our Sunday Schools, and especially of the Plymouth church [in Brooklyn, where Lincoln twice worshipped during visits to New York] (Mr [Henry Ward] Beechers) of which my Boy was a member, he needs, in these times of fearful trial, to use any legitimate means to incubate and energize the doctrine of a true "God fearing patriotism" and especially among our rising own youth throughout the land.

Permit me to add one word. My Father died here at the age of 87 praying for the blessing of Heaven upon yourself and our beloved adopted <u>Country</u>, he was one of the earliest signers of the <u>first</u> petition that was presented to the British Parliament praying for the abolition of the Slave trade.

We are <u>Scotch</u> and have been in this blessed land on 30 years and <u>our</u> "<u>Clan</u>" of relations, will muster on 50 votes, <u>loyal and true</u>, for your honoured name, the coming election, as they did on the previous one, and some of them have sealed their title to the "<u>good cause</u>" in many a hard fought field during the last three years.

And now may the God of Abraham Issac & Jacob be your <u>support</u> & <u>Comfort</u> and <u>everlasting succor</u>. And may our <u>eventual "peace"</u> be the "work of <u>righteousness</u>" in the "quietness and assurance <u>forever</u>."

I am honored Sir Your prayerful well wisher and

obt. Servant
John J. Meier

Brooklyn LI
51 Columbia St. Septr 2nd 1864

∽ *No formal reply from Lincoln has been found, but the Lincoln Papers do contain a draft in John Nicolay's handwriting, with a notation by Edward D. Neill, another presidential secretary, that the letter had been copied and sent to Meier (CW, VII: 538–539).*

Executive Mansion,
Washington, Sept 6, 1864.

Dear Sir

You write me under date of the 2d inst. that your boy who is at school in Dusseldorf, has for the last eighteen months been "saving up his pennies," and has sent you the proceeds, amounting to five dollars which you enclose, to "help the sick and wounded of our brave boys fighting for the glorious cause of truth and freedom" as he is himself "not yet old enough to fight."

The amount is duly received and shall be devoted to the object indicated. I thank your boy, not only for myself, but also for all the children of the nation, who are even more interested than those of us, of maturer age, that this war shall be successful, and the Union be maintained and perpetuated.

A Gift—with a Price

Baltimore September 4th 1864

His Excellency Abraham Lincoln
Prest. U.S. of America

Sir! I beg to be excused when I approach you with a small package it is my own work. I have been so happy, as to have made <u>seals</u> like this for our last <u>two</u> presidents and I have tried very often to be as happy, as to see you, in order that you may honor me with the order as I have always failed in gaining admission, and not been so fortunate as to speak to your excellency in person, I have taken the liberty and made a <u>Seal</u> for your own <u>use</u> on the same <u>plan</u> I have made it for Mr Fillmore and Mr Buchanan when they occupied the same position your Excellency does now. The price for the same, I will <u>leave</u> to your usual generosity, I shall be happy and highly honored by learning the package containing the <u>Seal</u> for our present & <u>future</u> President has met with satisfaction.

I have the Honor to be

Your Humble servant
J. Baumgarten
19 E. Fayette St, Baltimore

ᔇ *No reply is known . . . and there is no record of a payment.*

A Bible for Everyday Use

Newark, N.J. Sept 16th 1864

President Lincoln

Honored Sir. Having seen a notice in the paper of the beautiful Bible presented to you by the Col[ore]d. People of Baltimore, I thought it would be too bad to use that costly Bible—for daily reading so I write to say—we have several old ones and will be most happy to give you one for common use if you desire it.—

If you accept my offer & wish to avial [sic] yourself of one of our Bibles, address a line to "Essex." Newark. New Jersey and the Bible shall be forwarded by Express—
Very Respectfully Yours.—

Essex.

No reply is known. Lincoln probably was not convinced that a reply addressed only to "Essex" in Newark would be duly received.

The Largest Gift Ever

[T E L E G R A P H]

Boston Nov. 8, 1864

To Abraham Lincoln,
President of the United States
　　The mammoth Ox, Genl Grant is presented to you today Will you pass him over to the sailors fair as a contribution.

Alex. H. Rice

Lincoln replied as follows on the same day (CW, VIII: 96):

Executive Mansion,
Washington, Nov. 8, 1864.

Hon A. H. Rice
Boston, Mass
　　Yours received. I have no other notice that the ox is mine. If it be really so I present it to the Sailors Fair, as a contribution.

A. Lincoln

The animal was sold as proposed, and several weeks later Lincoln heard again from Alexander H. Rice.

[T E L E G R A P H]

Boston Nov 22, 1864.

My Dear Sir,
　　I have the pleasure of informing you that the Mammoth Ox, General Grant, which was presented to you on the 8th of the present month, by Carlos Pierce, Esq, of this City, and by you donated to the National Sailor's Fair on the ninth inst. has yielded upwards of three

thousand two hundred dollars to its treasury and that sum is held as your Contribution to this most just and patriotic object.

The Fair will close this evening, and its avails will be not far from Two Hundred Thousand Dollars.

I am, Dear Sir, With great respect

> Yours Very Truly
> Alex. H. Rice

To Abraham Lincoln, President of the United States

A Tree in Lincoln's Honor

West Point Nov. 8th 1864

My Dear Sir, The enclosed lines [an article from the New York *Commercial Advertiser* on "General Scott's Tree," planted in the old general's honor at West Point] suggested to me the idea of having a tree here, known as President Lincoln's tree. This morning therefore, at 8 o'clock, with the aid of my youngest daughter and son, I planted a tree in my garden, close to the flag-staff of my children, where they run up the Nation's flag on all occasions of National rejoicing.

My son threw in a few shovels of earth, my little girl ran up the flag, just over the tree, whilst I named it President Lincoln's Union Tree.

The tree is about the same age as your Administration, having come up from a seed in 1861. It comes of one of two trees raised by my predecessor, from two seeds, given him, by Old President Knote of Union College, some forty or more years ago.

It is a Gleditsia Triancanthos, or Honey-pad tree, as we called it in Virginia in my childhood. I selected it as emblematic, from its three pronged thorns, of having been a triple thorn yourself, in the side of the rebels, in that of their sympathizers at home, and in that of their supporters supporters [*sic*] abroad. It will long flourish after our heads are laid low and those of the children who assisted at its inauguration. It too must pass away; but, for our Union with its Institutions may a kind Providence inscribe on its temple, Esto Perpetua.

In closing, let me add, that my hopes and prayers are for you, as the representative of the principles under which our Republic alone can live. Whatever the result of this day [the letter was penned on election day] may be, it can change in nothing the confidence in the honesty of purpose and integrity of character, impressed upon me at our first interview and ever held to by me since.

Very Respectfully & Truly,
My Dear Sir, Yours
D. H. Mahan

Dennis H. Mahan was a professor of civil and military engineering at West Point. There is no record that this gesture was ever acknowledged; Lincoln's secretary merely filed it away under the heading "personal."

Thanksgiving Turkeys

Providence, R.I. Nov 21st 1864

Sir   I have taken the liberty of forwarding to you by Adams Ex. Co. two R.I. Turkeys for your Thanksgiving Dinner. They are "Narragansett" Turkeys celebrated in the New England and New York markets as being the best in the world.

Congratulating you upon the recent Election I am

Your obt. Svt
Walter C. Simmons

A. Lincoln President of the United States
Washington D.C.

Simmons was the son of a Rhode Island Senator. His letter was filed as having been acknowledged on November 29, but no copy of the response has surfaced.

For Christmas 1864: A Captured Rebel City

[T E L E G R A P H]

Savannah Ga Dec 22./1864
Via Ft. Monroe Va Dec 25.

His Excellency Prest. Lincoln.

I beg to present you as a Christmas gift the City of Savannah with 150 heavy guns & plenty of ammunition & also about 25.000 bales of cotton.

W. T. Sherman
Major Genl.

∽ *Lincoln replied to this famous letter the day after Christmas (CW, VIII: 181–182).*

Executive Mansion,
Washington, Dec. 26, 1864.

My dear General Sherman.

Many, many, thanks for your Christmas-gift—the capture of Savannah.

When you were about leaving Atlanta for the Atlantic coast, I was anxious, if not fearful; but feeling that you were the better judge, and remembering that "nothing risked, nothing gained" I did not interfere. Now, the undertaking being a success, the honor is all yours; for I believe none of us went farther than to acquiesce. And taking the work of Gen. [George H.] Thomas [a reference to recent Union successes in the Franklin and Nashville campaigns] into the count, as it should be taken, it is indeed a great success. Not only does it afford the obvious and immediate military advantages; but, in showing to the world that your army could be divided, putting the stronger part to an important new service, and yet leaving enough to vanquish the old opposing force of the whole—[Confederate General John Bell] Hood's army—it brings those who sat in darkness, to see a great light. But what next? I suppose it will be safer if I leave Gen. Grant and yourself to decide.

Please make my grateful acknowledgements to your whole army, officers and men.

Yours very truly
A. Lincoln.

∽ *When he received Lincoln's letter, Sherman wrote once again.*

In the Field, Savannah Jan 6 1865

To his Excellency
President Lincoln
Washington,

Dear Sir, I am gratified at the receipt of your letter of Dec 26, at the hands of General [John A.] Logan. Especially to observe that you appreciate the division I made of my army, and that each part was duly proportioned to its work. The motto, "Nothing ventured Nothing won" which you refer to is most appropriate, and should I venture too much and happen to lose I shall bespeak your charitable influence. I am ready for the Great Next as soon as I can complete certain preliminaries, and learn of Genl Grant his and your preferences of intermediate "objectives." With great respect

> Your servant
> W. T. Sherman
> Maj Genl.

An Honorary Degree from Princeton

> State Executive Committee Rooms,
> Trenton, N.J., Dec 23 1864

To His Excellency
The President—

My dear Sir: Permit me to congratulate you on the honor conferred upon you by our Board of Trustees on Tuesday last, Viz—that of the Honorary Degree of Doctor of Laws.

You have "doctored" so many old laws to make them better, and have had passed, so many good ones that it was a proper appreciation of your labors to have made you an L.L.D.

The best wish I can make is that the future will equal the past, and that you may continue to give leaden pills to the Rebels, and political ipecac to their sympathizers of the North while our house shall have been completely purged of them.

> Your old Friend & Obt. Svt
> J. R. Freese

∽ *Lincoln did not reply to this message from his old Illinois acquaintance, later a newspaper editor in New Jersey, whom Lincoln had only two months earlier named Commissioner of the Board of Enrollment for the state's second district. Lincoln made the appointment, he explained, because Freese was "wounded with me now, that I do not recognize him as he thinks I ought" (CW, VIII: 12, 25).*

An Album of Lithographs

> L. Prang & Co.
> Boston Dec. 24th 1864.

Abraham Lincoln,
President of the United States

Your Excellency, I do not want to bore you with a long letter expressing my high regard, my admiration, etc. etc. thinking that these feelings have become of late so very general as to be almost a matter of course.—I will therefore merely say that I thought, you might sometimes, in an hour of relaxation from your high duties, be pleased to see for yourself what we here down east are doing in the Arts of peace to entertain the people and at the same time to instruct and educate them; I beg leave to present to you an Album with specimens of my own publications, the acceptance of which would give me great satisfaction.

I am fully conscious that what I have to send are mere trifles compared to the great achievements all around us, and they might perhaps on that account be scarcely worthy [of] your attention, however as the commencement of a comparatively new industry in this Country, as Pioneers in a great field to be cultivated they will claim some regard.

I wish you a happy Christmas, health and success in your great labors for the benefit of my adopted Country and respectfully sign

Louis Prang

∽ *Neither Prang's album nor Lincoln's almost certain acknowledgment has survived, but it is likely that Boston's best-known printmaker sent a sample of his diverse work: portraits, war scenes, and what he called "beautiful art bits": album cards showing birds, butterflies, flowers, and autumn leaves. It is appropriate that the lithographer sent Lincoln one of the few holiday gifts received at the White House during the Civil War—for it was Prang who went on to invent the Christmas card (Marzio,* The Democratic Art, *98).*

Oranges from Louisiana

City of New York
December 28th 1864.

To His Excellency Abraham Lincoln
Washington, D.C.

Sir: I have the honor to enclose herewith, a receipt from the "Adams Express Company" for one box of Louisiana Oranges this day forwarded to your address.

These oranges were gathered from my own trees, and I hope they will reach you safely and in good condition.

I shall leave for Washington on tomorrow, and will have the honor to pay my respect to you in person. I am, Sir, with the highest respect

> Your obed. servt.
> John Touro

∽ *No reply has surfaced, nor is it known whether Touro's oranges were sufficient to gain him entry when he visited the White House. The year before, Touro had filed a claim with Lincoln for supplies seized by the Union army in Louisiana (*CW, VII: *492).*

A Cane of Many Sections

Cincinnati Dec 30th 1864

Hon Abraham Lincoln

Dear Sir My father being a Soldier of the Revolution and I having some knowledge of the War of Eighteen Hundred and Twelve, being Seventy five years Old on the above Date. I have been Led to Fix a value upon the union, Liberty and Independence of the States above all other Matters of an Earthly nature. Have twice voted for your Honor for the Chief Magistrate. Believeing that you are the Man, That God has Raised up and Appointed As Our Leader in the Putting Down the Greatest and Wickedest Rebellion that has ever Taken place in the World. And the Restoration to peace, Liberty, and union of All the Sections. From East to West North and South—

I have Made and Desire to present to you a Cane in some Measure Emblematical of What I hope Our Nation Will be before your Second term Expires. Being Composed of as Maney Sections and Pieces as there Ware States, and of a verry Beautifull Curled White Oak Not of the kind that Could be Split into Railes with Mall and wedge conveniently.—

The Sections are not Bound together by a Rope of Sand, But With a Rod of Iron—

Hoping you May Live to see Maney Happy Days after the Reunion is Established

> I am yours verry Truly
> Geo. C. Miller

∽ *Lincoln replied to Mr. Miller several weeks later (CW, VIII: 222).*

Executive Mansion,
Washington, January 18, 1865

My Dear Sir—Please accept my cordial thanks for the cane you were so kind as to send me, and the letter by which it was accompanied.

Yours truly,
A. Lincoln

George C. Miller, Esq.

New Socks from a Very Old Admirer

[January 7, 1865]

To My Much Esteemed President
Abraham Lincoln
    Dear Sir   Please allow an auld Lady of ninety one years of age to present to you a very humble testimony of esteem & confidence in the shape of a pair of socks knit with my own hands & allow me to say that I remember the trials passed through in revolution days. I lost two Brothers out of three that was in the servis of the country, besides Uncles & a number of cousins & my prayer to Him that doethe all things well, that holds the this [*sic*] nation in the hollow of his hand & hath continued my life to this time, & has enabled me to work almost dailey from the commencement of this rebellion to the present hour for the soldiers (God bless them) that you might be richly indowed with that wisdom which you have so much knowledg to enable you to beare so greate responsibilities & to do that that is for the good of our bleeding Country & I <u>do</u> pray that you may live to see this rebellion ended & with it slavery (which I <u>do</u> abominate) wiped from our land, & long there after to witness & enjoy the fruits of your labour—you will pardon this intrusion upon your time & believe me to be your friend & friend of my bleeding country;

Sarah Phelps

Groton, N.H. Jan 7. 1865.

ᔕ *Although one cannot imagine that Lincoln would have ignored the sentiments or the age of the writer, no acknowledgment of this gift has been located.*

An Unacknowledged Painting

Boston, Jan. 21, 1865.

To Abraham Lincoln,
President of the United States:

Sir—About the first of July, last year, what was deemed by critics and connisseurs [*sic*], artistically speaking, an admirable painting [see illustration, page 37], was sent by Adams's Express to your address at Washington; accompanied by a letter from me in behalf of the donors, whose contributions to the object in view amounted to upwards of five hundred dollars. This meritorious picture, executed by a most conscientious and excellent artist, was entitled "Watch Night—or, Waiting for the Hour." It represented a group of negro men, women and children waiting with heartfelt emotion and thrilling delight for the midnight hour of December 31, 1862, to pass, and the introduction of that new year which was to make them free. Many photographic copies were made of it, and it was by my advice that it was presented to you as the most fitting person in the world to receive it. Among those who subscribed to send it to you were Governor [John] Andrew [of Massachusetts] and a number of our most prominent citizens.

For some cause or other, no acknowledgement has been made, or at least received, of the receipt of the picture, or of my letter, which contained the names of the donors. As my friend Mr. Sumner assured me, on his return from Washington last summer, that he had seen the picture again and again at the White House, all anxiety has been relieved as to its safe arrival, and we are happy to know it is in your possession. But as the money raised to purchase it was collected by ladies who desire that the donors may be officially apprised of its legitimate application, I write in their behalf to say that it would relieve them of much embarrassment if you would be so obliging, either under your own signature or by the hand of one of your secretaries, as to send me a line, stating that the painting aforesaid was duly received by you.

I shall ever remember, with deep satisfaction, the private interview you were so kind as to accord to Mr. Tilton and myself, last June. Having full faith in your integrity of purpose, and inflexible determination to stand by every word and syllable enunciated by you in your emancipation proclamation, come what may, I have frequently had occasion, both in my editorial capacity and as a lecturer, to defend you against many sweeping accusations that have been brought against you, sometimes even on the anti-slavery platform. God be with you to the end, to strengthen, enlighten, inspire your mind and heart, and render your administration illustrious to all coming ages! God grant that it may be your enviable privilege to announce, ere long, that, by an amendment of the Constitution, slavery is forever abolished in the United States!

It is not my wish or purpose to meddle with any of your appointments; but you will pardon me if I respectfully suggest that, in any reconstruction of your Cabinet, New England, for her intelligence, wealth, enterprise, her mechanical, manufacturing and commercial power—her glowing and unswerving loyalty—is worthy to be represented in it. And as Mr. [William P.] Fessenden is soon to vacate the situation he holds as Secretary of the Treasury, I believe if Gov. Andrew, of this State, should be appointed his successor, he would bring to the place whatever of ability, industry, integrity, vigilance and efficiency it so imperatively requires. He is truly "a host in himself."

Yours, to break every yoke
Wm. Lloyd Garrision

෨ *Lincoln finally replied to the entreaty from the famous abolitionist on February 7, with the following letter written in John Hay's hand. Mary Lincoln apparently took the painting with her when she left the White House after her husband's assassination, but a copy by artist William Tolman Carlton was returned to the White House collection during the 1970s* (CW, VIII: 265–266; Kloss, Art in the White House, *152).*

Executive Mansion, Washington,
7 February, 1865.

My Dear Mr. Garrison

I have your kind letter of the 21st of January, and can only beg that you will pardon the seeming neglect occasioned by my constant engagements. When I received the spirited and admirable painting "Waiting for the Hour" I directed my Secretary not to acknowledge its arrival at once, preferring to make my personal acknowledgment of the thoughtful kindness of the donors; and waiting for some leisure hour, I have committed the discourtesy of not replying at all.

I hope you will believe that my thanks though late, are most cordial, and I request that you will convey them to those associated with you in this flattering and generous gift.

I am very truly

Your friend and Servant
A. Lincoln.

Wm. Lloyd Garrison Esq

A "Vetren" Sends his Stripes

Harrison landin[g] Virginy
March third 1865

mister ole Abe:

herbi Plese find inclosed won (1) Pare of reeinlistment Stripes I am a vetren which hev Bin warin sed Stripes. thinkin that as how U had reeinlisted i thot i wood Cut em Off & Send em to U hopin they ma cum handy. they Cost Forty (40) Sents i wood send U A pare with gold Stuf On the Ege of em if I cood git em them wons Costs A good Ele more tho. hev em Sode on with Blu thred

my Resins For Sendin em is these Firstly U Air my Stile of A man & Besides is Onist. Seconly U Air intitled to Sed Stripes For inlistin Again & things is verry hi now. I mus put Out my lite in a fu minuts. dont let up on them jonnys A darn bit ile stan Bi U til the darn Cuses is used up for won.

how is misis linkin now. i hope well Al the Rest of the Boys is well. Plese Rite direct to me, my name is

mr. william johnson
Co k 184th N.Y.V.
Harrisons landing Va.

P.s. ile git the Captin to direk this to U For i hent A verry good riter

Respeckfuly Ures truly
mr w.j.

(P.s. 2th) i Rote this On A hull Sheat Becos the Captin says it is Bisness Stile & this is Bisiness.

mr. w.j.

∽ There is no record of a reply.

A College Named in his Honor

Lincoln Ills. March 4th 1865

His Excellency A Lincoln
President of the United States

Dear Sir   By request of the president of the board of trustees of Lincoln University, whose address this will accompany I write to inform you more fully of the University and of the prosperity of this town, believing you feel a lively interest in it, on account of its being named for you before Presidential honors had any influence. Lincoln contains about twenty eight hundred inhabitants. Houses are going up almost daily, and it is expected that there will be from one to two hundred dwelling houses go up this season, mostly of a good quality, business has increased fully in proportion to the inhabitants. Our people although not very wealthy, are very enterprising, and are very anxious in fact determined to make the university a success. Messrs. Wyatt Gilett & I donated ten acres of land, that we were offered six thousand dollars for, and three thousand dollars in cash to it, several other persons one thousand each, and nearly all the citizens something. The friends of the town propose to build one wing of the building, and the church propose to endow it with $20000.00 as soon as $100,000.00 endowment fund is raised they to go on and finish the buildings. The school to commence as soon as this wing of the building is completed and $50,000.00 endowment fund is raised.

Our greatest difficulty will be to get sufficient funds to build a house that will do justice to the name and the place.

Hoping that we will have the pleasure of seeing you in our beloved Illinois ere the summer passes,

I am Very Respectfully

Your Obedient Servant
R B Latham

∽ Lincoln did not reply to this letter personally (it arrived only a few weeks before his death), but it brought him the news that the first college to be named in his honor was to be opened in the first town in the nation to carry his name. According to tradition, Lincoln had been present to personally christen the village of Lincoln, Illinois on August 29, 1853, by breaking open a pair of watermelons in the public square. Lincoln University—now Lincoln College—still operates there (LDBD II: 104).

This letter appears on page 250.

[7]
Official Business:
War, Race, and Politics

*T*HROUGHOUT THE war years, Abraham Lincoln was bombarded by friendly fire—and sometimes not-so-friendly fire as well—from armchair generals and home-front tacticians who were certain that by simply following their elaborate plans and recommendations, the President could successfully end the fighting, restore the Union, and settle the slavery question forever.

"There is . . . a throng of writers," White House secretary William O. Stoddard jeered, "who are ready to offer advice and even instruction upon the management of the war. It is marvelous," he added derisively, "how they can, theoretically, swing troops back and forth across the country. It is plain that they have all played the game of checkers, and have learned how to 'jump' the Confederate forces and forts with their men."

Lincoln's mailbag overflowed with such advice—yet, judging by the endorsements the surviving copies bear, the evidence is that the President was not always quite as skeptical about entertaining unsolicited policy suggestions as were his clerks. Letters from "official" military sources arrived routinely as well: not only from the generals reporting from campsites and battlefields, but from lower-rank officers begging to lay their own views and strategies before the Commander-in-Chief. Mail came, too, from both would-be spies and genuine prisoners of war, and once, even, from a group of frontier women convinced that they could do quite as well in uniform as their male counterparts.

Such was the "official" portion of Lincoln's White House correspondence—at least as we have categorized it here. It embraces war news, government business, political developments, and the evolution of race policy—in sum, the surviving record of the delicate balancing act Lincoln performed from 1861 to 1865 in order to harmonize his military, civil, and political prerogatives alike.

Of necessity, far more has been excluded from this chapter than could possibly be included: these crucial issues were, by far, the subjects most frequently addressed by correspondents during the Lincoln administration. But even a representative sampling suggests the overwhelming burdens and challenges confronting Lincoln every day of his beleaguered presidency.

From his own secretary of state, for example, came an early, presumptuous memorandum containing recommendations on how precisely to conduct policy—recommendations that were promptly rebuffed. From politicians throughout the country came advice on the draft, border state policy, recruitment of black soldiers, and the hiring and firing of generals. From both allies and enemies came suggestions on important appointments and prospects for future elections. And from whites and blacks alike came evocative thoughts on the future of former slaves in a rapidly changing America. Letters came not just from home but from overseas as well. So many came from France that the White House secretaries began taking French lessons from a "Professor Marix, a Russian Jew whose pronunciation had the St. Petersburg improvement on the Parisian dialect." The clerks understandably abandoned the lessons not long after beginning.

The inflammatory race question, predictably, aroused the public even more passionately than did the rebellion itself. Many examples of letters on this topic can be found elsewhere in this book, within chapters presenting either compliments or criticism. Included here are letters that address matters of policy—from figures as important as the great leader Frederick Douglass, who offered a plan to preserve the government's emancipation policy should the Democrats take back the White House in 1864; and as unknown as the ordinary "colored" soldier who wrote to make an eloquent plea for equal pay for blacks serving in the military.

As for whites who wrote to Lincoln to offer their views on the announcement of the Emancipation Proclamation in 1862, "they tell him," clerk Stoddard reported, "that his edict, his ukase, his decree, his firman, his venemous blow at the sacred liberty of white men to own black men is mere *brutum fulmen* . . . a dead letter and a poison that will not work. They tell him . . . that the army will fight no more, and that the hosts of the Union will indignantly disband rather than be sacrificed upon the bloody altar of fanatical Abolitionism." Clearly, the tidal wave of public opinion seriously worried the President: he would admit so in a frank, private letter to his vice president.

The Lincoln mailbag might have bulged even more copiously with official correspondence of the military kind but for the eventual imposition of a reporting system that discouraged military officers, even generals, from corresponding directly with the President. "The sack that Louis [Bargdorf] brings from the post-office," as Stoddard put it, "is not so large as it would have to be but for the fact that no subordinate military or naval officer communicates directly with the commander-in-chief. . . . [T]he men who make the movements do not report to him, and he does not meddle with the details of their work." Not that the President did not seek out the ciphered telegraphs that poured into the War Department. Lincoln spent a good deal of time, particularly late at night, reading the dispatches that arrived over the wire there. Thus, few such messages are included here, although many of the reports were evidently forwarded or taken back to the White House and there retained in the presidential files, even though many had been originally addressed to General-in-Chief Henry Halleck, or Secretary of War Edwin M. Stanton.

But there was no shortage of direct military advice from the civilian side. "This morning in the President's mail I came across some warlike documents," John Hay remarked early in Lincoln's first term. The President's mail would continue to bring such missives—in the thousands—throughout the next four years. "There is no end," Stoddard would comment, "to the suggestions of plans of campaigns and of proposed improvements in management." Unlike the compliments, complaints, and pleas that are presented elsewhere in this volume, these letters were designed to alert, inform, and arouse to action a president compelled as no president before him to juggle concurrent, potentially conflicting responsibilities as party leader, commander-in-chief, and precedent-shattering chief magistrate. Undoubtedly, inform and arouse him they did.

And occasionally, they elicited, too, one of the President's ingeniously crafted statements of policy or philosophy that has endured among Lincoln's finest works. For as William O. Stoddard remembered, many of "the few letters" Lincoln did write "were almost as if they had been addressed to the nation, rather than to individuals."

Some of the finest among them can be found on the pages that follow, as well as elsewhere in this book.

On How To Run the Government

Some thoughts for the President's consideration

April 1. 1861.

1st. We are at the end of a month's administration and yet without a policy either domestic or foreign.

2d This, however, is not culpable, and it has been unavoidable. The presence of the Senate, with the need to meet applications for patronage have prevented attention to other and more grave matters.

3d. But further delay to adopt and prosecute our policies for both domestic and foreign affairs would not only bring scandal on the Administration, but danger upon the country.

4th. To do this we must dismiss the applicants for office. But how? I suggest that we make the local appointments forthwith, leaving foreign or general ones for ulterior and occasional action.

5th. The policy—at home. I am aware that my views are singular, and perhaps not sufficiently explained. My system is built upon this idea as a ruling one, namely that we must

Change the question before the Public from one upon Slavery, or about slavery

for a question upon Union or Disunion.

In other words, from what would be regarded as a Party question to one of Patriotism or Union

The occupation or evacuation of Fort Sumter, although not in fact a slavery, or a party question is so regarded. Witness, the temper manifested by the Republicans in the Free States, and even by Union men in the South.

I would therefore terminate it as a safe means for changing the issue. I deem it fortunate that the last Administration created the necessity.

For the rest. I would simultaneously defend and reinforce all the Forts in the Gulf, and have the Navy recalled from foreign stations to be prepared for a blockade. Put the Island of Key West under Martial Law

This will raise distinctly the question of Union or Disunion. I would maintain every fort and possession in the South.

For Foreign Nations.

I would demand explanations from Spain and France, categorically, at once.

I would seek explanations from Great Britain and Russia, and send agents into Canada, Mexico and Central America, to rouse a vigorous continental spirit of independence on this continent against European intervention.

And if satisfactory explanations are not received from Spain and France,

Would convene Congress and declare war against them

But whatever policy we adopt, there must be energetic prosecution of it.

For this purpose it must be somebody's business to pursue and direct it incessantly.

Either the President must do it himself, and be all the while active in it; or

Devolve it on some member of his Cabinet. Once adopted, debates on it must end, and all agree and abide.

It is not in my especial province.

But I neither seek to evade nor assume responsibility.

William H. Seward

๛ Many historians have labelled this extraordinary memorandum as an attempt by the secretary of state to appoint himself America's prime minister. But if Seward harbored any illusions that Lincoln was too weak to run the government as it faced the secession crisis, the President's deft reply surely convinced him otherwise. Their exchange is among the most famous—and important—of Lincoln's presidency (CW, IV: 316–317).

Executive Mansion April 1, 1861

Hon: W. H. Seward:

My dear Sir: Since parting with you I have been considering your paper dated this day, and entitled "Some thoughts for the President's consideration." The first proposition in it is, "1st. We are at the end of a month's administration, and yet without a policy, either domestic or foreign."

At the beginning of that month, in the inaugeral [sic], I said "The power confided to me will be used to hold, occupy and possess the property and places belonging to the government, and to collect the duties, and imposts." This had your distinct approval at the time; and, taken in connection with the order I immediately gave General [Winfield] Scott [the aged Mexican War hero still in command of

Union forces at the time], directing him to employ every means in his power to strengthen and hold the forts, comprises the exact domestic policy you now urge, with the single exception, that it does not propose to abandon Fort Sumpter.

Again, I do not perceive how the re-inforcement of Fort Sumpter would be done on a slavery, or party issue, while that of Fort Pickens would be on a more national, and patriotic one.

The news received yesterday in regard to St. Domingo, certainly brings a new item within the range of our foreign policy [a Spanish warship had been dispatched on March 16 from Cuba to help Spanish colonists on San Domingo to annex that country]; but up to that time we have been preparing circulars, and instructions to ministers, and the like, all in perfect harmony, without even a suggestion that we had no foreign policy.

Upon your closing propositions, that "whatever policy we adopt, there must be an energetic prosecution of it"

"For this purpose it must be somebody's business to pursue and direct it incessantly"

"Either the President must do it himself, and be all the while active on it, or"

"Devolve it on some member of his cabinet"

"Once adopted, debates on it must end, and all agree and abide"
I remark that if this must be done, I must do it. When a general line of policy is adopted, I apprehend there is no danger of its being changed without good reason, or continuing to be a subject of unnecessary debate; still, upon points arising in its progress, I wish, and suppose I am entitled to have the advice of all the cabinet.

> Your Obt. Servt.
> A. Lincoln

Offering "Colored" Volunteers

New York, April 8th 1861.

Hon. Abraham Lincoln:—
Presd't U.S:—

Dear Sir:—In the present crisis, and distracted state of the country, if your Honor wishes colored volunteers, you have only to signify by answering the above note at 70 E. 13 St. N.Y.C., with instructions,

and the above will meet with prompt attention, whenever your honor
wishes them.

>Your very Obedient and
>Humble Servant.
>Levin Tilman.

∽ *No reply is known. The Lincoln administration did not begin recruiting blacks*
for the military for another two years.

The War Begins

[*T E L E G R A P H*]
Savannah Apl 13th 1861.

Mr A Lincoln
Fort Sumter has surrendered there is nobody hurt.

>W. H. Denslow

∽ *With this news—also received from official military sources—Lincoln learned*
that, for all intents and purposes, the Civil War had begun.

A Detective Offers Help

C O N F I D E N T I A L
Chicago April 21st 1861

To His Excellense A Lincoln
Prest of the U-S
Dear Sir   When I saw you last I said that if the time should ever
come that I could be of service to you I was ready—If that time has
come I am on hand—

I have in my Force from Sixteen to Eighteen persons on whose
courage, Skill & Devotion to their Country I can rely. If they with
myself at the head can be of service in the way of obtaining information of the movements of the Traitors, or Safely conveying your letters
or dispatches, or that class of Secret Service which is the most dangerous, I am at your command—

In the present disturbed state of Affairs I dare not trust this to the
mail—so send by one of My Force who was with me at Baltimore

[where the writer helped arrange the President-elect's safe passage through the city en route to Washington]—You may safely trust him with Any Message for me—Written or Verbal—I fully guarantee his fidelity—He will act as you direct—and return here with your answer

Secrecy is the great lever I propose to operate with—Hence the necessity of this movement (If you contemplate it) being kept <u>Strictly Private</u>—and that should you desire another interview with the Bearer that you should so arrange it—as that he will not be noticed—

The Bearer will hand you A Copy of A Telegraph Cipher which you may use if you desire to Telegraph me—

My force comprises both Sexes—All of Good Character—And well Skilled in their Business—

Respectfully yours
Allan Pinkerton

Lincoln evidently encouraged Pinkerton, for on May 2 the President sent this note to Secretary of State Seward: "Our Chicago detective has arrived; and I have promised to have you meet him and me here at 8. o'clock this evening." Pinkerton was subsequently attached to General McClellan's army, where his inflated estimates of enemy strength contributed to that commander's chronic reluctance to commit his troops to battle (CW, IV: 353).

Warnings from the Governor of Maryland

Executive Chamber
Annapolis, April 22nd 1861

To His Excellency, A. Lincoln.
President of the United States

Sir, I feel it my duty most respectfully to advise that no more troops be ordered or allowed to pass through Maryland and that the troops now off Annapolis be sent elsewhere, and I most respectfully urge that a truce be offered by you so that the effusion of blood may be prevented. I respectfully suggest that Lord Lyons [the British ambassador] be requested to act as mediator between the contending parties of our Country.

I have the honor to be

Very Respectfully
Your obt. Servant
Tho. H. Hicks

∾ *Three days before Governor Hicks wrote to Lincoln, a mob of pro-secessionist Marylanders had attacked Massachusetts soldiers marching through Baltimore, igniting riots in that city. But Lincoln angrily told a group of Baltimore citizens who came to the White House, "Our men are not moles, and can't dig under the earth; they are not birds, and can't fly through the air. There is no way but to march across, and that they must do." Lincoln directed Secretary of State Seward to tell the Maryland governor that the national highway through his state would continue to be used to move Union troops south, and to reject firmly the notion that a "domestic contention" could be "referred to any foreign arbitrament" (CW, IV: 341–342).*

A Union Man Worries

NY May 2d 1861.

To Abraham Lincoln,
President of the United States, Washington

For Gods sake, dont put your trust in the Union men of Maryland. As soon as it will be safe for them to rush to the standard of Jeff. Davis they will do so.

Oliver Dyer

∾ *No reply is known. Maryland teetered on the brink of disunion, but in the end did not secede. Lincoln administration restrictions on the civil liberties of state legislators attempting to convene there may have helped keep Maryland in the Union (Neely, The Fate of Liberty, 29–30).*

Death of his Lifelong Rival

[T E L E G R A P H]

Chicago June 3d. 1861

To President of U. S.
Hon Stephen A. Douglas is dead

R. T. Merrick

∾ *Richard Thomas Merrick was a Chicago Democrat and supporter of Douglas, Lincoln's archrival in politics and opponent for the presidency in 1860. Lincoln ordered the White House draped in black in honor of his lifelong foe (LDBD III: 46).*

Martyrdom of a Protégé

Mechanic[s]ville [N.Y.]
June 19th 1861

Mr Lincoln

Dear Sir   Pardon us the long delay in answering your kind and sympathizing letter. It has not occurred through want of inclination to write, but from the many calls made upon our time. The fact that Elmer succeeded in gaining the love & esteem of those with whom he was associated is to us one of great joy, and the reception of a letter, expressing such sentiments, from one whom we all so much respect is highly gratifying.

It would be useless for us to describe our feelings upon the receipt of the sad news of Elmers death. Although the blow was severe, however severe God only knows, yet through his goodness & mercy we are enabled to say "thy will not ours be done." The sympathy of all true Christians, and lovers of, that Country in whose defence he perished has done much to assuage the intensity of our grief. We sincerely believe that God has removed him from a life of strife to one of eternal peace.

He was indeed toward us all you represented him, kind loving & dutiful. Our present comfort and future happiness always seemed uppermost in his mind. But he is gone and the recollection of his goodness alone is left us. We trust he did not die in vain, but that his death will advance the cause in which he was engaged.

With these few words accept our most grateful thanks for your kindness to and interest you have always shown in our beloved son [.] May it never repent you.

We would always be pleased to hear from you.

We are with respect

Yours &c
E. D. Ellsworth

∽ *Ephraim D. Ellsworth was the father of Ephraim Elmer Ellsworth, a young Lincoln family friend who had recently become a colonel in the flamboyant Zouaves. Ellsworth was killed in Alexandria, Virginia, after ripping down a Confederate flag from a local hotel. He was instantly lionized as the first Union casualty of the War. Lincoln gave him a White House funeral and then sent his parents the following condolence letter, which inspired the above response (CW, IV: 385–386).*

Washington D.C.
May 25. 1861

To the Father and Mother of
Col. Elmer E. Ellsworth
My dear Sir and Madam, In the untimely loss of your noble son, our affliction here, is scarcely less than your own. So much of promised usefulness to one's country, and of bright hopes for one's self and friends, have rarely been so suddenly dashed, as in his fall. In size, in years, and in youthful appearance, a boy only, his power to command men, was surpassingly great. This power, combined with a fine intellect, an indomitable energy, and a taste altogether military, constituted in him, as seemed to me, the best natural talent, in that department, I ever knew. And yet he was singularly modest and deferential in social intercourse. My acquaintance with him began less than two years ago; yet through the latter half of the intervening period, it was as intimate as the disparity of our ages, and my engrossing engagements, would permit. To me, he appeared to have no indulgences or pastimes; and I never heard him utter a profane, or an intemperate word. What was conclusive of his good heart, he never forgot his parents. The honors he labored for so laudably, and, in the sad end, so gallantly gave his life, he meant for them, no less than for himself.

In the hope that it may be no intrusion upon the sacredness of your sorrow, I have ventured to address you this tribute to the memory of my young friend, and your brave and early fallen child.

May God give you that consolation which is beyond all earthly power. Sincerely your friend in a common affliction—

A. Lincoln

From His Confederate Counterpart
Richmond 6th July 1861

To Abraham Lincoln
President and Commander in Chief of the Army and
Navy of the United States
Sir Having learned that the Schooner Savannah, a private armed vessel in the service, and sailing under a commission issued by authority of the Confederate States of America, had been captured by one of the vessels forming the blockading squadron off Charleston Harbor, I directed a proposition to be made to the officer commanding that squadron for an exchange of the officers and crew of the Savannah for

prisoners of war held by this government "according to number and rank." To this proposition made on the 19th ulto, Captain Mercier the officer in command of the blockading squadron made answer on the same day that "the prisoners" (referred to) are not "on board of any of the vessels under my command—"

It now appears by statements made without contradiction in newspapers published in New York that the prisoners above mentioned were conveyed to that city, and have there been treated, not as prisoners of war, but as criminals: that they have been put in irons, confined in jail, brought before the courts of justice on charges of piracy and treason and it is even rumored that they have been actually convicted of the offences charged, for no other reason than that they bore arms in defence of the rights of this government and under the authority of its commission.

I could not without grave discourtesy have made the newspaper statements above referred to, the charge of this communication, if the threat of treating as pirates the citizens of the Confederacy armed for its service on the high seas had not been contained in your proclamation of April last—That proclamation however seems to afford a sufficient justification for considering these published statements as not devoid of probability—

It is the desire of this government so to conduct the war now existing, as to mitigate its horrors as far as may be possible: and with this intent its treatment of the prisoners captured by its forces has been marked by the greatest humanity and leniency consistent with the public obligation. Some have been permitted to return home on parol [sic]: others to remain at large under similar condition within this Confederacy; and all have been furnished with rations for their subsistence, such as are allowed to our own troops. It is only since the news has been received of the treatment of the prisoners taken on the Savannah, that I have been compelled to withdraw these indulgences, and to hold the prisoners taken by us in strict confinement—

A just regard to humanity and to the honor of this government now requires me to state explicitly, that painful as will be the necessity, this government will deal out to the prisoners held by it, the same treatment and the same fate as shall be experienced by those captured on the Savannah: and if driven to the terrible necessity of retaliation by your execution of any of the officers or crew of the Savannah, that retaliation will be extended so far as shall be requisite to secure abandonment by you of a practice unknown to the warfare of civilized man, and so barbarous as to disgrace the nation which shall be guilty of inaugurating it—

With this view, and because it may not have reached you, I now renew the proposition made to the commander of the blockading squadron to exchange for the prisoners taken on the Savannah an equal number of those now held by us, according to rank.

I am Sir, &c. &c.

> Jefferson Davis
> Prest. & Commander in Chief of the Army and Navy of the Confederate States of America

℃ *Lincoln did not respond to this extraordinary threat from his Confederate counterpart. It was merely filed: "Letter/From Jeff. Davis about crew of the privateer 'Savannah' and threatening retaliation." Davis never wrote to Lincoln again.*

A Journalist Volunteers To Spy

[August 14, 1861]

Hon. Abraham Lincoln
President of the United States

Being about entering upon a tour through the South, I propose to volunteer my services in supplying General Scott with whatever information of usefulness to him I shall be able to collect during my stay in Memphis, Richmond, New Orleans & other points I propose to visit. Not being personally acquainted with the General, I would respectfully ask you for a line of introduction to him. You will doubtless remember me as a newspaper-correspondent during the campaign of '58, in the fall of '59 in Eastern Kansas, last winter in Springfield etc. etc. I do not wish to enter the employ of the government, but, as already stated, will volunteer my services. I should have been glad to communicate my plans in detail to you, but I find it impossible to gain admittance, although I have sought it daily since Monday last. The same reason compels me to take this mode of addressing you.—

> Yours respectfully
> Henry Villard

℃ *Lincoln forwarded this letter to General Scott with the following comment: "I have only a slight acquaintance with Mr. Villard, as a gentlemanly newspaper corre-*

spondent, and as such I commend him to others." Villard went on his tour as scheduled and reported on it for the New York Herald. *But he did not confide in his* Memoirs *whether or not he also transmitted secret information to the Union military command. Villard's letter indicates how difficult it was for uninvited visitors—even those known to the President—to gain access to Lincoln at the White House without enduring long lines alongside favor-seekers and office-seekers.*

Reassurances from a Famous Showman

Lindencroft Bridgeport Ct
Aug 30th 1861

To His Excellency
Abraham Lincoln Prest &c

Honored Sir The late events which have occurred in this vicinity, concluding with the arrest of <u>Schnabel</u>, have rendered secessionists <u>so scarce</u>, I cannot find one for exhibition in my museum [Barnum's American Museum was renowned for its display of "curiosities" such as Tom Thumb and the Siamese twins Chang and Eng].

Those who one week ago were blatant secessionists are to day publicly announcing themselves as "in for the country to the end of the war." The "<u>Strong arm</u>" has a mighty influence here.

Truly yours
P. T. Barnum

ᔄ *No reply to the celebrated impresario is known.*

Death of Another Old Friend

[*T E L E G R A P H*]
Oct 21 1861.
Poolesville [Maryland]

To the President

Sir I have to inform you that Gen [Edward Dickinson] Baker was killed this afternoon at 5 oclock in an engagement with the enemy near Leesburg [the Battle of Ball's Bluff]. Knowing your great friendship & esteem of Gen Baker I lose no time in apprising you of our loss. He fell while leading on his command saying pleasant &

cheering words to the men his body we have brought to Poolesville & will bring it to Washington on Wednesday.

Francis G. Henry
Actg Brig QMG

☞ *Newspaper correspondent Charles Carlton Coffin later recalled, "I doubt if any other of the many tragic events of Lincoln's life ever stunned him so much as that unheralded message, which came over the wires while he was beside the [telegraph] instrument on that fateful day." Lincoln and Baker had been political friends in Illinois in the 1840s, and Baker had succeeded Lincoln in Congress. But their relationship went beyond the political: Lincoln's second son, Edward Baker Lincoln, who died in 1850, had been named for Lincoln's friend. President and Mrs. Lincoln attended the private funeral for the general on October 24, and the following day they received Baker's father, son, and nephew at the White House. Further proof of the Lincoln family's devotion to Baker came from the hand of the President's 11-year-old son, Willie, who composed his "first attempt at poetry" in the general's honor and had the result published in the Washington* National Republican *on November 4:*

> There was no patriot like Baker,
> So noble and so true;
> He fell as a soldier on the field,
> His face to the sky of blue.

(LDBD III: 214–215; Bates, Lincoln in the Telegraph Office, *96–97; Randall,* Lincoln's Sons, *93).*

A General Feels "Disgraced"

<u>*P R I V A T E*</u>

Fort Leavenworth
December 23 1861

To His Excellency
The President:

Dear Sir: I am very deeply mortified, humiliated, insulted and disgraced. You did me the honor to select me as a Major General and I am confident you intended I should have a Major Generals command. Yet strange as it may appear I am sent here into banishment with not three thousand effective men under my command, while one of the Brigadiers, General [Don Carlos] Buell, is in command of near one hundred thousand men in Kentucky. The only sin I have committed is my carrying out your views in relation to the retrograde movement from Springfield.

General McClellan writes me as follows:

"In regard to placing General Halleck in command of the Department of Missouri, that step was taken from the evident necessity of placing some one there who was in no manner connected for or against the unfortunate state state [sic] of affairs previously existing in that Department."

He does not however inform me, why a Brigadier, in Kentucky, is placed over one hundred thousand men and your Major General is banished to Kansas with three thousand.

So it appears that I have been deprived of a command suitable to my rank, for presuming to answer to the best of my ability, official questions put to me by the Secretary of War and the Adjutant General: for in no other way was I connected with the Fremont troubles—

If I have lost the confidence you once so kindly placed in me, I bow with humble submission, but if I have not, you owe it to my honor and to my Friends in Illinois, to place me in a different position.

On my arrival in Saint Louis Judge Davis, Judge Holt, Mr. Peck and Mr. Swett [all political friends of Lincoln] assured me that I had not been injured by your consent, that a change would be made immediately, and that I must say nothing on the subject, but leave it to them. I have waited in vain.

If you thought with General McClellan, that there was a political necessity for relieving me from command in Missouri, why should I not have been sent to Kentucky, where there was one hundred thousand men to command, and not to a wilderness with three thousand.

I have the honor to be,

> Very Respectfully
> Your mo. ob. servant
> D. Hunter
> Major General

∞ An exasperated Lincoln replied to David Hunter with the following letter on New Year's eve (CW, V: 84).

Executive Mansion, Washington,
Dec. 31, 1861.

Major General Hunter.

Dear Sir: Yours of the 23rd. is received; and I am constrained to say it is difficult to answer so ugly a letter in good temper. I am, as you intimate, losing much of the great confidence I placed in you, not from any act or omission of yours touching the public service, up to the time you were sent to Leavenworth, but from the flood of grumbling despatches and letters I have seen from you since. I knew you were being ordered to Leavenworth at the time it was done; and I aver that with as tender a regard for your honor and your sensibilities as I had for my own, it never occurred to me that you were being "humiliated, insulted and disgraced"; nor have I, up to this day, heard an intimation that you have been wronged, coming from any one but yourself. No one has blamed you for the retrograde movement from Springfield, nor for the information you gave Gen. Cameron; and this you could readily understand, if it were not for your unwarranted assumption that the ordering you to Leavenworth must necessarily have been done as a <u>punishment</u> for some <u>fault</u>. I thought then, and think yet, the position assigned to you is as resposible [*sic*], and as honorable, as that assigned to Buell. I know that Gen. McClellan expected more important results from it. My impression is that at the time you were assigned to the new Western Department, it had not been determined to re-place Gen. Sherman in Kentucky; but of this I am not certain, because the idea that a command in Kentucky was very desireable, and one in the farther West, very undesireable, had never occurred to me. You constantly speak of being placed in command of only 3000. Now tell me, is not this mere impatience? Have you not known all the while that you are to command four or five times that many?

I have been, and am sincerely your friend; and if, as such, I dare to make a suggestion, I would say you are adopting the best possible way to ruin yourself. "Act well your part, there all the honor lies." He who does <u>something</u> at the head of one Regiment, will eclipse him who does <u>nothing</u> at the head of a hundred.

Your friend as ever,
A. Lincoln

Recommending a General

[T E L E G R A P H]

Springfield, April 9, 1862.

A. Lincoln President,

We appeal to you to transfer Maj Genl John Pope to the regular army with his present rank as a token of gratitude to Illinois. Give one of her sons a position in the U.S. army who has so gloriously achieved the just reward we ask for him.

> Richard Yates Govr
> Wm Butler Treasr

∽ *Lincoln replied to Governor Yates and State Treasurer Butler, both old friends, as follows* (CW, *V: 186*).

Hon. R. Yates, & Wm. Butler   Washington,
Springfield, Ills.   April 10. 1862
I fully appreciate Gen. Pope's splendid achievements with their invaluable results; but you must know that Major Generalships in the Regular Army, are not as plenty as blackberries.

> A. Lincoln

A Plan To Reinforce the Army

Chesapeake Bay, July 6th 1862.

Mr. President.

After having been for three months in the rear of the army of the Potomac, superintending the business with it of the Sanitary Commission, I have just spent a day in Washington, where I had the honor of conversing with several gentlemen who are your advisers, or in your confidence. What I learned of the calculations, views and feelings prevailing among them, causes with me great apprehension.

In the general gloom, there are two points of consolation and hope, which grow brighter and brighter—opening my eyes suddenly, as I seem to have done, in the point of view of Washington, I may see these and their value, more clearly than those about you. One, is the trustworthy, patriotic devotion of the solid, industrious, home-keeping people of the country; the other, the love and confidence constantly growing stronger between these people and their president.

Here is the key to a vast reserved strength, and in this rests our last hope for our country.

Appeal personally to the people, Mr. President,—Abraham Lincoln to the men and women who will believe him, and the North will surge with a new strength against which the enemy will not dare advance. Then, can not fifty thousand men, now doing police and garrison duty, possibly be drawn off with safety, and sent within a month to McClellan? Add these to his present seven times tried force and he can strike a blow which will destroy all hope of organized armed resistance to the Law—Without these, the best army the world ever saw must lie idle, and in discouragement and dejection, be wasted by disease.

I am, Mr. President, Most Respectfully,

> Your obt. servant,
> Frederick L. Olmsted
> Ex. Sec'y
> San. Comm.

Abraham Lincoln,
President of the United States.

No reply is known. By 1862 Frederick Law Olmsted had already designed Central Park in New York, planned Prospect Park in Brooklyn, and was serving his second year as secretary general of the Sanitary Commission, which provided care to sick and wounded soldiers (Maxwell, Lincoln's Fifth Wheel, *10, 340–342).*

Landowner Wants Colonization

Tuesday Aug 19/62

Dear Sir There is an absolute necessity that colonization if intended to be made, should be commenced without further delay—or it will result badly.

The <u>rainy season</u> begins there [the Isthmus of Panama] about the 15th of November—If Emigrants are not there and some houses erected before the rains set in, they will be too much discouraged to do anything. The rainy season is also the time for planting & producing.

There are enough of colonists as I am informed, ready and anxious to go—immediately or as soon as a vessel can be made ready—

Will you see me tomorrow or this evening & see if we can arrange matters?

Very Respc
A. W. Thompson

To the President.

∽ *Lincoln was considerably interested in the idea of colonizing freed blacks at the time this letter was written. The writer, Ambrose W. Thompson, owned land in Chiriqui on the Isthmus of Panama, and although some of Lincoln's advisors warned that he was disreputable, the President approved a contract with him to relocate freedmen there, just eleven days before issuing the Emancipation Proclamation. In April 1863 the first 453 settlers sailed for their new home, but within a year 368 returned, after finding far less opportunity and far more disease than they had been led to expect. By 1864, John Hay reported that the President had finally "sloughed off the idea of colonization," concluding it was "a hideous & barbaric humbug." Historians have long debated the meaning of Lincoln's passing involvement in the notion: some argue it proved his innate racism; others insist it was merely a public relations effort to ensure popular acceptance of emancipation and black enlistment in the army. Yet there is no doubt that, for a time, Lincoln seriously entertained the idea (publicly, at least) of ridding America of its black population altogether (CW, V: 373, 414; ALE, 63; Dennett, Diaries and Letters of John Hay, 203).*

The Vice President on Emancipation

Bangor Sept. 25 1862.

My Dear Sir

I do not know, as in the multiplicity of the correspondence with which you are burthened, this note will ever meet your eye—But I desire to express my undissembled and sincere thanks for your Emancipation Proclamation. It will stand as the great act of the age. It will prove to be wise in Statesmanship as it is Patriotic. It will be enthusiastically approved and sustained and future generations will, as I do, say God bless you for this great and noble act.

Yours Sincerely
H. Hamlin

To the President

∽ *This letter is enormously revealing in that it demonstrates the severely limited role of the nineteeth-century vice president. It makes clear that not only was Hannibal Hamlin excluded from the deliberations over the emancipation policy; but also when the announcement came, he was not even in Washington—he wrote from his home in Maine. Equally revealing is Lincoln's response, which reveals him at his most uncertain over the effects of his thunderbolt proclamation (CW, V: 444).*

S T R I C T L Y   P R I V A T E .

Executive Mansion,
Washington, September 28, 1862

My Dear Sir: Your kind letter of the 25th is just received. It is known to some that while I hope something from the proclamation, my expectations are not as sanguine as are those of some friends. The time for its effect southward has not come; but northward the effect should be instantaneous.

It is six days old, and while commendation in newspapers and by distinguished individuals is all that a vain man could wish, the stocks have declined, and troops come forward more slowly than ever. This, looked soberly in the face, is not very satisfactory. We have fewer troops in the field at the end of six days than we had at the beginning—the attrition among the old outnumbering the addition by the new. The North responds to the proclamation sufficiently in breath; but breath alone kills no rebels.

I wish I could write more cheerfully; nor do I thank you the less for the kindness of your letter.

Yours very truly,
A. Lincoln.

Stung by Presidential Criticism

[*T E L E G R A P H*]

Head Qrs Army of Potomac
[Pleasant Valley] Oct. 25 6 pm 1862

His Excellency the President

In reply to your telegram of this date, I have the honor to state that from the time this Army left Washington on the 7th of Sept my Cavalry has been constantly employed in making reconnaissances, scouting and picketing. Since the battle of Antietam six Regiments have made one trip of two hundred miles, marching fifty five miles in one day while endeavoring to reach Stewart's Cavalry. General Pleasonton in his official report, states that he with the remainder of our available Cavalry while on Stewart's track marched seventy eight miles in twenty four hours. Besides these two remarkable expeditions our Cavalry has been engaged in picketing and scouting one hundred and fifty miles of river front, ever since the battle of Antietam, and has made repeated reconnaissances since that time, engaging the enemy on every occasion. Indeed it has performed harder service since the battle than before. I beg you will also consider that this same Cavalry was brought from the Peninsula where it encountered most laborious service, and was at the commencement of this campaign in low condition and from that time to the present it has had no time to recruit.

If any instance can be found where overworked cavalry has performed more labor than mine since the battle of Antietam I am not conscious of it.

Geo. B. McClellan
Maj. Genl.

ᔕ *McClellen was reacting to the following acerbic telegram from Lincoln, dispatched earlier in the day in reaction to a cavalry officer's claim that the army's horses were "absolutely broken down with fatigue and want of flesh" (Sears, The Civil War Papers of McClellan, 508; CW, V: 474, 477).*

Washington City, D.C.
October 24 [25]. 1862

Majr. Genl. McClellan

I have just read your despatch about sore tongued and fatiegued [sic] horses. Will you pardon me for asking what the horses of your army have done since the battle of Antietam that fatigue anything?

A. Lincoln

ᔕ *Not about to cede the issue entirely to his recalcitrant general, Lincoln wrote yet again in response to McClellan's accounting of cavalry activities.*

Executive Mansion, Washington,
Oct. 26. 1862.

Maj. Gen. McClellan

Yours in reply to mine about horses received. Of course you know the facts better than I, still two considerations remain. Stuart's cavalry outmarched ours, having certainly done more marked service on the Peninsula, and everywhere since. Secondly, will not a movement of our army be a relief to the cavalry, compelling the enemy to concentrate, instead of "foraging" in squads everywhere?

But I am so rejoiced to learn from your despatch to Gen. Halleck, that you begin crossing the river this morning.

A. Lincoln

Not "Radical" Enough

Washington Feb 24th 1863

President of the United States;

Dear Sir: We see that you are surrounded by Spies and men of evil intentions—and that you have been "weeping" over the apparent ruin of the Nation; and in the blackness of darkness you wonder if God has forsaken us.

"He has not; but God is just[.]" I wish you to carry out the plans you have been reflecting upon. Place them at once before Congress. The time is short and you <u>must</u> act, for the will of god must be done— He is about to Save this nation and Men are but straws in his way— What are you still afraid of the so called conservative element.—? Sir the Copperheads and rattlesnakes of the Nation are trembling for fear they will have to drink from the bitter cup. They have prepared; by advocating and sustaining wrong—yes they actually fear the Nation's ruin—, A powerful re-action will commence within three months which Shall sweep the Nation like a hurricane "On to Glory."

For years I have seen this struggle—and told my friends all about the plot for your assassination some three weeks before you were inagurated [sic]—Sometime you will know more of its magnitiude—and your strange escape. Yet had the plot succeeded it would not have changed in the least the struggle—except to have made it more violent; is the outset and relapse which we are just getting out of more painful,

Lincoln I know your good intentions; but I warn you as a friend to adopt at once those principles of strict right you have so often seen.

Adopt the plans called "Radical" which so many have urged—but bear in mind that the devils agents never do the Lords service from "choice" but may for selfish ends—let such men as [Benjamin F.] Butler and Jim Lane go on at once; if they make any selfish capital out of it "all right"   I have seen in "visions" this terrible net work for the strangling of freedom—they taint the very air you breathe for the city is swarming with them—and I wept for joy when the Angels showed me how God would destroy their power and save the Nation,—through their fear he will save them for they are not "totally despaired" but are "moral" cowards—they will be "clamorous" and accuse you of imbecility and want of action; as soon as they see out of the woods—for political purposes, "as you will soon die."

Unless you act as above pointed out or briefly hinted at; even though your political enemies shall out strip you in the race for freedom & union and you shall not be able to forgive yourself for the delay, let me beseech you—as a friend to fail not on your part in the great work so soon to commence.—"Keep this note one year and see if what I tell you dont take place—,"

I remain; Most Respectfully;

> Your Obedient Servant,
> G. F. Kelly

Lincoln did not reply to these criticisms, which arrived in an envelope marked "strictly private." He endorsed it "G. F. Kelly" and filed the letter away. The very next day the writer sent yet another long missive that began, "Then you think the letter I wrote you yesterday fanatical and wild. Still you had curiosity enough to carefully preserve it." Without indicating how he knew what Lincoln had done with the letter, Kelly went on to offer his services for the "salvation" of the country "without price," warning Lincoln to "do your duty 'for there is not an hour to lose.' " This letter, too, the President filed away, cryptically endorsing it "A vision."

Black Soldier Asks for Equal Pay

> Camp of the 54th Mass. Colored Regt.
> Morris Island. Dept of the South.
> Sept. 28th, 1863.

Your Excellency,
Abraham Lincoln:

Your Excellency will pardon the presumption of an humble individual like myself, in addressing you, but the earnest Solicitation of my Comrades in Arms beside the genuine interest felt by myself in the matter is my excuse, for placing before the Executive head of the Nation our Common Grievance.

On the 6th of the last Month, the Paymaster of the department informed us, that if we would decide to receive the sum of $10 (ten dollars) per month, he would come and pay us that sum, but that, on the sitting of Congress, the Regt. would, in his opinion, be <u>allowed</u> the other 3 (three). He did not give us any guarantee that this would be, as he hoped; certainly he had no authority for making any such guarantee, and we cannot suppose him acting in any way interested.

Now the main question is, Are we <u>Soldiers</u>, or are we <u>Labourers</u>? We are fully armed, and equipped, have done all the various Duties pertaining to a Soldier's life, have conducted ourselves to the complete satisfaction of General Officers, who were, if any[thing], prejudiced <u>against</u> us, but who now accord us all the encouragement and honour due us; have shared the perils and Labour of Reducing the first stronghold that flaunted a Traitor Flag; and more, Mr. President. Today the Anglo-Saxon Mother, Wife, or Sister are not alone in tears for departed Sons, Husbands and Brothers. The patient, trusting Descendants of Afric's Clime have dyed the ground with blood, in defense of the Union, and Democracy. Men, too, your Excellency, who know in a measure the cruelties of the Iron heel of oppression, which in years gone by, the very Power their blood is now being spilled to maintain, ever ground them to the dust.

But When the war trumpet sounded o'er the land, when men knew not the Friend from the Traitor, the Black man laid his life at the Altar of the Nation,—and he was refused. When the arms of the Union were beaten, in the first year of the War, and the Executive called more food for its ravaging maw, again the black man begged the privilege of aiding his Country in her need, to be again refused.

And now he is in the War, and how has he conducted himself? Let their dusky forms rise up, out [of] the mires of James Island, and give the answer. Let the rich mould around [Fort] Wagner's parapets be upturned, and there will be found an Eloquent answer. Obedient and patient and Solid as a wall are they. All we lack is a paler hue and a better acquaintance with the Alphabet.

Now your Excellency, we have done a Soldier's Duty. Why Can't we have a Soldier's pay? You caution the Rebel Chieftain, that the United States knows no distinction in her Soldiers. She insists on having all her Soldiers of whatever creed or Color, to be treated according to the usages of War. Now if the United States exacts uniformity of treatment of her Soldiers from the Insurgents, would it not be well and consistent to set the example herself by paying all her Soldiers alike?

We of this Regt. were not enlisted under any "contraband" act. But we do not wish to be understood as rating our Service of more Value to the Government than the service of the ex-slave. Their Service is undoubtedly worth much to the Nation, but Congress made express provision touching their case, as slaves freed by military necessity, and assuming the Government to be their temporary Guardian. Not so with us. Freemen by birth and consequently having the advantage of thinking and acting for ourselves so far as the Laws would allow us, we do not consider ourselves fit subject for the Contraband act.

We appeal to you, Sir, as the Executive of the Nation, to have us justly Dealt with. The Regt. do pray that they be assured their service will be fairly appreciated by paying them as American Soldiers, not as menial hirelings. Black men, you may well know, are poor; three dollars per month for a year will supply their needy Wives and little ones with fuel. If you, as Chief Magistrate of the Nation, will assure us of our whole pay, we are content. Our Patriotism, our enthusiasm will have a new impetus, to exert our energy more and more to aid our Country. Not that our hearts have ever flagged in Devotion, spite the evident apathy displayed in our behalf, but We feel as though our Country spurned us, now that we are sworn to serve her. Please give this a moment's attention.

James Henry Gooding

∽ *The writer was a member of the famous 54th Massachusetts Volunteer Infantry, the black regiment that won glory in its doomed charge against Confederate Fort Wagner in 1863. Gooding was also the only African-American soldier in that unit whose first-hand accounts of his days in the field have survived. Although he was a gifted writer, he probably sensed that a letter from a black man directly to the President might never be forwarded to its addressee by the White House staff. So he sent this request for equal pay for black troops through Harper Brothers, the New York publishers. Still, although others of his letters were regularly published in the New Bedford* Mercury, *and he wrote as well to Massachusetts Governor Andrew (who replied, albeit indirectly, through a white man who had forwarded Gooding's mail), he was not known in Washington, so it is doubtful that his plea was ever brought to Lincoln's attention. But even if it was, Lincoln forwarded it almost immediately to the War Department. This letter is not in the Lincoln Papers, where letters of any kind from black correspondents are all but unknown. Nevertheless, the Lincoln administration eventually did grant equal pay to its "colored" troops (Adams,* On the Altar of Freedom, *xxvii–xxxiii, 118–120; this letter appears courtesy of the National Archives, Record Group No. 94, Colored Troops Division, Letters Received, H133, CT 1863).*

"Behind the Curtain" in "Rebeldom"

Libby Prison Richmond Va Nov 12 1863.

To his Excellency
The President of the U.S.

Since my capture on the 30th of June '63 I have seen much of Rebeldom, behind the curtain, and have talked with a good many soldiers, conscripts, deserters, officers, and citizens. The result of all is, to my mind, that they—the masses are distinctly tired of the war, and that three fourths of all the people are anxious for its close on any counts. The officers and healthy men feel differently and desire hostilities to be continued to the last, as they say, unless their independence can be secured. They assure the soldiers and common people, that if subjugated, every mans property will be confiscated, and the farms and land given to the Negroes. I have been inquired of my a great many soldiers, conscripts, & citizens in relation to this and have always assured them that there will be no universal and indiscriminate confiscation, but that the property of men influential and active in the rebellion will be confiscated, to make good the losses of loyal men— whose property and homes have been destroyed and desolated by the Rebels—These persons say that if this were understood by the people the effect would be highly favorable and the opposition to the war would be nearly universal. Deserters from the rebels are very numerous, and will greatly increase before Christmas, as many soldiers assured me, of some of the Regts half the men have already deserted. The rebels cannot increase their forces in the field. They already have out every available man, and great numbers of conscripts are worthless as soldiers from physical infirmities. I have seen men with hollow chests—Hernia—and some even with but one Arm, men with an eye gone and a great many already worthless from general debility—and feeble constitutions, fit only for the Hospitals—The suffering among the people this month will be very great. Everywhere food is very desired: some places from scarcity where the evil is aggravated in all places from the depreciation of the currency and this is becoming greater every week—in July U.S. currency sold here at the rate of two confed. for one dollar U.S.—afterward it brought 2½—then 3—4—5—6—and <u>now</u> the authorities here pay seven for one! In July before the harvest flour was $35 per Bbl. corn $8 to $10 per bush[el]. <u>Now</u> Flour is $100 to $125 per Bbl. and Corn $15 per bush. And sweet potatoes cost is at this prison $10 for a common Water pail full—squash to $50 a bushel, and everything in the provision here is commanding price. The appreciation of the currency here is especially running the Rebellion into the ground. The Authorities see it and are in anxious consultation for some remedy, any financier, or even any intelligent merchant would be amused at the crude and absurd plans—that are suggested to save the Confederacy from the ruin that every reflecting man must see is inevitable. Their currency cannot be saved from entire prostration, utter worthlessness, and this fate will befall it immediately after a crushing defeat of either Lee or Bragg—The increase in the prices of provisions is not wholly due to any sudden scarcity but mostly dependent upon the depreciation of the currency. Meats of all kinds are very high. Yesterday the 11th of July [*sic*]—no meat was issued to our officers we had only half a pound of corn bread each for the twenty four hours—with water—the Rebel Commissary said he could get only 1000 lbs. of meat in the market and that was sent to the Hospitals. To day we have only corn bread and—about 3 each—very small sweet potatoes. The Authorities here say they do not know how they will be able to feed us[.] Were it not for purchases in the market at enormous prices and supplies from our homes our lives here would have been from the commencement a constant scene of suffering from hunger—I am confident that the defeat of either Lee or Bragg would cause the speedy collapse of the Rebellion, in the latter case the Army of the Cumberland could immediately destroy the railways and Public works at Atlanta & Augusta, and the vast amount of rolling stock collected at the former place from the Tennessee roads. The stock is stored on temporary tracks in the woods about two miles from the town. I saw it there, cars and Engines. From all I can learn of the sources of supply for Lee's army and Richmond, I form the opinion that the rout of Bragg would immediately compel the retirement of Lee and the speedy evacuation of this place. Lee would then have no point d'affaire north of Richmond and would probably be compelled to form a junction with the remains of Bragg's army at some point where food could be obtained, and it could not be here for such a force, as the most that can be done here is to feed, scantily too, the poorest population. I learn from an authentic source that the Rail

Roads in the South are calculated to last but four years—rails and rolling stock—already mutinous gangs of men are at work removing the rails that are worn and replacing these by those less worn from all side tracks and putting bad rails together over which the cars move very slowly. The general schedule speed is only ten miles an hour. It will be seen then that any considerable destruction of rolling stock and rails—will be a severe blow to the Rebels, as their means of transportation at present is wholly insufficient for their wants. Rails Listed and bent in tortured way can be straightened and fitted for use with little labor. To be rendered useless the[y] must be <u>crushed</u> at the points where they are hot, which is easily done——The officers in this prison are fed, at present, on corn bread, made of some sifted meal—a little such, a very few sweet potatoes and <u>nothing else.</u> They are earnest and unanimous in the wish that Rebel prisoners (officers, that is) should be put on precisely the same footing. We sleep on the floor without blankets, excepting a very few poor ones furnished to some of us and such as we get from friends and the Sanitary Commn. All officers arriving here now are turned into the prison without blankets, only one room in the prison has glass in their doors, all the rest are open to the free sweep of the north winds. There is no penitentiary in this or any other country that I have seen where every arrangement is not far superior to anything here, indeed any prison anything arranged like this where felons should be treated as we are would be regarded as infamous. Returned Rebel Officers have been here, and have freely spoken to us of the kind manner in which they have been treated, of their bountiful rations and their excellence and variety, while we are fed on corn bread, potatoes, & water! The officers are all perfectly willing to stay and suffer here, so long as the public good may require, but desire very earnestly that Rebel officers may be placed in <u>precisely</u> our situation. We have no fires to warm us—

This will be presented you by Dr Luck U.S.N. Very Respectfully

> Your obedient servt.
> Neal Dow
> Brig. Genl. U.S.V.

To his excellency Abraham Lincoln President of the U.S.A.

The Confederacy is now issuing fifty millions of dollars in their currency per month.

> N. Dow

⌒ *Of course, Lincoln could not respond to this extraordinary letter, which combined vivid and harrowing tales of prisoner mistreatment with valuable political and military intelligence. The lengthy communication, scrawled in tiny handwriting crowded onto two sheets of paper, was probably smuggled out of the prison by the doctor identified in the final paragraph.*

"Faith in God and Dry Powder"

Little Genesee Allegany Co N.Y.
March 28 1864

Father Abraham

I am 65 years old am able to do a fair days work (not the hardest kind of work) day after day—am willing to go to the army, or rather into some fort or garison, where there will be no long marches, was never a good traveler but <u>worker</u> will help you work out our national salvation will go free of any charge to Government except travel & rations   Avery Coon is a stout man of about my age—will go too to a Fort or Garison he may need the usual pay will be a good hand

We have Faith in God and dry Powder

Truly Yours
Daniel Edwards

⌒ *An endorsement on this letter indicates it may have been acknowledged on March 31, 1864; if so, "Father Abraham's" response has disappeared.*

A Poem on Emancipation

Washington, Apl 4th 1864

Mr. Lincoln.

Dear Sir. I enclose a poem of which you are the honored subject. The only favor I ask in return is your Autograph in duplicate. I desire it first, upon the enclosed piece of silk, which is to be placed in my wedding quilt. All the other Peachblossoms have a silk quilt ready for their wedding and why should not I? But mine is to exceed that of any <u>other</u> Peachblossoms. And as it cannot be finished without your autograph, and as the wedding can never take place until it <u>is</u> finished, I am sure you will not delay in complying with my very modest request. I also desire your autograph upon a slip of paper.

Yours politically, socially and religiously

Polly Peachblossom

Address "Republican Office" Washington D.C.

The Maul.
Inscribed to President Lincoln

I saw a boy in a "black-jack" wood,
 With a tall, lank, awkward "figger"
A-striking away with his heavy maul,
 By the side of a young slave "nigger["]:
And he said to himself, "I'll maul away,
 And cleave a path before me;
I'll hew <u>all</u> "black-jacks" out of my way
 Till the star of Fame shines o'er me."

I saw him again on a broad swift stream.
 But the maul this time was a paddle;
and I watched the tiny rain-bows gleam,
 As he made the waves skedaddle.
And he said, "I'll paddle away, away,
 Till space shall vanish before me;
And I yet shall live to see the day
 When the Star of Fame shines o'er me."

I saw him again with his mighty books,
 A-pondering Coke and Story:
And little there was in his homely looks
 To tell of his future glory.
But he said, "I'll master, I know I will,
 The difficult path before me;
I'll maul my way through the hard world still
 Till the Star of Fame shines o'er me[.]"

I saw him again when he rose to cope
    Hand to hand with the Western Giant;
And his eye lit up with a gleam of hope,
    On his sinewy strength reliant.
"I'll fight him" he said "with the mail of Luster
    Till he shrink and quail before me,—
Till he stand abashed in astonished truth,
    While the Star of Fame shines o'er me."

I saw him again in the White House chair
    A-writing the Proclamation,
And the pen he used was the heaviest maul
    In this rail-mauling nation.
And he said "tis the only way to make
    The traitors flee before us,
While the light it sheds will leave a wake
    That will shine when the sod grows o'er us."

I saw him again but the other day,
    And he shook my hand in greeting;
And little he thought how soon I'd write
    And tell the world of our meeting.
The hand I clasped has swung the maul,
    And my own has written its story.—
But never, I ween, could any hand
    Write half of its toil and glory.

                    Polly Peachblossom

Washington D.C.

∽ *No reply to the poem—or the request for an autograph to complete the writer's marriage quilt—has been located.*

The Proclamation inspired a number of amateur poets to dedicate verse to the Emancipator, including a New Yorker named Barry Gray, who concluded his verses by predicting that the Proclamation would "cause Humanity throughout the world,/ To bless and honor Abraham Lincoln's name,/And, more than marble face or statue could,/Will crown his memory with enduring fame" (Barry Gray to Lincoln, January 1863, Lincoln Papers).

Proof of Atrocities

Washington May 20th 1864

Abraham Lincoln
President of the United States

Sir: Enclosed please find the photographs [see illustration, page 34] of four returned prisoners whose likenesses were taken by order of the committee on the conduct of the war.

Some of these will form a part of the likenesses to be published in the forthcoming report on the condition of returned prisoners. Very respectfully

Yours &c &c
B. F. Wade

∽ The horrifying cartes de visite *sent by Sen. Benjamin F. Wade were designed to buttress the Ohio Republican's argument for the harshest retaliation against the South. The portraits of the skeletal prison survivors included two soldiers identified as having since died "from effects of treatment while in the hands of the enemy."*

News of Renomination

[T E L E G R A P H]

Baltimore June 8 1864.

A Lincoln Prest till 1868
    God bless & elect Abraham Lincoln

James M. Scovel

∽ Scovel was a Pennsylvania delegate to the National Union Party Convention which on the day of this letter nominated Lincoln for a second term.

A Contingency Emancipation Plan

Rochester: N.H. August 29th 1864

Hon Abraham Lincoln:
President of the United States:

Sir: Since the interview with which Your Excellency was pleased to honor me a few days ago, I have freely conversed with several trustworthy and Patriotic colored men concerning your suggestion that something should be speedily done to inform Slaves in the Rebel States of the true state of affairs in relation to them, and to warn them as to what will be their probable condition should peace be concluded while they remain within the Rebel lines: and more especially to urge upon them the necessity of making their escape. All with whom I have thus far spoken on the subject, concur in the wisdom and benevolence of the idea, and some of them think it practicable. That every slave who escapes from the Rebel States is a loss to the Rebellion and a gain to the Loyal Cause I need not stop to argue[;] the proposition is self evident. The negro is the stomach of the rebellion. I will therefore briefly submit at once to your Excellency the—the [*sic*] ways and means by which many such persons may be wrested from the enemy and brought within our lines:

1st Let a general agent be appointed by your Excellency charged with the duty of giving effect to your idea as indicated above: Let him have the means and power to employ twenty or twenty five good men, having the cause at heart to act as his agents: 2d Let these agents which shall be selected by him, have permission to visit such points at the front as are most accessible to large bodies of Slaves in the Rebel States; Let each of the said agts have power to appoint one sub agent or more in the locality where he may be required to operate: the said sub agent shall be thoroughly acquainted with the country—and well instructed as to the representations he is to make to the slaves: but his chief duty will be to conduct such squads of Slaves as he may be able to collect safely within the Loyal lines: Let the sub agents for this service be paid a sum not exceeding two doll[ar]s per day while upon active duty. 3dly in order that these agents shall not be arrested or impeded in their work, let these be properly ordered to report to the Generals Commanding the several Departments they may visit, and receive from them permission to pursue their vocation unmolested. 4th Let provision be made that the Slaves or Freed men thus brought within our lines shall receive subsistence until such of them as are fit shall enter the service of their country or be otherwise employed and provided for: 5thly Let each agent appointed by the General agent be required to keep a strict acct of all his transactions, of all monies received and paid out, of the numbers and the names of slaves brought into our lines under his auspices, of the plantations visited, and of everything properly connected with the prosecution of his work, and let him be required to make full reports of his proceedings at least once a fortnight to the General Agent. 6th Also, Let the General Agt be required to keep a strict acct of all his transactions with his agts and report to your Excellency or to an officer designated by you to receive such reports: 7th Let the General agt be paid a salary sufficient to enable him to employ a competent clerk, and let him be stationed at Washington—or at some other Point where he can most readily receive communications from and send communications to his agents: the General Agt should also have a kind of roving Commission within our lines, so that he may have a more direct and effective oversight of the whole work and thereby ensure activity and faithfulness on the part of his agents—

This is but an imperfect outline of the plan, but I think it enough to give your Excellency an idea of how the desirable work shall be executed.

Your Obededient Servant
Fred. Douglass

∾ *The extraordinary plan outlined here by black leader Frederick Douglass at Lincoln's suggestion was designed to ensure that as many slaves as possible would be freed under the terms of the Emancipation Proclamation, even if Lincoln were to lose his reelection to Peace Democrats who were likely to revoke his edict. Lincoln won, and the plan was scrapped, but Douglass insisted years later that the blueprint provided "evidence conclusive on Mr. Lincoln's part that the proclamation, so far at least as he was concerned, was not effected merely as a 'necessity,'" but also out of an earnest desire to end human bondage. This is the only known letter to Lincoln from Douglass (ALE, 89).*

Country Women Volunteer for the Army

Gallia Furnace [Ohio,] Sept 9 1864

Mr Abram Lincen

Dear Sir   I write you these few lines hoping you will consider it I appeal to you for aid there is fifteen young Ladies of the most worthy families that is in this part of the country we wish to do something for our Country we have been wanting to do something Ever since this Cruel war broke out but Circumstances will not permit it. but we cannot wait eny longer we must do something We have sent all that is Near and dear to us and we must help them in some way We are willing to be sworn in for one year or more eny lenght [*sic*] of time it makes No difference to us. But we must do something to help, save that Beautifful Flag that has Waved so long, oer the Land of the Free and the home of the brave   I could get up a Regt. in one day of young Ladies of high Rank but I hope you will give us pen something that is helping to save that old Flag We have but one young man in this Part of the Country most Evry man is gone out to help serve that Stary Banner end we must go to we live back in the Country so fur that we Cannot do much here has Evry thing is so quiet. I will Close now hoping you will do something for us I will not send you my full Name Now but if you will do anything for us you May have all your most Humble Servent

Miss Mollie E.

↶ "The men in the place have all gone," a secretary wrote on the back of this letter, "and the girls are anxious to go too." But no reply to this letter is known.

His Chiropodist on Re-election Prospects

760. Broadway
New York, Nov. 3d 1864

My Dear Friend. I just returned to this city after a trip of 9 days through Pennsylvania and New York State, and I am happy to inform you, that I am satisfied that I have done much good. I now think all is Right—and if we can reduce the Democratic Majority in this city, I shall be satisfied—as regards the Isrelites [sic]—with but few exceptions, they will vote for you. I understand them well, and have taken the precaution to see that they do as they have promised—I have secured good and trustworthy men to attend to them on Election Day—My men have been all the week seeing that their masses are proparly [sic] Registered—so that all will be right on the 8th ins.

As Regards Pennsylvania, if you knew all—You and your friends would give me much credit for I flatter myself I have done one of the Largest things that has been done in the Campaigne [sic] will explain it to you when I see you.

I wish to God all was over for I am used up, but 3 years ago, I promised I would Elect you, and if you are not it shall not be my fault.

Raymond [Henry J. Raymond, a New York editor] will inform you that I am doing all I can for Fenton [the Republican candidate for New York governor] but his chances are very Doubtfull [in fact Fenton, too, would win on November 8]—I should feel very bad if your chances was like his—I have much to say to you, but have been up almost every night—that I am used up, I hope to see you after the fun is over, when I hope you will say

"Well done, my good and faithful Servant."

With kind regards to Mrs. Lincoln.

Yours truly
I. Zacharie, Md

P.S. did you receive the oranges.

∽ *There is no record of a reply to this self-congratulatory letter from Lincoln's confidant and sometime unofficial emissary, Dr. Isachar Zacharie, a Jewish chiropodist who had successfully treated Lincoln's chronically painful feet (*CW, V: 436*).*

Congratulations on his Re-election

307 New Street
Philadelphia November 9. 1864.

His Excellency <u>Abraham Lincoln</u>
President of the United States:

Dear Sir: Praise <u>God</u>, from whom all blessings flow! The <u>Republic</u> is safe! From the fulness [*sic*] of my heart I congratulate you on your relection. God bless <u>you</u>! God bless your Administration! God bless the Republic!

Very Sincerely, Your friend,
Elizabeth E. Hutter

∽ *Elizabeth Hutter was president of the Northern Home for Friendless Children and Associated Institute for Soldiers' and Sailors' Orphans. She had sent Lincoln a gift in August 1863 (*CW, VI: 375–376*).*

[November 14, 1864]

To the Honorable Abraham Lincoln
Washington D.C.

Dear Sir. Please permit me although a poor man to congratulate you on your reelection as chief Magistrate of this Nation for another four years, for which I am truly thankful and your trustworthy servant will ever pray that you may be able to bring this rebellion to an and and we again be a happy and a prosperous Nation.

Very truly Your obedient servant
J. M. Belknap
Williston, Mass.

Lobbying for a New Chief Justice

Detroit Nov. 14. 1864

His Excely. the President

In common with all the leading members of our bar I feel a great desire that His honor Judge [Noah] Swayne [an associate justice on the court] may be appointed to vacant Chf. Justiceship. An extensive acquaintance with the bar of this and neighboring states enables me to say this is a common desire.

I am with great respect

Yours
H. H. Emmons

[*TELEGRAPH*]

Boston Nov 14 1864

His Excellency A. Lincoln

Frederick Fogg Boston should be made chief Judge, ask [Senator Charles] Sumner.

Richard W. Henshaw

ᔓ *Lincoln received countless such suggested nominations through the mail, but in the end he appointed his former treasury secretary, and on-again, off-again political rival, Salmon P. Chase to succeed Roger B. Taney as chief justice. Chase, too, had been urged on Lincoln by a number of correspondents—most of whom were from Chase's home state of Ohio.*

His Home State Ratifies End to Slavery

[T E L E G R A P H]

Springfield Ill Feby 1 1865

A Lincoln

The Legislature has by a large majority ratified the [Thirteeth] amendment to the Constitution   All suppose you have signed the joint resolution of Congress   Great enthusiasm

R. J. Oglesby
Gov

∽ *"This amendment is a King's cure for all the evils," Lincoln told a gathering of serenaders at the White House on the night this telegram was received. The New York* Tribune *reported: "He had the honor to inform those present that Illinois had already to-day done the work." On February 3 Massachusetts Governor Andrew wired to announce that his state, too, ratified the amendment "by a unanimous yea vote & nay vote . . . Democrats voting affirmatively." Maryland and New Jersey voted the same day, and slavery was on the road to final extinction (CW, VIII: 254).*

A General Resigns

5th Avenue Hotel
New York Apl 14/65

The President of the United States

My dear Mr Lincoln   When I last parted with you I made you a promise not to again urge my resignation for a week, at the end of which I was to report to you if I still desired to resign. Before the week expired you were reported sick so that I did not wish to annoy you with my affairs, and before I was satisfied that you were well enough to attend to general business, I learned that you had gone to the front, and I certainly did not feel authorised to trouble you there—But the time has now arrived when the services of many of our officers and men are not needed, particularly of those who have been for a long time idle—

In view of this fact I now tender my resignation—If I should be again wanted, you are of course, at liberty to command me—

I beg to thank you Mr President for your uniform kindness, encouragement and assistance, all of which have followed me through all my services during the rebellion—

I congratulate you upon the great success that has attended your labors as chief executive of our government, and pray that God may continue to inspire you with wisdom and justice in the final settlement of our national troubles—In the hope that you and yours may be blessed with health happiness and prosperity I remain, with great regard—

Sincerely your friend
A. E. Burnside

I beg to enclose the official resignation, as I promised to send it through you—A. E. B.

෨ *Lincoln never received this letter from Ambrose E. Burnside, onetime commander of the Army of the Potomac. The night the general sent it, Lincoln was shot. The letter arrived the next morning and was opened by the White House secretaries as the President's body lay in a nearby bedroom.*

This letter appears on page 287.

Gettysburg Nov. 2nd 1863

To His Excellency,
     A. Lincoln,
     President of the United States,
          Sir,
               The several States
having soldiers in the Army of the
Potomac, who were killed at the
Battle of Gettysburg, or have since
died at the various hospitals which
were established in the vicinity,
have procured grounds on a
prominent part of the Battle Field
for a Cemetery, and are having
the dead removed to them
and properly buried.

[8]

Presidential Invitations

*I*N MY PRESENT position," Abraham Lincoln told a disappointed crowd of well-wishers during one of his rare wartime forays outside Washington, "it is hardly proper for me to make speeches. Every word is so closely noted that it will not do to make trivial ones, and I cannot be expected to be prepared to make a matured one just now."

With these few words, uttered with undisguised self-consciousness in Frederick, Maryland, where Lincoln had quietly travelled in 1862 to visit a wounded general, one of history's greatest orators revealed his surprising reluctance to appear anywhere during his term of office that would require him to speak publicly. His stubborn resistance to leaving the nation's capital in wartime stood him in marked contrast to his twentieth-century presidential successors, for whom public appearances have become essential aspects of governing.

"If I were as I have been most of my life," Lincoln awkwardly added in that revealing little speech in Frederick, "I might perhaps, talk amusing to you for half an hour, and it wouldn't hurt anybody." But once he became president, Lincoln determined that such amusing presentations were no longer appropriate, and, worse, might well hurt everybody—including, perhaps, himself. "I am rather inclined," he admitted, "to silence."

Throughout the war, Lincoln resolutely rejected nearly every invitation that would require him to state official policy. Writing in 1864, one citizen unsuspectingly called on the President's "sense of public service and . . . personal disposition" to persuade him to attend an event. But it was precisely that sense of service—and a strong indisposition to make public appearances—that routinely elicited refusals. As he told more than one letter writer in response to such requests, "It is impossible for me to attend."

Seldom recalled is the fact that the Gettysburg Address, the most famous of all his presidential speeches, was much more than an example of his majestic writing and persuasive oratory. It was also an extraordinarily rare public appearance outside Washington by a president who felt it his duty to remain close to the White House, close to the War Department military telegraph, and far from the public spotlight, where he might be induced or compelled, as he admitted in an unfortunate offhand moment at Gettysburg, "to say foolish things." His Confederate counterpart, Jefferson Davis, made many public appearances during the Civil War, but in the North, Lincoln eschewed not only speechmaking opportunities but also charity fairs, grand musicales, religious ceremonies, public lectures, even a gymnastics exhibition—feeling, apparently, that even the briefest public appearance would throw his very dignity open to question.

Not that Lincoln remained entirely homebound during his presidency. He made several visits to the front to confer with his generals on war strategy. Once he even helped direct a naval engagement. On another occasion he braved enemy fire on the outskirts of Washington. And he toured a gun foundry in Cold Spring, New York, following a visit to aged former Union commander Winfield Scott at West Point. What was more, Lincoln was always available to visit the wounded at local military hospitals or to review troops as they marched through the capital.

But the President declined far more invitations than he accepted: invitations to rallies, meetings, even vacations; the chance to return to the scene of one of his greatest pre-presidential triumphs, Cooper Union in New York City; and the opportunity to return home to Springfield, Illinois, to rally support for the Union in the West. The Lincoln Papers are choked with the record of lost opportunities that our recent presidents would never allow to escape them. Historians have long suggested that Lincoln was in many ways the first modern president, not only in his concept of executive power but in his awareness of public opinion. But his correspondence suggests that he was far less conscious of the potential of a personalized presidency than has been supposed. He failed completely to comprehend the impact his presence might have exerted at war meetings and charity events from Boston to Chicago. And although he replied to the summons to his old hometown with a brilliant letter designed to be read aloud at a mass meeting there, had he delivered the remarks himself the result might have been recalled as one of Lincoln's great presidential addresses.

In his defense, Lincoln held office in an era in which presidential recalcitrance was de rigueur. Candidates for the nation's highest office were expected not to campaign in their own behalf and once elected to remain in Washington governing quietly. The exigencies of civil war, however unprecedented, did little to alter these traditions, at least as Lincoln viewed them. His annual message to Congress, for example, (the nineteenth-century equivalent of today's state of the union addresses) was sent to Capitol Hill by a messenger and read there by a clerk, not spoken by the President in person. Trained as a courtroom lawyer and famed as a stump speaker and debater, Lincoln made only a handful of formal speeches during his entire four years in the White House. The presidency silenced Abraham Lincoln—and kept him bound like a prisoner to Washington.

Lincoln doubtless believed that presidents were *supposed* to be one step removed from the people, separated not only by custom but by the electoral college that made their very election indirect. Fully aware of early questions about his dignity and fitness for high office, Lincoln may have been especially reluctant to break precedent and expose himself fully and frequently to the people.

In one of his rare visits outside Washington as president, Lincoln travelled to Philadelphia to attend a huge charity fair for the benefit of wounded soldiers. There he made several reluctant, forgettable speeches and toured the fairgrounds—nothing more. Returning home, he told his secretary only that "the ladies, he believed, had made several thousand dollars by placing him on exhibition." He seemed embarrassed by the experience, not energized.

What is remarkable is that Lincoln placed himself on exhibition so seldom—as the following letters show.

Offering a Summer Vacation

National Hotel
Long Branch, NJ
May 27th, 1861

To His Excellency
The President of the United States
    Dear Sir   Allow me the Honour of Tendering to yourself and suit[e] the Hospitalities of the National Hotel Long Branch this Summer as a most delightfull Summer retreat and having refurnished the above I flatter myself that I am fully competent to give yourself and suit[e] such Entertainment as would be required which I shall most cheerfully do Should your Excellency favour me with a visit.
    Waiting your Commands, I remain your Obednt Servant

D. P. Peters

Facing the threat of a Confederate invasion of the North, Lincoln hardly had the leisure to accept this invitation. But three months later Mrs. Lincoln, accompanied by her son Robert and her cousin Elizabeth Todd Grimsley, did visit Long Branch— perhaps accepting the invitation that had been tendered to the President (LDBD III: 60).

A Reception for a Naval Hero

Norfolk, Va. March 31 1863

His Excellency
To Abraham Lincoln & Lady
    You are respectfully invited to attend a Public Reception of Vice Admiral Farragut, to be given by the Citizens of Norfolk and Portsmouth, and vicinity, on the Evening of Monday, the 3rd inst., at MECHANICS' HALL, commencing at 7½ o'clock.

Committee of arrangements

Lincoln was visiting federal troops at the front until April 3 and thus could not consider accepting this printed invitation.

An Invitation Home

Hon Abraham Lincoln

Dear Sir   The unconditional union men in our State are to hold a Grand Mass Meeting at Springfield on the 3rd Day of September next. It would be gratifying to the many thousands who will be present on that occasion if you would also meet with them. It is stated in the public papers that you will visit the White Mountains [in Vermont] and perhaps you can make it convenient to extend your trip to Illinois. A visit to your old home would not be inappropriate if you can break away from the pressure of public duties.

We intend to make the most imposing demonstration that has ever been held in the Northwest. Many of the most distinguished men in the country have been, and will be invited to attend and I know that nothing could add more to the interest of the occasion than your presence

Can you not give us a favorable reply by return mail and oblige

Your obt Svt
James C. Conkling
Chairman &c

⌘ *Lincoln replied to this invitation as follows (CW VI: 399).*

Washington, D.C.,
August 20 1863

Hon. James C. Conkling
Springfield, Illinois

Your letter of the 14th. is received. I think I will go, or send a letter—probably the latter.

A. Lincoln

⌘ *In the end, Lincoln did not go—either to the White Mountains or home to Springfield. But true to his word, he did send a letter: not a perfunctory declination, but a near-oration crafted specifically to be read aloud at the public meeting. It was one of Lincoln's most persuasive uses of his pen to represent him at a major event he had decided not to attend (CW, VI: 406–410).*

Executive Mansion,
Washington, August 26, 1863.

Hon. James C. Conkling
My Dear Sir.

Your letter inviting me to attend a mass-meeting of unconditional Union-men, to be held at the Capital of Illinois, on the 3rd day of September, has been received.

It would be very agreeable to me, to thus meet my old friends, at my own home; but I can not, just now, be absent from here, so long as a visit there, would require.

The meeting is to be of all those who maintain unconditional devotion to the Union; and I am sure my old political friends will thank me for tendering, as I do, the nation's gratitude to those other noble men, whom no partizan malice, or partizan hope, can make false to the nation's life.

There are those who are dissatisfied with me. To such I would say: You desire peace; and you blame me that we do not have it. But how can we attain it? There are but three conceivable ways. First, to suppress the rebellion by force of arms. This, I am trying to do. Are you for it? If you are, so far we are agreed. If you are not for it, a second way is, to give up the Union. I am against this. Are you for it? If you are, you should say so plainly. If you are not for <u>force</u>, nor yet for <u>dissolution</u>, there only remains some imaginable <u>compromise</u>. I do not believe any compromise, embracing the maintenance of the Union, is now possible. All I learn, leads to a directly opposite belief. The strength of the rebellion, is its military—its army. That army dominates all the country, and all the people, within its range. Any offer of terms made by any man or men within that range, in opposition to that army, is simply nothing for the present; because such man or men, have no power whatever to enforce their side of a compromise, if one were made with them. To illustrate—Suppose refugees from the South, and peace men of the North, get together in convention, and frame and proclaim a compromise embracing a restoration of the Union; in what way can that compromise be used to keep Lee's army out of Pennsylvania? Meade's army can keep Lee's army out of Pennsylvania; and, I think, can ultimately drive it out of existence. But no paper compromise, to which the controllers of Lee's army are not agreed, can, at all, affect that army. In an effort at such compromise we should waste time, which the enemy would improve to our disadvantage; and that would be all. A compromise, to be effective, must be made either with those who control the rebel army, or with the people first liberated from the domination of that army, by the success of our own army. Now allow me to assure you, that no word or intimation, from that rebel army, or from any of the men controlling it, in relation to any peace compromise, has ever come to my knowledge or belief. All charges and insinuations to the contrary, are deceptive and groundless. And I promise you, that if any such proposition shall hereafter come, it shall not be rejected, and kept a secret from you. I freely acknowledge myself the servant of the people, according to the bond of service—the United States constitution; and that, as such, I am responsible to them.

But, to be plain, you are dissatisfied with me about the negro. Quite likely there is a difference of opinion between you and myself upon that subject. I certainly wish that all men could be free, while I suppose you do not. Yet I have neither adopted, nor proposed any measure, which is not consistent with even your view, provided you are for the Union. I suggested compensated emancipation; to which you replied you wished not to be taxed to buy negroes. But I had not asked you to be taxed to buy negroes, except in such way, as to save you from greater taxation to save the Union exclusively by other means.

You dislike the emancipation proclamation; and, perhaps, would have it retracted. You say it is unconstitutional—I think differently. I think the constitution invests its commander-in-chief, with the law of war, in time of war. The most that can be said, if so much, is, that slaves are property. Is there—has there ever been—any question that by the law of war, property, both of enemies and friends, may be taken when needed? And is it not needed whenever taking it, helps us, or hurts the enemy? Armies, the world over, destroy enemies' property when they can not use it; and even destroy their own to keep it from the enemy. Civilized belligerents do all in their power to help themselves, or hurt the enemy, except a few things regarded as barbarous or cruel. Among the exceptions are the massacre of vanquished foes, and noncombatants, male and female.

But the proclamation, as law, either is valid, or is not valid. If it is not valid, it needs no retraction. If it is valid, it can not be retracted, any more than the dead can be brought to life. Some of you profess to think its retraction would operate favorably for the Union. Why better after the retraction, than before the issue? There was more than a year and a half of trial to suppress the rebellion before the proclamation issued, the last one hundred days of which passed under an explicit notice that it was coming, unless averted by those in revolt, returning to their allegiance. The war has certainly progressed as favorably for us, since the issue of the proclamation as before. I know as fully as one can know the opinions of others, that some of the commanders of our armies in the field who have given us our most important successes, believe the emancipation policy, and the use of colored troops, constitute the heaviest blow yet dealt to the rebellion; and that, at least one of those important successes, could not have been achieved when it was, but for the aid of black soldiers. Among the commanders holding these views are some who have never had any affinity with what is called abolitionism, or with republican party politics; but who hold them purely as military opinions. I submit these opinions as being entitled to some weight against the objections, often urged, that emancipation, and arming the blacks, are unwise as military measures, and were not adopted, as such, in good faith.

You say you will not fight to free negroes. Some of them seem willing to fight for you; but, no matter. Fight you, then, exclusively to save the Union. I issued the proclamation on purpose to aid you in saving the Union. Whenever you shall have conquered all resistance to the Union, if I shall urge you to continue fighting, it will be an apt time, then, for you to declare you will not fight to free negroes.

I thought that in your struggle for the Union, to whatever extent the negroes should cease helping the enemy, to that extent it weakened the enemy in his resistance to you. Do you think differently? I thought that whatever negroes can be got to do as soldiers, leaves just so much less for white soldiers to do, in saving the Union. Does it appear otherwise to you? But negroes, like other people, act upon motives. Why should they do any thing for us, if we will do nothing for them? If they stake their lives for us, they must be prompted by the strongest motive—even the promise of freedom. And the promise being made, must be kept.

The signs look better. The Father of Waters [the Mississippi River] again goes unvexed to the sea. Thanks to the great North-West for it. Nor yet wholly to them. Three hundred miles up, they met New-England, Empire, Key-Stone, and Jersey, hewing their way right and left. The Sunny South too, in more colors than one, also lent a hand. On the spot, their part of the history was jotted down in black and white. The job was a great national one; and let none be banned who bore an honorable part in it. And while those who have cleared the great river may well be proud, even that is not all. It is hard to say that anything has been more bravely, and well done, than at Antietam, Murfreesboro, Gettysburg, and on many fields of lesser note. Nor must Uncle Sam's Web-feet be forgotten. At all the watery margins they have been present. Not only on the deep sea, the broad bay, and the rapid river, but also up the narrow muddy bayou, and wherever the ground was a little damp, they have been, and made their tracks. Thanks to all. For the great republic— for the principle it lives by, and keeps alive—for man's vast future,—thanks to all.

Peace does not appear so distant as it did. I hope it will come soon, and come to stay; and so come as to be worth the keeping in all future time. It will then have been proved that, among free men, there can be no successful appeal from the ballot to the bullet; and that they who take such appeal are sure to lose their case, and pay the cost. And then, there will be some black men who can remember that, with silent tongue, and clenched teeth, and steady eye, and well-poised bayonet, they have helped mankind on to this great consummation; while, I fear, there will be some white ones, unable to forget that, with malignant heart, and deceitful speech, they have strove to hinder it.

Still let us not be over-sanguine of a speedy final triumph. Let us be quite sober. Let us diligently apply the means, never doubting that a just God, in his own good time, will give us the rightful result.

> Yours very truly
> A. Lincoln.

Invitation to a Dance

[*TELEGRAPH*]
> Glades House via Boston Aug 28 1863

To Abram Lincoln.

Your friends send their respects to you and hope to have an answer by eight oclock tonight as the ladies are going to have a grand hop this night.

> "Lord Baltimore"

"By the request of the ladies.["]

Lincoln wrote on the envelope in which this peculiar telegram was received: "Baltimore—not answered."

Opening a New Theater

419 13th St. [Washington]
Monday Sep. 28th 63.

Your Excellency,

I desire very earnestly to have the honor of the presence of your Excellency at the opening of my new Theatre on Monday Oct 5th. The piece in view for the occasion is Shakespeare's Othello as adapted to presenting Messrs. [James William] Wallack and [Edward] Davenport in parts of nearly equal strength.

I have the honor to submit for your acceptance a double box with connecting door or any box or boxes in my theatre for the accommodation of your Excellency and the party accompanying you.

Should your Excellency prefer any of the other plays of Shakespeare within the repertoire of Messrs. Wallack and Davenport: Hamlet Richard III Macbeth; it will afford me, as well as these gentlemen, the greatest pleasure to concur with such preferences. Should the date above mentioned conflict with any different arrangement your Excellency may have in view, I will gladly with your permission postpone the day of opening one or two days to have the gratification of your presence.

It may not be amiss to state that Grover's Theatre is under the management of one who ever has and ever will do all that may be in his power to strengthen the devotion of his audience to the cause of the Union and your Excellencies [*sic*] Government in which purpose he has been warmly seconded by the artists in his employment.

I have again to renew the expression of my desire of last season that your Excellency will at any time avail yourself of the services of my Theatre; and any play or artist acceptable to your Excellency will meet with my immediate consideration.

Have the kindness to permit Mr. Nicolay to acquaint me with your wishes, of which no public use will be made, and sincere[ly] oblige

Your Servt
Leonard Grover

His Excellency Abraham Lincoln
President U.S.

☙ Throughout the war, theater was Lincoln's favorite, and usually his sole, recreation. He attended the opening of Grover's as invited, on October 6, 1863. In a three-week stretch the following winter, he returned to view, in quick succession, Richard III, Julius Caesar, The Merchant of Venice, Hamlet, Richelieu, The Fool's Revenge, *and* Richard III *yet again (LDBD III: 241–245).*

"A Few Appropriate Remarks":
The Summons to Gettysburg

Gettysburg Nov. 2nd 1863

To His Excellency A. Lincoln,
President of the United States,

Sir, The Several States having Soldiers in the Army of the Potomac, who were killed at the Battle of Gettysburg, or have since died at the various hospitals which were established in the vicinity, have procured grounds on a prominent part of the Battle Field for a Cemetery, and are having the dead removed to there and properly buried.

These Grounds will be Consecrated and set apart to this sacred purpose, by appropriate Ceremonies on Thursday the 19th instant,— Hon Edward Everett will deliver the Oration.

I am authorized by the Governors of the different States to invite you to be present, and participate in these ceremonies, which will doubtless be very imposing and solemnly impressive.

It is the desire that, after the Oration, You, as Chief Executive of the Nation, formally set apart these grounds to their Sacred use by a few appropriate remarks.

It will be a source of great gratification to the many widows and orphans that have been made almost friendless by the Great Battle here, to have you here personally! and it will kindle anew in the breasts of the comrades of these brave dead, who are now in the tented field or nobly meeting the foe in the front, a confidence that they who sleep in death on the Battle Field are not forgotten by those highest in authority; and they will feel that, should their fate be the same, their remains will not be uncared for.

We hope you will be able to be present to perform this last solemn act to the Soldiers dead on this Battle Field.

I am with great Respect, Your Excellency's

Obedient Servant,
David Wills
Agent for A. G. Curtin, Gov. of Penna. and acting for all the States.

᷇ Wills sent a second letter the same day, adding: "As the Hotels in our town will be crowded and in confusion at the time referred to in the enclosed invitation, I write to invite you to stop with me. I hope you will feel it your duty to lay aside pressing business for a day to come on here to perform this last sad note to our brave soldiers dead on the 19th instant." Lincoln accepted both invitations and spent the night of November 18 in a bedroom in Wills's home rewriting the "remarks" that would on November 19, 1863, emerge as the most famous presidential speech in American history: the Gettysburg Address.

An Opportunity Lost

New York, 23 Nov. 1863

His Excellency A. Lincoln
Prest. of the United States

Sir: If the engineers are ready, it is proposed to break ground on the Pacific Rail Road, on the 1st or 2nd of next month, at some point in Nebraska, through which, under the act of Congress, the line will pass. This inauguration of the work will be followed up by early measures to complete, as soon as possible, the grading of one hundred miles of road authorized by the Board of Directors to be put under contract.

In view of the vastness of the enterprise, and its probable influence on the political and commercial prosperity of the country, it would be very gratifying to receive a communication from you to be read on the occasion.

John A. Dix

᷇ There is no record of a reply to this request, or any set of remarks prepared or forwarded to the proposed ceremony—the kind of event no modern president would think of missing or ignoring. All Lincoln did was devote a few lines of his annual message to Congress to the enterprise, calling the "commencement of work . . . favorable to rapid progress and completion." For Lincoln, this was an opportunity lost (CW, VII: 42).

A Return Visit to Cooper Union

New York, November 28, 1863

To the President

Sir: A public meeting of citizens will be held at Cooper Institute on Thursday evening next, the 3rd December, in response to your call on the nation for additional volunteers.

We beg leave, on behalf of the Committee of Arrangements, to invite you to be present and to Encourage by your voice the active efforts of the loyal men of this City in support of the Union Cause.

We need scarcely say that your compliance will afford the highest gratification to the people of this city. With high Respects.

> George Opdyke
> Jos. Sutherland
> Benj. F. Mannierre
> Prosper M. Wetmore
> Spencer Kirby

Although Lincoln may have been tempted to accept this invitation—the proposed meeting was scheduled to be held at the scene of his first triumphant speech in New York City back in 1860—the President was at the time battling a mild case of smallpox and was confined to bed. As was his occasional custom, however, he declined not with a perfunctory note but with a ringing statement designed to be read aloud as a message at the meeting (CW, VII: 32).

> Executive Mansion,
> Washington,
> Dec. 2, 1863.

Messrs. George Opdyke, Jos. Sutherland,
Benj. F. Manierre, Prosper M. Wetmore
and Spencer Kirby, Committee.

Yours of the 28th. ult. inviting me to be present at a meeting to be held at the Cooper Institute, on the 3rd. Inst. to promote the raising of volunteers, is received. Nothing would be more grateful to my feelings, or better accord with my judgement than to contribute, if I could, by my presence, or otherwise, to that eminently patriotic object. Nevertheless the now early meeting of congress, together with a temporary illness, render my attendance impossible.

You purpose also to celebrate our Western victories [a purpose not mentioned in the committee's invitation, and evidently learned elsewhere]. Freed from apprehension of wounding the just sensibilities of brave soldiers fighting elsewhere, it would be exceedingly agreeable to me to join in a suitable acknowledgement to those of the Great West, with whom I was born, and have passed my life.

And it is exceedingly gratifying that a portion lately of the Army of the Potomac, but now serving with the great army of the West, have borne so conspicuous a part in the late brilliant triumphs in Georgia.

Honor to the Soldier, and Sailor everywhere, who bravely bears his country's cause. Honor also to the citizen who cares for his brother in the field, and serves, as he best can, the same cause—honor to him, only less than to him, who braves, for the common good, the storms of heaven and the storms of battle.

> Your Obt. Servt
> A. Lincoln

A Tribute to his "Beau Ideal"

New York Febry 9. 1864

His Excellency Abrm Lincoln
Prest United States

The Twenty-fifth Annual Re-union of the Eighth Ward Pioneer Clay Club, will be held at the Apollo Rooms, No. 410 Broadway on Wednesday evening, February 17th 1864.

I am directed by the Club to extend to you a most cordial invitation to be present on this interesting occasion, and unite with it in doing honor to the memory of him whose name we cherish and whose memorable declaration—"I will never consent to a dissolution of the Union, never, never, never," so entirely in keeping with his whole public character, will ever endear him in the hearts of a grateful people, as a noble patriot—a true statesman.

Trusting to receive your favorable response at as early a day as may be convenient, I am, sir, Very Respectfully

> Your obd't servt.
> Thos E. Gildersleeve
> Cord'g Secty.

∽ *It is almost unthinkable that Lincoln would fail to reply to an invitation to honor his political hero, even if he was compelled to decline. But if Lincoln responded to Gildersleeve's letter, the note has vanished (LDBD III: 240).*

A State Fair in Maryland

Baltimore March 17 1864
No 52 Cathedral St

To his Excellency Abraham Lincoln
President of the United States

Dear Sir   The Managers of the Maryland State Fair have unanimously invited you and Mrs Lincoln to attend the opening ceremonies of the Fair on monday April 18th at 8 pm; or on any other day, you may select, during the week of its continuance.

They have not without design appointed the 18th of April the anniversary of the never to be forgotten day of Maryland's humiliation, to inaugurate the opening of the Fair—the proceeds of which are to be devoted to the beneficent cause of the Sanitary & Christian Commissions, and they hope that the Chief Magistrate of the Republic will not decline to add dignity to the occasion by his presence.

It will give me pleasure to place at your disposal my carriage and the hospitalities of my house.

I am very respectfully

Your obt servt.
William J. Albert
President

ᔕ *Making one of his rare wartime forays from Washington, Lincoln accepted this invitation, taking note of the theme of "Maryland's humiliation" by reminding an audience there: "three years ago . . . soldiers could not so much as pass through Baltimore. The change from then till now, is both great, and gratifying" (CW, VII: 301).*

A 'Great Fair' in St. Louis

Rooms of the Mississippi Valley Sanitary Fair
Saint Louis, April 6, 1864.

To His Excellency, Abraham Lincoln,
President of the United States,

Sir: Among the effects of the rebellion which now curses the country, by making war against its loyal people and lawful authority, none are more patent to the human observer than the disease and suffering, which are visited upon the faithful soldiers of the Republic, whether in camp or in the field.

To assuage, in some degree, these results of a military course of life, especially in defense of the country in an unnatural civil war;—and to supply our gallant soldiers in the field with some of the comforts and luxuries of homes—the people of St. Louis and Missouri design holding a great Fair, commencing on the 17th day of May next—the profits of which are designed to be committed to the Western Sanitary Commission, for distribution among the real beneficiaries of their extended charity Extensive preparations are making for the occasion; which, it is hoped and believed, will be worthy of the title assumed for it—semi-national in its import—to wit: "The Mississippi Valley Sanitary Fair."

We cordially invite your Excellency to visit St. Louis at the time, and honor the occasion with your presence. Thousands of your friends, who might not otherwise feel constrained to be present, would be glad to meet you here. The loyal and liberty loving people of Missouri would extend to you a cordial welcome. It would be becoming in the President of the United States, to lend the sanction of his presence and countenance to observances having so sacred an object.

Trusting the public service and your personal disposition will allow and admit of your Excellency's compliande with this invitation, I beg to subscribe myself (for and in behalf of the Executive Committee, having the fair in charge,)

> Very Respectfully,
> Your obt Servt
> Alfred Mackay
> Corresponding Secretary

No reply has been found to this, yet another of the many appealing invitations Lincoln rejected during his presidency. A presidential appearance in border state Missouri would have received national attention; but Lincoln remained in Washington, as usual. He never once visited the Western Theater of the War (Lincoln Day By Day III: 258).

Honoring General Grant in New York

New-York, May 31st. 1864.

To The President,

Sir, The loyal citizens of New-York, without distinction of party, will convene in Mass Assemblage, on Union Square, on Saturday next, the Fourth of June, at 6 o'clock P.M. to give an expression of their gratitude to Lieutenant General Grant, for his signal services in conducting the National armies to victory; to reaffirm their devotion to the sacred cause of the Union, and to pledge their united energies to the support of the Government for the complete suppression of the Rebellion.

Lieutenant-General Scott has been invited to preside.

The undersigned have been instructed to solicit the honor of your presence and influence on an occasion of so much interest to the Country.

An early reply will oblige. Respectfully,

> Your Obedient Servants,
> F. A. Conkling
> Chas. H. Marshall and others

Once again declining a compelling opportunity to sway public opinion in overwhelmingly Democratic New York City, Lincoln declined this invitation with the following letter, probably written to be read aloud at the meeting. He would never visit New York again. Today a statue of Lincoln stands near the spot where this rally was organized (CW VII: 374).

> Executive Mansion,
> Washington, June 3, 1864.

Hon. F. A. Conkling
and others.

Gentlemen: Your letter inviting me to be present at a mass meeting of loyal citizens to be held at New York on the 4th inst., for the purpose of expressing gratitude to Lieutenant General Grant for his signal services, was received yesterday. It is impossible for me to attend. I approve, nevertheless, whatever may tend to strengthen and sustain Gen. Grant and the noble armies now under his direction. My previous high estimate of Gen. Grant has been maintained and heightened by what has occurred in the remarkable campaign he is now conducting; while the magnitude and difficulty of the task before him does not prove less than I expected. He and his brave soldiers are now in the midst of their great trial, and I trust that at your meeting you will so shape your good words that they may turn to men and guns moving to his and their support.

> Yours truly
> A. Lincoln

A Performer Invites Himself to the White House

Markham Hotel [Washington]
June 6. 1864

Abraham Lincoln Esqre

My dear Sir—The card you so kindly gave me this morning to
Professor Henry, obtained for me a very pleasant interview, but I regret
to say I was unable to procure the Lecture Room of the Institute.

Apart from the annoyance of leaving Washington, in consequence of the inability to obtain a Hall for my Lecture—it is a
double disappointment not to have had the honor of numbering you
among my patrons, and the object of my troubling you with these
lines, is to state that it will give me the greatest pleasure, in a very
informal and perfectly private manner, to set apart an hour any
evening this week you may suggest to present to Mrs Lincoln and
yourself, at your own residence, a few sketches that may possibly
interest and amuse you.

Very respectfully
Your obedient Servant
Stephen Massett

೧ *Massett, known professionally by the stage name "Jeems Pipes, of Pipesville,"
apparently piqued Lincoln's interest: the performer was indeed invited to the White
House to give the Lincolns a private demonstration of his "seriocomic lecture."
Entitled "Drifting About," according to a broadside that he enclosed with this
letter, it featured impersonations of such famous lecturers of the day as Henry Ward
Beecher and Ralph Waldo Emerson, all delivered with "creditable skill," as the
New York* World *had attested in a contemporary review. Although Lincoln later
confided to a visitor that Jeems was merely "a sort of mountebank, or comic
lecturer, or something of the kind," his performance in the Red Room, the visitor
recalled, "appeared greatly to amuse Mr. Lincoln," whose "voice and ringing
laugh" were "clearly distinguishable" from behind the closed doors. Lincoln even
urged Jeems to add to his repertoire an impression of someone who made whistling
noises while stammering, telling Jeems it would be "irresistably ludicrous," and
proceeding to demonstrate until Jeems could duplicate the imitation on his own
(Carpenter,* Six Months at the White House, *160–161).*

Summer at Saratoga

[*T E L E G R A P H*]
Saratoga Springs [N Y.,] July 29 1864.

President Lincoln

Can we expect the pleasure of your company on or before the fifth August

W. H. Deland & Co.
Union Hall

∽ *Lincoln did not go to the famous spa; instead he wired New York Governor Edwin D. Morgan on August 1 at Saratoga Springs: "Please come here at once. I wish to see you." (CW VII: 474.)*

A Rendezvous with Grant

[*T E L E G R A P H*]
Head Qrs 9th Corps in City Point
July 30th 1864 10:30 A.M.

His Excellency A. Lincoln
Prest U.S.

I will meet you at Fort Monroe Va tomorrow at the hour you designated.

U. S. Grant
Lt Genl

∽ *The exceptions to Lincoln's steadfast determination to remain in Washington managing the war were his occasional visits to confer with his generals at the front. Lincoln visited Grant at Fortress Monroe on Sunday, July 31, 1864 (LDBD III: 276).*

A "Monster" Music Festival

New York September 5th 1864

To the Honourable Abraham Lincoln
President of the United States

Sir   Your Excellency is respectfully invited to honour with your presence the first Annual Monster Festival and Concert of the Musical

Mutual Protection Union of New York, to be held at Jones' Woods on Monday Sept. the 19th commencing at 11 o'clock in the forenoon.

This Association, which has obtained a special Act of Incorporation and which now numbers over Eight Hundred members proposes to devote the surplus of its subscriptions after defraying its working expenses, aided by such funds as can be accumulated by means of an Annual Summer Festival and Winter Concert to carry out the object which will be briefly stated in the following paragraph.

In a community like ours, where the public taste for music is becoming rapidly developed, it is to its professors a great source of regret that there is no local institution where a thorough musical education can be obtained. The lack of which necessitates the trouble, expense and loss of time consequent on a journey to and from, and a residence of some years in Europe. To remedy this deficiency, to supply this want, which has been felt for some time, this society intends to raise funds by the methods above named, with which to build a Capacious and Elegant Hall wherein the performance of its Concerts will take place and to found a National School for Musicians, similar to the great European establishments where a most complete and thorough musical education shall be obtained at the lowest possible cost that will be remunerative.

The limits of this note do not admit of the advantages of such an institution, being more fully dwelt upon, but, the Society trusts that enough has been said in explanation to interest Your Excellency in the magnitude of their undertaking.

It is the Inaugural of the Monster Festival and Concert above alluded to, that your Excellency is solicited to favour by your personal attendance, if possible, and with great respect

We have the honour to be

> Your obedient Servants
> John P. Cooke, Chair.
> Theodore Thomas
> Carl Bergman
> Thomas Walker
> Henry D. Beissenherz
> D. Pehead, Secretary
> Office 155 Eldridge Street

Two complimentary tickets were enclosed with this invitation, according to a secretary's endorsement on the letter. But, preoccupied with war and politics, the President did not use them. No record has been found of a reply, but it was customary for such invitations to be accepted or declined with a letter, usually drafted by an aide and signed by the President. Lincoln's reply to this unusual invitation has yet to be uncovered.

Asking a Toast to his Favorite Poet

Treasury Department,
Second Auditor's Office,
January 24, 1865

Sir: The "Executive Committee of Management for the Celebration of the 106th Anniversary of the birth of Robert Burns" have instructed me, as their Secretary, to request the honor of your recognition of the genius of Scotland's bard, by either a toast, a sentiment, or in any other way you may deem proper. It takes place tomorrow. I am Sir

Your very obsvt
Alex. Williamson

Alexander Williamson, who had served as a tutor to Willie and Tad Lincoln a few years earlier, received in reply a brief memorandum from the busy president. According to the Washington Star, *"Mr. Williamson, remarking that the President's pressing duties had prevented him writing a letter or a toast in response to the invitation . . . read a hastily written memorandum which the President had sent him, in substance as follows: 'I cannot now frame a toast to Mr. Burns or to say to you aught worthy of his most generous heart and transcending genius."' In fairness to Lincoln, who loved Burns's work but in this reply seemed at best indifferent, Williamson had given him scant notice to prepare a formal toast (Washington* Star, *January 26, 1865).*

Anniversary of a Charity

Central Office,
U.S. Christian Commission
Philadelphia, January 24, 1865

His Excellency Abraham Lincoln
President of the United States

Dear Sir: The Third Anniversary of the United States Christian Commission, is to be held in the Hall of the House of Representatives at the Capitol next Sabbath Evening, the 29th inst., commencing at 7 o'clock.

Hon. William H. Seward is to preside, and distinguished gentlemen of the Army and Navy, the State and the Church, will address the Meeting.

Your presence with us, last year, added greatly to the interest of our meeting, and to its influence for good, throughout the country. It was an occasion never to be forgotten by those who were there. I am instructed to respectfully invite you to meet with us, this year also.

It is a great source of joy to us, as Americans and Christians, that our Government has not only surpassed the governments of all other times and nations in generous provision for the health and comfort of its Army and Navy, but has so cheerfully welcomed and encouraged the supplemental work of the Christian Commission amongst our brave men in their marches and battles, and in Hospital, Trench, and Camp. By this means, the people at home have been cheered and strengthened to give their sons, brothers and husbands to the War, many thousands have been rescued from the grave, and restored to the service; our forces have been steadied and strengthened for battle, and nerved to fight it out to the end, and an untold amount of suffering has been saved, and good done to our brave defenders.

Trusting for a favorable response, I remain

> Very Respectfully Yours,
> George H. Stuart
> Chairman

∽ *Lincoln accepted this invitation, and during the ceremonies was so impressed by the performance of a hymn by one Philip Philips that he scribbled a note on the back of his program and passed it to Chairman Stuart: "Near the close let us have 'Your Mission' repeated by Mr. Philips. Dont say I called for it." When the singer learned later that the President had requested the encore, he sent Lincoln a "little singing book for your little boy" and asked for a copy of the note the president had written the night of his performance, admitting: "the honor created in me a strong desire to have the request in writing." Peeved, perhaps, that Chairman Stuart had not heeded his insistence on anonymity, Lincoln is not known to have replied. Stuart wrote Lincoln again on February 1 to apologize for some of the remarks offered at the meeting, which he conceded "did not seem to us to be in good taste in such a presence." There is no record of the speeches made that night (CW, VIII: 245–246).*

A *Gymnastic Exhibition*

Washington, January 30th 1865

To His Excellency Abraham Lincoln
President of the United States

Sir, The undersigned being a committee deputed by the three hundred members of Brady's Gymnasium, respectfully request the honor of your attendance at Ford's Theatre, on the evening of Washington's birthday, which it is intended to commemorate by a grand gymnastic exhibition and ball to be given by them.

No labor nor expense has been spared upon the decorations and appointments, which will surpass in taste and elegance anything of the kind hitherto given in Washington.

Your acceptance of this invitation and its implied patronage of gymnasia, it is deemed, cannot fail to prove a stimulus to the youth of the country to cultivate the "mens sána in corpore sano [a sound mind in a sound body]."

We have the honor to be

Your Excellency's Most Obedient Servants
Richard C. Du Bois [and others]

ᔫ *Lincoln had ceased publicly observing Washington's birthday three years earlier. Although he did enjoy attending Ford's Theatre and saw several plays there during his presidency, he apparently did not have sufficient interest in the gymnasium movement, a growing health and fitness craze, to attend this demonstration.*

A *Ponderous Lecture*

Washington D. C. Jan'y 31, 1865

Your Excellency: To-morrow evening Wednesday Feby 1st Edwin Forrest, the eminent American tragedian is to be my guest, upon which occasion Mr. J. S. Wilson, Chief Clerk of the Gen. Land Office will deliver an address upon the "Senate of Rome, the House of Parliament of England, and the Senate of the U.S.!", and several prominent citizens are expected to be present. Your presence is most respectfully desired.

My residence is No 170 West Street, 4th door from High.

With great respect

Your obt. servant
Geo W. Miller

Although Lincoln admired Forrest, he likely would have found any excuse to avoid the tedious lecture described above. As it happened, the night of February 1 found the President at the White House being serenaded by a throng gathered there to celebrate the occasion of the Thirteenth Amendment to the Constitution abolishing slavery being sent to the states for their ratification.

A Washington's Birthday Celebration

[February 16, 1865]

The honor of your Company at the Soiree to be given by the Washington Literary and Dramatic Association on the evening of the 22nd of February next at Odd Fellows Hall in honor of the celebration of Washington's Birth Day is respectfully solicited.

> For the Committee
> A. Hart, Chairman

Lincoln did not attend the soiree described above. After years of heartfelt public tributes to Washington, Lincoln had, in fact, ceased invoking his name altogether after 1862—the same year his Emancipation Proclamation elevated him in many minds (including, perhaps, his own) to a new status as Washington's equal in history. In his final public statement on Washington, Lincoln had urged all Americans to observe his 130th birthday in 1862 by re-reading his Farewell Address. On February 22, a literal-minded citizen obliged by attempting to read it aloud from the galleries of Congress, prompting an overzealous guard to use force to restrain him. Lincoln had rushed to the guard's defense, insisting he was only trying to perform "his official duty." But he never called for a Washington's Birthday celebration again (Holzer, Washington and Lincoln Portrayed, 183; CW, V: 136).

A Final Visit to the Front

[T E L E G R A P H]
I N   C I P H E R

City Point Va Mar. 20th. 10 am 1865

His Excellency
A Lincoln Prest U.S.

Can you not visit City Point for a day or two? I would like very much to see you and I think the rest would do you good.

> Respectfully yours &c
> U. S. Grant
> Lt Genl

ᴑᴕ Lincoln replied as follows later the same day.

[T E L E G R A P H]

Washington, D. C., March 20 1865

"Cypher"
Lieut. Genl. Grant
City-Point Va.

Your kind invitation received. Had already thought of going immediately after the next rain. Will go sooner if any reason for it. Mrs. L. and a few others will probably accompany me. Will notify you of exact time, once it shall be fixed upon.

A. Lincoln

ᴑᴕ The next day Lincoln wired his son—then serving on Grant's staff—about his plans to visit the front, cautioning him: "Dont make public." And then, on March 23, he telegraphed Grant: "We start to you at One P.M. to-day." The trip of "a day or two" turned into a week or two, and by the time Lincoln returned to Washington on April 9 he had less than a week to live (CW, VIII: 367, 369, 372).

This letter appears on page 325.

April 5th 64.

Dere Abe I Received your
Little Check for 50.00 I Showed
it to mother She Cried Like a Child
Abe She is mity Childish heep of
trubles to us Betsy is very feble and
has to wait on hir which ort to have
Sum person to wait on hir we are
getting old we have a great many
to wait on of our Connections they
will Cum to See us while we Live
Abe Charlie has Reinlisted a
gain for three years or during the
war This is hard to his mother
Abe we had a horrible time a
munday of Caint it Broke up
got in to a fuss By a drunken
Soldier I Never Saw such a time
thare was 8 or 10 Killed in the
fight one you no doct yorke of
paris Edgar County young
E winkler was wounted

[9]

Family Matters

*I*F *LINCOLN* ever harbored the hope that letters from family members would provide him with relief from the demands and complaints that arrived in his usual correspondence, this hope was quickly, bitterly, and repeatedly dashed.

One might reasonably assume that Lincoln's voluminous and largely unpleasant mail was occasionally brightened by the arrival of a genial letter from a relative. But sadly, such was not the case—not ever. Astonishingly, not a single surviving letter from any member of the extended Lincoln or Todd families ever brought an unencumbered greeting, a birthday or holiday salutation, or even a straightforward wish for the President's health or success.

Instead, family correspondence mirrored the troubling mail that arrived from strangers: Lincoln's relatives relentlessly besieged him with complaints, criticism, and demands for jobs and favors. His wife's anti-Union relatives in the South, for example, asked special exemptions from the rules that restricted Confederates and their sympathizers. Todds in the North, meanwhile, most of them anti-Lincoln in their politics, nonetheless expected their share—perhaps more—of the federal patronage pot. Brothers-in-law did more than line up for appointments: one of them went on to misuse the office Lincoln awarded him; another had the audacity to ask for advance, secret notice of any imminent restoration of peace, he frankly admitted, so that he could sell his stocks at high prices and make a financial killing. After a while, Lincoln must have begun taking up letters from relatives with the same sense of foreboding with which he read the frequently distressing war news off the military telegraph. Family letters described battles every bit as painful to the beleaguered president.

Even the rare surviving letter from his wife, who travelled frequently—sometimes on shopping expeditions, occasionally to escape Washington's oppressive summer weather—seldom brought good cheer. A typical wire from Mary contained recriminations for Lincoln's failure to answer earlier notes, complaints about accommodations, and requests for money.

Lincoln's own relatives offered no more solace than did the Todds. They wrote heartbreaking reports describing his aged and apparently poorly tended stepmother, laying the blame with other family members; grumbled bitterly about their own imagined poor treatment on federal patronage; and blamed other relations for the bad feelings and irresponsibility that were rampant in the family. Like the Todds, most of Lincoln's surviving relatives on his mother's side—the Hanks family—were Democrats who were similarly convinced of their absolute right to special treatment from their Republican relative.

Lincoln had all but divorced himself from his own backwoods relations when he married Mary Todd in 1842, and his cousins' letters make the reasons for this distancing easier to understand. In education, ambition, and the mere ability to communicate coherently, his cousins lived worlds away from their distinguished relation. Once Lincoln achieved fame, even back in Illinois, where most of his people had settled, he very seldom saw them, and they exchanged letters with growing infrequency. "Mr. L. has neither brother nor sister, aunt or uncle, and only a few third cousins," Mary Lincoln once wrote dismissively. That did not stop even the most distant cousins from referring to their famous relative as "unkel"—no doubt hoping such familiarity would rebound to their benefit.

But Lincoln kept his distance. When his father lay dying in 1851, Lincoln conspicuously absented himself from the deathbed despite pleas from his kin that he come home. He did not bother to order a headstone erected over Thomas Lincoln's grave until his last visit to his stepmother's log cabin ten years later. Most incredibly of all, he made no effort ever to introduce his wife or his sons to the woman who had raised him after his natural mother had died. When Mary wrote to the old lady after Lincoln's assassination, she made sure to tell her, perhaps for the very first time, that the Lincolns' youngest child, Thomas "Tad" Lincoln, had been named for the President's father. Apparently no one had ever bothered to tell Sarah Lincoln. In a sense, the President's relatives were right to feel slighted by the onetime rail-splitter who rose from log cabin to White House: he deliberately, coolly cut all ties to them. Outside of his own tight circle—his wife and their sons—family mattered not at all to Abraham Lincoln, and he made little effort to conceal his indifference.

His best-remembered relation, aside from his stepmother, was Dennis Hanks, his cousin and step-brother-in-law ("I was the second man who touched Lincoln after his birth," Dennis was fond of boasting in later years). Dennis, who carried the news of Lincoln's death to Sarah in 1865, described himself that year as "an actor pretty much all my life in the scene" of his famous cousin's life, but the truth was, after Lincoln's ascent, Dennis rarely saw him. Still, his visit to Washington in March 1864, apparently unexpected, gave the President some nostalgic moments, according to those who witnessed their reunion. Dennis recalled finding him sitting "at an old desk worth about six bits"—his sturdy pigeonhole upright model—and that after he hollered into the room, "You're a pretty President, ain't ye," Lincoln rushed over "and just gathered me."

If he thought the visit would be purely social, Lincoln was in for a shock. Dennis proceeded to press him on political matters (the aftermath of a politically motivated riot back home), and probably pleaded for patronage assistance for his own ne'er-do-well sons-in-law (he would follow up these requests later by mail). Apparently feeling sorry for Dennis, Lincoln gave him his old silver watch (Dennis's had been lifted by a pickpocket on the train to Washington). Yet soon thereafter there came a deeply disturbing letter from the Illinois backwoods charging that Dennis had misappropriated funds Lincoln had sent for his stepmother's care.

All these Hanks and Lincoln family problems must have seemed minuscule, however, compared to those generated for the President by his wife's large brood of sisters. Mary's father had married twice and produced sixteen children. No fewer than four of Mary's sisters—Elizabeth Todd Edwards, Frances Todd Wallace, Ann Todd Smith, all from Springfield, and Margaret Todd Kellogg of Cincinnati—married men who later called on Lincoln for appointments or other favors once he reached the White House. Of one such effort Mary confessed that her sister "little knows what a hard battle, I had," and how close her sister's ungrateful husband had "come to getting nothing." In fact, Mary was an active conspirator on her relatives' behalf, emboldened by a political culture in which presidents routinely awarded patronage to their kith and kin. But Lincoln was likely surprised when a female from the Todd clan, Mary's devoted cousin Elizabeth Todd Grimsley, campaigned for a federal job for herself. Lincoln did not oblige her.

Worst of all, some of Mary's family had remained in the South and pledged loyalty to the Confederacy. Mary's half-sister Emilie married a Confederate general who was killed in action in 1863, and Mary went on to scandalize Washington by inviting Emilie to recuperate at the White House. Emilie departed, wrote later for further help, and proceeded to betray Lincoln's generosity by conducting herself disloyally and attempting to excuse her actions with a special pass she had secured from her brother-in-law.

In the entire archive of painful correspondence to Lincoln from or about his relatives, the one and only pleasant letter that has been found came not from a family member but from Lincoln's onetime Springfield barber, a black immigrant from the Caribbean named William Florville, who, with no criticism to proffer or favor to demand, wrote merely to compliment his old customer, to offer belated condolences over the death of Lincoln's son, Willie, and to pass on his assurances to Lincoln's surviving child that the pet dog he had left behind in Springfield was still thriving.

Family news as comforting never came from the family itself.

His Wife's Cousin Seeks Patronage Plum

P R I V A T E

Springfield Illinois
April 3rd 1861

Dear Lincoln.

I have received your favor of the 30th ultimo. I would not let the case of Cousin Lizzie trouble me if I were you No one will complain of you if you do not give her the appointment [as Springfield postmaster] while very many doubtless would complain of her appointment and would have much show of reason because the appointment of a lady would be unusual All I feel that I can properly say now is what I said to Cousin Lizzie that the emoluments of the office would be a great source of comfort to her and to Uncle & Aunt If they have a few years they will be dependent In my letter to Cousin Lizzie I said that I did not expect you would give her the appointment

So far as the election is concerned (I mean for Postmaster) it will amount to nothing. I understand that all the applicants but Ellis are opposed to submitting to a vote and it is charged that Ellis' friends on the North side of the town are anxious to have Ellis appointed so as to remove the office to that side of the town I have no reason to believe that there is any truth in this I only refer to it to show the feeling— There is a good deal of feeling among the different Candidates and their friends and no appointment you can make would be very satisfactory and if I were you I would please <u>myself</u>.

All that I can say is that I cannot urge upon you her appointment yet I would be glad if she is appointed. I do not feel that her appointment would subject you to more remarks than any one else while a very large portion of our community would be very much gratified by it—

I hope you will give Dr. [William] Wallace [Lincoln's brother-in-law] some good appointment and the appointment of both will do you no great harm I believe I have said enough to explain my feelings on this subject.

I wish to say one thing more that my personal attachment and respect for you which I have maintained for twenty years is as sincere now as it ever was notwithstanding our difference in politics and I hope you [have] every success, for you—and our common country.

Yours truly
John T. Stuart

Stuart was Lincoln's first law partner in Springfield in the 1840s. On March 30, the President had written him a private letter to express his concern over the desire of his wife's devoted cousin Lizzie to become Springfield postmaster. "The question . . . troubles me," he admitted. "You see I have already appointed William Jayne [a close family friend and a relative by marriage of his longtime political associate, Lyman Trumbull] a territorial governor, and Judge Trumbulls brother [Benjamin Trumbull] to a Land-office. Will it do for me to go on and justify the declaration that Trumbull and I have divided out all the offices among our relatives?" Only his brother-in-law, he wrote, was a justifiable exception: "Dr. Wallace, you know, is needy, and looks to me; and I personally owe him much." Lincoln did like the idea of a town referendum, which Stuart described, to endorse a consensus candidate for postmaster. But no such canvass was ever organized, and in the end Elizabeth Todd Grimsley, "Cousin Lizzie," did not get the patronage job she coveted (CW, IV: 303).

A Cousin's Aspirations Thwarted

PRIVATE

San Francisco
May 31. 1861.

Sir.   I feel compelled to write to you in reard [sic] to the appointment of L. M. Todd as Custom House Drayman.

He has not yet arrived here, but it has become known that he expects the appointment, and a formal protest has been sent to me against it, signed by the County Committee, and a large number of the Republicans of Solano County, where Mr. T. has resided, representing that he has been a most bitter and violent opponent of the Republican party up to the very day of the election and even longer, and that his appointment to any position of trust under your administration would be regarded as a gross insult and wrong to the Republicans of the County. An affadavit has also been sent to me signed by one of the protestants, a copy of which I take the liberty to enclose to you herewith, and which sets forth substantially the same facts. I am sorry to have to communicate such statements, but they have come to me in so many different ways, that I cannot doubt they are true. Several personal friends living in Suisun where Mr. T. has lived, inform me that the statements sent to me are correct beyond question. Such being the case, I shall take the liberty when Mr. T. arrives to withhold his appointment unless he can satisfy me that I have been misinformed. Until I can hear from you, and until he can so satisfy me

I hope for my credit and that of the party you will not insist upon my giving him the position. Admitting that all which is said of him is true, if still you desire on account of personal kindness or family feeling to do something for him, permit me to suggest that in giving the drayage contract to another party, I make a reservation of a certain sum to be paid over to Mr. Todd from the net profits, without his being known at all in connection with the appointment.

In the midst of your great cares I am very reluctant to trouble you with a personal affair like this, but in justice to you and myself I cannot do less.

General McDougall leaves here in the morning as one of our Senators. He has been known heretofore as a Democrat, and was elected by fusion of the Union Democratic and Republican votes of the Legislature—but in the present exigency you can count on him as a Republican Senator. That is, you will find him, if I do not mistake ready to go as far as the farthest in Sustaining Your Administration in enforcing the Laws, and maintaining the integrity of the Union. A great majority of the people of this State rejoice in the strong measures taken by Government to uphold its authority, and most earnestly hope to see no flinching until treason is effectually quelled. If any call should be made on this State for troops it would be responded to instantly—indeed one Regiment is nearly organized only in the hope of a call.

I have the honor to be Most respectfully

> Your obt svt
> Ira P. Rankin

To His Excellency Abraham Lincoln
President of the U.S.

∽ On April 5 Lincoln had written Rankin, collector of customs for the Port of San Francisco: "Lockwood M. Todd . . . is a cousin of Mrs. L. and she and I will be much obliged if the collector can give him the place he seeks." The Drayman's job could yield up to $2,500 a year. Faced with Rankin's resistance, Todd protested that he had "from a boy . . . been taught by our dear father to regard Mr. Lincoln as the best and purest of men." Nonetheless, Lincoln backed down and Rankin named his own brother to the job (he was later removed for corruption). Not until 1864 did Todd get an appointment from his famous relative: as captain and commissary of subsistence (CW, IV: 323; LFA, 8–10).

Another In-Law Seeks Commission

Fort Randall, Dakota Ty
August 27th 1861.

To the President

The stirring events occurring in different parts of the country, and the desire I have to contribute my share towards upholding and maintaining the Union & the Constitution of our Country, and to give you the proof of my devotion to yourself, the cause, & the policy you have pursued since your inauguration, urge me again to offer my services to you in any capacity in which I may be useful.

You are aware of my military education, and that I am amongst the oldest, if not the oldest, of the graduates of the U.S. Military Academy from our State, and that previous to my resignation in 1856, I served the Army for nearly twenty years, most of the time upon the Western frontier, & much of that time in command—My experience upon the frontier and knowledge of the character and habits of Western people, fit me in some degree to be of use in that part of the country, where more recently, operations have been most active, and if left to my choice, I would prefer a command in that field where my late friend Gen'l [Nathaniel] Lyon shown [sic] so conspicuous & fell so gloriously—But this is not so material—I am ready to go anywhere that my services can be made available, and am willing to devote my time, talents, energies & resources to that sacred cause which should & no doubt does, inspire all patriotic hearts—

I hope that you will approve my application to the Secretary of War for an appointment as either Brigadier or Major Genl. Many of my old associates & comrades have been thus honored & I believe I am as capable as most of them—& if so, that I may be directed to report to Genl Fremont for service in Missouri—will you please let Mr. Nicolay telegraph me, through A. S. Paddock, Secty of Nebraska, as soon as your decision is made.

Yours Truly
J. B. S. Todd

∽ *A month later, Lincoln added the name of J. B. S. Todd, his wife's cousin, to a list of appointments submitted by General McClellan. To make sure the secretary of war would not fail to notice the addition, Lincoln included the following note: "I sent, this morning, an order for Todd's appointment, on the back of Gen. McClellan's letter recommending three others. A. Lincoln." Todd was subsequently made Brigadier General of volunteers (CW, IV: 530; LFA, 11–12).*

Complaints about a Brother-In-Law

State of Illinois, Secretary's Office
Springfield October 21st 1861

Mr. A. Lincoln. President.

Dr. Sir. As we predicted, Joel A. Matteson, under a contract made between Ninian W. Edwards, commissary on the one part, and Dr Fowler and Mr Goodell on the other part, is now, <u>in person</u>, furnishing subsistence to the troops at Camp Butler; and claims the right to do so at the other encampments in this state. We again insist that this outrage against common decency be corrected. We protest that Mr Edwards is not, or ought not to be permitted to make such contracts, and we respectfully ask that he be assigned to duty elsewhere, and be required to contract directly with honest men, and not indirectly with thieves and scoundrels.

Respectfully Your friends
Jesse K. Dubois
William Butler
O. M. Hatch

His old Republican friends in Illinois were outraged when Lincoln's brother-in-law, a Whig turned Democrat, secured an appointment from the President as commissary of subsistence and then proceeded to award lucrative contracts to his fellow Democrat Matteson. Ninian Edwards was accused or profiting personally to the tune of $15,000, a princely sum for the time. Lincoln, who awarded the office to Edwards because he "needed it very much" to rescue him from "pecuniary embarrassment," came to regret the decision almost immediately. Edwards wrote Lincoln on October 27 to give him his "word of honor that I have done nothing except what I believe to be my duty for the public interest." Lincoln at first publicly backed his brother-in-law. Privately, however, the President was annoyed at Edwards for having provoked "harassing" letters like this one, which continued to arrive for two years. Lincoln believed that Edwards "could have spared me from this." The President's problems with this appointment would continue until 1863 (LFA, 8; ALE, 95–96).

Wife Chides Husband for Not Writing

[New York,] Nov 2d [1862]

My Dear Husband—

I have waited in vain to hear from you, yet as you are not <u>given</u> to letter writing, will be charitable enough to impute your silence, to the right cause. Strangers come up from W- & tell me you are well—which satisfies me very much—Your name is on every lip and many prayers and good wishes are hourly sent up, for your welfare—and McClellan & his slowness are as vehemently discussed. Allowing this beautiful weather, to pass away, is disheartening the North—

Dear little Taddie is well and enjoying himself very much—Gen and Mrs [Robert] Anderson [hero of Fort Sumter] & myself called on yesterday to see Gen [Winfield] Scott [retired general, then living at West Point]—He looks well, although complaining of Rheumatism. A day or two since, I had one of my severe attacks, if it had not been for Lizzie Keckley [Mrs. Lincoln's seamstress and companion], I do not know what I should have <u>done</u>—Some of <u>these periods</u>, will launch me away—All the distinguished in the land, have tried how polite & attentive, they could be to me, since I came up here—Many say, they would almost worship you, if you would put a fighting General, in the place of McClellan. This would be splendid weather, for an engagement. I have had two suits of clothes made for Taddie which will come to 26 dollars—Have to get some fur outside wrappings for the coachman's carriage trappings. Lizze [*sic*] Keckley, wants me to loan her thirty dollars—so I will have to ask for a check, of $100- which will soon be made use of, for these articles—I must send you, Taddie's tooth—I want to leave here for Boston, on Thursday & if you will send the check by Tuesday, will be much obliged—

One line, to say that we are occasionally remembered will be gratefully received by yours very truly

M. L.

I enclose you a note from Mr [Alexander T.] Stewart [New York retailer], he appears to be very solicitous about his young friend. Mr S. is so strong a Union man—& asks so few favors—if it came in your way, perhaps it would not be amiss to oblige—

There is no record that Lincoln answered this long letter, which begins with an effort to make the President feel guilty, then proceeds to offer advice on war strategy and ask for money, along with a favor for a store owner who, although she did not mention it here, had been patient with Mrs. Lincoln about overdue bills. In other words, it is a typical letter from Mary to Abraham Lincoln. The First Lady wrote again the following day on one subject she had somehow left out of her previous letter: race (Turner and Turner, Mary Todd Lincoln, 139–141).

[New York, November 3, 1862]

My dear Husband—

I wrote you on yesterday, yet omitted a very important item. Elizabeth Keckley, who is with me and working for the Contraband Association, at Wash [a relief group organized, Mrs. Keckley claimed, by herself, to provide help to freedmen facing poverty in the North] is authorized by the White part of the concern by a written document— to collect any thing for them—here that, she can—She has been very unsuccessful—She says the immense number of Contrabands in W- are suffering intensely, many without bed coverings & having to use any bits of carpeting to cover themselves—Many dying of want—Out of the $1000 fund deposited with you by Gen Corcoran [possibly Michael Corcoran], I have given her the privilege of investing $200 her[e] in bed covering. She is the most deeply grateful being, I ever saw, & this sum, I am sure, you will not object to being used in this way—The cause of humanity requires it—and there will be $800 left of the fund—I am sure, this will meet your approbation—The soldiers are well supplied with comfort. Please send check for $200 out of the fund—she will bring you on the bill

With much love
Yours &

Please write by return mail
[Written on the envelope:] Please write by return mail——with much love yours &c—Please answer by return mail & send c____"

ᑫ *There is no known reply.*

A Todd Pleads for her Son

Springfield Jan 7 1863.

Mr. Lincoln.

Dear Sir,   If you have any inclination, & opportunity to confer a favour on your old friends & relatives, we are ready now to afford you the pleasure we are aware you desire from such acts, the truth is, I ask it being unable to refrain, hoping you have something in your gift, or can procure for our son Lockwood who has been with us ever since he left Washn. with only occasional writing to do, hoping you would remember him, he had no means, & we are not able to assist him to return to Cala. where he could procure employment, all business men have their own friends for clerks—Lockwood wrote some months since to Mary inclosing a letter from Genl. Carlin to himself, to which he received no answer, the Genl. says he has twice since written to Washn. with similar results, he has allow'd his brother to attend to the business, yet hoping Lockwood would be appointed, he is not in town & I forget what it is unless something about the Commissary Dept. John [Lockwood's brother, J. B. S. Todd] may know—I think Mr. Lincoln you have no truer friends (tho perhaps not so efficient) as Dr. and his sons who have been so much with you, L. would risk his life for you, and still would doubtless—I am sorry to have been so prolix, knowing your time is precious, but I am not a business woman, but an anxious Mother, therefore I beg your clemency—

    May God bless, and assist you in your arduous duties is our prayer. Yours as ever

E. F. B. Todd

& Please present our love to Mary—

ℂ *The troublesome Lockwood Todd, an anti-Lincoln Democrat in politics, had to wait until 1864 for an appointment—his mother's assurances of loyalty notwithstanding (LFA, 10).*

Misconduct by his Son at Harvard

Cambridge, Mass. Dec. 9, 1862.

Hon. Abraham Lincoln,
President of the United States, Washington, D.C.
Dear Sir

    The faculty last evening voted 'that Lincoln, Junior, be publicly admonished for smoking in Harvard Square after being privately admonished for the same offense.' The word 'publicly' simply makes it my duty to inform you of the admonition, and I trust, sir, that you will impress upon him the necessity not only of attention to matters of decorum, but of giving heed to the private admonitions of his instructors.

> Very respectfully yours,
> Thomas Hill
> President of Harvard Coll.

∽ *If Lincoln reacted to this letter the way most parents then—and since—might be expected to respond, no record of a reprimand to his son Robert has ever come to light. If the President did scold Robert, the "junior" Lincoln in all likelihood destroyed the letter in later years, when his reclusiveness about family matters outweighed his sense of history. In this case, however, even the senior Lincoln seemed embarassed by this correspondence. Hill's letter cannot be found in the Lincoln Papers, and its absence strongly suggests that a mortified parent chose to discard rather than preserve it. The copy reproduced here was discovered in the papers of Harvard President Hill. Robert went on to graduate from Harvard in June 1864, and would later enter Harvard Law School. But first he desired a taste of army life, and for months after leaving school implored his parents to permit him to enlist. At the urging of Mary—frantic that she might thus lose yet another son—Lincoln resisted Robert's pleas, until he finally convinced the First Lady that "many a poor mother . . . has had to make this sacrifice." Even then, Robert would be coddled. On January 19, 1865, Lincoln wrote to General Grant not as "President, but only a friend," to ask whether Robert, "without embarassment to you, or detriment to the service," could "go into your Military family with some nominal rank, I, and not the public, furnishing his necessary means." Grant replied two days later that he would be "most happy" to welcome Robert into his entourage. Lincoln's eldest son—the only Lincoln child to live to maturity—went on to serve with Grant, return to law school, and later carve out a successful career as public servant (Secretary of War under two presidents) and business tycoon (president of the Pullman Company). He died in 1926 (Bentulek-Smith,* The Harvard Book, *54; CW, VIII: 223; LFA, 95).*

Complaints about his Brother-In-Law Heeded

Springfield May 25, 1863

Mr. Lincoln.

It is unpleasant to me, to complain to you,—I would not do it, only to justify or confirm what we have said. We protested against the appointment of Mr. Edwards as assistant Commissary: because of the influence of the men that had surrounded him for several years. All

that we then predicted—and more—has, I think, proven true. For-
tunes have undoubtedly been made, in an improper manner, I have no
doubt myself, though I cannot prove it.

Much complaint has been made of Captain [William H.]
Bailhache [quartermaster at Springfield]—that he too, is one of
them—it is certain that most of his contracts have been given to men,
that denounce your Administration, and sympathize with rebels.
These again are in easy, money making places, at home, our friends
are in the field. It ought not to be so.

Your friend
O. M. Hatch

ᔕᒧ *On May 29 Lincoln wrote to Hatch and other Springfield leaders: "Agree among
yourselves upon any two of your own number, one of whom to be Quarter-Master, and
the other to be Commissary, to serve at Springfield, Illinois, and send me their names,
and I will appoint them." Lincoln was finally ready to remove, or at least transfer, his
brother-in-law (CW, VI: 237–238).*

His Brother-in-law Defends Himself

PRIVATE & CONFIDENTIAL

Springfield Illinois
June 18 1863

My Dear Sir—Mr. Baker shows me your letter of the 15th—It
pains me very much to hear that I give you any trouble—I know that I
have not only kept my record correct, but I have taken extraordinary
pains to avoid giving any cause for complaint—I have let all contracts
strictly in accordance with law and have to swear that I have done so
without favoring any one—

Will it not remove cause of complaint, if the contracts in future
can be awarded by the Chief Commissary of this Department at Cincinnati? I would then only have to make payment under them—this
Col. Kilburn Chief Co 5 would be willing to do—

When I asked an office from you, (it was not this one) I needed it
very much—I can now do without it—I didnt wish to embarrass you.
If I am removed from here it will be said that there is good cause
for it—

Under my present orders, I can keep my office at Chicago, provided the arrangement that Col Kilburn may let the contracts is not
satisfactory—& rather than give you further trouble I will resign—I
will do what you think best.

You speak of your life long friends in Springfield—desiring a
change—I would like to ask you, if when you were a young man, I
was not your most devoted friend in more ways than one—Let Joshua
F. Speed, your own recollection [Edwards had first written "conscience," then he crossed it out], and a letter of yours written to me in
1842, before your marriage occurred—Again who was it, when it was
thought in 1840 that you would not be nominated for the legislature
publicly stated if any one was to be left out he should be—who was
your best friend when Baker, John Hardin & yourself were candidates
for a seat in Congress, again which of the two Butler or myself was
your best friend for years after that—

At the last Presidential Election although I differed with you I
made several speeches <u>with the approbation of your best political
friends</u>, in order to say what I thought of you—saying that if there
was a man living without a fault I believed you that man—This I can
prove.

I know that you thought when you Matteson & Trumbull were
candidates for the Senate, that I preferred Matteson to you—This was
not true for I stated publicly, that if there was any chance for you, I
preferred that you should be elected to either of them—and this too
although I differed with you in politics—I am sure you know me too
well to think that I would tell you an untruth. I know that others
make you believe otherwise—I mention these things to place myself
right—I am thankful to you for what you have already done—and in
your present situation I do not wish to add to your embarrassment —I
could mention something to show that I was ready and willing to
furnish when you were a young man, substantial evidence of <u>my
devoted attachment to you</u>—

If I have done anything improper I ought to be removed—I
would want an investigation from Judge Davis (who is here) or any
of your friends—

You have not a friend who is acquainted with the intricate relation existing between us in former times, who would not say that you
did right and acted nobly in aiding me when I needed it—For a proof
of this I refer you to Mr. Browning's & Judge Davis's letters—all
your old friends, Joseph Gillespie, Uncle Cyrus . . . A[.] Williams

Levant and others, have told me that you did what was right—No man of heart would say otherwise[.]

Very truly, yours as ever
N. W. Edwards

To his excellency, A Lincoln
President of U States

I never knew any one more unhappy than both my wife and myself, on acct. of the marriage of [indecipherable word]—and it seems that our troubles accumulate—

If Mr Vaughan had not been disappointed in getting a contract from Capt. Bailhasche, I dont believe any steps would have been taken in regard to me—I think still it will soon blow over—and especially if the contracts are all awarded at Cincinnati by the Chief Co 5—If you write that this shall be done I believe it will satisfy all parties At all events can you not try it and allow me to remain here—I am a strong friend of the Union—

I would also prefer not to make any contracts—I assure you again that I shall not be dissatisfied with anything you may think for the best—

∽ *As Lincoln had insisted in a letter written three days earlier, "I certainly do not suppose that Mr. Edwards has, at this time of his life, given up his old habits, and turned dishonest." But he hastened to add: "Springfield is my home, and there, more than elsewhere, are my life-long friends. These, for now nearly two years, have been harassing me because of Mr. E." As Lincoln saw it, his brother-in-law believed that if he and another beleaguered appointee "could keep their official record dryly correct . . . it was not any difference how much they might provoke my friends." In the end, despite this strong appeal for Lincoln's loyalty, Edwards was transferred to Chicago, a decision that strained but did not sever family relations (CW, VI: 275–276).*

Between Husband and Wife

[*T E L E G R A P H*]
New York September 22, 1863

A. Lincoln:

Your telegram received. Did you not receive my reply I have telegraphed Col McCullum to have the car ready at the earliest possible moment. Have a very bad cold and am anxious to return home as you may suppose. Taddie is well.

Mrs. Lincoln

∽ This telegram for Lincoln came after a series of wires to Mary making it progressively clear—after a half-hearted start—that he was eager for her return from a summer trip. The three telegrams that finally convinced her to hasten home follow (CW, VI: 469, 471, 474; Turner and Turner, Mary Todd Lincoln, 159–160).

Washington, D.C.,
Sep. 20 1863

Mrs. A. Lincoln
New-York

I neither see nor hear anything of sickness here now; though there may be much without my knowing it. I wish you to stay, or come just as is most agreeable to yourself.

A. Lincoln.

Washington, D.C.,
Sept. 21. 1863

Mrs. A. Lincoln
Fifth Avenue Hotel New-York

The air is so clear and cool, and apparently healthy, that I would be glad for you to come. Nothing very particular, but I would be glad see you and Tad.

A. Lincoln

Executive Mansion, Washington,
Sep. 22, 1863.

Mrs. A. Lincoln.
Fifth Avenue House New-York.

Did you receive my despatch of yesterday? Mrs. Cuthbert did not correctly understand me. I directed her to tell you to use your own pleasure whether to stay or come; and I did not say it is sickly & that you should on no account come. So far as I see or know, it was never healthier, and I really wish to see you. Answer this on receipt.

A. Lincoln

On the day this final, imploring wire was sent, Lincoln learned that his wife's half brother, Confederate General Ben Hardin Helm, had been killed at the Battle of Chickamauga. The President wrote the next day to inform Mary of the loss, and the First Lady finally hastened home to Washington (LDBD III: 209).

Family News from his Old Barber

Springfield Ills Decr 27th 1863

President Lincoln—

Dear Sir—I, having for you, an irresistible feeling of gratitude for the kind regards Shown, and the Manifest good wishes exhibited towards me, Since your residence in Washington City, as Communicated by Doctor [Anson] Henry [a Springfield physician] Sometime ago, and lately by his Excelency Governor Yates, have for the above reasons and our long acquaintance, thought it might not be improper for one so humble in life and occupation, to address the President of the United States.

Yet, I do so, feeling that if it is received by you (and you have time, for I know you are heavily Tax) it will be read with pleasure as a communication from Billy the Barber. This I express and feel for the truly great Man regards with corresponding favor the poor, and down troden of the Nation, to those more favored in Color, position, and Franchise rights and this you have shown, and I and my people feel greatful to you for it. The Shackels have fallen, and Bondmen have become freeman to Some extent already under your Proclamation. And I hope ere long, it may be universal in all the Slave States. That your authority may soon extend over them all, to all the oppressed, relieving them from their Bondage, and cruel Masters; who make them work, and fight, against the Government. And when so released, they would be glad I have no doubt, to assist in putting down the infamous Rebellion. May God grant you health, and strength, and wisdom, so to do, and so to act, as shall redown to his Glory, and the Good, peace, prosperity, Freedom, and happiness of this Nation. So that War Shall be known no more, that the cause or pretext for War be removed, that Rebellion and Secession Shall have no plea to make, and nothing to ask for, that all the States may not have an equal right to demand. Then, and not till then, will the Government be Steadfast and abiding, and for that reason, I hope and trust, that you may be chosen for a Second term to Administer the affairs of this Government. I think, after a four years experience, you are posted in matters relating thereto, and better calculated to carry out your own designs, and the wishes of the people, than any other man in this Nation. And the people here so think.

And if it Shall be the wish of the Men, who Support the Government, anxious to put down the Rebellion, Sustaining the Army, loving Freedom and the union, and who Sustain your acts, and your Administration, that you Should again accept the office of Chief Magistrate of this Nation, I hope you will not decline; but accept it, and put things and matters through, to their termination and when these troubles Shall end, the Nation will rejoice, the oppressed will Shout the name of their deliverer, and Generations to come, will rise up and call you blessed. (so mote it be) I was Sorry to hear of your illness [Lincoln had suffered a mild case of smallpox after returning from Gettysburg the previous month], and was glad when I learned that your health was improving. I hope by this time, you are able, or soon will be, to attend to your arduous business

I was Surprised at the announcement of the death of your son Willy. I thought him a smart boy for his age, so considerate, so manly; his knowledge and good Sence, far exceeding most boys more advanced in years. Yet the time comes to all, all must die.

I should like verry much to see you, and your family, but the privilege of enjoying an interview, may not soon, if ever come.

My family are all well. My son William is married and in business for himself. I am occupying the same place in which I was at the time you left. Tell Taddy that his (and Willys) Dog is alive and Kicking doing well he stays mostly at John E. Roll with his Boys Who are about the size now that Tad and Willy ware when they left for Washington

Your Residence here is Kept in good order. Mr. Tilton [who rented Lincoln's home] has no children to ruin things. Mrs Tilton and Miss Tilton are verry Strong Union Ladies and do a great deal for the Soldiers who are suffering so much for us & to sustain the Government

Please accept my best wishes for yourself and family, and my daily desires for yourself that your Administration may be prosperous, Wise, and productive of Good results to this Nation, and may the time soon come, when the Rebellion Shall be put down, and Traitors, receive their just recompence afterward, and the People be at Peace, is the Sincere feeling of your obt servant

William Florville the Barber

Of all the letters President Lincoln ever received from or about his family, or, for that matter, from his old Springfield hometown, none provided the pure praise and good wishes contained in this extraordinary letter from the Haitian-born barber Billy Florville, or Fleurville, whose literacy put that of Lincoln's own Illinois relatives to shame. Lincoln referred to him as "a colored barber here" and evidently regarded him affectionately. For years, Lincoln had helped Billy calculate his tax obligations on property he owned in Bloomington (CW, III: 518).

A Plea to a White House "Unkel"

Feb 2th 1864
Canyon vill Oregon

Dear unkel A. Lincoln

    after meditation over the past and the future and whot is to cumm I thought I coud not avail mi self a beter opurtunity than this to drop a few lines to let you know that I am still living yet and geting a long as well as the times will ad mit as to Helth thair is non beter fur the last three or four years I hav ben blest with the best of health I am still living her in oregon I think I will make this cuntry mi home I hav bin Travling a round fur sum time and I cant fine no better cuntry than this and I hav seteld down fur lif I expect I hav bin in washington terrytory and the British poseshion a fine cuntry fur minerl producks I hav ben over grat portion of oregon and california hav serched fur the hiden trashur found it not now I am satisfied to live on whot is loted to man. I dont no how the old folks at hom is geting a long it has ben som time since I hav herd from them I hop thair ar doin well I got a leter from Charley Hanks my Brothor he was at vicburg he is in the army brave Boy I wish & it was so that I coud be with him he inform me that he has ben in nine the hardest bateles that has ben fought now unkel he is the only Brother that I hav that is of my sise and I am her all a lone not a relation near me to stand by me throw the dangers of this world—and the onley thing that I ask in gods world fur you to send him on this cost of oregon it is in your power to doe soe if you will as fur my self I ask fur nothing I am well satisfied all though you hav given som of the best offices to men that I consider my self so peair to them her under mi nose I dont think you hav treated me rite all though you hav don your duty as a president wich you ar not to blame I hav allways hav loved you from Child hood and still think well ove you a miney a time hav I stoud up for you and hav ben curst for doing so in this country both parties is well devide I think thair will be wore times her yet som purty hard threates mad a gainst the union party I wish you wod send me som documentes so that I can post mi self with if thair is eny thing that I can doe fur you in this cuntry I am willing and so to doe if willing to lay down mi life fur you in defence of mu country if it is your wish I dont think I coud dy in a nobler cose but a Nuf of this you may think I am going to furre

Now unkel if I hav written eny thing that is Contrary to your wishes you will fur give me fur it I wont you to answer this if you please and you will be stow a grat favor and a ever lasting friendship direct your letter to Canyonvill douglas. co. oregon times is hard but a delitful winter I never hav seane a plesent er winter on the Posifick Cost when peace is maid I shall pay mi old frindes a visite and I shal be happy to col on you so good by yours in haiste

John T. Hanks

To his unkel A. Lincoln President of the united States

P.S. Charles Hanks is in the 8 Rigement of Illinois volunteears

J. T. H—

∽ *Dennis Hanks's son John had located in Oregon as early as 1860, at which time he asked his "uncle"—more accurately, his father's cousin—the President-elect, for advice on whether to stay or return to Illinois. "If your Father and Mother desire you to come home, it is a delicate matter for me to advise you not to do it," Lincoln wrote on September 24, 1860. "Still . . . if you are doing well, you better stick to it." John, like so many of Lincoln relatives, opposed him in politics. He did not support Lincoln's choice for an Oregon congressional seat, and no further known correspondence passed between the two until John wrote the above letter—to which Lincoln did not reply, as far as we know, John's plea for "documentes" notwithstanding (CW, IV: 120).*

Merchant Brother-in-law Asks Inside Information

friendly letter and <u>strictly confidential</u>

New York Feby 7th 1864

Mr Lincoln
   My Dear Sir   As I have never lived through a civil War—; I feel completely lost in a commercial point of view; I thought I would

trouble you with a letter for which I do hope you will take the trouble to read; and also pardon me for the liberty I have taken; and what ever your decision may be in reference to this letter you can rely on one thing that it will [be] kept strictly confidential and Secret

My effort in writing to you now is not for office place or position; but but [sic] simply to ask a very small favor of you; which if granted should never be the means of mortifying or embarrassing you in any way whatever; while I have been sorely afflicted to the very fullest in loosing three of my dear Children which was a very great blow to me; which you are capable of feeling for those afflicted; I have been prospered beyond my expectations; not in fat contracts of of [sic] the Government; but by steady perserverence and attention to my business no one can ever accuse me or my Children of owning <u>Shoddy property</u> I have much for the benefit of the little remnant of my Family that has been left me over a Hundred Thousand dollars; I commenced in the world like you did a poor Boy without Friends money or influence; and gradually climbed my way until now I would not take a cent less than $125,000.—for my little property it all consist in three Store Houses and ten Acres of land in Springfield and a part of old Jim Bassett Farm and my Stock of Goods at my diferant Stores

I now want to save that for my wife and little Children that has been spared me and the Children that I have taken to raise You are probably not aware of the sad affliction we have had since you left Springfield in the loss of our dear little Boy Lincoln who died last March

If you could at the proper time, give me a a [sic] little notice or a hint that things was likely to be brought to a close in our troubles; you could confer; and place me under everlasting obligation to you

I do not want or desire to know any of the Secrets of the administration; but simply a hint that it would be a good time for me to get my house in order; I have bought my Partners Interest in all of our business and paid him his money; I am selling at my diferant stores a half million goods annually for Cash; and a hint of 60 days or even 30 days would enable me to close out my stocks for money so that I would not loose any money; thus enabling me to escape without loss; If I should mention or even intimate any <u>confidence</u> that you might repose in me; dont you see that it would Thwart in my plans so you need not fear that for a moment; I shall remain here two weeks and if you think proper to drop me a line care of George Bliss No. 340 Broadway New York no one will ever know but what it would be a Family letter if they should see that the letter was from Washington; I

would like very much to see you in person but I know you are annoyed to death with visitors; and I feel a delicacy in being numbered
among that number

My business calls me among a great many People War Democrats
& Republicans in all points of the Country and manufacturing Districts; & a large majority are for you for the next four Years; but their is
a very strong under current among Politicians they would be glad to
upsett you; you know I told you that you would get the nomination at
Chicago [the 1860 nomination for his first term] and you did get it; I
hope once more to see you in person and spend hour socially with you;
not possibly before you visit Springfield if that should ever occur
again; you will please burn this letter and believe me as ever

Yours Truly
C. M. Smith

NB

If you should ever want to use me in any way command my services; I
have Just found Major Stuart going to Washington and I have requested him to hand you a letter

CMS

∽ *If Lincoln ever replied to this outrageous request for advance notice of peace, his
answer has never been located. Lincoln did not write at all to this brother-in-law after
September 18, 1863, when he advised Smith to name his newborn son after "the
General you fancy most," apparently in response to a request for suggestions, which
has since been lost. Smith, who was married to Mary Lincoln's sister Ann, earned his
fortune—which he evidently was scheming to multiply—selling what he advertised as
"The Best Ladies Goods in Illinois." Smith had given Lincoln, as president-elect, use
of a vacant room above his main establishment to write his first inaugural address. Yet
neither this favor, nor the honor he gave his famous brother-in-law by naming another
son for him, apparently entitled Smith to the inside information he requested. But
neither did Lincoln burn the letter, as requested. He simply placed it back in its
envelope, which he marked "C. M. Smith," and filed it away (CW, VI: 464; Baker,
Mary Todd Lincoln, 165; Angle, Here I Have Lived, 259–260).*

His Old Cousin Acknowledges Gift

April 5th 64

Dere Abe   I Receivd your Little Check for 50.00 I shoed it to
Mother [Lincoln's stepmother, and the writer's mother-in-law, Sarah

Bush Johnston Lincoln, then seventy-six years old] She cried Like a child Abe she is mity childish heep of truble to us Betsy [the writer's wife, Sarah Elizabeth Johnston Hanks] is very feble and has to wait on her which aut to have sum person to wait on her we are getting old We have a great many to wait on of our connections they will cum to see us while we Live

Abe Charles [the writer's son] has Reinlisted a gain for three years or During the war this is hard to his Mother Abe we had a horible time a Monday of court it Broke up got in to a fuss By a Drunkin soldier [a reference to a widely reported melee in Charleston, Illinois, involving Union soldiers and antiwar Copperheads on March 28, 1864] I never saw such a time Thare was 8 or 10 killed in the fight one you no Doct Yorke of paris Edgar County young E Winkler was wounded

Abe I Received a Letter from Sophia Lynch now John Lagmand is her Last husband She wants to no whether you and that Abe Lincoln hir cusin or Not is this not Strange to you it was to me hir Boys all in the army you nion [Union] Boys at Vixburg Abe you never have seen as strong a young boy as Charles Hanks I am mity fraid that [unintelligible word] will go into the army with Charles he is 15 years old a very stout Boy he can shoot as well as I can Abe Re member my Boys if you can I dont ask any thing how us your family Nothing more Drop me a few Lyns if you feel Like it

Yours Respectfully
D. H. Hanks

∽ *Dennis Hanks had been the closest thing to an older brother young Abraham Lincoln had during his Kentucky childhood. Later Dennis married into Lincoln's stepmother's family; the $50 that the President sent Hanks was expressly for her care. Although he frequently complained of ill health, Dennis did not die until 1892—when, at the age of ninety-three, he was struck by a carriage on the way home from a celebration of the anniversary of one of his long-dead cousin's greatest achievements—the Thirteenth Amendment to the Constitution (Coleman, Lincoln and Coles County, 226).*

Leniency for Confederate Todds

Judiciary Square Hosp April 27/64

Mr. President

Sir I enclose a Peice [sic] of paper taken from the Detroit Free Press stating that you gave Mrs Todd Mrs Lincoln sister a pass through

our lines with a Trunk of medicines and contraband goods and valuble
Papers now if this is so will you please have the ed of the Chronicle
confirm it or Condemn it and oblige for I dont believe our President
would do that pleese Answer yours

C. Stewart
Co. D 3d Michigan
Judiciary Square Hosp

∽ *The clipping that Stewart enclosed asserted that "Mrs. J. Todd White, a sister of
Mrs. Lincoln, who lately went South . . . had abused her pass and carried a large
quantity of contraband goods through to the enemy." The newspaper charged that the
nation's "hopes and prayers" had thus been "betrayed in the very White House."
Lincoln endured much criticism for his leniency with his wife's pro-Confederate
relatives.*

Mary Asks News about Goats

[T E L E G R A P H]

New York City, April 28, 1864

Hon. A. Lincoln
President United States
 We reached here in safety. Hope you are well. Please send me by
mail to-day a check for $50 deposited to me, care Mr Warren Leland,
Metropolitan Hotel, Tad says are the goats well?

Mrs Lincoln

∽ *Lincoln replied to this telegram on the same day (CW, VII: 320).*

Executive Mansion, Washington,
April 28. 1864.

Mrs. A. Lincoln
Metropolitan Hotel New-York
 The draft will go to you. Tell Tad the goats and father are very
well—especially the goats.

A. Lincoln.

Troubling News about his Stepmother

P R I V A T E

Charleston Coles County Illinois
October 18th 1864

Dear Uncle, This Leaves us all well but Grand Mother. She is quite puny. I write to inform you that Grand Mother has not and does not receive one cent of the money you send her Dennis & Chapman keep all the money you send her. She now needs clothing and shoes. they have the money in their Pockett & Uncle Dennis is cussing you all the time and abusing me & your best friends for supporting you they make you believe they are taking care of her which is not the case. I & my Mother [Matilda Johnston Hall Moore, Lincoln's stepsister] are now taking care of her and have for the past four years. If you wish her to have anything send it by check here to the bank of Charleston, or send none for I tell you upon the honor of a man she does not get it & he Dennis has threatened to put her on the county. I hope to hear from you soon. Brother Alfred [Hall] is wounded & badly, shot through the foot & now is in hospital at Quincy. he was wounded at Dallas Ga 27th of May last. I remain your nephew

John J. Hall

N.B. I have written you these plain truths by Gran Mothers request She has been asking me to do this for four years—please write soon

John J. Hall

∽ *If Lincoln replied to this disturbing letter, the response vanished with the last of the Lincoln family. Quite a different portrait of the elderly Mrs. Lincoln's life in the Hall home was painted by a niece three months later (Coleman, Lincoln and Coles County, 151–152).*

New Plea from "Cousin Lizzie"

Springfield Nov. 22d. 1864

My dear Mr Lincoln.

It is generally supposed there is to be a change in the Post Office here, and again I am an applicant for it, and write thus early to you, hoping you have not committed yourself to any one before you hear my arrangements. I write undeservedly to you, feeling and believing you will be willing to give me the office if you can consistently, and feeling also, that arrangements can be made which will be satisfactory not only to yourself but to the Republican friends.

Your objection before was, that a Post-Mistress in a place the size of Springfield would produce a dis-satisfaction, whereupon I immediately gave up all effort as you will remember. Perhaps your views on the subject have changed, and if so I should be very glad if you would so assist me, but if not, I could make an arrangement with some one of our good, reliable Republican friends, whereby I could receive benefits, and yet the office be given to him. I could get the names of hundreds of warm friends who would be happy to help me in either way, if you should think necessary so to do. I feel secure in saying, most of the leading <u>Republicans</u> would give me their countenance and names.

I thought of suggesting Father's name, but know that would again raise the cry about the "Todd Family" and therefore rather prefer not embarrassing you in that way.

Dear Mr Lincoln, you know my necessities, and I think, I know your disposition to assist me, so will not press the subject further upon you,

With much love to Mary and the boys, and in full hope of a favorable answer to my application I am truly

> Your affectionate cousin
> E. T. Grimsley

P.S. Please, Mr Lincoln, let me know your views at an early day—E.

ᴄᴏ *No letters are known to have been sent by Lincoln to Lizzie after August 24, 1863. If he replied to this fantastic scheme to hire a substitute postmaster for Springfield while giving Lizzie the "benefits," the response has vanished.*

More Disquieting News about his Stepmother

Charleston Ills. Jan. the 17th 65

Hon. A. Lincoln

Dear Uncle: I have been intending to write to you for some time, but felt so bad that I had not the heart to write to any one save my Husband. Our family have recently met with a great loss. God in his divine mercy has seen fit to take from our midst a kind and devoted Mother [Lincoln's stepsister]. She died on the 18th of Dec after an Illness of about 6 months in her death we have lost a devoted Mother one whose place can never be fild on this Earth. You also have lost a friend for Mother was indeed a friend to you and spoke of you often during her last moments. But we ought not to grieve too much for her for She died happy and left behind every assurance that she has gone hapy. Father [Lincoln's cousin, Dennis Hanks] takes her death very hard he is not well and I fear that he is not long for this world [Dennis lived until he was struck by a carriage at age ninety-three, twenty-seven years later] and it is heart rendering to think of having to give him up too. I was down to see Grand Ma Lincoln [the President's stepmother] on New years day. She seems to be failing fast [she, too, would outlive Lincoln] and is grieving her self to death about Mother. Poor woman how my heart aches for her. She was so destitute of every Comfort. She wants to leave there very bad and Come to my house and tells me that she is badly treated. I told her that it was impossible for me to take her just now for my house is small and not very Comfortable and my family is large but I told her to wait till my Husband comes home his time of Service expires the 17th of Feb. and then we would try to do something for her it looks too hard for as good a woman as She is to be Compeld to Spend her last days in <u>want</u> and <u>misery</u> and I for one will do as I always have done my part in her behalf and now want you to assist me by giving my Husband a situation so that he can support his family and get them a home and then we <u>will</u> take Grand Ma Lincoln and take good care of her as long as She lives if we should be spared that long. you can do this and not discommode yourself in the least and I think that Augustus [her husband, Augustus H. Chapman] deserves your favor he has always been a Strong Union man spent both time and money in your Elections has now been in the Army for 3 years and 3 months and would remain longer if his family was better Situated—during that time has never been sick a day or unfit for duty and has never had but one furlough home and that only for 15 days. has not made ennything but a living for himself and family and this is why I ask you for your assistance feeling sure that you would not deny me and then Gran Ma made me promise to write to you and tell you to do all you could for us for she would rather live with us than enny where else. The rest of the relations are all well.

The roling months have brought us the close of an other year. There has been much suffering throughout our land during that time. Many are the Vacant Chairs. Homes have been made desolate partings endured. Heart-Strings have been broken—and many widows and orphans have mourned for the loved ones lost. But let us look forward to a better future and welcome young '65 with bright hopes and pleasant anticipations let us hope that before its Close Smiling peace will return once more and Scatter its blessings through all our land.

Well I have written a much longer letter than I intended to trouble you with this time and if I have transgrest I hope you will forgive. If you feel disposed and can assist Augustus please let him hear soon he will be at home in about 6 weeks. Remember me kindly to your wife and children.

yours with love
Harriet A. Chapman

∽ *One can only imagine the dread with which Lincoln read the first few lines of this letter from his family home on the Illinois prairie. It is possible that his stepsister's daughter was exaggerating the old woman's circumstances, and that Lincoln quickly sensed this. He did nothing to help Mr. Chapman gain the security necessary to bring Sarah Bush Johnston Lincoln to live with the Chapman family. Twenty years earlier Lincoln had written to his stepmother, first bringing up the subject of her moving in with the Chapmans and urging her to "try it awhile" (CW, II: 112; Coleman, Lincoln and Coles County, 152).*

Husband and Wife's Final, Unhappy Trip

[*T E L E G R A P H*]
Executive Mansion Washington
April 2nd—[1865]

A Lincoln City Point
Arrived here safely this morning, found all well—Miss, Taddie & yourself very much—perhaps, may return with a little party on Wednesday—Give me all the news.

Mary Lincoln

∽ *As the war drew to a successful close, Mary had accompanied Lincoln on a last, triumphant trip to the front at the end of March. But after creating a humiliating public scene at a military review by "attacking her husband in the presence of officers," according to a horrified eyewitness, she returned to Washington, presumably on her husband's orders. Lincoln must have been appalled at the prospect that she now might return to the front, but he wired back the same day nevertheless.*

[*T E L E G R A P H*]

City Point, Va., April 2, 1865.

Mrs. Lincoln:

At 4:30 p.m. to-day General Grant telegraphs that he has Petersburg completely enveloped from river below to river above, and has captured, since he started last Wednesday, about 12,000 prisoners and 50 guns. He suggests that I shall go out and see him in the morning, which I think I will do. Tad and I are both well, and will be glad to see you and your party here at the time you name.

A. Lincoln.

∽ *The Confederate capital of Richmond fell the next day, prompting Mary to wire again.*

[*T E L E G R A P H*]

4 April 1865

A. Lincoln
City Point

Glorious news! Please say to Captain Bradford [skipper of the *River Queen*, a vessel that the President used for several wartime sea voyages] that a party of seven persons, leave here tomorrow & will reach City Point, on Thursday morning for breakfast—

Mrs Lincoln

∽ *If Mary hoped that Lincoln would wait for her before visiting the conquered Rebel capital, she would be disappointed. On the same day the above telegraph was sent, Lincoln departed for that city, where he was greeted exultantly by the city's liberated black population. Mary started back for Virginia anyway, and then, midway through this frantic effort to rejoin him, she learned that Secretary of State Seward had broken his arm and jaw in a carriage accident. Worried that her husband might now race back to Washington without her, she wired the following message to him.*

[T E L E G R A P H]

Fortress Monroe
April 6 [1865]
4 o'clock Thursday morning

A. Lincoln

If Mr Seward, is not too dangerously injured cannot you remain at City Point until we reach there at twelve noon to day. We have several friends on board [including Senator Charles Sumner and Robert Lincoln's future father-in-law, Senator James Harlan] & would prefer seeing you & returning on your boat, we are not comfortable here—

Mary Lincoln

If Lincoln replied to this wire, the copy has never come to light. But five hours after sending this middle-of-the-night entreaty, Mary telegraphed her husband one final time to complain anew about her accommodations aboard the steamer Monohasset. *It was the last communication Lincoln would receive from her, or from any member of his family, and, typically, it contained only demands and complaints. Eight days after it was sent, Abraham Lincoln, with his wife at his side, was assassinated (Turner and Turner,* Mary Todd Lincoln, *206–208, 211, 213–215; LDBD III: 322–327).*

[T E L E G R A P H]

Fortress Monroe
Apl 6 [1865] 9 a.m.

A. Lincoln—

If you are compelled to return before we see you, which I shall much regret, cannot you return on some other vessel, we are most uncomfortable on this & would like your boat—I know you would agree with me & we will be with you in six hours + at City Point

Mary Lincoln

This letter appears on page 341.

Feb 20, 1861

Mr Lincoln –
        May the hand of
the devil strike you
down before long –
You are destroying the
country
        Damn you – every
breath you take ~

                Hand of God
                against you

[10]

Threats And Warnings

WARD HILL LAMON, the longtime friend of Lincoln who accompanied him to Washington in 1861 and remained close to his side as often as he could in the ensuing four years, later admitted: "There was never a moment . . . up to the time of his assassination, that he was not in danger by violence." In Lamon's view, "his life was spared until the night of the 14th of April, 1865, only through the ceaseless and watchful care of the guards thrown around him." Lamon was one of them. He took to sleeping on the floor outside Lincoln's bedroom, John Hay remembered, armed "with a small arsenal of pistols & bowie knives."

The White House mailbag provided little solace. "Abuse, scurrility, threats," and "utter insanities," according to clerk William O. Stoddard, regularly characterized the contents of the tightly sealed bales of mail dumped on his desk each day. Stoddard called them "the brutalities, enmities, and infamies of the President's letter-bag."

Mary Lincoln's seamstress and companion, Lizzie Keckley, remembered that "frequent letters were received warning Mr. Lincoln of assassination." But the President "never gave a second thought to the mysterious warnings." The First Lady did not respond with the same indifference. "The letters," Lizzie recalled, "sorely troubled"

Mary until she began "to read impending danger in every rustling leaf, in every whisper of the wind." History, of course, proved her more prudent and prescient than her husband. Lincoln himself blithely confessed to a visitor in 1864 that by then threatening letters had "ceased to give me any apprehension," adding resignedly: "Oh, there is nothing like getting <u>used</u> to things."

There is ample evidence in the reminiscences of Lincoln's contemporaries of the frequency with which such threats were received at the White House. But there is disagreement about their ultimate disposition. One of Lincoln's secretaries insisted that he operated under strict instructions to keep all threatening letters from Lincoln's eyes. But another aide reported that he routinely delivered such letters to the President's desk. More than one contemporary testified that Lincoln kept all such letters in a bulging folder in a special pigeonhole in his battered, upright White House desk.

One revealing letter early in the administration came from Lamon himself, appalled at the sight of so many strangers swarming through the Executive Mansion daily. "I fear that there are eavesdroppers and traitors lurking about," he wrote. "I would suggest that no one be allowed upstairs except such as you permit after they're sending up their cards." Predictably, Lincoln ignored this eminently reasonable suggestion.

Twenty years later private secretary John G. Nicolay, too, admitted that danger to the President constantly preyed on the minds of his staff. "Of course," he conceded, "it was often discussed between his friends and himself. They would say, 'Now, Lincoln, you must look out and be constantly on your guard. Some crank is liable to come along and kill you.' His answer was, 'I will be careful. But I cannot discharge my duties if I withdraw myself entirely from danger of an assault. I see hundreds of strangers every day, and if anybody has the disposition to kill me he will find opportunity. To be absolutely safe I should lock myself up in a box.' "

Comfort came only with the realization that most of the anonymous threats and warnings that arrived at the White House came from deranged but hardly dangerous cranks. True potential assassins, the staff reasoned, would hardly write in advance to broadcast their intentions. A stoical Lincoln simply shrugged and declared "that if anybody was bad enough to kill him there was nothing on earth to prevent it."

Not that the secretaries did not try to remain alert. Edward D. Neill was concerned enough to retain in his files a letter from an acquaintance back in St. Paul who wrote to report a frightening rumor that the Knights of the Golden Circle, a secret organization, was plotting to murder Lincoln. The correspondent's advice was "to put the Prest. on his guard." Another letter preserved by Neill warned that Lincoln's blood would soon be shed unless he bent his "Stubborn Knee," a letter that ended with the ominous rhyme:

> This is the Last Warning Unto Thee Lincoln!!! That ever you will have from me.

Neill forever felt guilty that he did not more aggressively report the warnings that crossed his desk, including that from a Gloversville, New York, Lincoln foe who wrote: "God knows I have hated you, but God knows I cannot be a murderer. Beware of the ides of March." Lincoln was assassinated a month later.

Unfortunately, from history's point of view, most of the threats that arrived in Lincoln's mailbag were systematically destroyed, if we can believe William O. Stoddard, who insisted that the President absolutely "refused to be informed of letters which threatened personal violence." Obediently, Stoddard disposed of all the letters that told "stories of partisan bitterness and personal hatred; of the most venomous malice, seeking to shoot with personal arrows of abuse; of low, slanderous, meanness; of the coarsest, foulest vulgarity to which beastly men can sink; of the wildest, the fiercest and the most obscene ravings of utter insanity."

So quickly could Stoddard recognize and relegate to his trash baskets such correspondence, that on one occasion he aroused the ire of a visitor who witnessed Stoddard disposing of a letter and became convinced that he was treating the presidential mail disrespectfully. Stoddard loved the story—he repeated it in at least four of his memoirs—because it vindicated his decision to censor these threats. One version of the anecdote went like this:

> One day I and my paper cutter and my wastebaskets
> were hard at work when in came a portly, dignified,
> elderly man who sat down near me while waiting for an
> audience with Mr. Lincoln. He appeared to be some kind
> of distinguished person, perhaps a governor or something
> of that sort, and he watched me with an interest which
> evidently grew upon him. He became uneasy in his chair;
> he waxed red in the face. At last he broke out with:—

"Is that the way you treat the President's mail? Mr. Lincoln does not know this! What would the people of the United States think, if they knew that their communications to their Chief Magistrate were dealt with in this shameful manner? Thrown into the wastebasket! What does Lincoln mean? Putting such a responsibility into the hands of a mere boy! A boy!"

I had been all the while watching him as he fired up. Now there had been an uncommonly dirty mail that morning and I had put aside as I opened them a number of the vile scrawls. My critic had risen from his chair and was pacing up and down the room in hot indignation when I quietly turned and offered him a handful of the selected letters.

"Please read those, sir," I said, "and give me your opinion of them. I may be right about them. Do you really think that the President of the United States ought to turn from the affairs of the nation to put in his time on that sort of thing?"

He took the awful handful and began to read, and his red face grew redder. Then it was white with speechless wrath. Perhaps he had never before perused anything quite so devilish in all his life.

"You are quite right, sir," he gasped, as he sank into his chair again. "Young man, you are right! He ought not to see a line of that stuff! Burn it, sir! Burn it! What devils there are!"

In retrospect, the White House staff might have better served Lincoln by retaining and investigating such letters rather than destroying them. Edward Neill later remembered receiving one warning—which had been ignored at the time—from a writer with "knowledge of Booth's desire to do evil." Had Neill, Stoddard, and the others exercised more vigilance in response to such letters, Lincoln might never have been left so poorly guarded at Ford's Theatre on April 14, 1865. In all fairness to the secretaries, they had grown all but inured to such threats, so often did they read letters warning the President of violence that never came. And as William Stoddard testified, "the assassination idea" had "taken possession of so many minds that not many days" would pass "without the coming of some kind of epistolary threat or warning." When the genuine article finally arrived, it was simply too little, too late, to arouse the suspicion it deserved.

Post-Election Damnation

Fillmore La November 25th 1860

Old Abe Lincoln

God damn your god damned old Hellfired god damned soul to hell god damn you and goddam your god damned family's god damned hellfired god damned soul to hell and god damnation god damn them and god damn your god damn friends to hell god damn their god damned souls to damnation god damn them and god dam their god damn families to eternal god damnation god damn souls to hell god damn them and God Almighty God damn Old Hamlin to[o] to hell God damn his God damned soul all over everywhere double damn his God damned soul to hell

Now you God damned old Abolition son of a bitch God damn you I want you to send me God damn you about one dozen good offices Good God Almighty God damn your God damned soul and three or four pretty Gals God damn you

And by doing God damn you you

Will Oblige
Pete Muggins

∾ *This malevolent letter was part of an armful of correspondence that President-elect Lincoln intended to destroy before leaving Illinois for his 1861 inaugural. According to collector Oliver R. Barrett, who later purchased the material, Lincoln carried the bundle of mail into a cabinetmaker's shop located below his Springfield law office, and asked if he could dump it into the stove. The proprietor asked if he might instead be permitted to keep the letters, and Lincoln obliged (Sandburg,* Lincoln Collector, *45, 65).*

An Inaugural Warning

Lynchburg Va January 18th 1861

Hon Abraham Lincolmn [*sic*]
Springfield Ill.

Dear Sir   I have heard several persons in this place say that if you ever did take the President Chair that they would go to washington City expressly to kill you. for your wife and Children sake dont take the Chair if you do you will be murdered by some cowardly scoundrel have you had any application for this post if not I wish you would let me have it—if you take the Chair as the president of the United States but dont you take it. resign. if you dont you will be murdered I write you this as a friend I am a friend of yours please answer this letter so I can know whether I must go to washington City and raise a body of men to guard you.

Yours truly &c
R. A. Hunt

ᔕ *Lincoln did not reply to this offer. His March 4, 1861, inauguration was heavily guarded by swarms of armed troops under the command of General Winfield Scott.*

Vile Threats to the "Black Nigger"

Feb 14 1861

Sir

Mr Abe Lincoln

if you don't Resign we are going to put a spider in your dumpling and play the Devil with you you god or mighty god dam sundde of a bith go to hell and buss my Ass suck my prick and call my Bolics your uncle Dick god dam a fool and goddam Abe Lincoln who would like you goddam you excuse me for using such hard words with you but you need it you are nothing but a goddam Black nigger

yours &c
Mr. A. G. Frick

Tennessee Missouri Kentucky Virginia N. Carolina and Arkansas is going to secede Glory be to god on high

ᔕ *This letter, never before published in its entirety, was discovered in the files of the Chicago Historical Society.*

Invoking the Devil's Hand

Feb 20, 1861

Mr. Lincoln—

May the hand of the devil strike you down before long—You are destroying the country

Damn you—every breath you take—

Hand of God against you

Warnings from Baltimore

[February 22, 1861]

Dear Sir

I think it my duty to inform you that I was advised last night by a gentleman that there existed in Baltimore, a league of ten persons, who had sworn that you should never pass through that city alive— This may be but one of the thousand threats against you that have emanated from some paltry Southerners, but you should know it that your friends may be watchful while you are in the place as it was asserted positively to be the fact. God defend and bless you—The prayers of many go with you.

A Lady.

Friday Morning 11½ A.M.

ↄ *Lincoln had planned a public stop in Baltimore en route to his inauguration, but at the last minute he donned a long overcoat and an uncharacteristic slouch hat, changed trains under cover of darkness, and slipped through the city secretly—quite possibly in reaction to letters like this one (Cuthbert, Lincoln and the Baltimore Plot, xiv, xvi).*

An Inauguration Day Threat

[1861]

Abraham Lincoln Esq
Sir

You will be shot on the 4th of March 1861 by a Louisiana Creole we are decided and our aim is sure.

A young creole.
BEWARE

ↄ *This threat was another of the so called "Hot Stove" letters saved from destruction by a Springfield, Illinois cabinetmaker and later purchased by Lincoln collector Oliver R. Barrett from the cabinetmaker's daughter (Sandburg, Lincoln Collector, 45, 67).*

Warning from a Medium

Washington Oct 4 1862

Abraham Lincoln

I am your Heavenly Father and the God of all Nations and the same love and interest for the North as for the South and the same for the South as for the North I am not partial and have no respect of persons but desire the happiness of all my people wherever they be and will deal to that effect with them all I am the cause for the disruption between the North and the South for the sole purpose of breaking up the Kingdom divided against itself that an everlasting Kingdom may be built up with such a Basis such a foundation and that there will be no need of its overthrow the old world is dying out whilst the New is being born the new Era is commenced the Era of Righteousness and I am the cause of all this my will is being done daily with man because I know what is for the future good of all my people much better than they know and therefore what ever is occurring with you all is tending to a higher holier state when one man will not have a wish to trample upon their fellow man No it is time already that this Devilish power should be broken up forever and a better spirit to guide the earth inhabitants one that will be willing that all shall share equal in the bounties that I have placed within and without the globe that you dwell upon A horrible state of affairs has mans selfish nature brought about the Devil himself has had the control of affairs altogether to [*sic*] long And I the Father of the Universe the Creator of all things will hasten to unfold a better way that all that will follow shall reap a reward of so doing what is this better way you may enquire and I can readily explain to you that the best and only way for you to do under the existing state of things is to call together your mighty men the head officers and consider this whole thing whether there is not much time on both sides of the question whether you have not about as much evil in your system of things at the North as my people here at the South I wish you to weigh these things and see if there is not an equal balance the Devil has taught man that their neighbors was doing forever wrong and he was himself doing right and this comparatively speaking is the great cause of disharmony over the earth sphere the Devil has controlled affairs long enough And now I choose to take the affairs into my own hands and keep and conduct them in such a manner that I can deal out exact justice to all people that each one may have a home of their own an not be subject to being turned out doors because it is impossible for to pay rent whilst the landlords require such an unjust amount for there tenements also I wish to reregulate society that poor females will not have too subject themselves to the brutal passions of evil minded men for their living Oh what a pitiful condition my people are in   What a distracted excited most horrible situation has this monstrous Devil that was bred among the first born of the planet brought them two Oh my mercy my love for them has brought me to their rescue And as many as will hear my voice and hearken to me through this first born of this age will be saved from further destruction destruction of both soul and body take heed now wilst an opportunity is placed before you I am the God of God, the Lord of Lords

And my instrument the Messenger of Peace the Christ of this day is in the City stopping at the Fitzgeralds 476 Pensylvania Avenue Now Abram Lincoln I want you to call together 6 of your best men in the Army on the first day possible certainly as soon as Saturday and if impossible that day be sure and do so Monday next at 10 forenoon I want you to have this Medium present and I will tell you the 6 beside yourself just what to do that will speedily terminate this Devilish war now existing in your midst Now do as I tell you or if not you will have to suffer the consequences of not Hearing to me given through Lydia Smith the Medium for Jesus Christ and the Father God

Hearken to me all ye ends of the earth That may give you the immortal birth That you may reap a rich future reward By serving me the sovereign Lord

Lydia Smith Medium which I give through to all that will hear can be found at Mrs Fitzgeralds boarding house 476 Pensylvania Avenue

↬ *Not surprisingly, there is no record that Lincoln ever availed himself of the opportunity to hear the word of God through Lydia Smith the Medium.*

Danger from a "Wretch"?

[T E L E G R A P H]

Little Rock Ark
Oct 24 1863.
Via Memphis Oct 30

A Lincoln President, U.S.

A wretch of good address by name Dornby has gone to Washington

Fred'k Steele
Maj Genl

⌇ Nothing is known of the "wretch" Dornby, his mission to Washington, or Lincoln's response, if any.

"Your Days are Numbered"

New York
Jan 4th 1864

Abm Lincoln President,

The same who warned you of a conspiracy Novr. 18th 1862 is now compelled to inform you, that, "Your days are numbered," you have been weighed in the balance and found wanting. You shall be a dead man in six months from date Dec. 31st 1863.

Thus saith the good Spirit.

Joseph

⌇ Nothing further is known about this threat or its anonymous author.

Not from Horace Greeley

New York 1st June/64

Abraham Lincoln
President of United States,
Executive Mansion Wash. D.C.

Dear Sir. I have facts in my possession which I wish to reveal to you alone, in relation to a conspiracy against you & this glorious Union. When I reveal it to you, some of the most prominent men of the Democracy [the Democratic party] of this city will be brought out as Traitors & Conspirators. Please name a time for an interview.

Your obed Servt.
Horace Greeley

⌇ No doubt finding he had less trouble than usual reading this alleged note from Tribune *editor Greeley, whose penmanship was notoriously indecipherable, Lincoln scribbled on the reverse: "Forgery—in name of Mr. Greely [sic]."*

An Anonymous Warning to "Father Abram"

[Philadelphia, June 16, 1864]

Hagar's Appeal to Abram—

Look a here! Father Abram: They say You're Father of the Faithful; but I shan't believe it, unless you're Faithful yourself. Don't you go, and let "Old Sallie Seward," tempt you to turn us out in the Wilderness "without a pass"; Nor drive us from your bosom to sleep our last sleep on yonder bloody "Pillow" [a reference to the massacre of black troops by Confederates at Fort Pillow] without even a rag of a flag to cover us—haven't we served you well, for many years, as "Flowers of Wood (when Wood wasn't Hughing us) and drawers of water"? Why should you desert us now, because Old Sallie dont like the "Irre press ible Conflict" betwixt big I and little i [a reference both to Seward's famous prewar "irrepressible conflict" speech, and perhaps, too, to the administration's more recent suppression of some disloyal newspapers]

She hasn't much to boast on herself. Didn't she go a flirting with King Fair. and "Bim-lick,["] over the waters; and say it was only because she was afeard they would kill you, if she didn't; (I never believed you told her to do it, tho' she said you did) Now, I have been Faithful, though I was only a hand woman, and Ishmael has fought your battles when your other brave boy was safe in your tent "Out of the Drift." To be sure you have given us "bread and a bottle of Water" but that won't save us from death or starvation in the "Wilderness."

Ishmael is your son though he is dark complected, and I think you'll be mighty mean if you don't do something to save him from the "Beasts of that Forest" or give us a cure for the Polk powder we are forced to swallow.

You'd better look out, I can tell you, for if you don't treat us better, we'll take possession of the Land of Egypt and give you trouble in Care'o. If Ishmael once turns archer in earnest, remember there's a Prophet C. that says "His hand shall be against every man" as well as every man's hand against he and you'd better take care he don't turn his arrows against you. It would hurt my feelings dreadful bad, to hear the poor lad crying out in the bush, and dying by inches after being brot up in Old Abe's tent, and taught to believe that tho' he was "Son of the hand woman" he was still to be heir with the "Sons of the Free."

You and Sallie had better have "Let us alone" in the back tent than after taking me to your bosom to turn us out doors at Sallie's bidding. Thank God there are Welles men in the Wilderness and Hunter's near the Forrest [a reference to Union General David Hunter and Confederate General Nathan Bedford Forrest, who then stood accused of perpetrating, or at least countenancing, the Fort Pillow massacre] and if you wont hear our prayer the Angel of the Lord is not so deaf.

Now let the Sanitary Fair speak to you, on our behalf, if you don't like to listen to any other Fair One. She will tell you that, Black and White it makes no difference to her: She nurses, and tends us all without respect to color, or party color. Do you do the same Old Abe and Ishmael and I will be Faithful to the Faithful.

Your sorrowful Hagar.
"The voice of One Crying in the Wilderness."
"Prepare ye the Way of the Lord
Make his path Straight."

ᔈ *This long anonymous letter, addressed to "Father Abram Care of Uncle Sam," was posted at Philadelphia's Great Central Fair. Conceivably, the author of this stinging, but at times confusing, call for equal treatment of black soldiers had heard the President speak there before she wrote this attack. In the Bible Hagar is Abraham's concubine and the mother of Ishmael, with whom she was driven into the wilderness due to Sarah's jealousy. This letter was written shortly after the Battle of the Wilderness, a fierce battle between the armies of Grant and Lee that was known for its appalling death toll—a staggering casualty rate of 12–15 percent.*

Warning Against Assassination

Attica Wymong [*sic*] County N.Y.
Thursday morn 15: Sept 64

Abraham Lincoln
President of the
United States of America—
Washington. D.C.

My Dear Sir: Your existence and your life are in the grasp of a "Secret band of Traitors"—"Speculation" are the "Ring Leaders"— they <u>do</u> <u>not</u> <u>all</u> reside in <u>this Country</u>.

Your life is sought!—Our Country is in danger!!—

Forget not yourself, for one instant, Beware of <u>poisons</u>!—Beware of assassination!—

A week—A month, or perhaps Six months hence you will know & realize the value of this communication.

It is best you should not know me at this time—it is inexpedient—I am (however) <u>not</u> known as a politician, nor never was—Never held an office (coming from the people) & have no desire to—I do not seek thro. <u>this</u>, any remuneration, compensation, or appointment—But hope to save <u>your</u> <u>life</u>. <u>Our Liberty! Our Country!!</u>—

I ask you no favor except to remember the contents of this communication & to enable me to continue my observations of the <u>moving world</u>, unmolested. Use <u>great</u> <u>care</u> in repeating <u>anything</u> herein mentioned—

It is easy for you to know who I am—but not thro. any communication to me directly I am not old—I am not young—I know <u>you</u> <u>well</u>—you, do not know <u>me</u> (except thro other parties) I am known to Mr Seward, and I presume favorably—

I am not a member of <u>any</u> secret or public society—(so called) never was—Am not a <u>member</u> of the Masonic Order—but feel as could be—accident to the <u>frame</u> prevents my admission

I am <u>not</u> rich!—I do <u>not</u> seek for notoriety in this matter—no, nor any other

This place is <u>not</u> my residence tho. occasionally I happen around here—I shall be; or expect to be in Washington during the latter part of this month

Yours in Truth
Have <u>Care</u>
(135798642)

∽ *The President's secretaries filed away this three-page letter with the notation "Anonymous. Warning against poisoning assassination &c." There was no explanation for the series of numbers that accompanied the signature.*

To Rid the World of "the Monster"

[November 1864]

. . . When you remember the fearful, solemn vow that was taken by us, you will feel there is no drawback—Abe must die, and now. You can choose your weapons. The cup, the knife, the bullet. The cup failed us once, and might again. Johnson, who will give this, has been like an enraged demon since the meeting, because it has not fallen upon him to rid the world of the monster.

[Unsigned]

∽ *Assistant Secretary of War Charles A. Dana supposedly showed Lincoln this letter, one of a pair of letters allegedly discovered aboard a New York City streetcar. "He looked at them, but made no special remark," Dana remembered, according to Carl Sandburg's famous but sometimes fanciful biography. In fact, Dana marvelled, Lincoln "seemed to attach very little importance to them." The President kept a large envelope in his files, Dana testified, in which such threats were stored. On it was written in Lincoln's own hand: "Assassination." The orginal of this threat is lost (Sandburg, The War Years, IV: 135).*

Ravings from a "Prince of Peace"

January 2nd 1865

to your Honoreable Boddy in person
The President OVE THE UNITED STATES
ABRAHAM LINCON [sic]

May I presume to intrude my self upon your Notice on this August Assembly

God desires to Make this yeare:
THEE HAPPY NEW YEARE
THE 1 yeare YEARE OVE, Jubilee

I KNOW [unintelligible word] EPISTLE, AS A TOKEN OF MY UN-FEIGNED LOVE FOR YOUR FAITHFULNESS—OVER A FIEW THINGS I WILL MAKE THEE RULER-OVER—A KING-DOM FROM ABOMINATION AND SLAVERY—AND WAR—

If you heare The true Church ove GOD—GOD THEE SON AND GOD THEE HOLY GHOST

By Revelation to me direct Abraham Lincon WAS TO BE CHO-SEN president OVE THESE UNITED STATES Before your first Election and I called 2 persons to certify that you would be elected,

Also in this City I received A A [sic] Revelation the morning Before Abraham Lincoln Would be Re-elected

An Before, any Returnes ove votes I told a Missis Hurley an one other woman An a doctor WHO lives in this City that it was Reveald to me that morning that your Honorible Person would be Elected

Therefore you An All who Believe in GOD Must Know that God has laid his plastic hand upon me to Reveal Jesus Christ who says he would come The second time without sin unto salvation.

I declare unto All who will bow to you that I claime A patrimony in Booth hemispheres one Billion dollars one million immediately for my cervises up to the first day january 1865 for the Balance secure on Real Estate or Bonds in Each Hemisphere.

Also if you will have and Raise this Som to the Church Councill By my Appointment And you will Appoint Godly men to fill those offices OVE sacred trust you will Receive one million Dollars Secured to you By me

Before one yeare And the Greate feast to be Celebrated the Capital to be completed in June and then weight after messages sent to distinguished persons in escape in the Spring to offer and weight the Queene By your wife will be invited if she desires to share the Honour An her Roial family is Lord Lyons in this City your son can be sent if he will prepare for in addition for also if the Uropean people do come and visit and share Equally And A message I request for you And Lord Lions [British Ambassador Lord Lyons] and his Secretary petitioned by Gods Command to Donate to me one half ove one Billion And deposit the same And present Drafts or Check and Bonds By which I can Command the same At my pleasure

If so I will Reveale Christ Jesus And Explaine the mode ove his Crucifiction

Also I request you and yours to present to me twentfive thousand dollars youre self for youre Honor is Solicited to meet Church and Congress And By my Request fur A meeting Next Sabbath at the Capital And deliver Summons By tickets being sold this week to pay the twenty five thousand dollars, also I desire to Appoint, By your Concent twelve persons in Government and you can I must visit my friends and prepare they way North but if you will fulfull you can Be crown in the fut[ur]e

I am Elias Gove THEE, PRINCE OVE PEACE

⇚ Not surprisingly, Lincoln endorsed this letter "Crazy-Man." What is astounding is that his staff allowed the diatribe to reach his desk in the first place. Perhaps it was a kind of holiday-week joke played on the President by his secretaries. The same ranting correspondent had sent a similar threatening letter on New Year's Day, 1864, a letter Lincoln had filed under a more benign heading: "Foolery."

Notes to Introduction

1. William O. Stoddard, "Face to Face with Lincoln," ed. William O. Stoddard, Jr., *Atlantic Monthly* (March 1925): 333.

2. William O. Stoddard, Jr., ed., *Lincoln's Third Secretary: The Memoirs of William O. Stoddard* (New York: Exposition Press, 1955), 208.

3. Helen Nicolay, *Personal Traits of Abraham Lincoln* (New York: The Century Co., 1912), 182.

4. *Ibid.*, 182–183.

5. Helen Nicolay, *Lincoln's Secretary: A Biography of John G. Nicolay* (New York: Longmans, Green & Co., 1949), 75; for Jackson's inauguration, see Margaret Klapthor *et al*, eds., *The White House: An Historic Guide* (Washington: White House Historical Association, 1973), 24, 119.

6. Anne C. Rose, *Victorian America and the Civil War* (Cambridge: Cambridge University Press, 1992), 197; Henry Adams, *Democracy: An American Novel* (1880; reprint, New York: New American Library, 1961), 22.

7. Harold Holzer, Mark E. Neely, Jr., and Gabor S. Boritt, *The Lincoln Image: Abraham Lincoln and the Popular Print* (New York: Scribner's, 1984), 197–200; Philip Shaw Paludan, *"A People's Contest": The Union and the Civil War, 1861–1865* (New York: Harper & Row, 1988), 12–13.

8. Henry J. Raymond quoted in Francis B. Carpenter, *Six Months at the White House with Abraham Lincoln* (New York: Hurd & Houghton, 1866), 129.

9. Theodore C. Blegen, ed., *Abraham Lincoln and His Mailbag: Two Documents by Edward D. Neill, One of Lincoln's Secretaries* (St. Paul: Minnesota Historical Society, 1964), 46.

10. *Ibid.*

11. Henry Rood, ed., *Memories of the White House: The Home Life of Our Presidents from Lincoln to Roosevelt, Being Personal Recollections of Colonel W. H. Crook . . .* (Boston: Little, Brown & Co., 1911), 27; Carpenter, *Six Months at the White House*, 281; Helen Nicolay, *Lincoln's Secretary*, 82.

12. Helen Nicolay, *Lincoln's Secretary*, 83; Carpenter, *Six Months at the White House*, 281–282; Rufus Rockwell Wilson, ed., *Intimate Memories of Lincoln* (New York: Primavera Press, 1945), 604.

13. John F. Trumbull to Lincoln, March 12, 1864, Abraham Lincoln Papers, Library of Congress; hereafter cited as Lincoln Papers; Benjamin P. Thomas, *Abraham Lincoln: A Biography* (New York: Alfred A. Knopf, 1952), 458.

14. Thomas D. Jones, *Memories of Lincoln* (New York: Press of the Pioneers, 1934), 7.

15. Harold G. and Oswald Garrison Villard, eds., *Lincoln on the Eve of '61: A Journalist's Story by Henry Villard* (New York: Alfred A. Knopf, 1941), 27.

16. *Ibid.*, 27–29.

17. Helen Nicolay, *Lincoln's Secretary*, 36.

18. *Ibid.*, 4, 13; Louis A. Warren, "John G. Nicolay, 1832–1901," *Lincoln Lore* No. 718 (January 11, 1943); Mark E. Neely, Jr., *The Abraham Lincoln Encyclopedia* (New York: McGraw-Hill, 1982), 224–225; hereafter cited as *ALE*. For examples of letters addressing Nicolay as "George," see C. Woolfolk to Nicolay, February 12, 1861; "Cole" to Nicolay, December 19, 1861, in Lincoln Papers. On the pronunciation issue, the author relies on a conversation with Wayne C. Temple of Springfield, who knew Helen Nicolay and asked her how the family name should be pronounced.

19. Helen Nicolay, *Lincoln's Secretary*, 27.

20. *Ibid.*, 30; Warren, "John G. Nicolay."

21. Helen Nicolay, *Lincoln's Secretary*, 34, 41, 85; see William Dean Howells, *Life of Abraham Lincoln* (1860; reprint, Springfield, IL: Abraham Lincoln Association, 1938).

22. Helen Nicolay, *Lincoln's Secretary*, 74; William O. Stoddard, Jr., ed., *Lincoln's Third Secretary: The Memoirs of William O. Stoddard* (New York: Exposition Press, 1955), 90.

23. Roy P. Basler et al., eds., *The Collected Works of Abraham Lincoln*, 9 vols. (New Brunswick, NJ: Rutgers University Press, 1953–55), IV: 49; cited hereafter as *CW*; Helen Nicolay, *Lincoln's Secretary*, 38, 41.

24. Roscoe Thayer, *The Life and Letters of John Hay*, 2 vols. (New York: Houghton-Mifflin, 1908), I: 87.

25. Helen Nicolay, *Lincoln's Secretary*, 76, 85; Tyler Dennett, ed., *John Hay: From Poetry to Politics* (New York: Dodd, Mead, 1933), 35.

26. Wilson, *Intimate Memories*, 336; Frank J. Williams, "John Hay and Abraham Lincoln: A Retrospective," *Books at Brown* 35–36, 16 [Hay's comments on Washington were written in 1861]; Dennett, *John Hay*, 35; Tyler Dennett, ed., *Lincoln & The Civil War in the Diaries and Letters of John Hay* (New York: Dodd, Mead, 1939), 172, 234, 241; William Seale, *The President's House: A History*, 2 vols. (Washington: White House Historical Association, 1986), I: 380. For an example of an amusing Hay endorsement, see Otho Hinton to Lincoln, January 1, 1864 (endorsed "Essay"), Lincoln Papers; Emanuel Hertz, *The Hidden Lincoln . . .* (New York: Viking Press, 1938), 307.

27. Louis A. Warren, "John Milton Hay, 1838–1905," *Lincoln Lore* No. 707 (October 19, 1942); *ALE*, 141.

28. Benjamin P. Thomas, "The President Reads His Mail," *Lincoln Herald* 55, No. 1 (Spring 1953): 30–31; Robert T. Lincoln to John G. Nicolay, undated fragment in the Lincoln Papers.

29. P. J. Staudenraus, ed., *Mr. Lincoln's Washington: Selections From the Writings of Noah Brooks, Civil War Correspondent* (New York: Thomas Yoseloff, 1967), 254; William O. Stoddard, *Abraham Lincoln: The True Story of a Great Life* (New York: Fords, Howard & Hulbert, 1884), 243; George Alfred Townsend, *The Life, Crime and Capture of John Wilkes Booth . . .* (New York: Dick & Fitzgerald, 1865), 58–59; Donald B. Cole and John J. McDonough, eds., *Benjamin Brown French: Witness to the Young Republic—A Yankee's Journal, 1828–1870* (Hanover, NH: University Press of New England, 1989), 395; Seale, *The President's House*, I: 380, opp. 394; Wayne C. Temple and Justin G. Turner, "Lincoln's 'Castine': Noah Brooks—'The Close of Lincoln's Career,' " *Lincoln Herald* 73, No. 3 (Fall 1971): 169; Dennett, *Diaries and Letters of John Hay*, 178, 187.

30. Helen Nicolay, *Lincoln's Secretary*, 85–86; Stoddard, Jr., *Lincoln's Third Secretary*, 7.

31. Stoddard, Jr., *Lincoln's Third Secretary*, 58.

32. *Ibid.*, 59.

33. *Ibid.*, 65.

34. *Ibid.*

35. William O. Stoddard to William H. Herndon, December 27, 1860, Lincoln Papers.

36. Stoddard, Jr., *Lincoln's Third Secretary*, 71, 77, 81, 90.

37. Staudenraus, *Noah Brooks*, 254; Stoddard, Jr., *Lincoln's Third Secretary*, 134–135.

38. Stoddard, Jr., *Lincoln's Third Secretary*, 91; Stoddard, *The True Story of a Great Life*, 343–344; Temple and Turner, "Lincoln's 'Castine,'" 169.

39. See John G. Nicolay and John Hay, *Abraham Lincoln: A History* (New York: The Century Co., 1890).

40. William O. Stoddard, *Lincoln at Work: Sketches from Life* (Boston: United Society of Christian Endeavor, 1900), 75–76; Stoddard, Jr., *Lincoln's Third Secretary*, 94.

41. Stoddard, *Lincoln at Work*, 66, 72–73, 79, 103; William O. Stoddard, *Inside the White House in War Times* (New York: Charles L. Webster, 1890), 27; Wilson, *Intimate Memories of Lincoln*, 228; Stoddard, Jr., *Lincoln's Third Secretary*, 94.

42. Stoddard, Jr., *Lincoln's Third Secretary*, 93.

43. Stoddard, *Lincoln at Work*, 79; Stoddard, Jr., *Lincoln's Third Secretary*, 109.

44. Stoddard, *Lincoln at Work*, 72, 81; Stoddard, *Inside the White House*, 27.

45. F. Sterling Bertram to Lincoln, November 9, 1864; Richard Yates to Lincoln, n.d.; undated fragment, all in Lincoln Papers.

46. Blegen, *Abraham Lincoln and His Mailbag*, 48; Chicago *Herald*, December 25, 1887; Stoddard, *Lincoln at Work*, 75, 79.

47. Stoddard, Jr., *Lincoln's Third Secretary*, 107; Stoddard, *Lincoln at Work*, 73, 75.

48. Stoddard, Jr., *Lincoln's Third Secretary*, 108; Stoddard, *Lincoln at Work*, 81; Roud, *Recollections of Col. W. H. Crook*, 16.

49. Stoddard, Jr., *Lincoln's Third Secretary*, 56–57; David C. Mearns, *The Lincoln Papers: The Story of the Collection with Selections to July 4, 1861*, 2 vols. (Garden City, NY: Doubleday, 1948), I: 42.

50. Thomas, *Abraham Lincoln*, 166; Mearns, *The Lincoln Papers* I: 41; Stoddard, *Inside the White House*, 24.

51. Helen Nicolay, *Personal Traits of Abraham Lincoln*, 189; Roud, *Recollections of Col. W. H. Crook*, 15; S. T. Glover to Lincoln, October 25, 1861, Lincoln Papers; *CW* II: 81; Mearns, *The Lincoln Papers* I: 35.

52. Thomas, *Abraham Lincoln*, 465–466; *CW* VI: 17; Dennett, *Diaries and Letters of John Hay*, 225; Helen Nicolay, *Lincoln's Secretary*, 86.

53. Stoddard, *Lincoln at Work*, 78; Dearborn *Independent*, February 7, 1925, clipping in The Lincoln Museum, Fort Wayne, Indiana.

54. Stoddard, Jr., *Lincoln's Third Secretary*, 111, 115; Stoddard, *Inside the White House*, 218.

55. Blegen, *Abraham Lincoln and His Mailbag*, 4–5.

56. Earl Schenck Miers, et al., eds., *Lincoln Day by Day: A Chronology, 1809–1865*, 3 vols. (Washington: Lincoln Sesquicentennial Commission, 1960), III:

129; hereafter cited as *LDBD*; Nicolay to Edward D. Neill, n.d., Neill Papers, Minnesota Historical Society; Neill to Lincoln, January 28, 1863, Lincoln Papers.

57. Blegen, *Abraham Lincoln and His Mailbag*, 8–9, 36; Huntley Dupre, *Edward Duffield Neill: Pioneer Educator* (St. Paul: Macalester College Press, 1949), 66–67; Mark E. Neely, Jr., and Harold Holzer, *The Lincoln Family Album* (New York: Doubleday, 1990), 80–81; hereafter cited as *LFA*.

58. Blegen, *Abraham Lincoln and His Mailbag*, 12; Nicolay to Neill, August 28, 1864, Neill Papers, Minnesota Historical Society; Nicolay to Lincoln (with message on envelope for Neill), August 30, 1864, Lincoln Papers.

59. Blegen, *Abraham Lincoln and His Mailbag*, 12, 26, 47. Blegen's booklet includes two papers by Neill, "Reminiscences of the Last Year of President Lincoln's Life," and "President Lincoln's Mail Bag."

60. Blegen, *Abraham Lincoln and His Mailbag*, 47–49; Wilson, *Intimate Memories of Lincoln*, 603.

61. Wayne C. Temple, "Charles Henry Philbrick: President Lincoln's Private Secretary from Illinois College," ms.

62. *Ibid.*; Hay to Nicolay, August 26, 1864, in Dennett, *Diaries and Letters of John Hay*, 213.

63. Stoddard, *Inside the White House*, 219; Hay to Nicolay, September 24, 1864, in Dennett, *Diaries and Letters of John Hay*, 213; also 214–216; Charles Philbrick to Ozias M. Hatch, December 30, 1864, in Illinois State Historical Library, Springfield.

64. Helen Nicolay, *Lincoln's Secretary*, 87; Temple, "Charles Henry Philbrick"; Thomas, *Abraham Lincoln*, 482; *ALE*, 141, 224, 291. A month before the assassination, clergyman Theodore Cuyler recommended Neill as "a candidate for superintendent of the interests of loyal refugees." See Cuyler to Lincoln, March 14, 1865, in the Neill Papers, Minnesota Historical Society.

65. Louis A. Warren, "The Executive Mansion Secretariat," *Lincoln Lore* No. 1061 (August 8, 1949); R. Gerald McMurtry, "A. Lincoln & Son," *Lincoln Lore* No. 1457 (July 1959); undated clippings in the Lincoln Museum, Fort Wayne, Indiana; Wilson, *Intimate Memories of Lincoln*, 230; Jay Monaghan, "Lincolniana: Who Made the Fingerprints?" *Journal of the Illinois State Historical Society* 42, No. 2 (June 1949): 209, 212.

66. Blegen, *Abraham Lincoln and His Mailbag*, 47.

67. Willard L. King, *Lincoln's Manager: David Davis* (Chicago: University of Chicago Press, 1960), 228.

68. Louis A. Warren, "Lincoln's Secretary, John G. Nicolay," *Lincoln Lore* No. 1040 (March 14, 1949).

69. David C. Mearns, "The Lincoln Papers," *Abraham Lincoln Quarterly* 4, No. 8 (December 1947): 373–375. Robert could be generous: he gave his father's handwritten message on "Indian Barbarities" to Neill, so that it could be deposited in the Minnesota Historical Society. See Robert T. Lincoln to Neill, November 20, 1868, Neill Papers.

70. Ida Tarbell, *All in a Day's Work: An Autobiography* (New York: Macmillan, 1939), 169–170. Robert's friend Nicholas Murray Butler also heard him say he wanted to burn some of his father's papers. See Nicholas Murray Butler, *Across the Busy Years: Recollections and Reflections*, 2 vols. (New York: Scribner's, 1939–40), I: 375–376. For Robert's travels with the trunks of his father's papers, see John S. Goff, *Robert Todd Lincoln: A Man in His Own Right* (Norman, OK: University of Oklahoma Press, 1969), 254.

71. Mearns, "The Lincoln Papers," 373; Mearns, *The Lincoln Papers* I: 103, 135–136.

72. Helen Nicolay, *Lincoln's Secretary*, 239–245, 267–268; Temple and Turner, "Lincoln's 'Castine,'" 169. Brooks's report appeared in the Sacramento *Union* on August 2, 1865.

73. *Ibid.*, 304–311; Warren, "John George Nicolay, 1832–1901"; *ALE*, 224–225. The best history of the early biographies, including Nicolay and Hay's, is Benjamin P. Thomas's *Portrait for Posterity: Abraham Lincoln and His Biographers* (New Brunswick, NJ: Rutgers University Press, 1947).

74. Louis A. Warren, "John Milton Hay"; Dennett, *Diaries and Letters of John Hay*, 247; Thayer, *The Life and Letters of John Hay*, II: 405.

75. Blegen, *Abraham Lincoln and His Mailbag*, 17–23.

76. Temple, "Charles Henry Philbrick."

77. Louis A. Warren, "Lincoln's Three Secretaries," *Lincoln Lore* No. 412 (March 11, 1937).

78. Blegen, *Abraham Lincoln and His Mailbag*, 41; Helen Nicolay, *Lincoln's Secretary*, 231–232; Thayer, *Life of John Hay* I: 219–220.

79. Blegen, *Abraham Lincoln and His Mailbag*, 50.

Sources for Chapter Prologues

Chapter 1

CW, IV: 219.
Fellman, *Inside War,* 66.
Neely, *The Fate of Liberty,* 29.
Stoddard, *Inside the White House,* 32.
Villard and Villard, *Lincoln on the Eve of '61,* 16.

Chapter 2

R. George to Lincoln, January 29, 1863, Lincoln Papers.
Andrew Jackson to Lincoln, January 17, 1865, Lincoln Papers.
Thomas D. Jones to Nicolay, August 11, 1861, Lincoln Papers.
Moses Kelly to John G. Nicolay, March 13, 1861, Lincoln Papers.
Mrs. M.B. Oakes to Lincoln, June 15, 1862, Lincoln Papers.
Stoddard, *Inside the White House,* 28.
Stoddard, *Lincoln at Work,* 76.
Stoddard, *The Table Talk of Abraham Lincoln,* 7.
New York *Tribune,* February 15, 1939.
Ward, *Abraham Lincoln: Tributes from His Associates,* 103.

Chapter 3

CW, V: 444; VIII: 356.
Holzer, "Tokens of Respect."

Chapter 4

Stoddard, *Inside the White House*, 33.
Stoddard, *Lincoln at Work*, 74.
Stoddard, Jr., ed., *Lincoln's Third Secretary*, 170.

Chapter 5

Edward Bates to Lincoln, November 17, 1863, Lincoln Papers.
Bruce, *The Launching of Modern American Science*, 306.
Bruce, *Lincoln and the Tools of War*, 76–79, 131, 135–136, 185, 311.
Chittenden, *Recollections of President Lincoln*, 419–420.
Current, *The Lincoln Nobody Knows*, 177–178.
Nicolay to Therena Bates, February 9, 1863, Lincoln Papers.
Nicolay, Helen, *Lincoln's Secretary*, 60.
Stoddard, *Lincoln at Work*, 76.
Stoddard, Jr., ed., "Face to Face with Lincoln," 334–335.
Wilson, *Intimate Memories of Lincoln*, 398.

Chapter 6

J. Baumgarten to John G. Nicolay, October 3, 1864.
Carpenter, *Six Months at the White House*, 93, 113.
George Cassaru to Lincoln, September 25, 1862, Lincoln Papers.
CW, IV: 122–123.
William Lloyd Garrison to Lincoln, January 24, 1865 and February 13, 1865,
    Lincoln Papers.
Leonard Grover to Lincoln, February 20, 1864, Lincoln Papers.
Holzer, "Tokens of Respect."
Charles Lieb to Lincoln, February 1, 1863, Lincoln Papers.
Mrs. David Newhall to Lincoln, March 4, 1864, Lincoln Papers.
William O. Snider to Andrew Curtin, April 6, 1864.
Stoddard, *Inside the White House*, 60.
Stoddard, *Lincoln at Work*, 79.
W.W. Thomas to Lincoln, April 3, 1853, Lincoln Papers.
New York *Tribune*, May 5, 1939.
J.G. True to Lincoln, October 6, 1861, Lincoln Papers.
Isachar Zacharie to Lincoln, May 13, 1864, Lincoln Papers.

Chapter 7

Bates, *Lincoln in the Telegraph Office*, 113–123.
Dennett, *Diaries and Letters of John Hay*, 17.
Stoddard, *Inside the White House*, 33–34.
Stoddard, *The Table Talk of Abraham Lincoln*, 7.
Stoddard, Jr., ed., *Lincoln's Third Secretary*, 82–170.

Chapter 8

Bates, *Lincoln in the Telegraph Office*, 211–216.
Blegen, *Abraham Lincoln and His Mailbag*, 28–29.
CW, V: 450; IV: 209; VII: 16–17; VIII: 171.
Alfred Mackay to Lincoln, April 6, 1864, Lincoln Papers.

Chapter 9

Baker, *Mary Todd Lincoln*, 202–203.
Coleman, *Lincoln and Coles County*, 136, 154, 212–213, 230–231.
Hertz, *The Hidden Lincoln*, 274–283.
LFA, 7–14, 56–57, 72–73, 84.
Strozier, *Lincoln's Quest for Union*, 53–54, 164.
Turner and Turner, *Mary Todd Lincoln*, 105.

Chapter 10

Blegen, *Abraham Lincoln and His Mailbag*, 15, 41–42.
Carpenter, *Six Months at the White House*, 63.
Cuthbert, *Lincoln and the Baltimore Plot*, xvii.
Dennett, *Diaries and Letters of John Hay*, 236.
Eisenschiml, *Why Was Lincoln Murdered?* 247, 504.
Keckley, *Behind the Scenes*, 118.
Alexander Ramsay to Edward D. Neill, November 6, 1864, Neill Papers.
Des Moines *Register*, December 25, 1887, clipping in the Lincoln Museum,
    Fort Wayne, Indiana.
Rood, *Recollections of Col. W.H. Crook*, 20–21.
Stoddard, *Inside the White House*, 31.
Stoddard, *Lincoln at Work* 74–75.
Stoddard, Jr., ed., "Face to Face with Lincoln," 333.
Teillard, Recollections of Abraham Lincoln, 47.
Thomas, "The President Reads His Mail," 33.

The following abbreviations are used for book titles frequently cited in textual comments:

ALE   *The Abraham Lincoln Encyclopedia*
CW   *The Collected Works of Abraham Lincoln*
LDBD *Lincoln Day by Day*
LFA   *The Lincoln Family Album*
LTW   *Lincoln and the Tools of War*

Bibliography

Adams, Virginia M., ed. *On the Altar of Freedom: A Black Soldier's Civil War Letters From the Front.* New York: Warner Books, 1991.

Angle, Paul M. *"Here I Have Lived": A History of Lincoln's Springfield.* Rev. ed. Chicago: Abraham Lincoln Association, 1971.

Baker, Jean. *Mary Todd Lincoln: A Biography.* New York: W. W. Norton, 1987.

Barnes, John S. "With Lincoln From Washington to Richmond in 1865." *Appleton's Magazine* 9 (May 1907): 515–524; 742–751.

Basler, Roy P. et al., eds. *The Collected Works of Abraham Lincoln.* 9 vols., New Brunswick, NJ: Rutgers University Press, 1953–55.

Basler, Roy P., ed. *The Collected Works of Abraham Lincoln: First Supplement, 1832–1865.* New Brunswick, NJ: Rutgers University Press, 1990.

———. *President Lincoln Helps His Old Friends.* Springfield, IL: Abraham Lincoln Association, 1977.

Basler, Roy P., and Christian O. Basler, eds. *The Collected Works of Abraham Lincoln: Second Supplement, 1848–1865.* New Brunswick, NJ: Rutgers University Press, 1990.

Bates, Homer. *Lincoln in the Telegraph Office.* New York: The Century Company, 1907.

Bentuiek-Smith, William, ed. *The Harvard Book: Selections from Three Centuries.* Rev. ed., Cambridge: Harvard University Press, 1982.

Bernstein, Iver. *The New York City Draft Riots: Their Significance for American Society and Politics in the Age of the Civil War.* New York: Oxford University Press, 1990.

Blegen, Theodore C., ed. *Abraham Lincoln and His Mailbag: Two Documents by Edward D. Neill, One of Lincoln's Secretaries.* St. Paul: Minnesota Historical Society, 1964.

Blue, Frederick J. *Salmon P. Chase: A Life in Politics.* Kent, OH: Kent State University Press, 1987.

Braden, Waldo C. *Abraham Lincoln, Public Speaker.* Baton Rouge: Louisiana State University Press, 1988.

Brooks, Noah. "Personal Reminiscences of Lincoln," *Scribner's Monthly* 15 (1877/78): 561–569; 677–681.

Bruce, Robert V. *Lincoln and the Tools of War.* Indianapolis, IN: Bobbs-Merrill, 1956.

————. *The Launching of Modern American Science, 1846–1876.* New York: Alfred A. Knopf, 1987.

Butler, Nicholas Murray. *Across the Busy Years: Recollections and Reflections.* 2 vols. New York: Charles Scribner's Sons, 1939–40.

Carman, Harry J., and Reinhard H. Luthin. *Lincoln and the Patronage.* New York: Columbia University Press, 1943.

Carpenter, Francis B. *Six Months at the White House with President Lincoln.* New York: Hurd & Houghton, 1866.

Chittenden, Lucius E. *Personal Reminiscences, 1840–1890.* New York: Richmond, Croscup & Co., 1893.

————. *Recollections of President Lincoln and His Administration.* New York: Harper & Bros., 1891.

Cole, Donald B., and John J. McDonough, eds. *Benjamin Brown French: Witness to the Young Republic: A Yankee's Journal, 1828–1870.* Hanover, NH: University Press of New England, 1989.

Coleman, Charles H. *Abraham Lincoln and Coles County, Illinois.* New Brunswick, NJ: Scarecrow Press, 1955.

Cullinan, Howell. "William O. Stoddard as a Reporter in 1859 Started First Boom [For Lincoln]." Clipping in the Lincoln Museum, Fort Wayne, Indiana.

Current, Richard N. *Lincoln and the First Shot.* New York: J.B. Lippincott, 1963.

————. *The Lincoln Nobody Knows.* New York: McGraw-Hill, 1958.

Cuthbert, Norma B., ed. *Lincoln and the Baltimore Plot of 1861, From Pinkerton Records and Related Papers.* San Marino, CA: Huntington Library, 1949.

Dennett, Tyler. *John Hay: From Poetry to Politics.* New York: Dodd, Mead & Co., 1933.

————, ed. *Lincoln and the Civil War in the Diaries and Letters of John Hay.* New York: Dodd, Mead & Co., 1939.

De Young, Dirk P., "Lincoln's Secretary Talks of His Chief." *Dearborn Independent*, February 7, 1925.

Donald, David H., ed. *Inside Lincoln's Cabinet: The Civil War Diaries of Salmon P. Chase.* New York: Longmans, Green & Co., 1954.

Dorris, Jonathan Truman. *Pardon and Amnesty Under Lincoln and Johnson.* Chapel Hill, NC: University of North Carolina Press, 1953.

Dupre, Huntley. *Edward Duffield Neill: Pioneer Educator.* St. Paul, MN: Macalester College Press, 1949.

Eberstadt, Charles. *Lincoln's Emancipation Proclamation.* New York: Duschnes Crawford, 1950.

Eisenschiml, Otto. *Why Was Lincoln Murdered?* Boston: Little, Brown & Co., 1937.

Fellman, Michael. *Inside War: The Guerilla Conflict in Missouri During the Civil War.* New York: Oxford University Press, 1989.

Goff, John S. *Robert Todd Lincoln: A Man in His Own Right.* Norman, OK: University of Oklahoma Press, 1969.

Grant, Ulysses S. *Personal Memoirs.* 2 vols. New York: Charles L. Webster, 1892.

Hamilton, Charles and Lloyd Ostendorf. *Lincoln in Photographs: An Album of Every Known Pose.* Rev. ed. Dayton, OH: Morningside Books, 1985.

Hay, John. "Life in the White House in Lincoln's Time." *Century Magazine* 151 (November 1890): 33–37.

————. *Letters of John Hay and Extracts from His Diary.* Washington, D.C.: n.p., 1908.

Helm, Katherine. *The True Story of Mary, Wife of Lincoln.* New York: Harper & Brothers, 1928.

Hertz, Emanuel. *The Hidden Lincoln: From the Letters and Papers of William H. Herndon.* New York: Viking Press, 1938.

Holzer, Harold. "Lincoln at the Front: Abraham Lincoln Visits the Battlefields of the Civil War." *Blue and Gray Magazine* 1 (February–March 1984): 47–54.

———. "Tokens of Respect and Heartfelt Thanks: How Abraham Lincoln Coped with Presidential Gifts." *Illinois Historical Journal* 77 (Autumn 1984): 177–192.

Holzer, Harold, Mark E. Neely, Jr., and Gabor S. Boritt. *The Lincoln Image: Abraham Lincoln and the Popular Print.* New York: Scribner's, 1984.

"How Lincoln Chose a Secretary," *Success Magazine,* n.a., n.d. Clipping in the Lincoln Museum, Fort Wayne, Indiana.

Jones, Thomas D. *Memories of Lincoln.* New York: Press of the Pioneers, 1934.

Kantor, Alvin Robert, and Marjorie Sered Kantor. *Sanitary Fairs: A Philatelic and Historical Study of Civil War Benevolence.* Glencoe, IL: SF Publishing, 1992.

Keckley, Elizabeth. *Behind the Scenes: Or, Thirty Years a Slave, and Four Years in the White House.* 1868. Reprint. Buffalo, NY: Stansil & Lee, 1931.

King, Willard L. *Lincoln's Manager, David Davis.* Chicago: University of Chicago Press, 1960.

Kloss, William. *Art in the White House: A Nation's Pride.* Washington: White House Historical Association, 1992.

Kunhardt, Philip B., Jr. *A New Birth of Freedom: Lincoln at Gettysburg.* Boston: Little, Brown, 1983.

"Letter Reveals Lincoln Knew He Was Great: Hay Wrote Herndon in '66 of President's Arrogance . . . ," n.a. New York *Tribune,* February 15, 1939.

"Lincoln Had Fourth White House Secretary," New York *Times,* January 9, 1949.

McMurtry, R. Gerald. "A. Lincoln & Son." *Lincoln Lore* No. 1457 (July 1959).

———. "Lincoln Newspaper Clippings." *Lincoln Lore* No. 1550 (April 1967).

McPherson, James M. *Battle Cry of Freedom: The Civil War Era.* New York: Oxford University Press, 1988.

Marzio, Peter. *The Democratic Art: Chromolithography 1840–1900—Pictures for a 19th-Century America.* Boston: David R. Godine, 1979.

Maxwell, William Quentin. *Lincoln's Fifth Wheel: The Political History of the United States Sanitary Commission.* New York: Longmans, Green & Co., 1956.

Mearns, David C. "The Lincoln Papers." *Abraham Lincoln Quarterly* 4 (December 1947): 369–385.

———. *The Lincoln Papers: The Story of the Collection with Selections to July 4, 1861.* 2 vols. Garden City, NY: Doubleday, 1948.

Miers, Earl Schenck, ed. *Lincoln Day by Day: A Chronology, 1809–1865.* Washington, D.C.: Lincoln Sesquicentennial Commission, 1960.

Mitgang, Herbert. *Abraham Lincoln: A Press Portrait.* Chicago: Quadrangle Books, 1971.

———. "Garibaldi and Lincoln." American Heritage 26 (October 1975): 34–39, 98–101.

Monaghan, Jay. *Diplomat in Carpet Slippers: Abraham Lincoln Deals with Foreign Affairs.* New York: Bobbs-Merrill, 1945.

———. "Lincolniana: Who Made the Fingerprints?" *Journal of the Illinois State Historical Society* 42 (June 1949): 209–212.

———, ed. *Lincoln Bibliography 1839–1939.* 2 vols. Collections of the Illinois State Historical Library 31, Bibliographic Series Volume 4. Springfield, IL: Illinois State Historical Library, 1943.

Neely, Mark E., Jr. *The Abraham Lincoln Encyclopedia.* New York: McGraw-Hill, 1983.

———. *The Fate of Liberty: Abraham Lincoln and Civil Liberties.* New York: Oxford University Press, 1991.

Neely, Mark E., Jr., and Harold Holzer. *The Lincoln Family Album: Photographs from the Personal Collection of a Historic American Family.* New York: Doubleday, 1990.

Nicolay, Helen. *Lincoln's Secretary: A Biography of John G. Nicolay.* New York: Longmans, Green & Co., 1949.

———. *Personal Traits of Abraham Lincoln.* New York: The Century Company, 1912.

Nicolay, John G. *A Short Life of Abraham Lincoln.* New York: The Century Company, 1904.

Nicolay, John G., and John Hay. *Abraham Lincoln: A History.* 10 vols. New York: The Century Company, 1890.

Paine, Albert Bigelow. *Th: Nast–His Period and His Pictures.* New York: Macmillan, 1904.

Paludan, Philip Shaw. *"A People's Contest": The Union and the Civil War, 1861–1865.* New York: Harper & Row, 1988.

Pease, Theodore Calvin, and James G. Randall, eds. *The Diary of Orville Hickman Browning.* 2 vols. Springfield, IL: Illinois State Historical Library, 1925.

Pfanz, Donald C. *The Petersburg Campaign: Abraham Lincoln at City Point, March 20–April 9, 1865.* Lynchburg, VA: H. E. Howard, Inc., 1989.

Pratt, Harry F. *The Personal Finances of Abraham Lincoln.* Springfield, IL: Abraham Lincoln Association, 1943.

Quinn, Camille A. *Lincoln's Springfield in the Civil War*. Macomb, IL: Western Illinois University, 1991.

Randall, Ruth Painter. *Lincoln's Sons*. Boston: Little, Brown & Co., 1955.

Rice, Allen Thorndike, ed. *Reminiscences of Abraham Lincoln by Distinguished Men of His Time*. New York: North American Review, 1888.

Rood, Henry, ed. *Memories of the White House: The Home Life of Our Presidents from Lincoln to Roosevelt, Being Personal Recollections of Colonel W. H. Crook. . . .* Boston: Little, Brown & Co., 1911.

Rose, Anne C. *Victorian America and the Civil War*. Cambridge: Cambridge University Press, 1992.

Rubinger, Naphtali. *Abraham Lincoln and the Jews*. New York: Jonathan David, 1962.

Sandburg, Carl. *Abraham Lincoln: The War Years*. 4 vols. New York: Harcourt, Brace & Co., 1939.

————. *Lincoln Collector: The Story of Oliver R. Barrett's Great Lincoln Collection*. New York: Harcourt, Brace & Co., 1950.

Seale, William. *The President's House: A History*. 2 vols. Washington: White House Historical Association, 1986.

Sears, Stephen W., ed. *The Civil War Papers of George B. McClellan: Selected Correspondence, 1860–1865*. New York: Ticknor & Fields, 1989.

Segal, Charles M., ed. *Conversations with Lincoln*. New York: G. P. Putnam's Sons, 1961.

Shaw, Archer H., ed. *The Lincoln Encyclopedia*. New York: Macmillan, 1950.

Staudenraus, P. J., ed. *Mr. Lincoln's Washington: Selections from the Writings of Noah Brooks, Civil War Correspondent*. New York: Thomas Yoseloff, 1967.

Stoddard, William O. *Abraham Lincoln: The True Story of a Great Life*. New York: Fords, Howard & Hulbert, 1884.

————. *Inside the White House in War Times*. New York: Charles L. Webster, 1890.

————. *Lincoln at Work: Sketches from Life*. Boston: United Society of Christian Endeavor, 1900.

————. "Lincoln's Great Genius for Detail." *Success Magazine*, December 29, 1898.

————. *The Table Talk of Abraham Lincoln*. New York: Frederick A. Stokes, 1894.

Stoddard, William O., Jr., ed. "A Journalist Sees Lincoln, by William O. Stoddard," *Atlantic Monthly* 135 (February 1925): 171–177.

———, ed. "Face to Face with Lincoln, By William O. Stoddard." *Atlantic Monthly* 135 (March 1925): 333.

———, ed. *Lincoln's Third Secretary: The Memoirs of William O. Stoddard.* New York: Exposition Press, 1955.

Strozier, Charles B. *Lincoln's Quest for Union: Public and Private Meanings.* New York: Basic Books, 1982.

Tarbell, Ida. *All in a Day's Work: An Autobiography.* New York: Macmillan, 1939.

Teillard, Dorothy Lamon, ed. *Recollections of Abraham Lincoln 1847–1865, by Ward Hill Lamon.* 2d ed. Washington: 1911, reprint of 1895 ed. pub. by A.C. McClurg.

Temple, Wayne C. *Abraham Lincoln and Others at the St. Nicholas.* Springfield, IL: St. Nicholas Corp., 1968.

———. "Charles Henry Philbrick: President Lincoln's Private Secretary from Illinois College." Unpublished ms.

Temple, Wayne C., and Justin G. Turner. "Lincoln's 'Castine': Noah Brooks —'The Close of Lincoln's Career.'" *Lincoln Herald* 73 (Fall 1971): 163–180.

Thayer, William Roscoe. *The Life and Letters of John Hay.* 2 vols. Boston: Houghton Mifflin Co., 1908.

Thomas, Benjamin P. *Abraham Lincoln: A Biography.* New York: Alfred A. Knopf, 1952.

———. *Portrait for Posterity: Lincoln and His Biographers.* New Brunswick, NJ: Rutgers University Press, 1947.

———. "The President Reads His Mail." *Lincoln Herald* 55 (Spring 1953): 30–32.

Townsend, George Alfred. *The Life, Crime and Capture of John Wilkes Booth.* New York: Dick & Fitzgerald, 1865.

Trefousse, Hans L. *Andrew Johnson: A Biography.* New York: W. W. Norton, 1989.

Turner, Justin H., and Linda Levitt Turner. *Mary Todd Lincoln: Her Life and Letters.* New York: Alfred A. Knopf, 1972.

Villard, Harold G., and Oswald Garrison Villard, eds. *Lincoln on the Eve of '61: A Journalist's Story by Henry Villard.* New York: Alfred A. Knopf, 1941.

Ward, William Hayes, ed. *Abraham Lincoln: Tributes from His Associates.* New York: Thomas Y. Crowell, 1895.

Warren, Louis A. "John George Nicolay, 1832–1901." *Lincoln Lore,* No. 718 (January 11, 1943).

———. "John Milton Hay, 1838–1905." *Lincoln Lore*, No. 707 (October 19, 1942).

———. "Lincoln Sees Hackett Play Falstaff." *Lincoln Lore* No. 1289 (December 21, 1953).

———. *Lincoln's Gettysburg Declaration: "A New Birth of Freedom.* Fort Wayne, IN: Lincoln National Life Foundation, 1964.

———. "Lincoln's Secretary, John G. Nicolay." *Lincoln Lore* No. 1040 (March 14, 1949).

———. "Lincoln's Solicitude for His Stepmother." *Lincoln Lore* No. 1175 (October 15, 1951).

———. "Lincoln's Three Secretaries." *Lincoln Lore* No. 412 (March 1, 1937).

———. Lincoln's Youth: *Indiana Years Seven to Twenty-One, 1816–1830.* New York: Appleton, Century, Crofts, 1959.

———. "The Executive Mansion Secretariat." *Lincoln Lore* No. 1061 (August 8, 1949).

Williams, Frank J. "John Hay and Abraham Lincoln: A Retrospective." *Books at Brown* 35–36 (1988–1989): 11–22.

Wilson, Rufus Rockwell, ed. *Intimate Memories of Lincoln.* Elmira, NY: The Primavera Press, 1945.

———, ed. *Lincoln Among His Friends.* Caldwell, ID: Caxton Printers, 1942.

———. *Lincoln in Portraiture.* New York: Press of the Pioneers, 1935.

Zilversmit, Arthur, ed. *Lincoln on Black and White: A Documentary History.* Malabar, FL: Robert E. Krieger Publishing Co., 1983.

Public Collections Consulted

The Library of Congress, Washington, D.C.
The National Archives, Washington, D.C.
The Lincoln Museum, Fort Wayne, Indiana.
Lilly Library, Indiana University, Bloomington
The Chicago Historical Society
Lincoln Memorial University, Harrogate, Tennessee
The Lincoln Shrine, Redlands, California
The Forbes Collection and Museum, New York City
The New-York Historical Society
The Illinois State Historical Library, Springfield
The Minnesota Historical Society
The Illinois State Archives

Index